Lecture Notes in Computer Science 7083

Commenced Publication in 1973
Founding and Former Series Editors:
Gerhard Goos, Juris Hartmanis, and Jan van Leeuwen

W0227335

Iulian Ober   Ileana Ober (Eds.)

SDL 2011: Integrating System and Software Modeling

15th International SDL Forum
Toulouse, France, July 5-7, 2011
Revised Papers

 Springer

Volume Editors

Iulian Ober
Université de Toulouse, IRIT
118 route de Narbonne
31062 Toulouse, France
E-mail: iulian.ober@irit.fr

Ileana Ober
Université de Toulouse, IRIT
118 route de Narbonne
31062 Toulouse, France
E-mail: ileana.ober@irit.fr

ISSN 0302-9743   e-ISSN 1611-3349
ISBN 978-3-642-25263-1   e-ISBN 978-3-642-25264-8
DOI 10.1007/978-3-642-25264-8
Springer Heidelberg Dordrecht London New York

Library of Congress Control Number: 2011940214

CR Subject Classification (1998): D.2, C.2, D.3, F.3, C.3, K.6, D.2.4

LNCS Sublibrary: SL 5 – Computer Communication Networks and Telecommunications

Typesetting: Camera-ready by author, data conversion by Scientific Publishing Services, Chennai, India

Printed on acid-free paper

Springer is part of Springer Science+Business Media (www.springer.com)

Preface

This volume contains the papers and invited contributions presented at the 15th International Conference on System Design Languages (SDL Forum), which took place in Toulouse, France, on July 5–7, 2011, under the organization of the University of Toulouse and the Institute de Recherche en Informatique de Toulouse (IRIT).

The SDL Forum has been held every two years for the last three decades and is one of the most important events in the calendar for anyone from academia or industry involved in system design languages and modelling technologies. It is a primary conference event for the discussion of the evolution and use of these languages. The most recent innovations, trends, experiences, and concerns in the field are discussed and presented. The SDL Forum series addresses issues related to the modelling and analysis of reactive systems, distributed systems, and real-time and complex systems such as telecommunications, automotive, and aerospace applications. The intended audience of the series includes users of modelling techniques in industry, research, and standardization contexts, as well as tool vendors and language researchers.

By adopting a new name as the International Conference on System Design Languages, the conference aims to mark its opening towards all the languages and paradigms of system design.

The program of this year's conference featured three invited talks, two tutorials, and sixteen regular papers. The first talk, in chronological order, was given by Prof. Dorina Petriu from Carleton University, Ottawa, Canada. Her talk, titled "Model-Based Performance Analysis of Service-Oriented Systems" focused on the OMG standard "UML Profile for Modeling and Analysis of Real-Time and Embedded systems" (MARTE) and the way it is used for adding performance annotations and performing analysis on service-oriented models described in UML. The second talk, titled "SCADE: A Comprehensive Framework for Critical System and Software Engineering", was given by Thierry Le Sergent, SCADE System and SCADE Suite Product Manager at Esterel Technologies, Toulouse, France. This talk discussed some of the recurrent problems in system engineering and provided insight into the solutions adopted in Esterel's new system design suite. The third talk was given by Rick Reed, Chairman of the SDL Forum Society and long time contributor to the ITU-T standards into which the SDL Forum community remains strongly rooted. Titled "SDL-2010: Background, Rationale and Survey", his talk brought up the most up-to-date information on the new version of SDL prepared by the ITU-T.

The tutorial part of the program focused on two model-based technologies of high practical interest. The first tutorial, animated by Juha-Pekka Tolvanen, from MetaCase, Finland was titled "How to Implement Domain-Specific Modeling Languages: Hands-on". The participants to this tutorial learned about domain-specific modeling and code generation, where these technologies can best be used and how to apply them effectively to improve software development. The second tutorial, given by Maxime Perrotin, Eric Conquet, Julien Delange, André Schiele, and Thanassis Tsiodras, from the European Space Agency (ESA), presented "TASTE: A Real-Time Software Engineering Tool-Chain". TASTE stands for "The ASSERT Set of Tools for Engineering", in reference to the European FP6 program where it finds its roots. It consists in an open-source tool-chain dedicated to the development of embedded, real-time systems. TASTE tools are responsible for putting everything together, including drivers and communication means and ensuring that the execution at runtime is compliant with the specification of the system real-time constraints.

The regular program of the conference featured 16 paper presentations. The topics of these papers span from the traditional interest topics for SDL Forum participants, such as the SDL and related languages, testing, services, and components to a wide range of presentations on domain specific languages and applications, going from use case maps to train station models or user interfaces for scientific dataset editors for high performance computing.

Acknowledgements

The conference and this volume could not exist without the contributions of various actors. We thank in particular the authors of the high quality regular contributions. We also express our gratitude to the members of the Program Committee for their commitment and their contributions during the reviewing process. The organization of SDL 2011 was assisted by sponsorship and support from the University of Toulouse, the Midi-Pyrénées Region (France) and PragmaDev.

August 2011   Iulian Ober
                                                                    Ileana Ober

Organization

SDL 2011 is organized by the University of Toulouse and the Institute de Recherche en Informatique de Toulouse (IRIT) in collaboration with the SDL Forum Society.

General Co-chairs

Ileana Ober	IRIT, University of Toulouse, France
Iulian Ober	IRIT, University of Toulouse, France

Board of the SDL Forum Society

Chairman:	Rick Reed (TSE, UK)
Secretary:	Reinhard Gotzhein (University of Kaiserslautern, Germany)
Treasurer:	Martin von Löwis (Hasso-Plattner-Institut, Germany)

Program Committee

Daniel Amyot	University of Ottawa, Canada
Attila Bilgic	Ruhr-University of Bochum, Germany
Marius Bozga	Verimag, University of Grenoble, France
Rolv Braek	NTNU, Norway
Reinhard Brocks	HTW Saarland, Germany
Jean-Michel Bruel	IRIT - University of Toulouse, France
Laurent Doldi	Aeroconseil, France
Anders Ek	IBM Rational, Sweden
Stein-Erik Ellevseth	ABB Corporate Research, Norway
Joachim Fischer	Humboldt University of Berlin, Germany
Pau Fonseca i Casas	Technical University of Catalonia, Spain
Emmanuel Gaudin	PragmaDev, France
Birgit Geppert	Avaya Labs, USA
Abdelouahed Gherbi	University of Quebec, Canada
Reinhard Gotzhein	University of Kaiserslautern, Germany
Jens Grabowski	University of Goettingen, Germany
Peter Graubmann	Siemens, Germany
Øystein Haugen	SINTEF, Norway
Peter Herrmann	NTNU, Norway
Dieter Hogrefe	University of Goettingen, Germany
Michaela Huhn	Technical University Braunschweig, Germany
Clive Jervis	Motorola, USA
Ferhat Khendek	Concordia University, Canada
Tae-Hyong Kim	KIT, Korea

Table of Contents

Components and Services

Specification and Description Language (SDL)

Domain Specific Languages (Part 2)

Model-Based Performance Analysis of Service-Oriented Systems (Invited Talk)

Dorina C. Petriu

Department of Systems and Computer Engineering,
Carleton University, Ottawa, Ontario, Canada
http://www.sce.carleton.ca/faculty/petriu.html

Abstract. Quantitative performance analysis of service-oriented systems can be conducted in the early development phases by transforming a UML software model extended with performance annotations into a performance model (such as queueing networks, Petri nets, stochastic process algebra) which can be solved with existing performance analysis tools. The OMG standard "UML Profile for Modeling and Analysis of Real-Time and Embedded systems (MARTE)" can be used for adding performance annotations to a given UML model.

The talk discussed the type of MARTE performance annotations and the principles for transforming annotated software models into performance models. Such a transformation must bridge a large semantic gap between the source and target model for two main reasons: performance models concentrate on resource usage and abstract away many details of the original software model, and the performance model requires platform information which is not contained in the software application model. The starting point for the performance model derivation is a platform independent model (PIM) of a SOA system representing the process workflows, architecture of the components offering services, and behavior of the runtime scenarios chosen for evaluation. The PIM is transformed into a platform specific model (PSM) by weaving platform services through aspect-oriented modeling techniques. Other research challenges will be also discussed, such as merging performance modeling and measurements and analyzing performance effects of SOA design patterns.

I. Ober and I. Ober (Eds.): SDL 2011, LNCS 7083, p. 1, 2011.
© Springer-Verlag Berlin Heidelberg 2011

SCADE: A Comprehensive Framework for Critical System and Software Engineering

Thierry Le Sergent

SCADE System and SCADE Suite Product Manager
Esterel Technologies, Toulouse, France
http://www.esterel-technologies.com/

Abstract. The International Council on Systems Engineering (INCOSE) defines system engineering as an interdisciplinary approach and means to enable the realization of successful systems. It focuses on defining customer needs and required functionality early in the development cycle, documenting requirements, and then proceeding with design synthesis and system validation.

The main challenges of System Engineering are related to providing non-ambiguous and coherent specification, making all relevant information readily available to all stakeholders, establishing traceability between all activities, and providing the appropriate level of verification and validation. Model Based technology can play a central role in System Engineering. Among the benefits, MBSE shall avoid duplication of information, parallel evolution of data between system teams and software teams, hence reducing the nightmare of information resynchronization.

I will introduce the SCADE System product line for embedded systems modeling and generation based on the SysML standard and the Eclipse Papyrus open source technology. SCADE System has been developed in the framework of Listerel, a joint laboratory of Esterel Technologies, provider of the SCADE tools, and CEA LIST, project leader of MDT Papyrus.

From an architecture point of view, the Esterel SCADE tools are built on top of the SCADE platform which includes both SCADE Suite, a model-based development environment dedicated to critical embedded software, and SCADE System for system engineering. SCADE System includes MDT Papyrus, an open source component (under EPL license) based on Eclipse. This allows system and software teams to share the same environment. Furthermore, and thanks to Eclipse, other model-based tools can be added to the environment.

The SCADE System modeler focuses on ease of use, hiding the intricacies of UML profiling to the system engineers. Hence, domain views that have been consistently requested by the system engineering users, such as a tabular view to describe blocks and interfaces, are added to the tool. The core functionality of the Papyrus SysML modeler has also been augmented with requirements traceability and automatic production of system design documents.

Once the system description is complete and checked, the individual software blocks in the system can be refined in the form of models in SCADE Suite and SCADE Display, or for some of them in the form of manually developed source code. SCADE System avoids duplication of efforts and inconsistencies between system structural descriptions made of SysML block diagrams, IBD and BDD, and the full software behavioral description designed through both

I. Ober and I. Ober (Eds.): SDL 2011, LNCS 7083, pp. 2–3, 2011.

SCADE Suite and SCADE Display models.   Automatic and DO-178B Level A qualified code generation can be applied to the SCADE Suite and SCADE Display models. Moreover, the SCADE System description can be used as the basis to develop scripts that will automatically integrate the complete application software.

SDL-2010: Background, Rationale, and Survey

Rick Reed

TSE, The Laurels, Victoria Road, Windermere,
LA23 2DL,United Kingdom
rickreed@tseng.co.uk

Abstract. This invited paper concerns a revised version of the ITU-T Specification and Description Language standard, which is scheduled to be consented for approval by ITU-T during 2011. In this document and ongoing ITU-T work, the revised version is called SDL-2010. The current standardized (or in ITU-T terminology Recommended) version at the time of initially writing this paper (April 2011) was called SDL-2000. The paper gives some historical background on the development of the language. The paper includes rationale for the update of the language and the revised organization of the language standard. After the history, there is a description of the new organization followed by some details of the changed feature set of a revised version SDL-2010 compared with SDL-2000. The paper concludes with a snapshot of the status of the SDL-2010 standard.

The purpose of this paper is to provide an overview introduction to the revision of the ITU-T Specification and Description Language called SDL-2010.[1]

The Specification and Description Language has a long history as a published standard going back to 1976 [1], but other than corrections and some re-organization of material in 2002 [2], the language standard has remained stable since the publication of SDL-2000 in 1999 [3]. Considering that previously the language had been revised in 1980, 1984, 1988, 1992 and an addendum to the 1992 version in 1996 [4–8], this is the longest period of stability in the evolution of the language, as can be seen in Fig. 1. As explained in Sect. 1.1, this stability is to some extent due to changed market circumstances in the last decade. One incentive for a revised version of the language is to remove some differences between the language standard and implementations provided by tools: in particular some of the aspects of data introduced in SDL-2000 that have not been implemented (see Sect. 1.2), nesting of diagrams (see Sect. 1.3), and features without SDL-2000 semantics from the United Modeling Language (see Sect. 1.4). The resulting feature set is outlined in Sect. 1.5.

The organization of the standard documents is described in Sect. 2, followed by more detailed description in Sect. 3 of some features added or deleted. Finally the paper closes with the status at the time of writing in sect.4.

---

[1] The content of this paper is not entirely new because it reports work that has been in progress for some time in the domain of ITU-T standardization, but although some material has been made available as ITU-T temporary documents and some material presented at SAM-2010, it has not been widely published.

I. Ober and I. Ober (Eds.): SDL 2011, LNCS 7083, pp. 4–25, 2011.

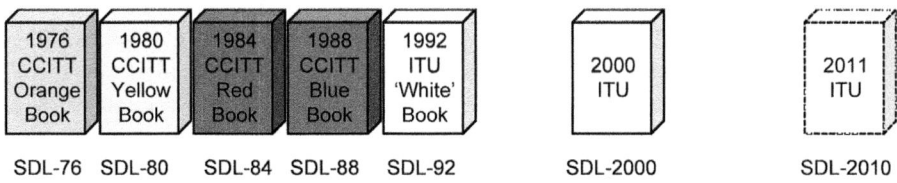

Fig. 1. Specification and Description Language publication dates

1   Background for the Development of SDL-2010

SDL-2000 was completed in 1999 with versions of the ITU-T Recommendations Z.100, Z.105, Z.107 and Z.109. The main document was Z.100 [3] with Z.105 and Z.107 [9, 10] covering use of ASN.1 [11] with the SDL-2000, and Z.109 [12] covering use with the Unified Modeling Language (UML)[13]. A revised Common Interchange Format for SDL-2000 in ITU-T Recommendation Z.106 [14] supplemented these in the year 2000. Since then there have been some minor updates to these Recommendations. The text was reorganized in 2002 so that Z.100 [2] describes the graphical language, and the parts of the textual (SDL/PR phrase representation) that are alternatives to graphical representation (SDL/GR) were moved to the interchange format in Z.106[15]. At the same time a number of corrections and a few minor changes were made. In 2003 an Amendment [16] was issued to incorporate two new Annexes B and C that concern backwards compatibility and conformance to the standard. In 2007 Z.100 was republished incorporating all agreed amendments [17]. The changes have been minor: either re-organization or correction of flaws in the 1999 version, so that essentially SDL-2000 has not changed and has remained stable.

1.1   Status of SDL-2000

When SDL-2000 was being developed, right up until the ITU-T meeting at which it was approved there were two sizable software organizations that were promising to produce tools to support SDL-2000 in 2000 or 2001: Telelogic and Verilog. A merger of these two organizations in Telelogic was announced before the end of 1999, so that some competition was removed in the tool market. Although these commercial tools already supported some of the features of SDL-2000 by 2000, it is now unlikely that there will ever be a tool that approaches full support of SDL-2000 in its final form [15, 17–19]. Even the tool that best supported SDL-92, Cinderella, reached a position by 2007 when it would probably never offer full SDL-2000 support, because it has a smaller (at least in value terms) share of the ITU Specification and Description Language tool market and had to offer compatibility with Telelogic as the market leader at that time. Cinderella collaborated with Humboldt University that previously had not entered into the commercial tool market. The Humboldt SDL-tool implemented many of the features of SDL-2000 on a trial basis to test the feasibility of various ideas - indeed some features such as nested packages were implemented specifically to support feature requests promoted by Humboldt for OMG related work. In 2003 SOLINET announced the SAFIRE tool set, claiming that it is based on Z.100. In late 2004 PragmaDev, which previously supported a dialect called SDL-RT announced support also of Z.100. All four organizations (Cinderella, PragmaDev, SOLINET/SAFIRE, Telelogic) had commercial tools available in May 2006, though SOLINET/SAFIRE had ceased to be involved in ITU or SDL-Forum activities and the future of the language. By November 2008 all Telelogic products and services had become part of the IBM Rational Software portfolio, and the main tool vendors were IBM, PragmaDev and Cinderella (probably in order of market value at that time). At the time of writing all three of these vendors still offered Specification and Description Language tools.

Since 1999 the general market perception has developed. In 1999, part of the rationale for developing Z.109 as a UML profile for the ITU Specification and Description Language was because UML was perceived as a major competitor to the ITU language. Within the telecommunications industry some organizations were divided internally between those that favoured the ITU Specification and Description Language and fans of UML. A decade later the perspective is quite different, because the issue is not seen as whether to use UML or SDL-2000 (and other ITU languages), but how to use these together. In retrospect it would be easy to say this was always the way it was seen - but to be truthful this was not the case especially in 1997 and 1998 when SDL-2000 was being formulated. However, it is now clear that the state machine specification part of UML 2.1.2 is not really a complete language in itself, because of the semantic and syntactic variations that are allowed, and that to make its use practical an (implicit or explicit) profile for UML has to be used. The revised Z.109 profile of 2007 [20] is geared to the needs of the telecommunications industry by mapping UML 2.1.2 [13] onto the more precise (and therefore more practical) Z.100 semantics and (where UML 2.1.2 gives notation options or no specific notation or no notation) binding to the Z.100 syntax.

It is not by accident that the situation has been reached today where UML and ITU System Design Languages are seen as complementary rather than competing. Between 1999 and 2004 there was a significant involvement of ITU System Design Language experts in the ongoing development of UML, in particular for UML 2.0. The ITU languages have the good features of being well-defined and having action semantics that ensure specific behaviours. UML is good at object modelling and has proven to be a success at providing a framework for using different languages together - a feature that the ITU languages (for historical reasons) lack. Rather than defining new precise action languages for UML, or adding a framework scheme and object modelling to the ITU System Design Languages, the sensible way forward from a telecommunications system engineering point of view is to combine these features of both approaches.

It was therefore not a surprise to see the industry use tools that combine UML with the SDL-2000 semantic engine. This was the perspective of several major telecommunications manufacturers, and therefore the general direction of industry.

However, the situation with SDL-2000 after over a decade is unsatisfactory for all parties. Despite the 1996-1999 intention to ensure the language standard and tool support should be closely aligned (of course, ideally the same), this has not been the reality right through to the start of 2011. The language available to users is effectively SDL-92 with the 1996 addendum plus some of the features of SDL-2000 (which features depending on which tool is used) and often using legacy syntax for data. It was to ensure users are still able to produce SDL-models that are valid according to the standard that Annex B was added to Z.100 for SDL-2000, which allows the legacy syntax supported by tools.

Not only was SDL-2000 not fully supported, but also as UML and other languages such as the ITU-T User Requirements Notation [21], become more commonly used, there have been changing expectations of the facilities offered by the Specification and Description Language. Some, such as UML-like syntax, do not seem to be required. Others, that are not included in SDL-2000 such as timer supervised states, seem to be desirable.

1.2   The Data Issue

A data model that provides data with both sets of values (as in ASN.1) and operations is essential for any language that is to provide executable models or implementations. SDL-2000 made a major change to the way that data was defined: the algebraic axiom approach was removed from the user language, leaving just a constructive data approach (as in most programming languages). At the same time object data types were added. Leaving aside whether reference (object) data is actually needed and the "modernized" syntax in SDL-2010, whether SDL-2000 data is the best approach is reconsidered.

An SDL-2000 user is faced with the option of using either ASN.1 or SDL-2000 to define data types. If ASN.1 is used SDL-2000 provides a built-in set of operators. Similarly the built-in SDL-2000 data types provide a set of defined operators. The only real advantage of the SDL-2000 data types over ASN.1 is an arguably nicer syntax. The language could be made simpler by removing the SDL-2000 data types, but this would not be acceptable for legacy reasons.

Tools that produce target code for SDL-2000 are usually proprietary products of larger companies. Commercial tools usually implement ASN.1[2] and SDL-2000 data in one of two ways: providing translation to another programming language (usually C or C++), or producing code for a virtual machine and providing an emulator for that machine (written in some other language like Java or C). The advantage of either of these approaches is that they are target machine independent. However, there remains the issue of interfacing code from SDL-2000

---

[2] Whether ASN.1 compilation is done in a separate tool or not is a tool issue, not a language issue.

with other code, especially device and message handlers and possibly the Real Time Operating System (RTOS).

An alternative is to open up the language to external data types. In fact this was envisaged in SDL-92, with the **external** data syntax, but (as seen from MSC [22] and UML experience) it is difficult to define a language that can use the declarations and expression syntax in a plug-compatible way. Moreover, Z.121 [23] now provides an MSC to SDL-2000 data binding. Also from the user viewpoint the meaning of an expression in SDL-2000 would depend on the actual data language used, which may not be clear from context. As with MSC, there are requirements on any data language used, so that data is compatible with essential features such as timers. Despite these issues, from a user point of view using a data expression notation from another language can be a practical approach (as evidence see SDL-RT). The plan therefore for SDL-2010 was to first ensure SDL-2000 data is supported, and then define a way of providing a binding to other language syntaxes such as Java, C (or C++) or the data language of SDL-RT.

1.3   Diagram Structure

It has been agreed for some time that although the Specification and Description Language has both a graphical (SDL/GR) and textual (SDL/PR) presentation form coupled by a common abstract grammar, the primary presentation form is graphical, and the textual form is used mainly as an interchange format. Specifications in the language therefore usually consist of a number of diagrams. While in SDL-2000 it is permitted that diagrams for inner components are drawn nested inside the diagrams for the enclosing component, in practice this is not done for two reasons: in general the resulting diagram would be too large, and full tool support is not provided. Even though tools support the printing of such nested diagrams to some extent, diagrams are usually generated separately, and for any reasonable size of system the nested diagrams become too extensive to handle, read or comprehend. Instead inner diagrams are referenced from enclosing diagrams, so that each diagram is a reasonable size. Tools support this approach.

On the other hand, the semantics of the language is defined in terms of a single hierarchical model in the abstract syntax, in which the referenced diagram replaces each reference (after eliminating any duplicates). In SDL-2000 the change from references to the hierarchy is theoretically done by transformations to a nested concrete syntax and then this concrete syntax is mapped to the abstract syntax. In SDL-2010 the change from references to the hierarchy is done by mapping referenced diagrams directly to the abstract grammar. In the concrete syntax the nested graphical form (which is not generally tool supported for diagrams in any case) is no longer part of the language. This is a worthwhile simplification, because the concrete grammar does not have to describe both forms and intermediate transformation. To some extent, moving SDL/PR to Z.106 in 2002 enabled this change.

1.4   Features without Formal Semantics

Some features (such as comments, paging, create lines, multiple type references) do not add to the semantics of an application model, but are provided to allow annotation to be presented for the benefit of engineers. While these features should be checked for consistency, tools otherwise ignore them. In SDL-2010 these features are separated from the extended finite state machine parts of the language.

In particular, the Association feature was added in SDL-2000, to allow UML-like associations to be shown between types (or "classes" in UML terminology). This had no semantic meaning in SDL-2000, and is arguably now better covered by using UML tools and applying the UML profile in Z.109.

1.5   Feature Deletion, Retention and Extension

So where does this leave SDL-2000?

As for previous versions (SDL-88, SDL-92) the language definition has had several years of stability, and it was appropriate to consider what change should be made for the new version. First scheduled for consent in 2008, the revision was initially named SDL-2008. This date was not achieved. At the September 2009 ITU-T meeting it was renamed SDL-2010, the expected year for consent at that time. Though still not completed in December 2010, it was then decided (reaffirmed April 2011) not to change the name again: work had progressed sufficiently for completion in 2011 to seem certain.

As for previous revisions, one objective was to simplify the language. A new objective was to have a clearly defined basic SDL: the SDL-Task Force (a small consortium outside ITU-T) was ostensibly set up with this objective, but that organization had by October 2005 effectively ceased to exist, and the target of this group was not an SDL-2000 subset. In addition extension proposals for the language had come from many sources such as the SDL-RT, the SDL-Task Force, and industry users. There were also ideas considered previously but not incorporated into SDL-2000 and a few ideas to support UML profiling. There were some additions made in SDL-2000 compared to the previous SDL-92 version that had **not** been widely implemented, such as object data, the UML class symbol for types and UML-like associations. Some features, such as exception handing had been implemented in just one tool. These largely unimplemented features were considered for deletion.

Because SDL-2000 is a richer language than SDL-92 it was agreed there was no point in retaining features that have not been widely supported or used. On the other hand, features that are widely used should not be deleted, even if a better alternative exists or is proposed, because it has been found this kind of change leads to significant legacy problems.

A pragmatic approach has been taken: some features are being deleted and some potentially useful ones (based on the participating expert contributions tempered by user and tool vendor feedback) were added. The way Recommendations are approved at ITU-T has changed since 1999, so that significant comments can now be made and handled in a more open way during the approval

stage. One criterion for feature retention or addition is compatibility with UML.
There are two reasons for this: UML is a coherent framework for binding ITU-T
languages together so SDL-2010 needs to be consistent with the UML model,
and secondly the language provides the needed precise action semantics to UML.
The creation of a UML profile for the telecommunications action language in
Z.109 (06/07) [20] for SDL-2000 was obviously a key determinant for this compatibility, and generated a few necessary or highly desirable changes to Z.100.

The current draft has been prepared on the assumption that exception handling[3] is deleted (while keeping the timers on remote procedures). Object data
is for the time being removed, but further study is in progress. Esoteric features
(such as name class) are removed. In addition the Association feature and the use
of UML class symbols for types are removed. An overview of the set of features
of SDL-2010 is given in Sect. 3.

The net result is (as for previous versions) SDL-2010 contains both existing
language features implemented in tools, and additional language features that
(if and when supported) will enhance the language. The composite state feature
does not exactly fit into either of these categories. In SDL-2000 composite states
replaced the **service** concept of SDL-92, but is both a more powerful concept
than **service** and more compatible with UML, though currently lacking tool
support. For SDL-2010, returning to the SDL-92 **service** was not an option, because UML compatibility would be diminished, and deleting the feature was not
an option either, because the SDL-92 **service** maps to an aggregate composite
state. Moreover, the way an SDL-2000 state machine behaves is defined in terms
of the way an instance of a composite state type behaves, and in SDL-2010 this
underlying model is clarified and strengthened in the revised description of state
machines.

2   Organization of the SDL-2010 Language Standard

This section outlines the organization of the SDL-2010 standard.

In SDL-2000 there was already a successful clear separation of abstract
grammar, concrete grammar and shorthands (further considered in Sect. 2.1).
SDL-2010 takes a further step by separating concerns as described in Sect. 2.2
into documents for the core language (see Sect. 2.3), full coverage of the abstract grammar (see Sect. 2.4), shorthand notation (see Sect. 2.5) and data (see
Sect. 2.6) into separate documents, while retaining the separate document for
ASN.1 use (see Sect. 2.7) and the common interchange format (see Sect. 2.8).

2.1   Shorthand Transformation Models

Since SDL-88 and in SDL-92 and SDL-2000, transformation models have been
used to define a number of language features, where a given concrete syntax is

---

[3] Exceptions are still raised by certain constructs (such as indexing OutOfRange),
but cause the further behaviour of the system to be undefined because they are not
handled.

transformed into another concrete syntax. These features are called "shorthand" productions. While these features are often so useful and practical that they are essential, they are not essential in a theoretical sense, as the transformed concrete syntax can (usually) be used instead of the shorthand version. In fact the abstract syntax and language semantics are (or at least should be) defined only for concrete syntax that cannot be transformed. It is this canonical syntax that is mapped to abstract ayntax. The semantics and (as far as possible) constraints are expressed in terms of the abstract syntax.

An objective in SDL-2010 is to keep the core of the language as small as possible (and therefore easier to understand), and as far as possible separate the description of the transformation models from the core parts of the language. This is reflected in a reorganization of the SDL-2010 standard compared with SDL-2000 (see below).

2.2   Reorganization of the Documents for the Language Standard

SDL-2010 is reorganized so that core features are defined within the Z.101 part of the language definition, with the remaining (retained) more complex language features described in subsequent parts (Z.102, Z.103, Z.104, Z.105 and Z106). In the new organization Z.100 is re-utilized to provide an overview of the set of Recommendations.

Anyone who has been tracking the language for a number of years will be aware that this structure for the language definition is not new: the 1988 version (SDL-88) defined "Basic SDL" and then a number of additional features that extended "Basic SDL". This structure does not invalidate tools and applications that use the "full" language, while providing an identifiable subset. Some of the proposed benefits of having a clearly defined subset were:

- It makes it easier to teach and learn the basics of the language;
- It makes it easier to produce and maintain tools that can handle such a subset;
- If all tools that claim to support the standard have to support this subset, it gives a level of guaranteed portability.
- Such a subset would characterize essential "SDLness".

Getting agreement on what should and should not be in such a subset is not an easy task. There will be many different opinions backed up by different experiences and value judgements. Work already existed, such as studies at ETSI, which could lead a consensus result, so it was argued the potential benefits (some of which are outlined above) would justify the effort. Eventually it was agreed there were insufficient participants really interested in formally defining a subset, so that explicit definition of such a subset was not a specific objective for SDL-2010.

The objective of the reorganization has been separation of concerns. The essential behaviour of a system defined using SDL-2010 depends on the extended finite state machine model of Rec. Z.101 (coupled with the behaviour of expressions of Rec. Z.104). The other Recommendations Z.102, Z.103, Z.104, Z.105

and Z.106 provide language features that (respectively): make the language more comprehensive, make the language easier and more practical to use, provide the full data model and action language, enable ASN.1 to be used, and define the interchange format. A summary of the distribution of features over the main Recommendations Z.101 to Z.104 is given in Table. 1.

2.3   Basic SDL-2010 - Z.101

Recommendation Z.101 contains the part of the Specification and Description Language Recommendations for SDL-2010, that covers core features such as agent (block, process) type diagrams containing agent instance structures with channels, diagrams for extended finite state machines and the associated semantics for these basic features. A state machine is a composition of states of an agent: that is, a composite state, which is an instance of a state type. For that reason, state types and composite states are part of the basic language.

Most of the abstract grammar of SDL-2000 is covered by Basic SDL-2010. The abstract grammar that is not covered is for specialization (also known as inheritance) of types, the additional types of stimulus for an input (priority input, enabling condition, continuous signal, remote procedures and remote variables), synonyms and the generic definition features. These and macros are covered in Z.102.

The example given in Fig. 2 illustrates Basic SDL-2010 use, but is not intended to be useful as it specifies a kind of write only memory.

In Basic SDL-2010 the system model is based on type definitions: agent instances are type based instances and the state machine of an agent is a type based state. The page structure is part of the concrete syntax, but in Basic SDL-2010 each diagram contains only one page. Multiple pages and agent diagrams (instead of type based agent instances) are shorthand notations. The key contents of Basic SDL-2010 are:

- Lexical rules including revised frame use and page numbers;
- Revised framework, package use and referenced definitions;
- Agent (system, block , process) types and state types;
- Typebased agents, procedures, channels and signals;
- State transition graphs with start and state nodes with inputs and saves;
- Transitions: each to a nextstate, join;stop or return node;
- Task (assignment), create (agent), procedure call, output (signal), and decision actions;
- Timers and key data features.

Each diagram is restricted to one page, and there are no agent diagrams (only agent types and typebased agents).

In the example an <sdl specification> is a <system specification>, which is a <typebased agent definition> that in turn is a <typebased system definition> associated with a <package use area>. The system symbol references the system type Syst defined in package Pkg. In package diagram Pkg, the system type symbol references the system type Syst . In the system type diagram Syst, the

Table 1. Features in Z.101, Z.103, Z.103 and Z.104

Feature	Z.101 Basic	Z.102 Comprehen.	Z.103 Shorthand	Z.104 Data
Lexical rule, frame use, page numbers	X	UCS Chars.		
Framework, packages, referenced definitions	X			
Agent types, state types	X			
Typebased agents, procedures	X			
Channels, interfaces, signals	X			
State transition graphs: start, state with input/save	X			
Transitions to; nextstate, join, stop, return	X			
Actions; tasks, create, proc. call, output, decision	X			
Timers, Data (overview)	X			
Macros		X		
Substate entry/exit points		X		
Aggregate states (fork/join)		X		
Type context parameters		X		
Specialization/inheritance		X		
Virtuality		X		
Remote procedures/variables		X		
Spontaneous transitions, continuous signals, priority inputs		X		
Statement lists in tasks		X		
Generic systems: select, transition option			X	
Various syntax alternatives			X	
Comment symbol, create line			X	
Text extension symbol			X	
Multiple page diagrams			X	
Statement lists in tasks			X	
Agent diagrams			X	
State graph in agent (type)			X	
Implicit channels, optional names			X	
* state/input/save, implicit input			X	
Predefined data package				X
Textual procedure/operator body				X
Data encoding (see text)				X

14   R. Reed

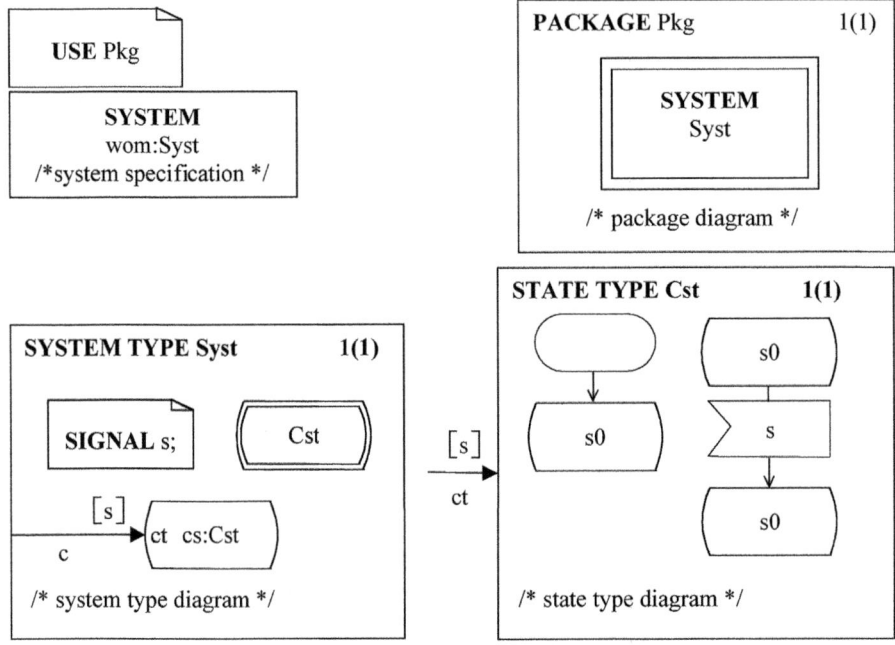

Fig. 2. System wom in Basic SDL-2010

state symbol represents the state machine based on the (composite) state type
Cst. In Basic SDL-2010 an agent type (system, block or process) never contains
a state graph, but only contains other (typebased) agents and (if the agent type
has a state machine) a typebased state machine. In this case the (composite)
state type of the state machine is referenced locally by the state type symbol
containing Cst. The referenced state type Cst gives the state graph.

In SDL-2000, the transformations (from agent diagrams to agent references
using implicit agent types, and from a state graph at the agent level to reference an implicit state type for the state machine of the agent containing for
the graph) were hidden within the general description of agents. In SDL-2010
the more concise, usual forms are not defined in Basic SDL-2010. Instead the
transformations are given in Z.103 and result in Basic SDL-2010.

2.4   Comprehensive SDL-2010 - Z.102

Recommendation Z.102 contains a part of the Specification and Description Language Recommendations for SDL-2010 that extends the semantics and syntax
of the Basic language in Rec. Z.101 to cover the full abstract grammar and
the corresponding canonical concrete notation. This includes features such as
type inheritance, continuous signals, enabling conditions, and aggregate states.
Other features of Comprehensive SDL-2000 are important to complete the

language: virtual types, parameterized types with context parameters, remote procedures/variables, generic systems (select, optional transition), macros and Unicode handling. Features without full abstract grammar are:

Inheritance (specialization) which allows one type to be a specialized sub-type of another type, so that it inherits properties, structure and the way instances behave from the parent super-type while additional properties, structure and actions can also be added. There is an optional parent identifier defined in the abstract syntax to link the specialized type to the parent type. However, the abstract grammar part given by the *Semantics* description of a specialized type definition is still largely in terms of combining the content of the super-type with the content of the specialized definition described by reference to concrete syntax items and is mostly unrevised from SDL-2000 (and probably SDL-92).

Virtuality where a type marked as **virtual** defined within an enclosing type is inherited in any sub-type of the enclosing type, and as a virtual type is allowed to be redefined in the sub-type. The redefined type can be marked either **redefined** in which case it is virtual and is allowed to be redefined in a sub-type of the sub-type, or marked **finalized** in which case redefinition is not allowed. Virtuality is currently handled at the concrete syntax level: there (currently) is no associated abstract syntax.

Context parameters are another feature handled at the concrete syntax level. In this case a copy is made of the body of the base type with context parameters and the actual parameters are substituted for the formal parameters rather like macro parameter substitution, but with type checking on the actual parameters. With all the parameters bound, the resulting body is used to define a type.

Remote procedures/variables are defined in terms of an implicit signal exchange between the caller and the owner of the procedure/variable with the caller waiting in an implicit state for a response. For simplicity, these are described in terms of models that use Basic SDL-2010 concrete grammar, but in principle they could (with some effort) be redefined in terms of abstract grammar.

Select and optional transition provide concrete syntax for including/excluding parts of diagrams based on the value of a <simple expression>: Boolean in the case of **select** used in agent structure diagrams, and typically Boolean or Integer for a <transition option area> of a state graph. It is possible to statically evaluate a <simple expression> during the <sdl specification> analysis and the resulting *SDL-specification* is determined from the selected parts. Consequently there is no abstract grammar for this feature.

Macros and Unicode handling are both carried out on the system model before the full validity and meaning of the resulting system is considered. They are therefore not the same as shorthand notations. The handling of Unicode is a lexical issue resulting in unique tokens for each name. Macros can be defined anywhere, have global scope and are expanded before other analysis results: the division of the <sdl specification> into diagrams and and/or files is (in theory) ignored, so there is no abstract grammar.

2.5   Shorthand Notation and Annotation in SDL-2010 - Z.103

Recommendation Z.103 contains the part of the Specification and Description Language Recommendations for SDL-2010 that adds shorthand notations (such as asterisk state) that make the language easier to use and more concise, and various annotations that make models easier to understand (such as comments or create lines), but do not add to the formal semantics of the models. Models transform shorthand notations from the concrete syntax of Rec. Z.103 into concrete syntax of Rec. Z.102 or Rec. Z.101. The key additional features are:

- Agent diagram (has an implied agent type)
- Agent with state graph (has an implied state type)
- Asterisk input/save, implicit transition
- Signallist, interface as stimulus/on channel
- Asterisk state, multiple state appearance
- Multiple diagram pages
- Various syntax alternatives
- Create lines, comment area, text extension.

The example given in Fig. 3 is a redefinition of the wom system using the features of Shorthand SDL-2010. Compared with Fig. 2 only one diagram is now required, because the types are implied.

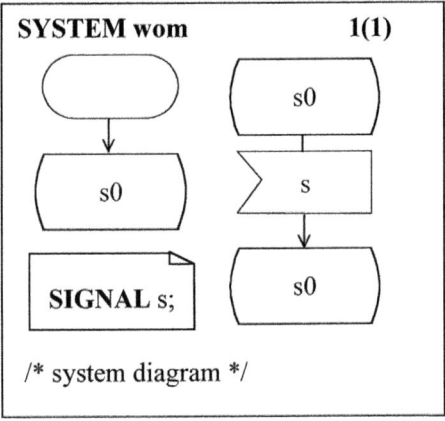

Fig. 3. System wom in Shorthand SDL-2010

2.6   Data and Action Language in SDL-2010 - Z.104

Recommendation Z.104 contains the part of the Specification and Description Language Recommendations for SDL-2010 that adds the data and action language used to define data types and expressions. In SDL-2010 it is allowed to use different concrete data notations, such as the SDL-2000 data notation or C with bindings to the abstract grammar and the Predefined data package. The underlying data model is fundamental to behaviour and provides sorts of data such as

Boolean and Integer that are used in other language features. For that reason this underlying model and an overview of predefined data sorts and constructs is given in Z.100 annex D.

The SDL-2000 Z.104 [18], which concerns the encoding of data, was initially incorporated into Z.104 for SDL-2010. A key feature is applying encoding rules for ASN.1 and it has therefore been decided to move this material to Z.105.

2.7   SDL-2010 Combined with ASN.1 Modules - Z.105

Recommendation Z.105 provides a mapping for ASN.1 modules to features defined in rest of the Specification and Description Language Recommendations for SDL-2010, so that the ASN.1 modules define data items that can be used with the rest of SDL-2010. This is unchanged from SDL-2000 except the data type definitions are moved to Z.104 for SDL-2010. However, since the publication of Z.104 [18] in 2004, there has been a standardized why of invoking encoding/decoding rules, which is described in paper [24]. An ASN.1 CHOICE in an ASN.1 module can be imported as an interface. For example, if an ASN.1 module named MyASN1 contains a CHOICE named MyMessages, this can be imported using the package use area:

> **USE** MyASN1/**INTERFACE** MyMessages;

attached to the system diagram. If MyMessages is defined in MyASN1 as:

```
MyASN1
        DEFINITIONS AUTOMATIC TAGS ::=
BEGIN
-- definitions including
        MyMessages ::= CHOICE {
                connect Destination,
                sendInfo Information,
                disconnect ConnectionRef}
-- the data types mentioned above such as Destination
-- and Information visible here.
END
```

this implies the SDL-2010 **interface**:

```
interface MyMessages {
        signal   connect ( Destination ) ,
                 sendInfo ( Information ) ,
                 disconnect ( ConnectionRef ); }
```

The user therefore has a simple and direct way of defining in ASN.1 the signals to be used in the SDL-2010 model. The channel that carries the signals of the interface can be defined with **interface** MyMessages as a <signal list> associated with the channel. The set of encoding rules used on the channel are specified after the channel name with (for example, for Packed Encoding Rules) **encoding PER**.

2.8   Common Interchange Format for SDL-2010 - Z.106

Recommendation Z.106 provides alternative textual syntax for the graphical syntax items defined in Z.101 to Z.105 that can be used as a Common Interchange Format (CIF) between SDL-2010 tools. The basic level of CIF provides only a textual equivalent of graphical items. The full CIF is intended for the interchange of graphical SDL-2010 specifications (SDL/GR) so that the drawings are recognizably the same.

2.9   Formal Definition (Annex F to Z.100)

The initial plan is that no formal definition be provided for SDL-2010, due to a lack of resources to modify the existing model or generate a new one. Instead the published Z.100 Annex F for SDL-2000 is referenced. It is therefore noted that this is out of date, but in combination with the obsolete 2007 version of Z.100 (for SDL-2000) [17] it provides a more formal definition for SDL-2000 than currently available for SDL-2010. Most of SDL-2010 is intended to be unchanged from SDL-2000, therefore Annex F to Z.100 with [17] provides more detail than Z.100 to Z.106 for most SDL-2010 features. If there is an inconsistency between Annex F to Z.100 for SDL-2000 and other parts of Z.100 to Z.106 for SDL-2010, it is either because there is an error in Z.100 to Z.106 or because there is a specific change to SDL-2010 compared with SDL-2000. If a change from SDL-2000 is not documented in Z.100 to Z.106, further study is needed to determine if the inconsistency is an error or intended.

If work is done to replace the formal definition, alternatives are to update the existing model or completely replace it with a new one, in which case a different approach (such as metamodelling) might be considered.

3   Changed, New and Deleted Features

A number of changes in SDL-2010 compared to SDL-2000 are the result of reviewing and rewriting to divide the text into several Recommendations. Some changes, such as removing nested diagrams, resulted in both deletion and a rewrite of retained text. Changes, such as making pages part of the diagram syntax, required additional syntax rules as well as modifying existing rules. The items described here only cover changes that are significant new or deleted items. For example, although the text on statement lists has had a major revision, there was no intention to change the language – only to improve Recommendation text, therefore this change is not described here.

3.1   Synonym as a "Read Only Variable"

A <synonym definition> represents a *Variable-definition* in the context in which the synonym definition appears with special property that the variable is read-only. The <synonym name> represents the *Variable-name*. Writing to the variable is not possible, because <synonym> is not allowed where assignments could take place. The concrete syntax is not changed and synonyms can be used as in SDL-2000. The revised semantics better matches implementation by means of a variable containing the synonym value, which can easily be changed if the value is changed.

3.2   Lower Bound of Agent Instance Sets

It is allowed to specify a *Lower-bound* on agent instance sets as in Fig. 4, which by default is zero matching SDL-2000. If the same Natural is used for the initial, maximum and lower bound, the set is fixed, which was not possible to specify in SDL-2000. A *Stop-node* in an instance set that is already at the *Lower-bound* causes the exception OutOfRange to be raised, but the number of active instances can be found from the integer built-in expression **active(this)** or **active(ais)** where ais is an agent instance set. The new syntax is:

<number of instances>::=([<initial number>][,[<maximum number>][,<lower bound>]])

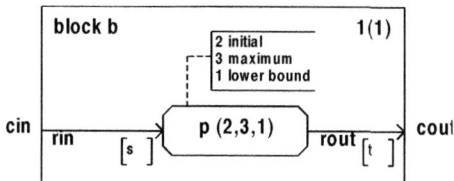

Fig. 4. Process instance set with a lower bound

3.3   Input and Save via Gate

In SDL-2010 when a signal is placed in an input port, it is stored with the identity of the gate on which it arrived at the destination agent. This allows the transition taken to be determined by the gate as well as the signal identity. The example in Fig. 5 is used to illustrate the feature. Assume an instance of signal s is the next signal in the input queue.

In state s0, if s arrived via g1 the next state is s1. If s did not arrive via g1 the next state is s2. Only one input or save can contain s **via** g1 for the same state. Only one input or save can contain s (without a gate).

In state s1, if s arrived via g2 the next state is s2. If s did not arrive via g2, the signal remains in the input queue (if these are the only transitions from s1, until a signal s arrives via g2).

In state s2, if s arrived via g3 the signal remains in the input queue. If s did not arrive via g3, the next state is s3.

If there is no explicit input or save for s without a gate, there is still an implicit input for s without a gate back to the same state. In a process (rather than a process type) diagram, the name of a channel to the process is used for the via. In the implicit process type for the process, this is transformed to the implicit gate connected to the channel.

20   R. Reed

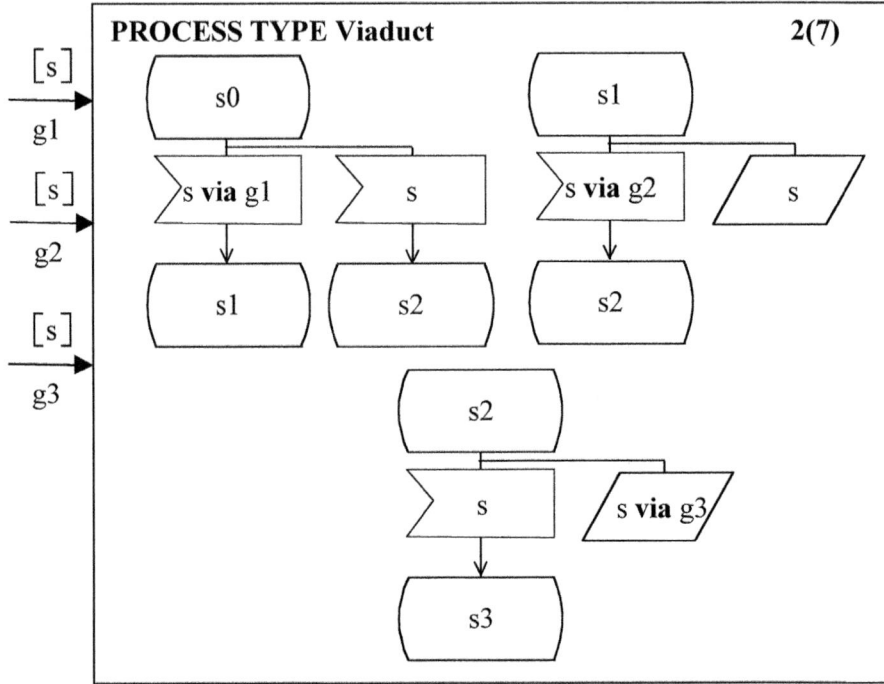

Fig. 5. **PROCESS TYPE** Viaduct using the input via gate feature

3.4   Multiple Priority Levels of Input

In SDL-2000 inputs can be with or without priority, but there are no levels of input priority. Priority inputs of a state are considered for enabling signals in the input port for consumption before other inputs without priority. In SDL-2010 there are multiple levels of priority and inputs with highest priority are considered first. If there are no signals for a priority level, inputs with the next priority are considered until either a signal is enabled or all priority inputs have been considered, after which inputs without priority are considered. Priority is specified by a *Priority-name* given as a `Natural` value, but note that zero is the *highest* priority, one is lower and the *highest* number given has the *lowest* priority. The reason is to be consistent with the existing SDL-2000 *Priority-name* for *Continuous-signal* where zero is taken first. However, if the <priority name> is omitted this implies a number one greater than the highest number explicitly given: that is, the lowest priority. A priority input without a gate, takes precedence over a lower priority input with a gate or an input with a gate without priority. The new syntax is:

<priority input list>::=<priority stimulus>{,<priority stimulus>}*
<priority stimulus>::=<stimulus>[<priority clause>]
<priority clause>::= **priority** [<priority name>]

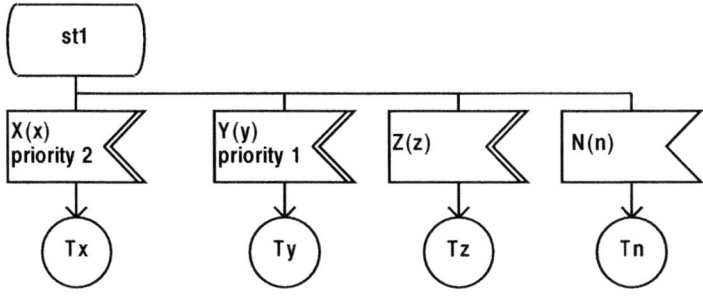

Fig. 6. Multiple levels of input priority

For the example in Fig. 6 assume the signals X, Y, Z and N each with one parameter saved in x, y, z and n respectively. Assume state st1 is reached with the input port containing in order of arrival signals N, Y, Z and X. Assume the connectors Tx, Ty, Tz and Tn connect to transitions that terminate in state st1. The input for Z has an implied *Priority-name* of 3. The signal Y is enabled and consumed because this input has the highest priority and Ty is taken. When st1 is reached again signal X is enabled if no Y signals have arrived in the meantime, and on next occasion signal Z (assuming no X or Y signals have arrived). Signal N is only enabled if there are no signals X, Y or Z in the input port when in state st1. If the inputs for two or more signals have the same input priority, the signal that arrived first is consumed.

3.5   Timer Supervised States

SDL-2010 is extended to cover timer supervised states. If state has a <state timer area> (see syntax below), the *State-node* has a *State-timer*. The timer is set entering the state and reset entering a *Transition*, except for an empty *Transition* to the state (for example from an implicit transition). If the timer expires while in the state, the timer signal is immediately consumed: it is a higher priority input than any other input. The *Transition* for the <transition area> of the <state timer area> is taken. The syntax is:

<state timer area>::=<plain input symbol> **contains** <state timer>
                      is followed by <transition area>
<state timer> ::= **state timer** <time expression> | **set** <set clause>

A <state timer> with **state timer** <time expression> as in Fig. 7 uses an implicit timer for the state, whereas **set** <set clause> uses a defined timer which can have a default duration. If the state is a composite state, the timer expiration is treated in the same way as a signal causing an exit from the composite state.

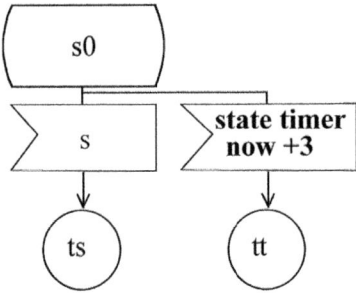

Fig. 7. Timer supervised state with an implicit timer

3.6   Deleted Features

As mentioned above, nested diagrams are no longer part of the standardized concrete syntax. Instead each diagram is referenced from the parent. Associated with this change, <specification area> that was an optional graphical depiction of the relationships between <system specification> and <package>s is deleted. These features were not supported by tools in a consistent way, or as defined in the Recommendations.

SDL-2000 included UML-like concrete syntax for type references and also UML-like associations. These were not well supported and added nothing to the semantics of the language: they just made the language Recommendation more complex and difficult to understand.

Since SDL-92 there has been a mechanism called *nameclass* for defining a generator for a set of names of literals or operators of a data type. This is used to define the literals for the Integer data type, character strings for the Charstring data type, and similarly for the literals of Bitstring, Real, Duration and Time. The nameclass feature is used with **spelling**, which provides the character string that corresponds to the spelling of the nameclass literal. While these are essential for the Predefined data types, there is no need to provide them as a feature of the user language. These have therefore been moved to Annex A of Z.104 to be used only (like axioms) for the definition of the Predefined data types. It is therefore no longer expected that tools support these features.

For the time being object data types are no longer part of the language. However, similar data types are widely used in other languages and the purpose of including them in SDL-2000 was to provide the advantages of reference computing. The further study plan for SDL-2010 is to reconsider how object data types are incorporated into the language, leading to a revision of Z.104 and/or the drafting of an additional Recommendation. One key issue is to minimize (preferably eliminate) dynamic binding of data types.

4   Conclusion

The status of SDL-2010 as this paper was initially being written in April 2011 was that a reasonable draft existed for Z.100 to Z.105, so that it was not unrealistic to expect a final draft to be consented for initiation of the ITU-T approval process at the start of September 2011. By the time this paper was presented in July 2011, improved drafts were available, to be circulated for review and comment up to and including the ITU-T meeting starting in the last week of August 2011.

On the other hand, as this paper was being revised for publication there were still issues in the existing drafts to be corrected and further discussed. The concept of support for specifying channel delay values was accepted, but the text needed to be finalized. Work has started on a further Recommendation, probably to be approved in 2012, to include in SDL-2010 **ref** and **own** variables and parameters that are associated with a reference to a value. Also, work has not really started on revising Z.106. So there was still work to do, and the reader is advised to check if the September 2011 date was met, or whether there is a further delay until 2012.

Another concern is tool support. There has been little innovation in tools for the language in the last few years. This is probably because the major source of income for tool providers has been the telecommunications industry, and despite the rapid growth of the Internet, companies such as Nortel, Nokia, Sony Ericsson and Motorola have had trading difficulties. No matter how good SDL-2010 is, if there is a lack of funds for tool development SDL-2010 is likely to remain theoretically interesting, but only implemented to the same subset as SDL-2000. The good news is that this subset is probably a bigger percentage of SDL-2010 than it was of SDL-2000, as I estimate more has been deleted than added in the revision.

Finally, if you read this paper, and would like to participate in the language review process, contact the author. This applies even if September 2012 has already passed, because there is a review period during the ITU-T approval process, and there is a defined maintenance procedure subsequent to publication by ITU-T. It is expected that the language will evolve further to meet user needs.

References

1. CCITT Orange Book, Programming Languages for Stored-Programme Control Exchanges, vol. VI.4, ITU, Geneva, pp. 3–23 (1977) ISBN 92-61-00421-0
2. ITU-T – International Telecommunication Union: Recommendation Z.100 (08/02): Specification and Description Language (SDL), Geneva, Switzerland (August 2002), http://www.itu.int/rec/T-REC-Z.100-200208-S/en
3. ITU-T – International Telecommunication Union: Recommendation Z.100 (11/99): Specification and Description Language (SDL), Geneva, Switzerland (November 1999), http://www.itu.int/rec/T-REC-Z.100-199911-S/en
4. CCITT Yellow Book, Functional Specification and Description Language (SDL). Man Machine Language (MML), Recommendations Z.101 – Z.104 and Z.311 – Z.341, vol. VI Fascicle VI.7, ITU, Geneva (1981)
5. CCITT Red Book, Recommendations Z. 100 to Z. 104: Specification and Description Language, ITU, Geneva (1985)

6. ITU-T – International Telecommunication Union: Recommendation Z.100 (11/88): Specification and Description Language (SDL), Geneva, Switzerland (November 1999), http://www.itu.int/rec/T-REC-Z.100-198811-S/en

7. ITU-T – International Telecommunication Union: Recommendation Z.100 (03/93): CCITT Specification and Description Language (SDL), Geneva, Switzerland (March 1993), http://www.itu.int/rec/T-REC-Z.100-199303-S/en

8. ITU-T – International Telecommunication Union: Recommendation Z.100 Addendum 1 (10/96): Corrections to Recommendation Z.100, CCITT Specification and Description Language (SDL), Geneva, Switzerland (March 1993), http://www.itu.int/rec/T-REC-Z.100-199610-SAdd1/en

9. ITU-T – International Telecommunication Union: Recommendation Z.105 (11/99): SDL combined with ASN.1 modules (SDL/ASN.1), Geneva, Switzerland (November 1999), http://www.itu.int/rec/T-REC-Z.105-199911-S/en

10. ITU-T – International Telecommunication Union: Recommendation Z.107 (11/99): SDL with embedded ASN.1, Geneva, Switzerland (November 1999), http://www.itu.int/rec/T-REC-Z.107-199911-W/en

11. ITU-T – International Telecommunication Union: Recommendation X.680-X.695 (11/08): Information Technology - Abstract Syntax Notation One (ASN.1) & ASN.1 encoding rules, Geneva, Switzerland (November 1999), http://www.itu.int/rec/T-REC-X.680-X.693-200811-P/en

12. ITU-T – International Telecommunication Union: Recommendation Z.109 (11/99): SDL combined with UML, Geneva, Switzerland (November 1999), http://www.itu.int/rec/T-REC-Z.107-199911-S/en

13. Object Management Group: Unified Modeling Language, http://www.omg.org/spec/UML/ and http://www.omg.org/spec/UML/2.1.2

14. ITU-T – International Telecommunication Union: Recommendation Z.106 (11/00): Common interchange format for SDL, Geneva, Switzerland (November 2000), http://www.itu.int/rec/T-REC-Z.106-200011-S/en

15. ITU-T – International Telecommunication Union: Recommendation Z.106 (08/02): Common interchange format for SDL, Geneva, Switzerland (August 2002), http://www.itu.int/rec/T-REC-Z.106-200208-I/en

16. ITU-T – International Telecommunication Union: Z.100 (2002) Amendment 1 (10/03): Backwards compatibility and compliance, Geneva, Switzerland (October 2003), http://www.itu.int/rec/T-REC-Z.100-200310-SAmd1/en

17. ITU-T – International Telecommunication Union: Recommendation Z.100 (11/07): Specification and Description Language (SDL), Geneva, Switzerland (November 2007), http://www.itu.int/rec/T-REC-Z.100-200711-I/en

18. ITU-T – International Telecommunication Union: Recommendation Z.104 (10/04): Encoding of SDL data, Geneva, Switzerland (October 2004), http://www.itu.int/rec/T-REC-Z.104-200410-I/en

19. ITU-T – International Telecommunication Union: Recommendation Z.105 (07/03): SDL combined with ASN.1 modules (SDL/ASN.1), Geneva, Switzerland (July 2003), http://www.itu.int/rec/T-REC-Z.105-200307-I/en

20. ITU-T – International Telecommunication Union: Recommendation Z.109 (06/07): SDL-2000 combined with UML, Geneva, Switzerland (June 2007), http://www.itu.int/rec/T-REC-Z.107-200706-I/en

21. ITU-T – International Telecommunication Union: Recommendation Z.151 (11/08), User Requirements Notation (URN) – Language definition, Geneva, Switzerland (November 2008), http://www.itu.int/rec/T-REC-Z.151/en

22. ITU-T – International Telecommunication Union: Recommendation Z.120 (02/11), Message Sequence Chart (MSC), Geneva, Switzerland (February 2011), http://www.itu.int/rec/T-REC-Z.120/en
23. ITU-T – International Telecommunication Union: Recommendation Z.121 (02/03), Specification and Description Language (SDL) data binding to Message Sequence Charts (MSC), Geneva, Switzerland (February 2011), http://www.itu.int/rec/T-REC-Z.121/en
24. Reed, R.: Data encoding for SDL in ITU-T Rec. Z.104. In: Amyot, D., Williams, A.W. (eds.) SAM 2004. LNCS, vol. 3319, pp. 80–95. Springer, Heidelberg (2005)

TASTE:
A Real-Time Software Engineering Tool-Chain Overview, Status, and Future

Maxime Perrotin[1], Eric Conquet[1], Julien Delange[1],
André Schiele[1], and Thanassis Tsiodras[2]

[1] European Space Agency, ESTEC, Keplerlaan 1,
2201AG Noordwijk, The Netherlands
{Maxime.Perrotin,Eric.Conquet,Julien.Delange,
Andre.Schiele}@esa.int
[2] Semantix Information Technologies, K. Tsaldari 62,
11476, Athens, Greece
ttsiodras@semantix.gr

Abstract. TASTE stands for "The ASSERT Set of Tools for Engineering", in reference to the European FP6 program where it finds its roots. It consists in an open-source tool-chain dedicated to the development of embedded, real-time systems. TASTE addresses the modelling and deployment of distributed systems containing heterogeneous software and hardware components; it focuses on the automation of tedious, error-prone tasks that usually make complex systems difficult to integrate and validate. TASTE relies on two complementary languages, AADL and ASN.1, that allow to create embedded systems which functional parts are made of C, Ada, SDL, SCADE, Simulink and/or VHDL code.

Keywords: ASN.1, SDL, MSC, TASTE, SCADE, AADL, VHDL.

1 Introduction

TASTE stands for "The ASSERT Set of Tools for Engineering", in reference to the European FP6 program where it finds its roots. **It consists in an open-source tool-chain dedicated to the development of embedded, real-time systems**. TASTE addresses the modelling and deployment of distributed systems containing heterogeneous software and hardware components; it focuses on the automation of tedious, error-prone tasks that usually make complex systems difficult to integrate and validate.

The philosophy is to let the user only focus on his functional code, letting him write it in the language of his choice, may it be a modelling language or a low-level implementation language. TASTE tools are responsible for putting everything together, including drivers and communication means and ensuring that the execution at runtime is compliant with the specification of the system real-time constraints.

To achieve this, **TASTE relies on two simple modelling languages** that give enough power to capture all the essential elements of a system that are required to

I. Ober and I. Ober (Eds.): SDL 2011, LNCS 7083, pp. 26–37, 2011.

generate the tasks, threads, and glue around the user functional code. These two languages are **AADL and ASN.1**.

Once a set of carefully selected system properties has been captured using these two languages, the core of the system's subcomponents can be developed using C, Ada, SDL (with RTDS or ObjectGEODE), SCADE, Simulink, VHDL, or any combination of these languages. Without any major overhead in the code, **TASTE will produce binaries that can be directly executed on several supported targets**: native Linux, Real-time Linux (Xenomai), Leon2/RTEMS, and Leon2/ORK.

In addition, TASTE provides many powerful features that help the end user building and validating his system. TASTE is implemented in a way that it is open to extensions ; for example it is possible in a dedicated mode to interact with TASTE-generated binaries using Python scripts or interactive user interfaces ; it is possible to stream and plot data, to trace internal message exchanges at runtime using message sequence charts (MSCs), to generate documentation, to analyse schedulability, code coverage, etc. TASTE is all but monolithic, contrary to many existing modelling tools which rely on a single modelling paradigm. It has several independent components, which can be used together in an homogeneous way, or which can be taken separately and used in a different development environment.

2 Scope

TASTE addresses what we call "heterogeneous computer-based systems", with a particular focus on embedded systems. The main characteristics of these systems are the following:

- They have limited resources;
- They have real-time constraints;
- They contain applications of very different natures (control laws, resource management, protocols, failure detection);
- Parts of the system are developed by different companies;
- They communicate with hardware (sensors and actuators);
- They contain heterogeneous hardware (e.g. with different endianness);
- They can be distributed over several physically independent platforms;
- They may run autonomously for years;
- They may not be physically accessible for maintenance (satellites)

Contrary to "ordinary", desktop-based software, which can be specified and developed by software engineers, our systems require the expertise of external actors such as scientists who define control laws, and for whom the specific challenges of software design – making sure all tasks will run in time, handling resources – are of little interest. Usually these people, who are the key people in the definition of embedded systems, are not able to write "good" software themselves. Very often, they will for example prototype their algorithms using a tool (e.g. Simulink) and then pass the models to software engineers who will code and integrate them for the embedded platform. Little automation is done, and there can be important delays between the mock-up and the release of the actual software. Maintenance and modifications are always difficult in that scheme.

The scope of TASTE is targeting this area, where non-software people need to be able to build the software part of system without too much hazardous and uncontrolled dependency on other people for what concerns interfaces, resource management, and real-time issues.

3 Case Study

In this section we introduce a case study that highlights each step of the TASTE process and many of the toolset features. The idea is to be very concrete about what TASTE can do for a project, and give some explanations about our technological choices.

3.1 Specification of the System

In this system, we want to control a robotic arm using an exoskeleton [1]. The exoskeleton is a set of sensors that an operator puts around his arm to detect movements and transfer them through electrical signals to a computer. The computer receives the sensor data and transforms it into a set of commands sent to a distant mechanical arm. The objective is to allow remote control of robots with a "convenient" user interface.

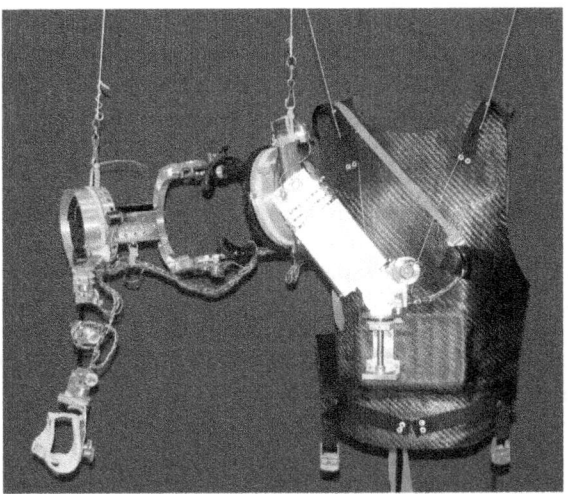

Fig. 1. ESA Exoskeleton

The exoskeleton is connected to an acquisition board (PCI 6071E)[1] , which is placed in an industrial PC. The PC is running Linux with the Xenomai[2] hard real-time extensions . There exists an open-source device driver for the acquisition board called "comedi"[3] , which means that for this setup we did not have to develop any specific low-level device driver.

Regarding the other end of the system, we used an existing 3D model that simulates the movements of a real robotic arm based on commands passed through an UDP (Ethernet) link.

The requirements are to develop an application that:

1. Polls the acquisition board and plot the input data for monitoring
2. Upon reception of sensor data, execute a control law
3. Send the resulting commands to the 3D model.

3.2 The Challenge

Following the TASTE approach, we want to put the focus here on the engineering of the functional aspects of the system rather than on software implementation details.

Independently from any constraints, we consider that the best way to address this problem is to model the control law using Matlab Simulink, and the overall orchestration of the system using the SDL language[4]. The combination is good

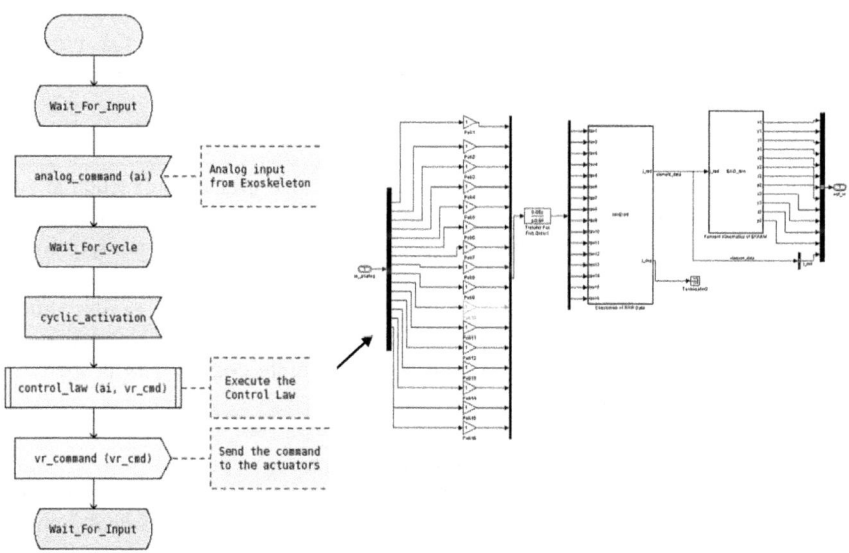

Fig. 2. The SDL-Simulink combination to model the system behaviour

---

[1] http://sine.ni.com/nips/cds/view/p/lang/en/nid/1042
[2] http://www.xenomai.org/
[3] http://www.comedi.org/
[4] We are using the Real-Time Developer Studio tool from http://www.pragmadev.com

because it puts together the simplicity of SDL to capture a behaviour using a workflow-like notation that anybody can read, and the power of Simulink to model and simulate a control law.

Without any tool support, implementing such a system is actually quite challenging, for the following reasons:

1. SDL-generated code has to be interfaced with device drivers;
2. Sensors send binary data in a format that is not compatible with SDL or Matlab abstract data types;
3. Actuators need commands to be formatted in packets which format is unknown to SDL or Matlab;
4. SDL-generated code has to be interfaced with Simulink-generated code;
5. The runtime (Linux with Xenomai) has to be configured;
6. If we want to plot data at runtime, some tools have to be found and configured.

These reasons partly explain why in practice the use of modelling tools and code generation is very limited in real projects, and why manual coding is preferred – developers would need to keep a deep knowledge of modelling tools and their (evolving) code generation strategy in order to integrate all components.

Several aspects of the complexity are obviously not related to the use of modelling tools: communication with hardware implies to encode and decode messages at binary level, which is difficult to implement and test, operating system tasks have to be created and configured, scheduling analysis has to prove that the system is feasible, etc. All these aspects have to be carefully addressed when developing a real-time system.

3.3   The TASTE Approach: AADL and ASN.1

In order to automate the integration of components and create an executable system, TASTE relies on two complementary languages: AADL and ASN.1. AADL is used to capture the system logical and physical architecture, while ASN.1 is used to express formally all the messages exchanged by the various system interfaces.

These languages are simple and powerful – in fact, there exists almost no alternative to them in terms of capabilities and tool support[5] . TASTE makes extensive use of AADL and ASN.1 in order to generate code, verify properties, and make sure the system will run as it was specified.

3.3.1   AADL to Capture the System Architecture

AADL is a language designed to capture the characteristics of system components and their relations. It addresses the logical architecture and the physical architecture of the system. The logical architecture is an abstract representation of the system where mostly the functional blocks are considered, while the physical architecture contains concrete software artefacts: processes, threads, and hardware: processors, memory, busses.

---

[5] For various reasons, UML, SysML, XML and IDL have not been considered as appropriate as they lack critical features or tool support to fulfil the needs we expressed.

AADL is textual, but can also be graphically represented. One of the main interests in AADL resides in its capability to be extended with formally-specified properties.

If we take for example our control law block, its AADL specification is:

```
SYSTEM Control_law
    FEATURES
        Control_law : PROVIDES SUBPROGRAM ACCESS FV::Control_law
          {
             Taste::RCMoperationKind => unprotected;
          };
    PROPERTIES
        Source_Language => SIMULINK;
END Control_law;

SUBPROGRAM FV::Control_law
    FEATURES
        in_analog : IN PARAMETER DataView::Analog_Inputs
          { Taste::encoding => NATIVE; };
        out_vr    : OUT PARAMETER DataView::VR_Model_Output
          { Taste::encoding => NATIVE; };
END FV::Control_law;
```

Each property is defined in an AADL "property set", which specifies a set of allowed values as well as the elements to which the property applies. This way, any existing AADL parser can automatically verify the consistency of properties used in the model just as if they were native keywords of the language. For example, the "Source_Language" property is defined this way:

```
Source_Language : Supported_Source_Languages applies to (system);
Supported_Source_Languages: type enumeration
    (Ada95,
     ASN1,
     Blackbox_Device,
     C,
     GUI,
     RTDS,
     SCADE6,
     SDL_ObjectGeode,
     Simulink,
     System_C,
     VHDL,
     ACN);
```

3.3.2 ASN.1 to Capture Data Types and Their Encoding Rules

ASN.1 is a simple textual language dedicated to data types description. With a concise syntax, it allows to express types and constraints (ranges, optional fields, etc.). It is used industrially in many applications (telecommunication, aeronautics, etc.) and is a well-established standard. The strong point about ASN.1 is that it is supported by a wide variety of mature tools, including open-source tools. ASN.1 permits a non-ambiguous representation of types in a language which is independent from implementation languages, and allows to derive automatic marshallers that follow any kind of binary encoding rules. This characteristic of ASN.1 makes it today the only valid "data modelling" solution to address embedded system issues when focusing on communication between heterogeneous components. The bold reference to DataView::Analog_Inputs in the AADL model above leads to an ASN.1 type:

```
-- Analog inputs are 16 voltage lines in range 0 to 6 volts
Analog-Inputs ::= SEQUENCE (SIZE(16)) OF REAL (0.0 .. 6.0)
```

In order to be able to derive the appropriate marshallers for this data, a separate model is used to specify how the physical device will place bits in memory when encoding the raw values:

```
Analog-Inputs[size 16] {
        dummy [encoding IEEE754-1985-64, endianness little]
}
```

3.4 The Graphical TASTE Model

AADL models exist either in textual or graphical form. TASTE provides an editor to capture the system attributes in such a way that at no point it is necessary to manually write AADL code. The complete system looks this way:

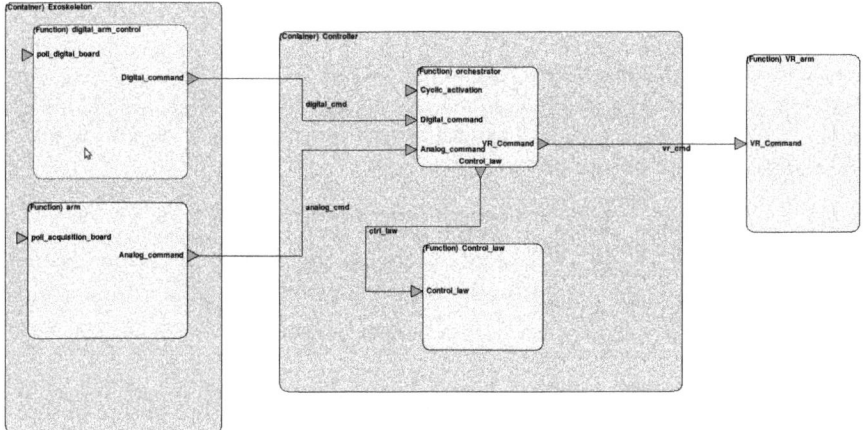

Fig. 3. System logical architecture

In the picture above, the "arm" block on the left corresponds to the input sensors of the exoskeleton, while "VM_arm" function on the right corresponds to the 3D model. In between, the "controller" container in the middle contains the various software functions that interact with the hardware blocks, i.e. the SDL and the Simulink blocks.

Each element of the model contains specific attributes. Interfaces can be cyclic, sporadic, protected (mutual exclusion), or unprotected. We also associate to each function an implementation language and context parameters (allowing configuration information to be captured at model level and used in the implementation code).

What is important is that all these attributes are used by TASTE model transformation tools, that follow a set of rules in order to go from a system abstract model down to a set of tasks and threads that comply with the system requirements.

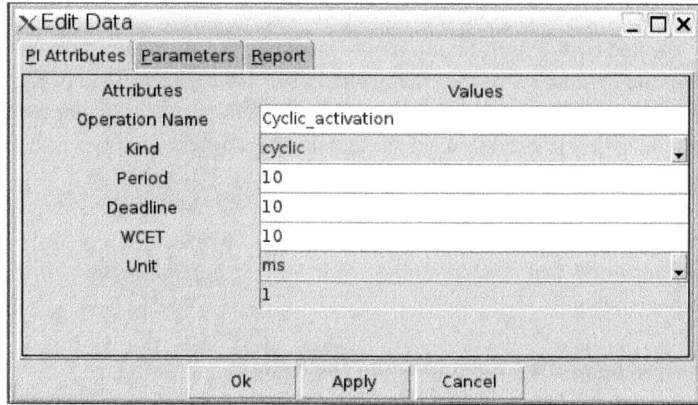

Fig. 4. Attributes of the cyclic_activation interface

3.5 Model Transformation and Code Generation

3.5.1 Generation of Code or Model Skeletons

One of the major features of TASTE is to be able to let the user work on functional code (or models) without having to know how to connect it to the rest of the system.

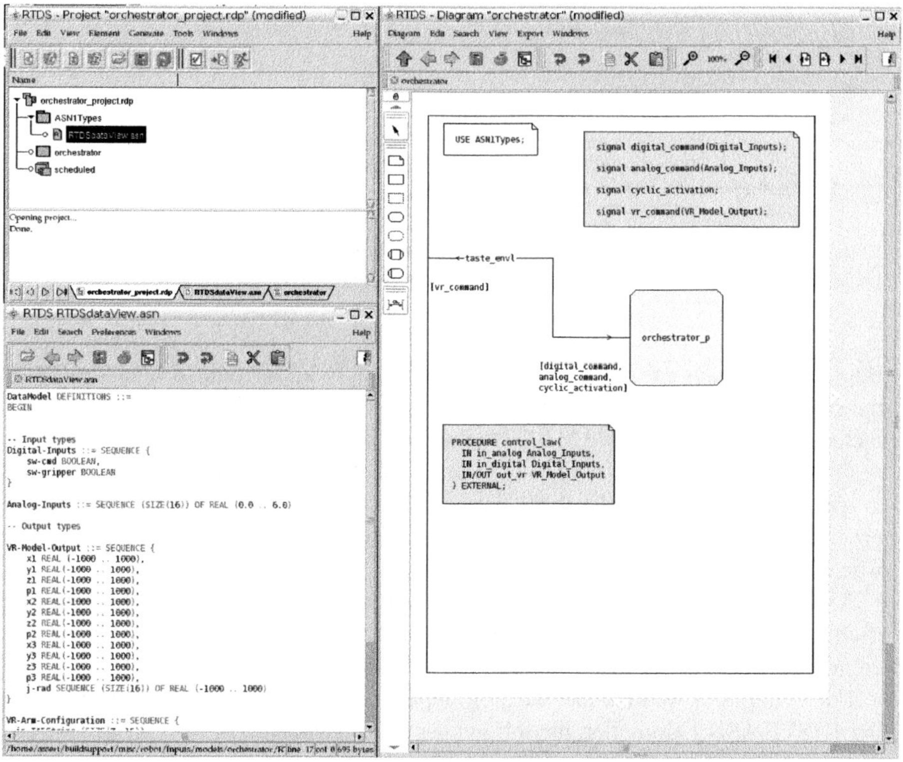

Fig. 5. TASTE-generated RTDS skeleton

For this purpose, TASTE generates application-level skeletons in the implementation language selected by the user, be it a native language (C, Ada) or a modelling language. If we take the example of the SDL block we have defined, and that we called "orchestrator", TASTE generated a complete RTDS project file, including an SDL empty system with a pre-defined set of signals and abstract data types in line with the original ASN.1 data model.

The same feature is provided for Simulink, SCADE, C, Ada, VHDL, and ObjectGEODE. TASTE is extensible by design and in principle any tool can be added to the list, provided that it also comes with a code generator that fulfils embedded system requirements.

3.5.2 Processing of the Model to Build the System

TASTE components make use of the user captures properties. Following some pre-defined rules, the input AADL logical model of the system is transformed into a corresponding physical model. The rules are usually straightforward. For example, if the user specifies a block that contains protected interfaces, it is automatically translated into a shared resource with mutual exclusion on the interfaces. If the user specifies a cyclic interface, then a periodic thread will be specified, etc.

```
THREAD arm_arm
FEATURES
            analog_command : OUT EVENT DATA PORT
DataView::Analog_Inputs_Buffer.impl;
END arm_arm;

THREAD IMPLEMENTATION arm_arm.others
PROPERTIES
            Initialize_Entrypoint_Source_Text => "init_arm";
            Compute_Entrypoint_Source_Text =>
"po_hi_c_arm_poll_acquisition_board";
            Dispatch_Protocol => Periodic;
            Period => 1 ms;
            Compute_Execution_Time => 0 ms .. 1 ms;
            Source_Stack_Size => 100 KByte;
            Deployment::Priority => 1;
END arm_arm.others;
```

Based on this physical model, it is possible to apply a variety of analysis using off-the-shelf tools. Among other, we may cite of course scheduling analysis (TASTE includes the CHEDDAR and MAST tools), memory sizing, etc.

Once this physical model of the system is created, an AADL compiler is invoked to generate low-level code that "wraps" the actual user code inside threads or processes, and that handles semaphores, communication, and access to device drivers when needed.

ASN.1 tools are used to automatically convert data at code level between languages (SDL, Simulink, C, Ada), as well as to generate binary encoders and decoders to communicate at packet level with external devices.

For example, if we take the "Analog_Inputs" data type seen before, once given to the TASTE ASN.1 Compiler, the following code is generated:

```
typedef struct {
    double arr[16];
} asn1SccAnalog_Inputs;

#define asn1SccAnalog_Inputs_REQUIRED_BYTES_FOR_ENCODING     128
flag asn1SccAnalog_Inputs_ACN_Encode (
                const asn1SccAnalog_Inputs* val,
                BitStream* pBitStrm,
                int* pErrCode,
                flag bCheckConstraints);

flag asn1SccAnalog_Inputs_ACN_Decode(
                asn1SccAnalog_Inputs* pVal,
                BitStream* pBitStrm,
                int* pErrCode);
```

The definition of the Encode and Decode functions provides all the routines to transform data between the C structure and the packet (binary buffer) expected by the actual device. TASTE ASN.1 compilers generate effective, compact code that is compliant with embedded system constraints and coding standards (no dynamic memory allocation, no dependency on any external code, no system calls, etc.).

3.6 Runtime Features

TASTE generates binaries that target a set of supported platforms, ranging from native x86 processors running Linux to embedded Leon2 (SPARC) processors with a real-time operating system. All operating system operations are handled by

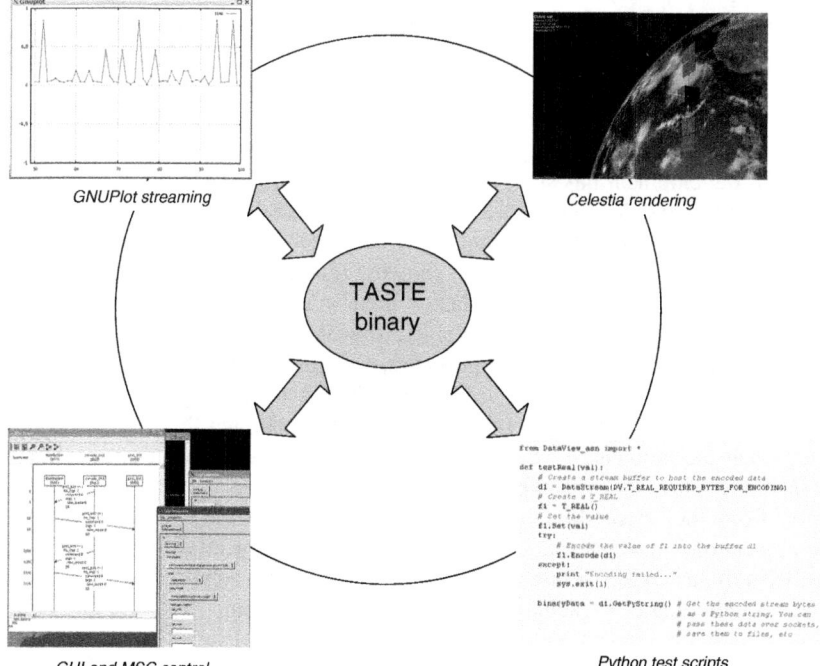

Fig. 6. TASTE runtime features

TASTE – the generated binary can be directly downloaded on target without any manual intervention.

TASTE provides many additional features at runtime. They are summarized in the following picture. In particular, a strong emphasis has been put on the possibility to write and execute test scripts automatically written using the Python language.

4 Conclusion and Future

The complete setup running is pictured below, showing the exoskeleton (on the left) sending data to the computer running the TASTE-generated binary, which in turn translates the sensor information to command a 3D model of the robotic arm. The next step is to replace this 3D model by the real arm. This case study showed how TASTE could easily be used in an environment using real hardware and that it was not limited to small software experiments. In particular, the use of drivers together with our ASN.1-based data modelling technologies showed excellent performance and opens doors to many other kinds of applications.

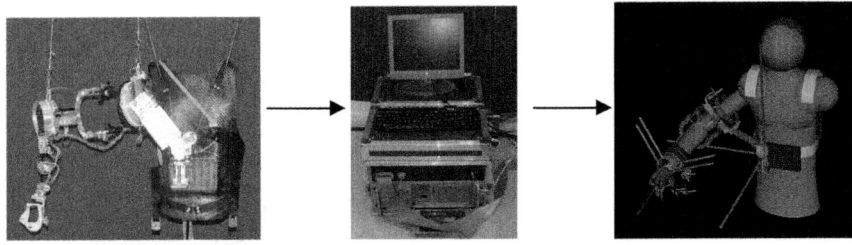

Fig. 7. Complete case study setup

TASTE development has started at the end of the ASSERT project, in 2008[2]. In three years of active development[6], it has reached a level of maturity which allows it to be used in operational projects and many complex case studies cases have already been performed by various companies, showing that TASTE today has no competitor for the technical issues it addresses. Dissemination outside R&D teams is however a tedious task – much more difficult than technical aspects. As of today, TASTE is freely released for all experimental purposes, and some of the companies involved in the tool already provide commercial support. But in order to guarantee a long-term continuation of the project, a further step has to be done, and this is one of our main objectives at the moment. TASTE can live as a product or as a set of separate tools, and several companies have expressed some interest in disseminating the technology outside from the space domain. We are willing to continue funding the TASTE development and make sure it will bring help to many projects which suffer from the so-called software crisis. In the meantime, we are continuously looking for innovative ideas and technologies to include them within the tool-chain.

---

[6] The development team mainly comprises ESA, Semantix Information Technologies, Ellidiss and ISAE, with significant contributions from UPM and ENST.

References

1. Schiele, A., Visentin,: The ESA Human Arm Exoskeleton for Space Robotics Telepresence. In: Proceeding of the 7th International Symposium on Artificial Intelligence, Robotics and Automation in Space, i-SAIRAS 2003, NARA, Japan, May 19-23, 2003 (1981)
2. Perrotin, M., Conquet, E., Dissaux, P., Tsiodras, T., Hugues, H.: The TASTE Toolset: turning human designed heterogeneous systems into computer built homogeneous software. In: ERTS 2010, Toulouse (2010)

Synthesizing Software Models:
Generating Train Station Models Automatically

Andreas Svendsen[1,2], Øystein Haugen[1], and Birger Møller-Pedersen[2]

[1] SINTEF, Pb. 124 Blindern, 0314 Oslo, Norway
[2] Department of Informatics, University of Oslo, Pb. 1080 Blindern, 0316 Oslo, Norway
{andreas.svendsen,oystein.haugen}@sintef.no, birger@ifi.uio.no

Abstract. This paper presents an approach for automatic synthesis of software models. Software models are increasingly being used for representing software applications at a high abstraction level, and source code can usually be generated from these models. Creating application models can be a tedious task, and thus the presented approach automates this task. Based on a formal definition of the domain-specific language (DSL) and user-defined properties, we generate intended application models. These models can then be subject to further manual extensions or used as is. The approach is illustrated by a DSL from the train domain, and the automatic synthesis of train station models.

Keywords: Model synthesis, domain-specific language, Train Control Language, Alloy.

1 Introduction

Traditionally, software models have been used to document software applications to give an overview of complex software systems. However, software models are now increasingly being used for representing the applications themselves, and from these models source code can be generated. This raises the level of abstraction and allows analysis to be performed on the models in question. Model analysis is particularly useful for proving certain properties of a system or e.g., performing model-based testing which involves generating test-cases for the application.

Domain-specific modeling (DSM) makes use of domain-specific languages (DSL) to describe concepts and how these concepts are related in particular domains. Code generators are used to generate implementation code from the models. Thus, domain engineers can build models, representing applications, with only concepts and relations from the domain, without being concerned about implementation details. As we will see later, the Train Control Language (TCL) is a domain-specific modeling language for modeling train stations and generating configuration code for controlling the signaling system on the station. TCL models only cover the concepts of train stations and hide all the implementation details. Model analysis is also performed on TCL models to simulate and test properties of the models to detect design flaws.

Even though domain-specific modeling languages can automate the production of software applications [11], building applications models can still be a tedious task. Automating the task of building models can therefore be advantageous in several

I. Ober and I. Ober (Eds.): SDL 2011, LNCS 7083, pp. 38–53, 2011.

ways, e.g., software applications can be produced quicker and more reliable, and a number of software models can be created to validate and verify a code generator.

In this paper we present an approach for automatically synthesizing software models based on user-specified properties. We use a formal definition of the DSL to define the legal set of application models. This set of application models is then further restricted by user-defined properties representing the kind of models to be generated. One model is then selected and presented for the modeler. The model can either be used as is, or extended as desired by the modeler.

The contribution of this paper is as follows: We give a description of an approach for synthesizing software models automatically based on a formal definition of the DSL and user-defined properties. The approach is illustrated by using a real example from the train domain, TCL, where train station models are generated automatically.

The outline of the paper is as follows: Section 2 gives some background information about DSLs, TCL and the formal language Alloy. Section 3 gives an overview of the approach for synthesizing software models and Section 4 describes the approach using the TCL example domain. Section 5 gives some general discussion while Section 6 presents some related work on this topic. Finally, Section 7 summarizes the paper before future work is given in Section 8.

2 Background

Before describing the approach, we first introduce certain technologies. First, we explain the main concepts of DSLs, before we give a short overview of TCL. Then we present the formal language Alloy, which is used to find and produce intended DSL models.

2.1 Domain-Specific Language

A domain-specific language is a programming or modeling language tailored for a particular application domain. A DSL hides the implementation details, and thus raises the level of abstraction, covering only the concepts and the relations between the concepts of the domain. Domain-specific programming languages are usually defined by grammars (or embedded within general purpose languages), while domain-specific modeling languages are defined by metamodels. In this paper we will focus on domain-specific modeling languages.

A DSL is defined by an abstract syntax, a concrete syntax and well-defined semantics. The abstract syntax specifies the structure of the application models, involving the model elements in the application and how they are related. A metamodel is a model which defines the abstract syntax of the DSL, specifying the concepts in the language and how they are related. The concrete (graphical) syntax defines how the abstract syntax is presented to the user. There is often, but not always, a direct mapping between the abstract and concrete syntax, in form of having each concept in the metamodel being related to a (graphical) symbol. The semantics of the DSL defines the construction and the operational behavior of the application. This is often defined by constraints, restricting the legal set of models and their behavior.

DSLs are usually accompanied by code-generators and frameworks. A code-generator translates the application model into another representation, which can either be executable source code or configuration code that is used by the framework. The DSL presented in the next subsection, TCL, is a graphical DSL for modeling train stations and generate configuration code for a framework which controls train station signaling systems.

2.2 Train Control Language

Train Control Language is a domain-specific modeling language for modeling train stations and generating train station configuration code for train station signaling systems [7, 17]. TCL has been developed in cooperation with ABB, Norway, to automate the development of signaling system source code. TCL is defined by a metamodel (see Fig. 1) and has been developed as an Eclipse plug-in with a graphical editor and code generators.

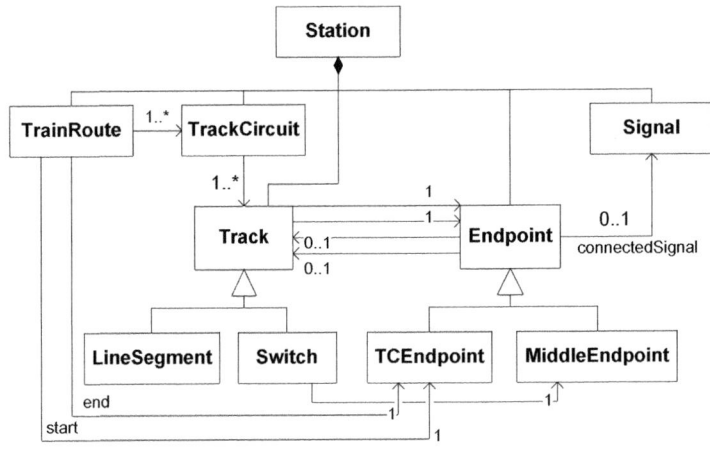

Fig. 1. TCL metamodel excerpt

As defined by the TCL metamodel, Station is the top concept, containing all the other concepts. A *TrainRoute* is a route a train must obtain before it can move into or out of a station. A TrainRoute is divided into *TrackCircuits*, which defines a certain amount of Tracks where a train can be located. A Track can either be a *LineSegment*

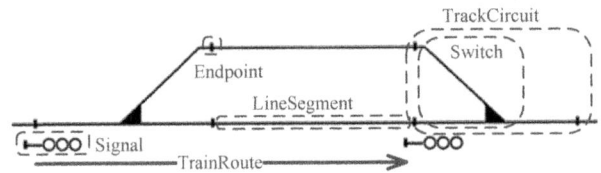

Fig. 2. TCL concrete syntax with meta-information

or a *Switch*, which are connected by Endpoints. A TrainRoute starts end ends at a *Signal*, which will only give green light if the requested TrainRoute is available for the train. The concrete syntax of TCL is illustrated in Fig. 2.

Based on the metamodel, a graphical editor and code generators have been developed using Eclipse Modeling Framework (EMF) [6], Graphical Modeling Framework (GMF) [9] and MOFScript [13]. The TCL graphical editor is illustrated in Fig. 3 with a model of a two-track station. Note that the rectangles on the top of the model represent the train routes and track circuits in the station. A TCL model is created by dragging model elements from the tool palette (to the right) onto the canvas (middle) and setting the properties of these model elements (property view at the bottom). When the station is complete according to the specification, code can be generated (buttons on top). Note that the purpose of this figure is to illustrate the graphical editor, and the details of it are not important for this paper.

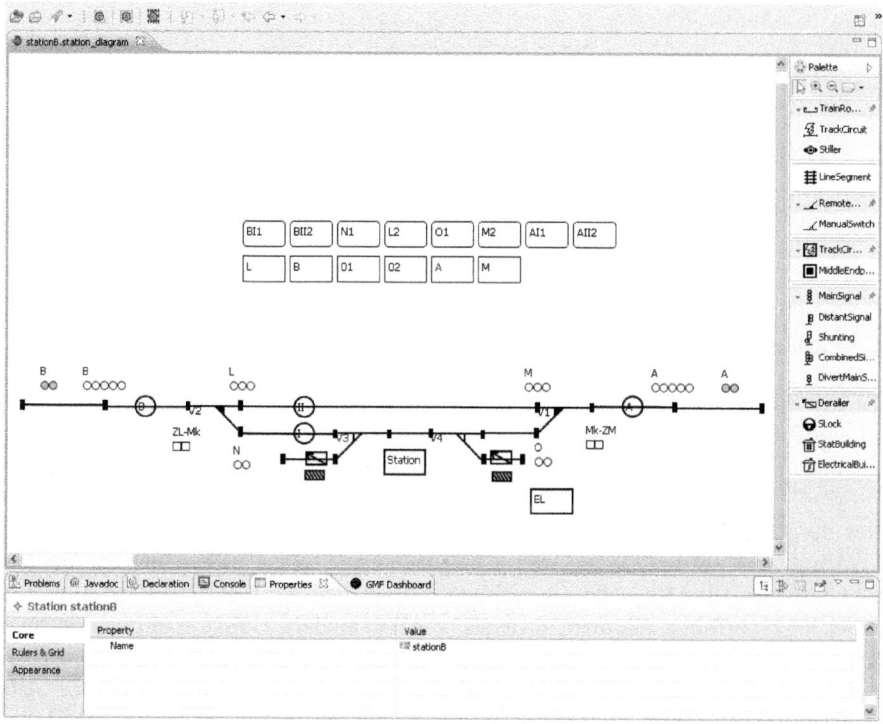

Fig. 3. TCL graphical editor

A TCL model consists of two parts: A repository model, containing the abstract syntax, and a diagram model storing the location of each element on the canvas. TCL includes algorithms for calculating the diagram model based on the repository model. This allows the graphical diagram model to be reconstructed if the repository model is exposed to changes.

Basic TCL model elements can be composed to form logical entities. The entities we use in this paper are *StationTracks* and *SideTracks*. A StationTrack denotes one of the main tracks in a station, where a two-track station consists of two such tracks. A SideTrack consists of a Switch together with other model elements to form a place to park trains or carriages. StationTracks and SideTracks are illustrated in Fig. 4.

TCL also allows the developer to perform analysis on train station models. Using a formal definition of the semantics defined in Alloy (see next subsection), analysis such as simulations, finding maximum of trains allows simultaneously, and checking whether train routes can be obtained to allow unsafe train movement, can be performed. We will later in this paper see how we can use this analysis to generate station models that have certain dynamic properties. We refer to [16] for further information about analysis of train station models.

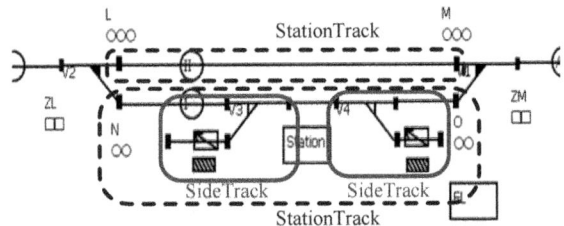

Fig. 4. StationTrack and SideTrack

2.3 Alloy

Formal validation and verification of a system involves using mathematical notation to express the system precisely, to prove the correctness of it. Traditionally, formal methods have required extensive knowledge of mathematical techniques and theorem proving, and have been a time-consuming task with a high cost. Formal analysis is therefore not as widely used as it ought to be.

Alloy is a light-weight declarative language using relational calculus for modeling a system formally [10]. Alloy is supplied with an analyzer tool, which based on first-order logic performs automatic analysis of Alloy models. Unlike traditional theorem-proving, the Alloy Analyzer only performs analysis within a user-specified scope, restricting the number of elements of each type in the model. Thus, the Alloy Analyzer only guarantees for the analysis within the scope, meaning that solutions may still exist in models within larger scopes. However, the small scope hypothesis ensures that if a solution exists, it will be within a small scope size [3], such that such analysis is sufficient.

An Alloy model typically consists of *signatures*, *fields*, *facts*, *predicates* and *assertions*. Signatures represent the types used in the model, which will be populated by the Alloy Analyzer when searching for a solution. A type hierarchy can be modeled by having a signature extending another signature. Signatures contain fields, which represent references between signatures. Facts consist of global constraints that must hold for all solutions. Predicates consist of local constraints that must hold if the predicate is processed, much like operations in other languages. Assertions consist of constraints that claimed to hold if the assertion is processed. Fig. 5 illustrates some of the concepts and the concrete syntax of an Alloy model, showing a signature and a fact involving the Track element in TCL. The signature defines a Track, which have two fields, *start* and *end*, referring to Endpoint. The fact, consisting of global constraints, states that there exist no tracks in the solution, such that the fields start and end refer to the same Endpoint.

```
abstract sig Track extends Element {
    start: one Endpoint,
    end: one Endpoint
}

fact {
    no t:Track, e:t.start, e2:t.end | e in e2
}
```

Fig. 5. Signature and fact involving a Track in TCL

When the Alloy Analyzer searches for a solution, it populates all signatures in the model with model elements up to the user-specified scope. E.g. if the scope is three for the signature Track, the Alloy Analyzer will populate this signature with at most three instances. There are two kinds of analysis available: Searching for a solution model satisfying a predicate or searching for a counter-example to an assertion. If no solution is found, or if the solution model is not as expected, the constraints in the model can be adjusted, leading to an incremental specification of the system.

3   Model Synthesis

The intention of model synthesis is to generate models automatically based on specifications. There are several purposes of generating application models automatically, such as reducing development time of these models by generating a basis which can be extended. Furthermore, for verification of a compiler, or when performing model-based testing of a system, there is a need for a larger set of application models as input. Modeling large sets of models is a time-consuming task that can be automated using model synthesis.

A metamodel defines the concepts of a language and the relations between these concepts. Modeling application models based on a metamodel involves creating instances of the concepts in the metamodel and relating them to each other according to the rules in the metamodel. In principle this approach can be followed when generating application models automatically. However, metamodels are usually not strict enough to only cover intended models, meaning that models without any semantic value can also be generated. Therefore, there is a need for further specification of the semantics of the DSL and the intended models to prohibit generating unintended models.

Based on a strict specification, representing additional constraints on the metamodel, arbitrary models can be generated by instantiating the metamodel according to the specification. In most cases there is a need for particular kinds of models, and consequently arbitrary models are not desired. A guided generation of models based on user-defined properties is therefore necessary.

Models in DSLs with a graphical concrete syntax consist of a diagram model in addition to the repository model (abstract syntax). Only building the repository model might be sufficient as input for model-based testing or verification of code-generators, but it is not sufficient if the model is supposed to be manually extended or verified. Therefore, there is a need for a layout algorithm to calculate relative positions to all elements in the model, such that diagrams can be generated from the model. Our example, TCL, includes such an algorithm, as described in Section 2.2.

Our approach uses Alloy for the formal specification of the metamodel with additional constraints. Since Alloy is a declarative language, further constraints, representing certain properties of the desired solution model, can simply be added. The formal specification is therefore extended to include user-defined properties of the solution model. The Alloy Analyzer is then used to find solution models corresponding to the Alloy model (including all user-specified properties). These solution models are then transformed such that they correspond to the metamodel, resulting in a model in the DSL. The approach is illustrated in Fig. 6. The starting point is the metamodel which is transformed into an Alloy model (step 1), according to the approach described by Kelsen and Ma [12]. This involves converting each metaclass to a signature and each association to a field. Additional constraints, including user-defined properties are added, and the Alloy Analyzer is invoked to provide a solution model (step 2). This solution model is then transformed to a model which corresponds to the metamodel (step 3), and if the DSL has a graphical concrete syntax, the diagram model is generated (step 4).

4   Synthesizing TCL Models

In this section we describe the details of the approach by illustrating it using TCL as an example domain. TCL is used for modeling a variety of train stations with some common structure. Examples of variations of stations are the number of StationTracks, numbers of SideTracks, number of TrackCircuits per StationTrack, direction of Station and SideTracks and optional Signals. E.g., we have stations with two StationTracks, two SideTracks, where the station is directed towards the bottom and SideTracks in both directions (see Fig. 3). Traditionally, developing source code for such a station required weeks of development. This has been shortened down to hours by modeling the station using TCL and generating the code from the model. However, this can further be reduced to minutes of modeling if a basis model can be generated.

User-defined properties

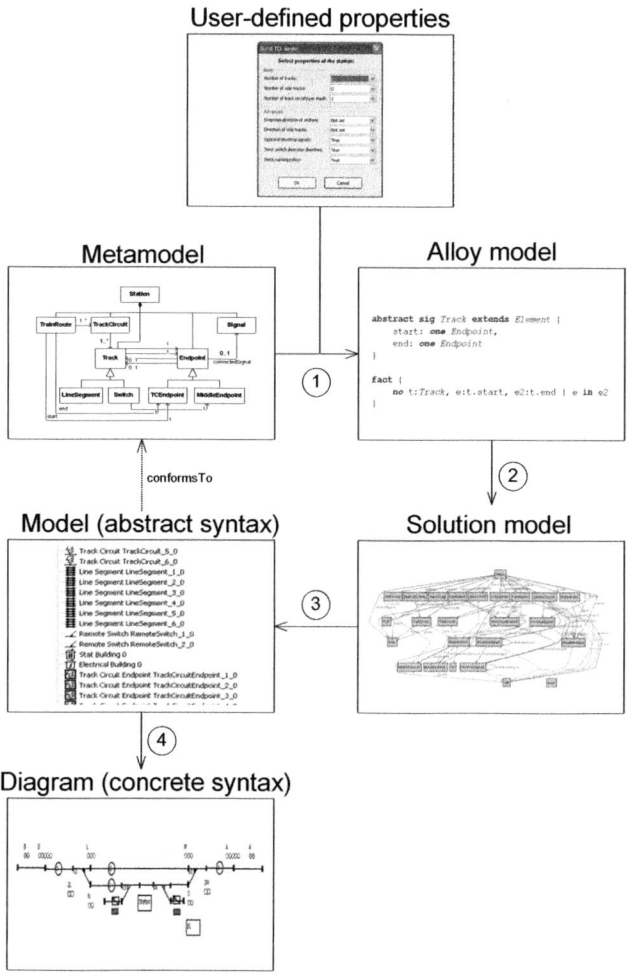

Metamodel

Alloy model

①

conformsTo

Model (abstract syntax)

Solution model

③

④

Diagram (concrete syntax)

Fig. 6. Overview of the approach

4.1 Generating TCL Models

Fig. 7 shows the graphical user interface (GUI) which initiates the synthesis of TCL
models. The GUI is used to retrieve the user-specified properties to guide the
generation of the station models. The properties are divided into a basic section and
an advanced section. Within the basic section, the numbers of tracks (StationTracks),
SideTracks and TrackCircuits per track are selected. The number of tracks can either
be 2, 3 or 4. In addition, as we will discuss later, there are possibilities to select the
number of tracks that will satisfy having 2, 3 or 4 trains on the station simultaneously.
Furthermore, the number of SideTracks can be set to 0, 1 or 2, and the number of
TrackCircuits per track can be between 1 and 4. Within the advanced section the
direction of the station can be set to UNSET, UP and DOWN, the direction of the

SideTracks can be UNSET, RIGHT, LEFT and BOTH (if two SideTracks). UNSET in both of these involves not restricting the model with the direction, giving a random value of these properties. Furthermore, optional signals can be added, strict direction of the switches in the station can be selected, and strict naming policy can be selected. The latter involves extra post-processing of the names of the model elements.

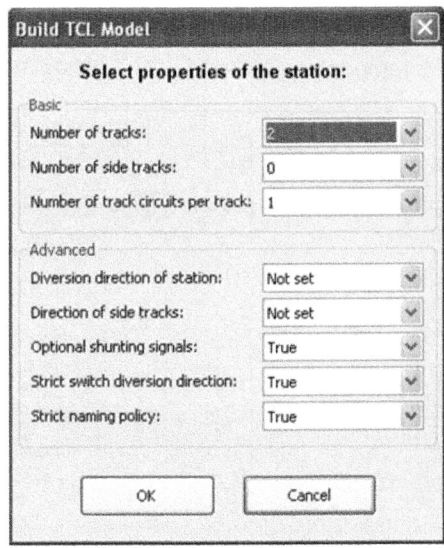

Fig. 7. Build TCL model GUI

As illustrated in Fig. 6, our basis is the Alloy model, which is partly generated from the metamodel of the DSL. The Alloy model consists of signatures and fields generated from the metamodel, facts containing further restriction to the DSL such that only intended models can be generated, an empty predicate to find a model that satisfies all the facts, and user-defined constraints based on the GUI in Fig. 7. For each user-defined property that is selected from the GUI additional constraints are added to the Alloy model, ensuring that only models with these properties can be generated. Since Alloy is a declarative language, it will find a solution that satisfies all constraints (facts) regardless of the order of the constraints.

To demonstrate the approach in practice we show three generated stations with different sets of properties selected from the GUI. Fig. 8 illustrates the result of selecting 3 tracks (StationTracks), 0 side tracks and 1 track circuit per track. The advanced settings were set to default, such that e.g. the direction of the station was random (either UP or DOWN). Fig. 9 illustrates the result of selecting 3 tracks, 2 side tracks, 1 track circuit per track and LEFT direction of the side tracks. Fig. 10 illustrates the result of selecting a station with 2 tracks, 0 side tracks and 3 track circuits per track (i.e. two extra endpoints on each StationTrack and extra track circuit rectangles). Note that the role of these figures is to show the structure of the generated station models, and it is therefore not required to understand the details of them.

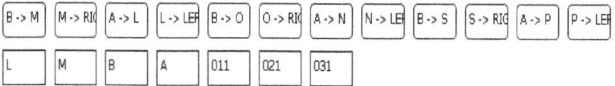

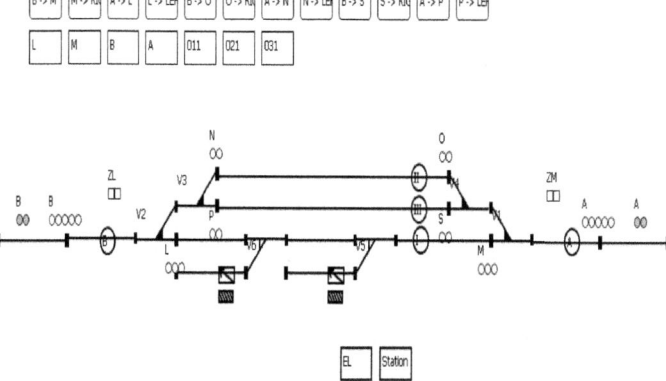

Fig. 8. Three-track station

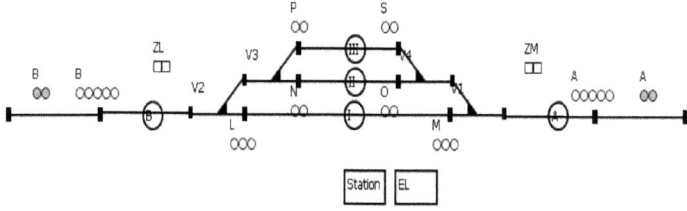

Fig. 9. Three-track station with two SideTracks

4.2 Adding Dynamic Properties

We have so far described the synthesis of station models based on static properties, i.e. number of tracks etc. To take this a step further we introduce dynamic properties when generating these models. We define dynamic properties as a quality that can only be determined by dynamic analysis, such as model simulation. Dynamic analysis requires a well-defined operational semantics, identifying the unambiguous behavior of the application model. Using such dynamic analysis, certain properties of the model can be checked or simulated before the model is generated. The procedure will then typically be to synthesize a model and then analyze it to check whether a desired property holds for the model. If a property does not hold, a new model is synthesized where the structure of the model is changed to satisfy the property. This procedure is repeated until the generated model completely satisfies the property.

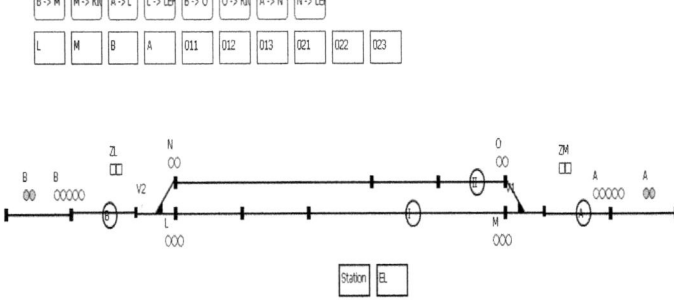

Fig. 10. Two-track station with extra TrackCircuits

TCL defines the dynamic semantics of TCL models as train movement into and out of the station, where trains have to allocate a train route before they can move through the station by occupying subsequent track circuits. As mentioned in Section 2.2, see [16] for more information about the dynamic analysis of TCL.

The dynamic property we have added into the synthesis of train station models is the requirement for the station to handle a number of trains simultaneously. When planning a train station, it is useful to know the throughput of the station, and whether it meets the requirements. The number of tracks of the station can give an indication of how many trains the station can handle simultaneously, but it can not guarantee for the results. However, performing analysis of the station model to simulate the train movement through the station can ensure the number of trains allowed simultaneously.

The analysis of TCL models includes checks for how many trains a given station model can handle concurrently. This analysis consists of predicates to simulate whether the station can handle two, three or four trains. Our model synthesis has the option of generating a station which can handle two, three or four trains simultaneously (see Section 4.1). We reuse the analysis performed on TCL models by first generating a small station and then checking whether it can handle the required number of trains. If the result of the analysis confirms that the station model is sufficient, the model is returned to the user. On the other hand, if it is not sufficient, another larger station model is generated and analyzed. This procedure is repeated until the station model is confirmed to be sufficient.

From the TCL model synthesis we get a two-track station if we choose a station that can handle three trains. Fig. 11 illustrates the generated station with annotated trains to show the result of the model analysis. Note that all the user-defined properties (see Fig. 7) were set to default, except the number of tracks, where we selected "Handling 3 trains".

4.3   Optimizing Alloy Models

The Alloy Analyzer performs complete analysis within the user-specified scope (number of element of each type). Complete analysis involves populating all possible models and discarding the ones where the constraints (facts) do not hold. Therefore, when the scope increases, the number of possible combinations to form solution models, and thus the analysis time, increases exponentially.

The TCL models generated in this paper consists of 62 (three-track station), 82 (three-track with two side tracks) and 61 (two-track with three track circuits per track) elements. Models of this size require quite a substantial analysis time to be built. Therefore, optimization of the Alloy models is required. We have implemented an optimization technique where we replace fields with constant functions, where the fields can be calculated before the analysis is performed. These constant functions are denoted *partial instances*. The difference from using fields is that the Alloy Analyzer does not need to populate instances to check all possibilities of relating fields, but can rather use a constant function to get the relation.

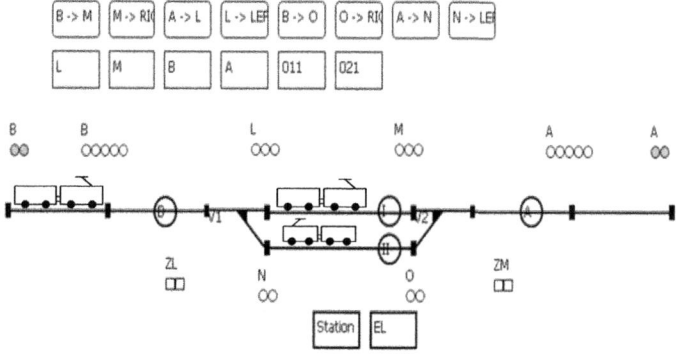

Fig. 11. Station model handling three trains

Fig. 12 illustrates the difference between using a field and partial instance for the *buildings* relation from *Station* to *Building*. In the partial instance, Station is referring two sub-signatures of Building directly, while using field for this relation involves having the Alloy Analyzer calculating the relation on analysis time.

Using field:

```
one sig Station extends Element {
    buildings: Building
    . . .
}
```

Using partial instance:

```
fun buildings[]:Station->Building {
    Station->StatBuilding_0 +
    Station->ElectricalBuilding_0
}
```

Fig. 12. Partial instance example

Using partial instances to optimize the TCL models in Alloy yields a building time that is an order of magnitude less than the building time for the original model. Building a three-track station with two side tracks (see Fig. 9) requires about 16-32 seconds (SAT solving time can be quite variable).

5 Discussion

In this paper we have seen that we can generate application models automatically based on a well-defined specification of a DSL. We have used Alloy to define the semantics of the DSL and illustrated the approach using TCL. However, the approach is not limited to either TCL or Alloy. TCL is, like many other DSLs, defined by a metamodel. Kelsen and Ma [12] have described an approach for defining formal semantics for a DSL in Alloy in order to perform analysis and generating solution models. Thus, this approach applies in general to other DSLs as well. Alloy is used primarily because of its uniform notation and its automatic analyzer. The principle of our approach is to define a strict specification of the system, and generate an arbitrary model which conforms to that specification. Alloy is providing the tool support for this approach, but the approach is not limited to Alloy.

The advantages of performing model synthesis are, as mentioned before, that the cost of developing applications can be reduced, several applications can be generated to test a code generator etc. Developing application models manually consists of time-consuming and repeating work. This work, as shown in this paper, can be automated. However, developing a system for performing model synthesis is far from trivial. An unambiguous specification of the DSL is required, which only allows intended application models. This requires not only detailed knowledge about the system itself, but also about how to define such specifications. In this paper we have used Alloy as specification language and TCL as example DSL, and thorough knowledge of both is required. However, defining the unambiguous specification is performed once for each DSL, while numerous application models can be synthesized automatically once the specification is in place. We therefore see this approach significant if the number of applications is large.

As we have discussed in Section 4.3, Alloy suffers from the *state space explosion* problem, meaning that the number of instances grows exponentially. This limits the size of the models that can be generated. Therefore, we presented optimization techniques, which have been implemented, to reduce the analysis effort needed. However, the analysis time still grows exponentially when the models increase in size. TCL is designed for small and medium-sized stations, where typical stations have two or three tracks. We have seen that the model synthesis in this paper easily can handle such station models of more than 80 model elements, which is sufficient for many DSLs.

Allowing guided model synthesis based on dynamic properties, such as station models handling three trains simultaneously, gives added value to the generated models. Application models can be automatically generated, that otherwise would have to be built and analyzed manually. Using Alloy as a specification language provides the possibility also to specify the operational semantics of the DSL, which can then be used for such analysis.

Notice that the user-specified properties of the generated models not necessarily define exactly the required model for a given application. However, using the model synthesis will generate a model that is close to the target application model. Further extension of this model is then possible. Note that performing such extension requires less effort and is more reliable than building a model from scratch or copying and extending an old model.

6 Related Work

Ehrig et al. [5] present an approach for generating application models using instance-generating graph grammars. They derive graph grammar rules from the metamodel, which is used to generate objects and relations between them. These rules are executed an arbitrary number of times until all models within a given scope are generated. This approach is similar to our approach, since they also perform model synthesis starting with the metamodel. However, our approach does not require the definition of graph grammar rules, but is based on the definition of declarative constraints. Using the Alloy Analyzer also provides instantiation of the application models with less effort.

Anastasakis et al. [1] describe an approach, which is extended by Shah et al. [15], to generate application models based on UML models. They transform a UML model to Alloy to find a solution model, which is transformed back to an application model conforming to the original UML model. Our basis is not UML, but rather a DSL, but this is, however, not a limitation.

Sen et al. [14] use Alloy to generate models for black-box testing. They transform a metamodel to Alloy, and use both random and guided generation of instance models. Their work is intended to generate a large set of instance models for testing purposes, while our approach also includes user-specified properties when generating the models. Furthermore, we introduce the possibility to synthesize application models based on dynamic properties.

White and Schmidt [18] present an approach for transforming configuration rules from feature models into a constraint satisfaction problem. They then use a constraint solver to derive the correct application configuration, and they provide a cost function to the constraint solver to select optimal configurations. Their approach is implemented an Eclipse plug-in called *Fresh*. Even though our approach is not based on feature models, it is similar. Our user-defined properties serve the same purpose as the feature model.

Several other works use Alloy for performing analysis. Kelsen and Ma [12] give a comparison between traditional formal methods and using Alloy to perform analysis on modeling languages. Anastasakis et al. [2] use Alloy to analyze model transformation rules and whether the target model is well-formed. Baresi and Spotelini [4] use Alloy for analyzing graph transformation systems. Gheyi et al. [8] specify a theory for feature models in Alloy and use this to perform analysis.

7 Conclusion

This paper has presented an approach for performing automatic model synthesis. Using a formal definition of the semantics of a DSL, described in Alloy, we generate application models. Guided model synthesis was presented by extending the Alloy model with required user-defined properties of the generated model. We also introduced the possibility of using dynamic analysis to guide the model synthesis.

The approach was illustrated using a DSL from the train domain to generate train station models automatically. We have seen that development time of such models can be reduced from hours to minutes using this approach. Furthermore, generating a huge set of application models for testing purposes (testing a code generator, using with model-based testing, etc.) can be performed automatically using this approach.

8   Future Work

As future work we will extend the user-defined properties, in particular the dynamic ones, to be able to generate a larger set of stations models with more variety. This will give more choices for synthesizing station models and thus require less work extending the generated models.

Further future work involves performing case-studies and implementing the approach using other DSLs. This will give further confidence in the usefulness of the approach.

Acknowledgements. The work presented here has been developed within the MoSiS project ITEA 2 – ip06035 part of the Eureka framework and the CESAR project funded by ARTEMIS Joint Undertaking grant agreement No 100016.

References

1. Anastasakis, K., Bordbar, B., Georg, G., Ray, I.: On Challenges of Model Transformation from Uml to Alloy. In: Software and Systems Modeling, vol. 9, pp. 69–86. Springer, Berlin (2010)
2. Anastasakis, K., Bordbar, B., Küster, J.M.: Analysis of Model Transformations Via Alloy. In: Baudry, B.. Faivre, A., Ghosh, S., Pretschner, A. (eds.) 4th International Workshop on Model Driven Engineering, Verification and Validation. Springer, Nashville (2007); Conjunction with MODELS 2007
3. Andoni, A., Daniliuc, D., Khurshid, S., Marinov, D.: Evaluating the "Small Scope Hypothesis". MIT CSAIL MIT-LCS-TR-921 (2003)
4. Baresi, L., Spoletini, P.: On the Use of Alloy to Analyze Graph Transformation Systems. In: Corradini, A., Ehrig, H., Montanari, U., Ribeiro, L., Rozenberg, G. (eds.) ICGT 2006. LNCS, vol. 4178, pp. 306–320. Springer, Heidelberg (2006)
5. Ehrig, K., Küster, J., Taentzer, G.: Generating Instance Models from Meta Models. In: Software and Systems Modeling, vol. 8, pp. 479–500. Springer, Berlin (2009)
6. EMF, Eclipse Modeling Framework (Emf),
   http://www.eclipse.org/modeling/emf/
7. Endresen, J., Carlson, E., Moen, T., Alme, K.-J., Haugen, Ø., Olsen, G.K., Svendsen, A.: Train Control Language - Teaching Computers Interlocking. In: Computers in Railways XI (COMPRAIL 2008), Toledo, Spain (2008)
8. Gheyi, R., Massoni, T., Borba, P.: A Theory for Feature Models in Alloy. In: First Alloy Workshop, Portland, United States, pp. 71–80 (2006)

9. GMF, Eclipse Graphical Modeling Framework (Gmf),
   http://www.eclipse.org/modeling/gmf/
10. Jackson, D.: Software Abstractions: Logic, Language, and Analysis. The MIT Press, Cambridge (2006)
11. Kelly, S., Tolvanen, J.-P.: Domain-Specific Modeling: Enabling Full Code Generation. John Wiley & Sons, Inc, Chichester (2008)
12. Kelsen, P., Ma, Q.: A Lightweight Approach for Defining the Formal Semantics of a Modeling Language. In: Busch, C., Ober, I., Bruel, J.-M., Uhl, A., Völter, M. (eds.) MODELS 2008. LNCS, vol. 5301, pp. 690–704. Springer, Heidelberg (2008)
13. Oldevik, J.: Mofscript Eclipse Plug-In: Metamodel-Based Code Generation. In: Eclipse Technology Workshop (EtX) at ECOOP 2006, Nantes (2006)
14. Sen, S., Baudry, B., Mottu, J.-M.: Automatic Model Generation Strategies for Model Transformation Testing. In: Paige, R.F. (ed.) ICMT 2009. LNCS, vol. 5563, pp. 148–164. Springer, Heidelberg (2009)
15. Shah, S.M.A., Anastasakis, K., Bordbar, B.: From Uml to Alloy and Back Again. In: Lúcio, L., Weißleder, S. (eds.) 6th International Workshop on Model-Driven Engineering, Verification and Validation, ACM, Denver (2009)
16. Svendsen, A., Møller-Pedersen, B., Haugen, Ø., Endresen, J., Carlson, E.: Formalizing Train Control Language: Automating Analysis of Train Stations. In: Comprail 2010, Beijing, China (2010)
17. Svendsen, A., Olsen, G.K., Endresen, J., Moen, T., Carlson, E., Alme, K.-J., Haugen, O.: The Future of Train Signaling. In: Busch, C., Ober, I., Bruel, J.-M., Uhl, A., Völter, M. (eds.) MODELS 2008. LNCS, vol. 5301, pp. 128–142. Springer, Heidelberg (2008)
18. White, J., Schmidt, D.C.: Automated Configuration of Component-Based Distributed Real-Time and Embedded Systems from Feature Models. In: 17th Annual Conference of the International Federation of Automatic Control, Seoul, Korea (2008)

Exploring Early Availability Requirements Using Use Case Maps

Jameleddine Hassine[1] and Abdelouahed Gherbi[2]

[1] Department of Information and Computer Science, King Fahd University of Petroleum and Minerals, Dhahran, Kingdom of Saudi Arabia
jhassine@kfupm.edu.sa
[2] Departement de Génie Logiciel, École de Technologie Supérieure, Montreal, Canada
Abdelouahed.Gherbi@etsmtl.ca

Abstract. Non-functional aspects including time constraints, distribution and fault tolerance are critical in the design and implementation of distributed real-time systems. As a result, it is well recognized that non-functional requirements should be considered at the earliest stages of system development life cycle. The ability to model non-functional properties (such as timing constraints, availability, performance, and security) at the system requirements level not only facilitates the task of moving towards real-time design, but ultimately supports the early detection of errors through automated validation and verification. In this paper, we introduce a novel approach to describe availability features in Use Case Maps (UCM) specifications. The proposed approach relies on a mapping of availability architectural tactics to UCM components. We illustrate the application of our approach using the In Service Software Upgrade (ISSU) feature on IP routers.

1 Introduction

The modeling and analysis of requirements are very challenging during the development of complex systems. In order to cope with these tasks, scenario driven approaches are very effective amongst requirement engineering techniques due mainly to their intuitive representation. Scenarios are a well established approach to describe functional requirements, uncovering hidden requirements and trade-offs, as well as validating and verifying requirements. The Use Case Maps language (UCM), which is part of the ITU-T standard User Requirements Notation (URN) Z.151 [1], is a high-level visual scenario-based modeling language that can be used to capture and integrate functional requirements and high-level designs at early stages of the development process. UCM models allow the description of both functional and architectural requirements at a high level of abstraction.

Non-functional aspects such as *timing*, *availability*, and *reliability* are often overlooked during the initial system design, considered as non-related behavioral issues, and consequently, described in separate models. The ability to model and analyze non-functional requirements supports the detection of design errors during the early stages of a software development life cycle. This contributes significantly in reducing the cost of later redesign activities in case of unsatisfactory reliability and performance. The standard UCM language [1] does not describe semantics involving time. This leaves

I. Ober and I. Ober (Eds.): SDL 2011, LNCS 7083, pp. 54–68, 2011.

room for different interpretations of timing information, such as the time needed for a transition or a responsibility to complete. In order to address this issue, we have extended the UCM language with timing constraints [2,3] allowing for quantitative analysis (such as Schedulability Analysis) at a high level of abstraction [4,5]. In a related work, Petriu et al. [6] have augmented the UCM language with performance related data such as arrival characteristics for start points, probabilities/weights on branches, plugins and dynamic stubs. The resulting models can then be used to generate Layered Queueing Network (LQN) performance models. However, the use of the UCM language to model dependability aspects [7] like availability, fault-tolerance, and security remain unexplored.

The main motivation of this work is to support the modeling and analysis techniques of dependability [7]. In particular, we focus on the need for an approach to model and validate availability requirements at the very early stages of system development. In this paper, we aim at the following purposes:

- provide a literature review of the existing approaches to system (high) availability and discuss their relevance to high level requirements description.
- enhance our previous set of UCM-based availability features introduced in [8]. We introduce metamodels to describe the proposed availability extensions.
- extend our ongoing research towards the specification of of a comprehensive UCM-based framework for the description, simulation, and analysis of real-time systems [2,3,4,5,8,9].

The remainder of this paper is organized as follows. The next section provides an overview of existing high availability approaches. In Section 3, we present and discuss the proposed UCM-based availability annotations. An example of ISSU (In Service Software Upgrade) is presented in Section 5. Finally, conclusions are drawn in Section 6.

2   Availability Requirements

Several definitions of availability have been proposed. The ITU-T recommendation E.800 [10] defines the availability as the ability of an item to be in a state to perform a required function at a given instant of time, or at any instant of time within a given time interval, assuming that the external resources, if required, are provided. Avizienis et al. [7] argue that availability is an attribute of dependability and define it as being the readiness for a correct service.

Moreover, availability requirements might be very stringent as in highly available systems used to provide telecommunication services (a.k.a 5 nines (99,999%)). The Service Availability Forum (SAF)[1] focuses on the issues related to high availability requirements. SAF supports the delivery of highly available carrier-grade systems through the definition of standard interfaces for availability management [11], software management [12] and several other high availability middleware services [13].

---

[1] SAForum: http://www.saforum.org

Bass et al. [14] have introduced the notion of tactics as *architectural building blocks* of architectural patterns. The authors [14] have provided a comprehensive categorization of availability tactics based on whether they address fault detection, recovery, or prevention. Figure 1 shows these four categories:

1. **Fault Detection.** tactics are divided into (1) *Ping/Echo* (which determines reachability and the round-trip delay through the associated network path); (2) *Heartbeat* (which reports to system monitor when a fault is incurred), and (3) *Exception* (which detects faults such as divide by zero, bus, and address faults).

2. **Fault Recovery-Preparation and Repair.** tactics are divided into (1) *Voting* (A voter component decides which value to take in a redundant environment); (2) *Active Redundancy* (called also *hot redundancy*, refers to a configuration where all redundant spare maintain synchronous state with the active node(s)); (3) *Passive Redundancy* (called also *warm redundancy*, refers to a configuration where redundant spare(s) receive periodic state updates from active node(s)), and (4) *Spare* (called also *cold redundancy*, refers to a configuration where the redundant spares remain out of service until a fail-over occurs). It is worth noting that the application of one tactic may assume that another tactic has already been applied. For example, the application of *voting* may assume that some form of redundancy exists in the system.

3. **Fault Recovery-Reintroduction.** tactics are divided into (1) *Shadow* (refers to operating a previously failed component in a *shadow mode* for a predefined duration of time); (2) *Rollback* (allows the system state to be reverted to the most recent consistent state), and (3) *State Resynchronization* (ensures that active and standby components have synchronized states).

4. **Fault Prevention.** tactics include (1) *Removal from Service* (refers to the fact of placing a system component in an out-of-service state for the purpose of mitigating potential system failures); (2) *Transactions* (which are typically realized using *atomic commit protocols*), and (3) *Process Monitor* (monitors the health of a system).

In this work, we adopt these availability tactics [14] as a basis for extending the Use Case Maps language with availability annotations. These tactics have been proven in practice for a broad applicability in different industrial domains. In a closely related work to Bass et al. [14], Hatebur et al. [15] defined a set of patterns for expressing and analyzing dependability requirements, such as confidentiality, integrity, availability, and reliability.

Many approaches have been proposed to tackle the issue of annotating models with information needed for availability. Mustafiz et al. [16] have proposed a probabilistic model-based approach for analyzing the safety and reliability of requirements based on use cases. Each interaction step in a use case is annotated with a probability reflecting its chances of success, and a safety tag if the failure of the step hampers the system safety. On the UML front, Bondavalli et al. [17] have proposed a comprehensive approach for availability analysis of UML specifications. Dal Cin [18] has proposed a UML profile for specifying and capturing reliability and availability requirements, aimed at supporting the quantitative evaluation of the effectiveness of a fault tolerance strategy. However,

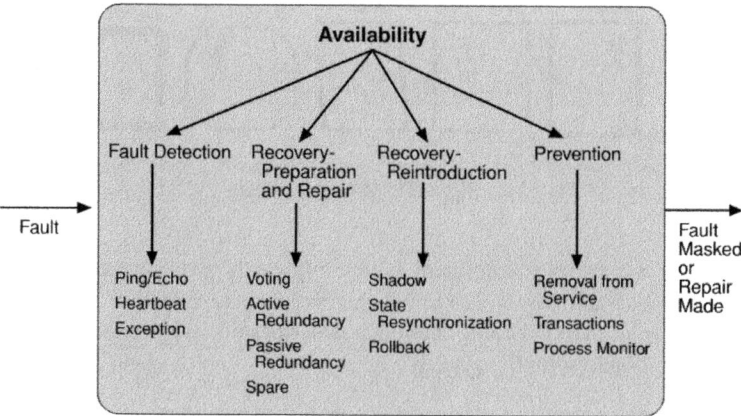

Fig. 1. Availability Tactics [14]

the profile lacks support for modeling the interactions between dependability mecha-nisms and system components. More recently, Bernardi et al. [19,20] have proposed to add a profile for Dependability Analysis and Modeling (DAM) to MARTE. Another OMG standard specifying UML extensions for a variety of non-functional properties is the *Profile for Modeling Quality of Service and Fault Tolerance Characteristics and Mechanisms* (QoS&FT) [21]. QoS&FT defines specific QoS catalogs for several non-functional properties such as performance, security or reliability.

3 Availability Modeling in Use Case Maps

In this section, we implement the availability tactics proposed by Bass et al. [14] in the Use Case Maps language.

3.1 Use Case Maps Architectural Features

One of the strengths of UCMs resides in their ability to bind responsibilities to archi-tectural components. The default UCM component notation is generic and abstract al-lowing for representing software entities (e.g., objects, processes, databases, or servers) as well as non-software entities (e.g., actors or hardware). In the ITU-T standard [1], a UCM component is characterized by its kind (Team, object, agent, process, actor) and its optional type (user-defined type), may contain other component definitions or be contained in other component definitions.

Figure 2 illustrates these component kinds:

– A *Team* is the most generic component, used as a container for sub-components of any kind. Teams are operational groupings of system-level components.
– *Objects* are data or procedure abstractions that are system-level components to sup-port the system comprehension.

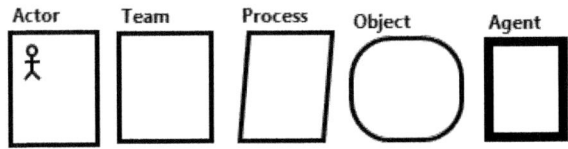

Fig. 2. UCM Components

- A *Process* is an active component, which implies the existence of a control thread.
- An *Agent* is an autonomous component, which acts on behalf of other components.
- An *Actor* is an external component that describes an entity, either human or artificial, that interacts with the system.

UCM component relationships depend on scenarios to provide the semantic information about their dependencies. Components are considered to be dependent if they share the same scenario execution path even though no actual/physical connections are drawn between components.

3.2 UCM Fault Detection Modeling

In order to model the fault detection tactic, we extend UCM architectural features with physical/logical links between components. Figure 3 illustrates an UCM architecture that is composed of three components, two bidirectional and one unidirectional physical links (*Link1* (bidirectional) and *Link2* (unidirectional) connecting *Component1* and *Component2*; and *Link3* (bidirectional) connecting *Component2* and *Component3*).

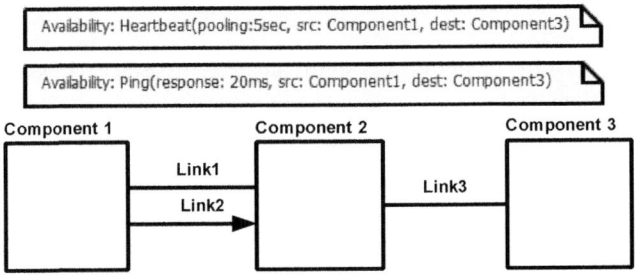

Fig. 3. UCM Physical Links

Ping/Echo/Heartbeat Tactics: *Ping/Echo/Heartbeat* tactics can be used to determine how long it takes to detect a fault. This can be achieved based on the round-trip time and the number of missed Pings/Heartbeats. In order to describe ping/echo/heartbeat availability requirements, we have reused the UCM *Comment* constructor. Each availability-related description or condition is modeled by a UCM comment that is preceded by the keyword *Availability*. In this paper and contrary to our initial UCM fault detection modeling presented in [8], where *Ping*, *Echo*, and *Heartbeat* tactics are associated with physical links, we have chosen to associate these tactics with the UCM model. This choice would allow for the introduction of indirect/logical connectivity between different participating components. Hence, helping to maintain end-to-end fault detection mechanism between not directly connected components. For example, *component1* and *component3* in Figure 3 are indirectly connected and a ping can be initiated between them.

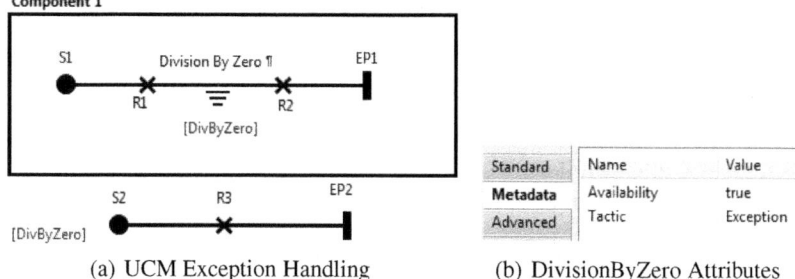

(a) UCM Exception Handling   (b) DivisionByZero Attributes

Fig. 4. UCM Exception Handling

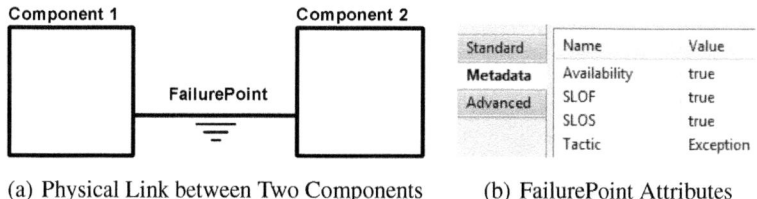

(a) Physical Link between Two Components   (b) FailurePoint Attributes

Fig. 5. UCM Physical Link Failure

Exceptions: Exceptions are handled at the scenario path level. Exceptions may take place after any responsibility along the UCM execution path. Figure 4(a) illustrates an example of exception handling mechanism to deal with a division by zero that may occur after executing responsibility *R1*. This exception is described using the *failure point* annotation and would trigger the execution of another UCM path called *Exception Path* (i.e., when the boolean precondition *DivByZero* at start point *S2* is satisfied) leading to the execution of responsibility *R3*. The exception path may be handled either by the same component, another component, or left for future design refinement (i.e., not bound to any component as illustrated in Figure 4(a)). To indicate that such an exception is being handled part of an availability requirement strategy, we associated an *Availability* and a *Tactic* attribute to the *Division By Zero* failure point. Figure 4(b), produced using *jUCMNav* tool [22], illustrates these two attributes.

Physical links may also be subject to failures, which can be described using the *failure point* annotation as illustrated in Figure 5(a). The occurrence of such failures can be treated using a separate scenario path (i.e., the same way as an exception). A physical

60   J. Hassine and A. Gherbi

link failure may be associated with a set of alarms. For instance, a SONET[2] (Synchronous Optical NETworking) link may be subject to critical alarms such as SLOS (Section Loss of Signal) or SLOF (Section Loss of Frame). These alarms can be described using metadata as illustrated in Figure 5(b).

3.3 UCM Modeling of Fault Recovery and Repair

It focuses mainly on redundancy modeling in order to keep the system available in case of the occurrence of a failure. To model redundancy, we annotate UCM components with the following attributes:

- *Group Id*: A system may have many spatially redundant components of different types. The group Id is used to identify the group to which a component belongs in a specific redundancy model.
- *Role*: Denotes whether a component is in *active* or *standby* role.
- *Redundancy Type*: Determines the redundancy type as *hot, warm,* or *cold*.
- *Protection Type*: The minimal redundancy configuration is to have one active and one redundant node (commonly referred to as *1+1* redundancy). Cases where one spare is used to protect multiple active nodes, are referred to as *1:N*. Cases where multiple spares are used to protect multiple active nodes, are referred to as *M:N*.
- *Voting Function*: Denotes whether a component plays a voting role in a redundancy model using a boolean value.

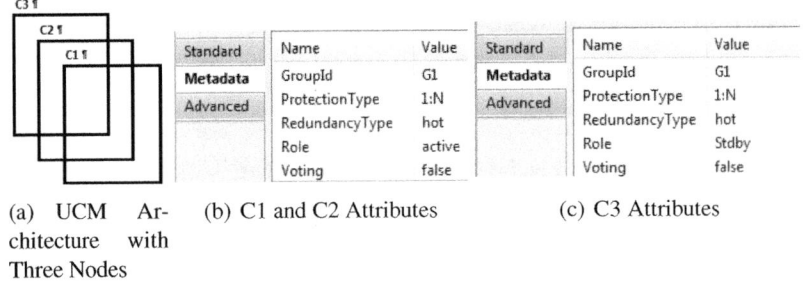

(a) UCM Architecture with Three Nodes (b) C1 and C2 Attributes (c) C3 Attributes

Fig. 6. UCM Node Protection

Figure 6 illustrates an example of a system with three components *C1*, *C2*, and *C3* participating in one hot redundancy configuration (i.e., Group ID: *G1*). *C1* and *C2* are in active role (i.e. Role: *Active*) while *C3* is in standby role (i.e., Role: *Stdby*). None of these three components is taking part in voting activity (i.e., Voting : *false*).

Physical links redundancy can also be annotated with the following attributes:

- *Group Id* used to identify the group to which a physical link belongs.
- *Role* denotes whether a link is in *active* or *standby* role.
- *Protection Type* refers to *1+1, 1:N*, or *M:N* protection types.

---

[2] Telcordia GR-253-CORE, SONET Transport Systems: Common Generic Criteria.

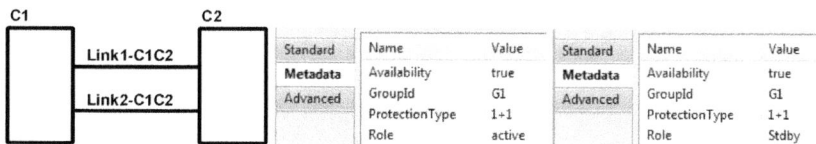

(a) UCM with One Redun- (b) Link1-C1C2 Attributes (c) Link2-C1C2 Attributes
dant Link

Fig. 7. UCM Link Protection

Figure 7 shows a UCM architecture having two components *C1* and *C2* connected physically using two links: one active (i.e., *Link1-C1C2*)) and one standby (i.e., *Link2-C1C2*).

It is worth noting that such annotations are static and cannot be modified at run-time. Therefore, if a component needs to change its role, for instance because of the occurrence of a switchover, it should be documented as part of the scenario execution path. Section 5 illustrates such scenario.

3.4 UCM Modeling of Fault Recovery-Reintroduction

The presented annotations deal with the static description of availability requirements. The operational implications of such availability requirements, in case of failure for instance, can be described using the UCM scenario path as discussed in Section 3.2. Figure 8 illustrates a feature configuration scenario on a dual route processor (RP) system. The feature configuration details are embedded in a plugin bound to the static stub *FeatureConfiguration* and are not shown here. The introduction of a new feature may result in having the active and standby route processors (respectively *RP1* and *RP2*) in Out-of-Sync state. The detection of such situation would trigger an exception path (i.e., precondition *OutOfSych* is satisfied) and causes both RPs to synchronize again (using responsibilities *StateSynchronization* between AND-Fork and AND-Join constructs). The failure point *OutOfSynchronization*, the start point *SP2*, and responsibility *StateSynchronization* are part of the availability strategy (see Figure 8(d)).

Similarly, *Shadow* and *Rollback* tactics can be described using the metadata associated to responsibilities.

3.5 UCM Fault Prevention Modeling

Annotations presented in Sections 3.2 and 3.3 can be used to accommodate this category. Indeed, responsibilities can be annotated with availability metadata specifying a removal from service property. Figure 9 illustrates a UCM scenario of placing a component in an out-of-service state by shutting it down (i.e., responsibility *Shutdown*) to prevent potential system failures in case the component is running low in memory.

Similarly, responsibilities can be annotated with availability metadata about their transactional properties. Figure 10 provides a scenario of updating a database record using a two-phase-commit type of transaction (a.k.a *2PC*). Failing to ensure the two

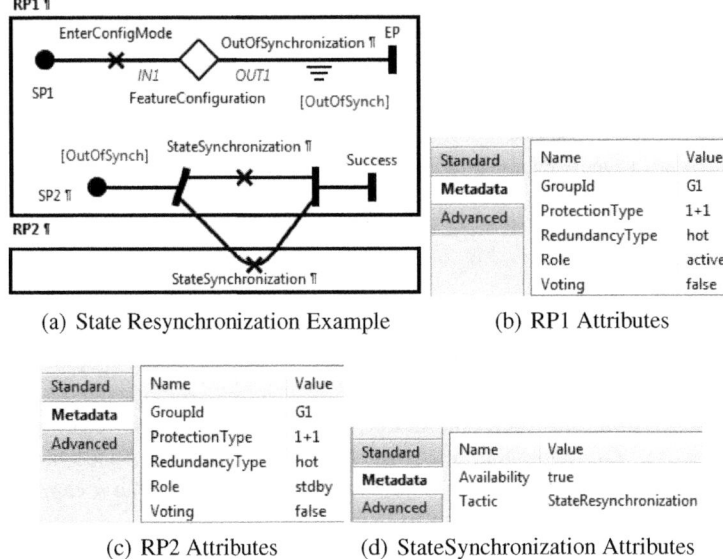

(a) State Resynchronization Example   (b) RP1 Attributes

(c) RP2 Attributes   (d) StateSynchronization Attributes

Fig. 8. Fault Recovery-Reintroduction Example

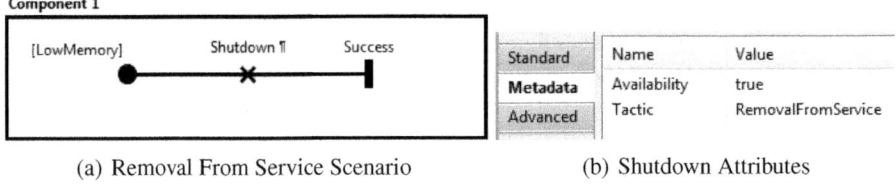

(a) Removal From Service Scenario   (b) Shutdown Attributes

Fig. 9. UCM Fault Prevention Modeling

phase commit requirement, would trigger a rollback (i.e., responsibility *Rollback*) to undo the update. Finally, processes can be annotated with health monitoring capabilities as described in Section 3.2.

4   UCM Availability Metamodels

In this section, we describe our UCM availability extensions using abstract grammar metamodels. Concrete grammar metamodels, which includes metaclasses of the graphical layout of UCM elements in addition to the abstract metaclasses (with attributes, relationships, and constraints), are not discussed in this paper since they have no semantic implication.

Figure 11 illustrates the abstract grammar of the UCM specification. *UCMspec* serves as a container for the UCM specification elements such as *Component* and

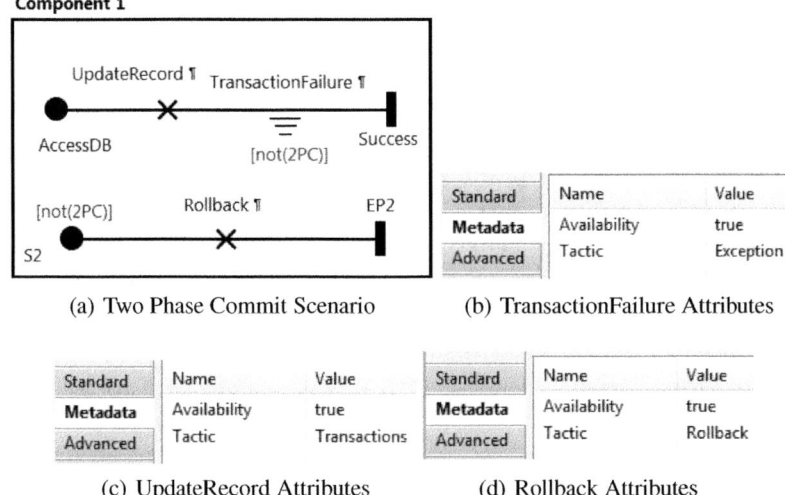

(a) Two Phase Commit Scenario   (b) TransactionFailure Attributes

(c) UpdateRecord Attributes   (d) Rollback Attributes

Fig. 10. UCM Fault Prevention Modeling

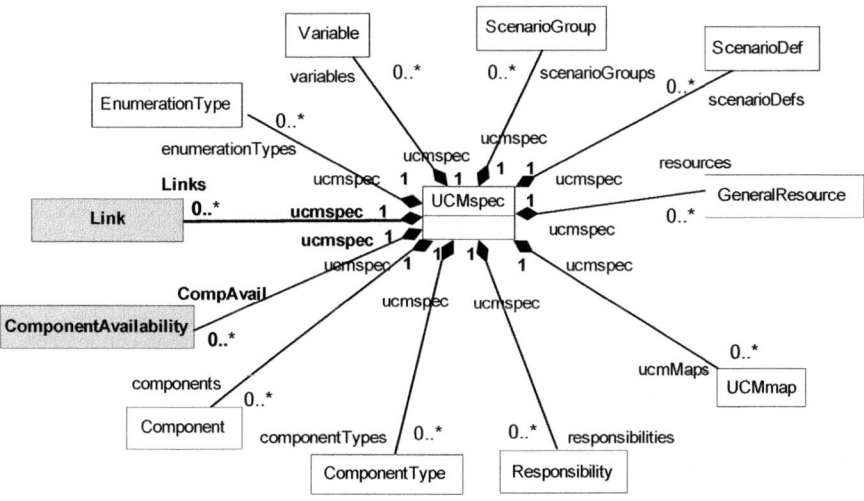

Fig. 11. Abstract Grammar: UCM Specification

GeneralResource. The new proposed availability elements (*Link* and *ComponentAvailability*) are shown as gray metaclasses.

Figure 12 illustrates the availability concepts of the core abstract metamodel of the UCM language. Path-related and plug-in binding-related concepts are not shown because they do not impact our availability extensions. Five new enumeration metaclasses are introduced:

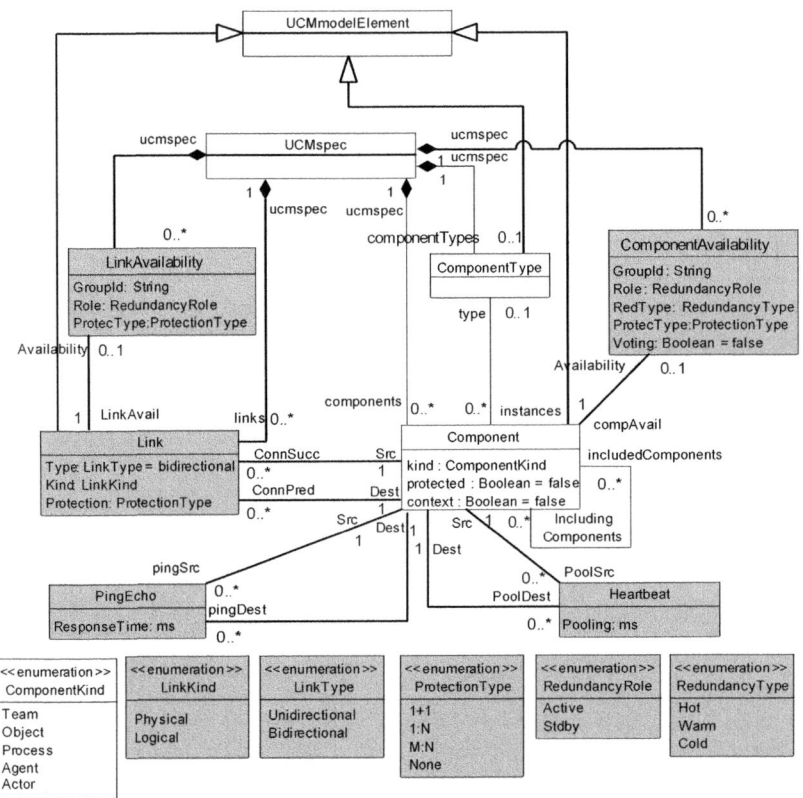

Fig. 12. Abstract Grammar: UCM Availability Metamodel

- **RedundancyRole:** Specifies whether a component or a link is in *Active* or *Stdby* role.
- **RedundancyType:** Specifies the component redundancy type as *hot*, *warm* or *cold*.
- **LinkType:** Specifies whether a link is *Unidirectional* or *Bidirectional*.
- **LinkKind:** Specifies whether a link is *Physical* or *Logical*.
- **ProtectionType:** Specifies the protection type as 1+1, 1:N, M:N, or None.

Five new metaclasses are introduced:

- **Link**, a subtype of *UCMmodelElement*, defines the connections between participating UCM components. A link is described using the following attributes: (1) *Type* of type *LinkType*, (2) *Kind* of type *LinkKind*, and (3) *Protection* of type *ProtectionType*. A link has two associations with *Component*: one to specify the source component and one to specify the destination component.
- **ComponentAvailability** defines component availability attributes: (1) GroupId of type *String*, (2) *Role* of type *RedundancyRole*, (3) *RedType* of type *Redundancy-Type*, (4) *ProtecType* of type *ProtectionType*, and (5) *Voting* of type Boolean.

- **LinkAvailability** defines link availability attributes: (1) GroupId of type *String*, (2) *Role* of type *RedundancyRole*, and (3) *ProtecType* of type *ProtectionType*.
- **PingEcho** defines the response time (i.e., *ResponseTime*) in milliseconds.
- **Heartbeat** defines the poolling rate (i.e., *Pooling*) in milliseconds.

5 Illustrative Example: In Service Software Upgrade (ISSU)

Network availability has become an increasingly important issue for service providers and their customers. A significant cause of downtime is planned maintenance and software upgrades. Many router vendors, such as Cisco Systems [23], offer *In Service Software Upgrade (ISSU)* capabilities to allow service providers to migrate from one software version to another while the system remains in service (i.e., with minimal disruption to existing Layer 2 and Layer 3 customer traffic). A software upgrade may be introduced in the following situations:

- **Bug fixes**: It involves generally a patch to a specific component of the system. The impact is local and does not cause a state change. The affected processes are restarted and replaced.
- **Minor/Major upgrade**: It involves generally state and architectural changes (e.g., introduction of a new feature release, new software design).

Hitless ISSU is an availability tactic that leverages the component redundancy (active and passive) to achieve non-service-affecting upgrades to software. Figure 13(a) shows a UCM scenario of upgrading a dual RP (route processor) IP router from an old software version to a new version. The router operates in a hot redundancy configuration, *RP1* being the active route processor and *RP2* being the standby. The first step in performing an upgrade is to copy the new software version on the file systems of both RPs (i.e., responsibility *CopyNewVersion*). Then load the new version on *RP2* (i.e., the standby RP), which may result into a failure because of an incompatible or corrupted software. Figure 13(d) illustrates the corresponding failure path, where the old version is loaded back on *RP2*. If the new version is loaded successfully, *RP2* is then reset and it should come up in a SSO (Stateful Switch Over) mode. If it failed to synchronize with the active RP, a failure path is taken (Figure 13(e)) and the old version is loaded back on *RP2*.

The second step is to perform a switch over in order to make *RP2* as active and *RP1* as Standby). ISSU assumes that there should be no changes to any configuration settings or network connections during the upgrade. Any changes to configuration is considered as an exception or even a failure if it causes a service disruption. In this scenario, losses are reported to the administrator so he can re-apply the missing configuration again (Figure 13(f)). The next step is to accept the new version within a specific period of time (i.e., UCM Timer *acceptVersion*), otherwise a rollback to the old version will be performed upon the timer expiry. If the result of the upgrade is satisfactory, the final step would be to commit the new version using responsibility *CommitVersion*.

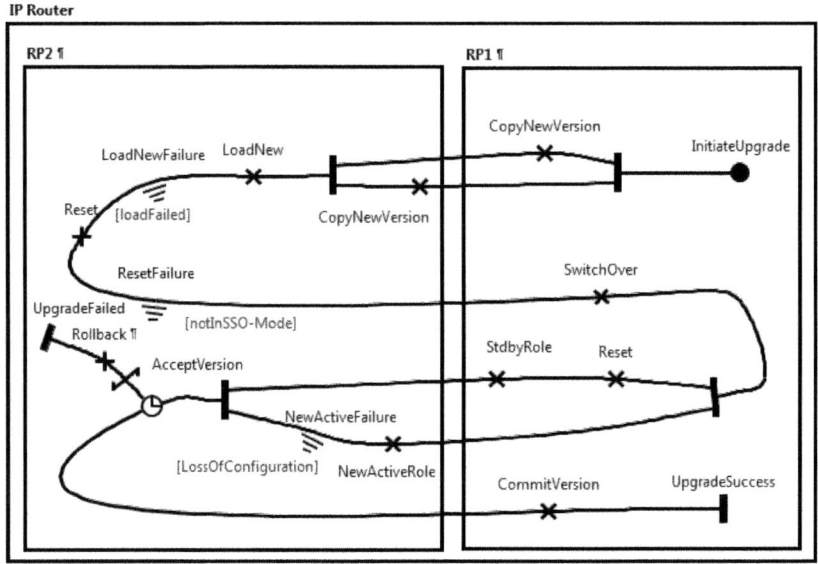

(a) ISSU Root Map

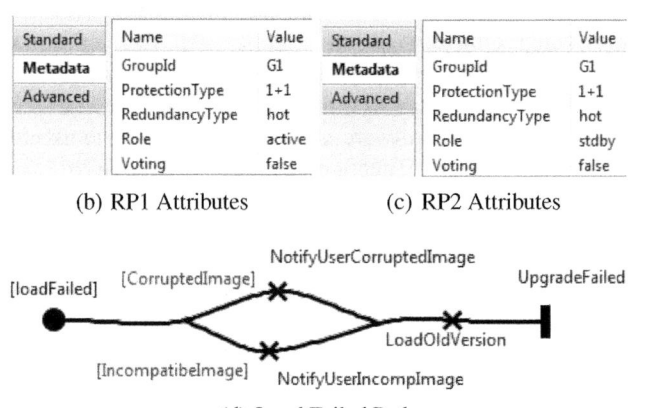

(b) RP1 Attributes   (c) RP2 Attributes

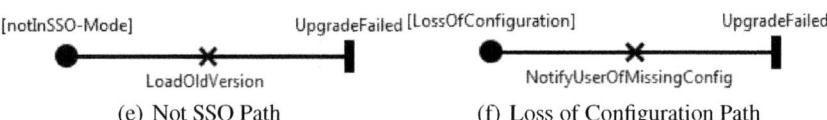

(d) Load Failed Path

(e) Not SSO Path   (f) Loss of Configuration Path

Fig. 13. In Service Software Upgrade (ISSU)

6 Conclusion

In this work, we aim at defining a new approach to model availability requirements at the very early stages of the system development. To this end, we introduced an extension to the Use Case Maps language. The new features we introduced in UCM cover all availability tactics proposed by Bass et al. [14] in a flexible manner. The extended UCM allows for further model refinement and smooth moving towards more detailed design models. In our future work, we aim at exploring how to map UCM high availability concepts into SAF's AMF configurations [11]. Our goal is to enable conducting qualitative and quantitative analysis of availability requirements at a very early stage of system development.

Acknowledgment. Dr. Jameleddine Hassine would like to acknowledge the support provided by the Deanship of Scientific Research at King Fahd University of Petroleum & Minerals (KFUPM) for funding this work through project No. FT101011. Dr. Abdelouahed Gherbi acknowledges the support of the Natural Sciences and Engineering Research Council of Canada (NSERC) through its Discovery Grants program.

References

1. ITU-T: Recommendation Z.151, User Requirements Notation (URN) (2010)
2. Hassine, J., Rilling, J., Dssouli, R.: Timed use case maps. In: Gotzhein, R., Reed, R. (eds.) SAM 2006. LNCS, vol. 4320, pp. 99–114. Springer, Heidelberg (2006)
3. Hassine, J., Rilling, J., Dssouli, R.: Formal verification of use case maps with real time extensions. In: Gaudin, E., Najm, E., Reed, R. (eds.) SDL 2007. LNCS, vol. 4745, pp. 225–241. Springer, Heidelberg (2007)
4. Hassine, J.: Early Schedulability Analysis with Timed Use Case Maps. In: Reed, R., Bilgic, A., Gotzhein, R. (eds.) SDL 2009. LNCS, vol. 5719, pp. 98–114. Springer, Heidelberg (2009)
5. Hassine, J.: AsmL-Based Concurrency Semantic Variations for Timed Use Case Maps. In: Frappier, M., Glässer, U., Khurshid, S., Laleau, R., Reeves, S. (eds.) ABZ 2010. LNCS, vol. 5977, pp. 34–46. Springer, Heidelberg (2010)
6. Petriu, D., Amyot, D., Woodside, M.: Scenario-based Performance Engineering with UCM-NAV. In: Reed, R., Reed, J. (eds.) SDL 2003. LNCS, vol. 2708, pp. 18–35. Springer, Heidelberg (2003)
7. Avizienis, A., Laprie, J.C., Randell, B., Landwehr, C.: Basic Concepts and Taxonomy of Dependable and Secure Computing. IEEE Transactions on Dependable and Secure Computing 1(1), 11–33 (2004)
8. Hassine, J.: Early Availability Requirements Modeling using Use Case Maps. In: 8th International Conference on Information Technology: New Generations (ITNG 2011), Modeling and Analysis of Dependable Embedded and Real-time Software Systems Track, April 11-13, pp. 754–759. IEEE Computer Society, Las Vegas (2011)
9. Hassine, J., Rilling, J., Dssouli, R.: Abstract Operational Semantics for Use Case Maps. In: Wang, F. (ed.) FORTE 2005. LNCS, vol. 3731, pp. 366–380. Springer, Heidelberg (2005)
10. ITU-T: E.800: Terms and Definitions related to Quality of Service and Network Performance including Dependability (2008)
11. Forum, S.A.: Application Interface Spec. Availability Management Framework SAI-AIS-AMF-B.04.01

12. Forum, S.A.: Application Interface Spec. Software Management Framework SAI-AIS-SMF-A.01.02
13. Forum, S.A.: Application Interface Spec. Overview SAI-Overview-B.05.03
14. Bass, L., Clements, P., Kazman, R.: Software Architecture in Practice. Addison-Wesley Longman Publishing Co., Inc., Boston (2003)
15. Hatebur, D., Heisel, M.: A Foundation for Requirements Analysis of Dependable Software. In: Buth, B., Rabe, G., Seyfarth, T. (eds.) SAFECOMP 2009. LNCS, vol. 5775, pp. 311–325. Springer, Heidelberg (2009)
16. Mustafiz, S., Sun, X., Kienzle, J., Vangheluwe, H.: Model-Driven Assessment of System Dependability. Software and Systems Modeling 7, 487–502 (2008)
17. Bondavalli, A., Cin, M.D., Latella, D., Majzik, I., Pataricza, A., Savoia, G.: Dependability Analysis in the Early Phases of UML-based System Design. Comput. Syst. Sci. Eng. 16(5), 265–275 (2001)
18. Cin, M.D.: Extending UML towards a Useful OO-Language for Modeling Dependability Features. In: The Ninth IEEE International Workshop on Object-Oriented Real-Time Dependable Systems, WORDS 2003 Fall, pp. 325–330 (October 2003)
19. Bernardi, S., Merseguer, J., Petriu, D.C.: Adding Dependability Analysis Capabilities to the MARTE Profile. In: Busch, C., Ober, I., Bruel, J.-M., Uhl, A., Völter, M. (eds.) MODELS 2008. LNCS, vol. 5301, pp. 736–750. Springer, Heidelberg (2008)
20. Bernardi, S., Merseguer, J., Petriu, D.: A Dependability Profile within MARTE. Software and Systems Modeling, 1–24 (2009)
21. OMG: Object Management Group. UML Profile for Modeling Quality of Service and Fault Tolerant Characteristics and Mechanisms. OMG document formal. V1.1/08-04-05 (April 2008)
22. jUCMNav: jUCMNav Project (tool, documentation, and meta-model) (2011) (last accessed, June 2011)
23. Cisco: Cisco IOS High Availability(HA)-In Service Software Upgrade (2006), http://www.cisco.com/en/US/prod/collateral/iosswrel/ps6537/ps6550/prod_presentation0900aecd80456cb8.pdf (accessed May 28, 2011)

Paprika: Rapid UI Development of Scientific Dataset Editors for High Performance Computing

Didier Nassiet, Yohan Livet, Marc Palyart, and David Lugato

CEA / CESTA
33114 Le Barp - France
{didier.nassiet,yohan.livert,marc.palyart,david.lugato}@cea.fr

Abstract. The increasing demand for numerical simulation software leads to productivity bottlenecks in the development of scientific dataset editors. New methods must be found to improve the time to market and the maintainability of these software applications. In this paper we present Paprika, an Eclipse-based application which tackles this problem through two approaches, both of them relying on model-driven engineering techniques. The first is a generative approach where a tailored scientific dataset editor is created for each numerical simulation. The second approach provides a generic editor, which uses reflective interfaces. We present the implementation of these approaches and assess them using results from an empirical study.

1 Introduction

In the context of high performance scientific computing, the specification of a complete and coherent dataset has always proved to be a difficult task for the end user of a computing code. For years, human input has been necessary to fulfill that task, usually provided by the developer of the numerical simulation as the person with the best knowledge of the parametrization of the algorithms. To reduce the degree of involvement of the developers and to expand the community of end users, graphical user interfaces were developed by specialists.

These specific editors integrate hard coded rules for managing the inputs of the scientific dataset specified by the simulation software developer. This co-development method allow the end user—assuming an exhaustive phase of manual validation—to produce complete and coherent datasets for the application. However, the dispersion of the knowledge between the HPC application and its user interface is a real challenge for long term maintainability and traceability, especially when the lifetime of a simulation software—in the order of several decades—is compared to the frequency of software technologies renewal for user interfaces. Given that a software simulation and its dataset must be upgraded at the same pace, the maintenance of the editor implies the availability of dedicated skills.

The increasing number and diversity of scientific simulation applications are outpacing the renewal of financial and human resources available for GUI development. At the CEA (French Atomic and Alternative Energy Commission), both

I. Ober and I. Ober (Eds.): SDL 2011, LNCS 7083, pp. 69–78, 2011.

to meet the goal of strengthening the coherence between a simulation code and its dataset editor and to preserve the separation of concerns, we have explored two ways for improving development productivity of scientific dataset editors. First the automatic generation of editors by model transformation, and second the development of a generic editor which uses reflective interfaces to extend its editing domain to several types of dataset. Along each of these two paths for improvement, and as in [1] and many recent works on rapid UI, we chose to adopt a model-driven engineering approach to tackle our search for productivity in the development of scientific dataset editors. This paper presents the results of this two-pronged approach, a software suite called Paprika, centered on a *numerical* metamodel dedicated to scientific data modeling. The technology of Paprika is based on the Eclipse Modeling Framework (EMF) and is packaged as an Eclipse RCP application (the Paprika studio). The main contribution of Paprika can be summed up as follows: ① a modeling process dedicated to scientific computing based on two Domain Specific Modeling Languages—named *numerical* and *GUI*—and ② a set of Eclipse plug-ins for the generation of the editors.

The rest of this paper is organized as follows: Section 2 describes the operating process of Paprika. Section 3 presents its implementation in Eclipse and the various available tools. In Section 4, we compare the two approaches according to five criteria. Finally, Section 5 describes future work and perspectives.

2   The Paprika Process

Use of Paprika includes two essential activities: the modeling of a scientific dataset and the construction, on the basis of a model, of a graphic editor. Figure 1 shows the overall operating process of Paprika.

2.1   Modeling of the Scientific Dataset

We have defined *numerical*, a DSML dedicated to the representation of a scientific dataset implemented in the form of an EMF metamodel[2]. A simplified view of its metamodel is presented in Figure 2. At the highest level, the *numerical* metamodel provides:

- the data types, to meet the needs of factorization and reuse of data between several datasets. These types are of three kinds: *predefined*: integer, real, boolean, character string, enumerations; *simple*, i.e. extending a predefined type, for example the "Angle" type by extension of the "real" predefined type; or *structured* to form compound types from other types. A range value can be specified for a simple data type: default value, minimal and maximal values, increment. It is also possible to associate a simple data type with a physical quantity, for example a frequency, and to set the unit used by default. The structured data types are constructed by the aggregation of predefined and/or simple types. Two structured types can be linked by an inheritance relationship (specialization of a type) or by a reference relationship, with or without containment.

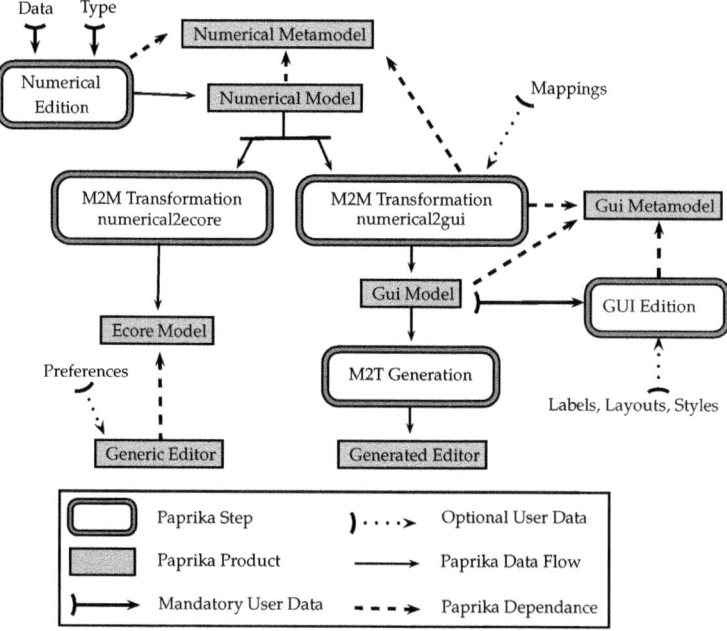

Fig. 1. Paprika simplified operating process

- the data, to define the dataset model. Data are always attached to a pre-defined, simple or structured type. The supply of predefined types by the *numerical* metamodel makes it possible to define data directly without necessarily defining types beforehand. Data may be isolated or grouped with other data in recursive data blocks.

2.2   Automatic Generation of the Editor

For the automatic generation of the editor, a DSML implemented with EMF was defined to model graphical user interfaces. Its metamodel is presented in Figure 3. The main components of this *GUI* metamodel are: basic graphical controls (widgets), content panels and layout managers. In order to give the Paprika user an opportunity to customize the generated editor, we chose to break the editor construction phase down into three distinct steps:

- the model to model (M2M) transformation step starts with the dataset *numerical* model and all the mapping rules between model elements and *GUI* metamodel. This results in an *GUI* model of the editor;
- the optional step for the *GUI* model customization makes it possible to enrich the model with the addition or modification of labels, layouts and styles;

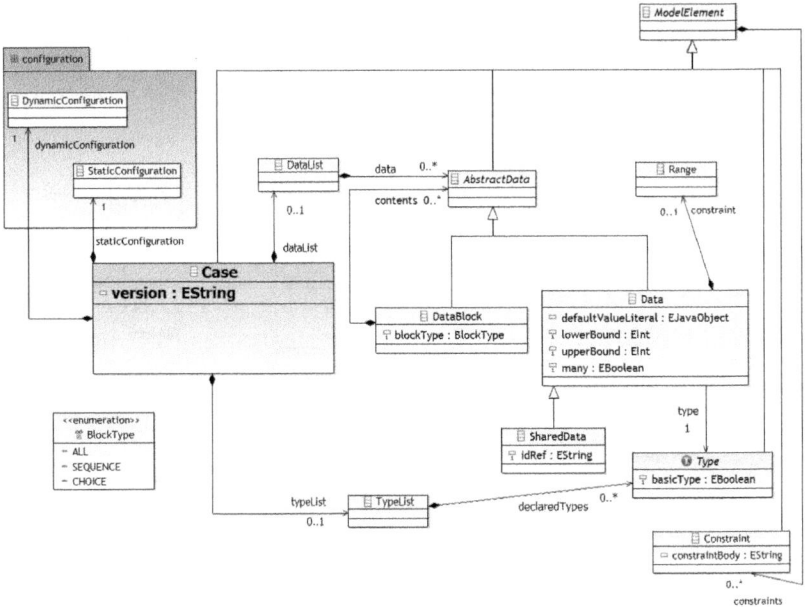

Fig. 2. Simplified view of the *numerical* metamodel

- the model to text (M2T) transformation step starts with the *GUI* model and generates a dataset editor. The compliance with the initial *numerical* model is ensured by the integration of the EMF validation framework in the generated editor.

2.3   Paprika Generic Editor

For this step in the process, an Eclipse multi-page generic editor was designed and written in SWT/JFace, for the edition of any instance of the *numerical* model in the form of master-detail blocks. To inherit the modeling components brought by the EMF.Edit layer, the databinding and the XMI persistence framework[2], we initially pass through an M2M transformation of the *numerical* metamodel to the *ecore* metamodel. The elements of the *numerical* metamodel are either carried over directly into the *ecore* model or carried over in the form of Paprika annotations. The generic editor integrates an annotation processor provided by Paprika ① to reconstitute the hierarchical structure of the data blocks in the form of editor pages and separate master-detail blocks, and ② to use the information on types, default values and scientific units exclusive to the *numerical* model. The layout algorithms and the mapping rules between the data model elements and the SWT/JFace widgets are implemented in the editor itself. However, an extension of the Eclipse preferences system enables the end user to customize the final rendering of the generic editor. The Paprika generic editor automatically handles the databinding between the editing domain and the presentation layer

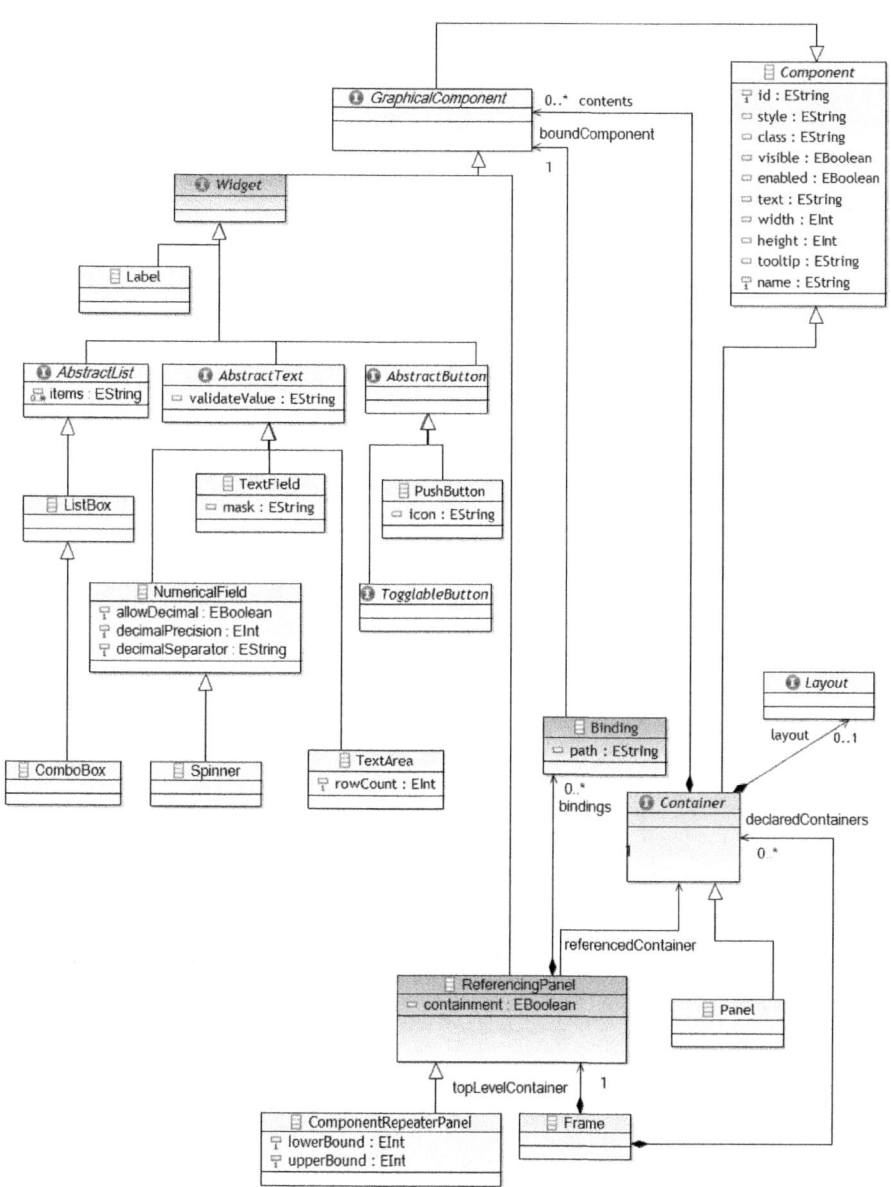

Fig. 3. Simplified view of the *GUI* metamodel

and helps the user for data input thanks to the Undo/Redo mechanism and to the integration of EMF validation.

3   Implementation and Use

The two major achievements of our work include the Paprika studio and the Paprika generic editor, implemented in the form of Eclipse plug-ins.

3.1   Paprika Studio

The *Paprika studio* is implemented as an Eclipse RCP application, the structure of which is illustrated in Figure 4 above. It essentially consists in a navigator of scientific dataset modeling projects (1) and a *numerical* model editor (2); a M2M transformer; an *gui* model editor (3); a dataset editor generator. The generated editors, either GWT(Google Web Toolkit) applets[3] or Eclipse SWT/JFace editors, can be used directly in the studio through its integrated preview mode. The Paprika studio detects any potential obsolescence between a *numerical* data model and a generated editor from that model and flags the obsolete editor models directly in the project navigator. The definitions of data types can be shared between several dataset models through the Paprika management of data types libraries: this is an essential feature regarding our needs for productivity as it makes it possible to model a whole domain of scientific data and to reuse such modeling between several dataset models within the same domain. The technologies used by the Paprika studio include the oAW (openArchitectureWare), Xpand and Xtend tools [4] for the model transformations. The generation phase of the editors is directly implemented in Java.

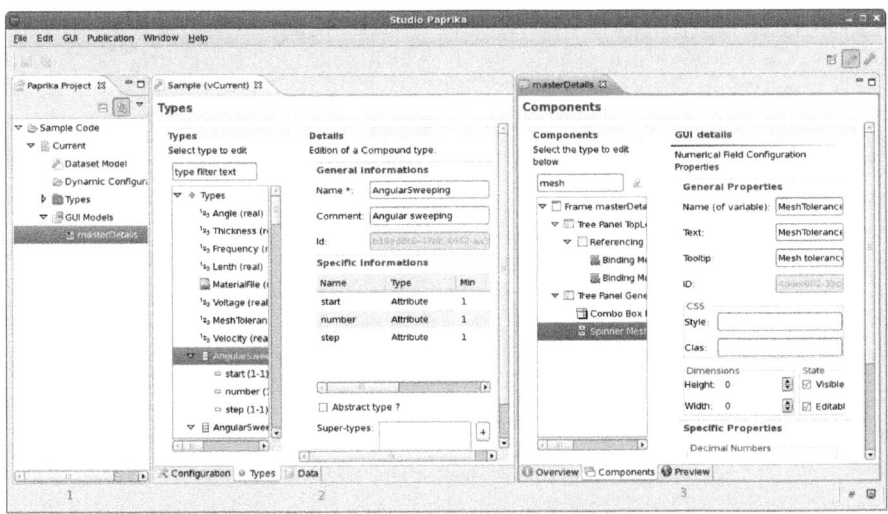

Fig. 4. The Paprika studio, an Eclipse RCP application

3.2   Paprika Generic Editor

The *Paprika generic editor* cannot be dissociated from the M2M transformation component, which handles the transformation of a *numerical* model into an equivalent *ecore* model: this Eclipse plug-in is based on the M2M ATL technology [5] and on the work of openArchitectureWare on the EMF Generic Form Editor. The Paprika generic editor is a multi-page Eclipse editor, each page (1) being created dynamically from the first level data blocks in the *numerical* model, the data sub-trees being handled by dedicated master-detail blocks (2). EMF validation (3) and editing domain are fully implemented to assist the user with respect to data input and to support the Undo/Redo mechanism. Figure 5 shows the Paprika generic editor, implemented as a dedicated Eclipse plug-in.

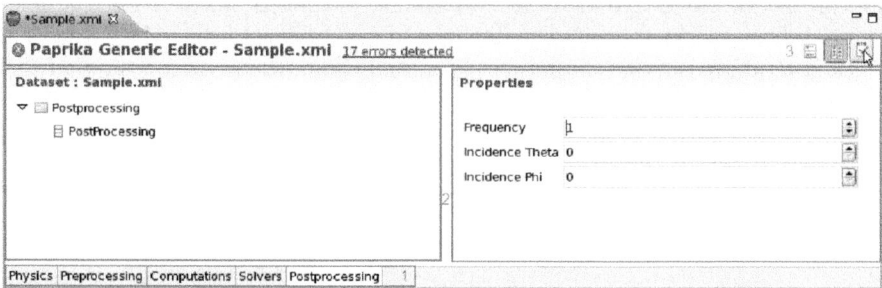

Fig. 5. The Paprika *numerical* generic editor

3.3   Demonstration

To increase the final ease of use, the model-driven engineering technologies used in Paprika are provided through a seamless integration within the Eclipse platform. As a demonstration, we have published a screencast[1] broken down into three sequences: ① the modeling of a *numerical* data domain, ② the automatic generation of a corresponding dataset editor in the form of a GWT applet, and ③ the use of the Paprika generic editor on the same data model.

4   An Empirical Study

4.1   Evaluation Method and Criteria

Our search for productivity in the development of scientific dataset editors identified two possible paths for improvement, namely the increase of versatility through the programming of a generic editor, and the automatic generation of an editor from a dataset model. We compared the generic and generative approaches against the traditional handwritten one. In order to actually assess these three development methods, each one must be characterized by a set of criteria. For this evaluation we have defined the following five criteria:

---

[1] http://www.youtube.com/watch?v=S_Q9nU2QWeU

1. *availability*: time-to-market characteristic of a dataset editor, i.e. the time between the expression of needs and the editor delivery. This criterion is induced from the productivity constraint.
2. *versatility*: capability of an editor to produce datasets from different scientific domains.
3. *usability*: ease of use, consistency, efficiency and customization levels brought to the end user by an editor.
4. *maintainability*: capability of an editor to easily and quickly take into account corrections and/or upgrades.
5. *total cost of ownership (TCO)*: integrates, on a significant period of time, initial cost, return on investment, operating costs, return on information technology.

According to these five criteria, two trainee engineers and three experienced engineers were asked to rate the different approaches regarding their experience with several projects on the subject. Figure 6 shows the average results of these evaluations: on this chart, values range from *one* (poor result) to *five* (excellent result).

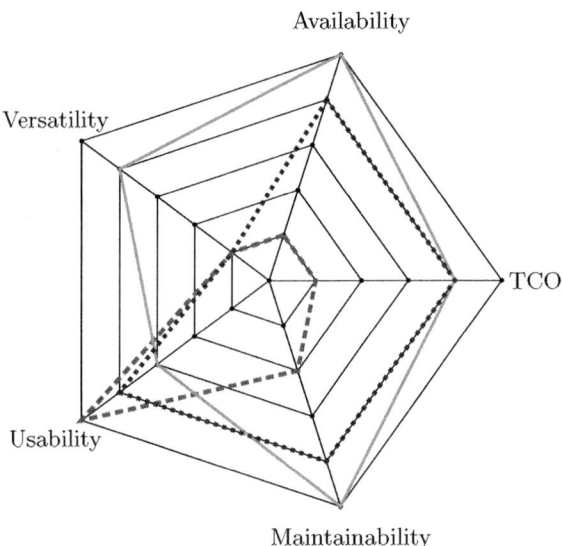

Fig. 6. Evaluation results on three UI development methods: handwritten (red, dashed), generic (green, plain), generative (blue, dotted)

4.2 Results Analysis

The strong point of the traditional programming method is, unsurprisingly, the possibility to fit the user required ease of use. That objective is generally reached at the expense of the availability and maintainability of the editor. The versatility of a *handwritten* editor is thereby wiped out. This approach suffers from a poor score on TCO, due to a significant lack of return on technology and to high initial and operating costs.

The generative approach increases the availability of the editor thanks to the automation of the most time-consuming development phases, and its maintainability by delegating the maintenance tasks upstream to the modeling phase. These gains, however, come at the cost of versatility because a generated editor remains totally linked to a specific data model. Regarding the criterion of usability, the generative approach remains behind the traditional approach: however, by integrating UI standards and best practices directly into the generator, we can rate it relatively high on this point. The initial cost inherent in this approach being largely offset by its significant contribution to the return on information technology, through innovative model-driven engineering technologies, this method gets a high rating on the TCO criterion.

If we consider the Paprika generic editor as a final product, the two strengths of the generic approach are its immediate availability and its maintainability. By design, its comes with a high versatility which enables it to edit any type of dataset in compliance with the *numerical* metamodel. On the other hand, the generic editor loses a bit in usability in comparison to an automatically generated editor. As it shares with the generative approach the same technology-driven innovations, the generic approach can get the same score on the TCO criterion.

The choice of a development method to meet as closely as possibly the needs of an end user will depend on the context, the allocated resources and the priority given to the project. Moreover, these three methods are not mutually exclusive but are to a large extent complementary. For instance, the generic editor can be deployed as an immediate alternative—or even for the purposes of prototyping—to a generated or handwritten editor. In the same manner, the presentation layer of a generated editor can be completely rewritten in a traditional way to obtain better usability of the editor interface.

5   Conclusion and Perspectives

In this paper we have presented and compared two ways of obtaining graphic editors in order to manipulate scientific dataset. Regarding the generic editor, improvements are planned with a special focus on its usability. For instance, we consider the development of a second generic editor with graphical editing capabilities, such as a mesh data editor. Consideration will also be given to the opportunity to adapt Paprika to the new technologies progressively brought in by the Eclipse 4 project [6] such as: Eclipse application modeling, user interface modeling, declarative widgets and styles, convergence between the Web and desktop applications. Finally, Paprika is expected to be integrated into a global approach for the development of numerical simulation applications based on modeling[7]. This approach aims to address and progressively abstract other facets of high performance computing application development such as parallelism management, model validation and calibration or code generation for upcoming hybrid supercomputers.

Acknowledgements. We sincerely thank Benjamin Cabé for his expertise on the Eclipse Modeling Framework and his contribution to the design and implementation of Paprika.

References

1. Schramm, A., Preußner, A., Heinrich, M., Vogel, L.: Rapid UI Development for Enterprise Applications: Combining Manual and Model-Driven Techniques. In: Petriu, D.C., Rouquette, N., Haugen, Ø. (eds.) MODELS 2010. LNCS, vol. 6394, pp. 271–285. Springer, Heidelberg (2010)
2. Gronback, R.: Eclipse Modeling Project: A Domain-Specific Language (DSL) Toolkit. Addison-Wesley Professional, Reading (2009)
3. Google Web Toolkit, http://code.google.com/webtoolkit/
4. Haase, A., Völter, M., Efftinge, S., Kolb, B.: Introduction to openarchitectureware 4.1.2. In: MDD Tool Implementers Forum, Zürich (2007)
5. ATL : ATL Transformation Language, http://www.eclipse.org/atl/
6. e4 Project, http://www.eclipse.org/e4/
7. Palyart, M., Lugato, D., Ober, I., Bruel, J.-M.: Le calcul hautes performances: un nouveau champ d'application pour l'ingénierie des modèles. Génie Logiciel, GL & IS 97, 41–46 (2011)

Verifiable Coverage Criteria for Automated Testing

Sergey Baranov[1], Vsevolod Kotlyarov[2], and Thomas Weigert[3]

[1] St. Petersburg Inst. for Informatics and Automation of the Russian Academy of Sciences,
St.Petersburg, Russia
snbaranov@googlemail.com
[2] Saint-Petersburg State Polytechnic University,
St. Petersburg, Russia
vpk@ics2.ecd.spbstu.ru
[3] Dept. of Computer Science, Missouri University of Science and Technology,
Rolla, MO, USA
weigert@mst.edu

Abstract. A key question for system testing of a software product is how to determine that the semantics of its requirements is adequately realized in the given implementation, or alternatively to find a series of concrete counter-examples demonstrating the violation of (a) particular requirement(s). An adequate test suite will aid in this determination. This paper formulates three types of requirements coverage criteria to establish the adequacy of a test suite. The suggested approach to system testing was validated in a number of medium and large size industrial projects.

Keywords: Requirements verification, requirement coverage, integration testing and verification.

1 Introduction

Current practice of industrial testing of software products utilizes different criteria for test coverage [1] to assess product quality. In this paper, we interpret "product quality" to mean how closely the product matches its requirements. "Test coverage" in this context refers to the extent by which the test suite covers the functional requirements of the system under development.

The key question is how to assess that the requirements are adequately realized in the implementation or, alternatively, to find concrete counter-examples which demonstrate that one or more requirements have been violated. The main difficulty stems from the fact that although each source requirement is typically mapped onto a respective test run result, the adequacy of mapping a requirement onto a test is usually not formally established. In industrial software development, this gap is partially filled with test reviews and/or inspections [2]. However, the subjective nature of these activities leaves ample room for residual product defects.

Various technologies of formal requirements verification have been developed, see for example [3], and aim at ensuring correctness and consistency of the source requirements. However, these technologies have so far yielded only limited impact on the quality of industrial software products. [3] uses deductive methods to generate a

I. Ober and I. Ober (Eds.): SDL 2011, LNCS 7083, pp. 79–89, 2011.

set of symbolic scenarios and to select a minimal subset of these scenarios intended to cover the behavioral requirements. In contrast to model checking, symbolic verification allows to analyze many concrete behaviors with a single symbolic scenario thereby substantially reducing the state space that needs to be explored.

This paper formulates three coverage criteria which we argue ensure that a test suite covers the product requirements. These are: the functional criterion, the structural criterion, and the tolerance range criterion. According to the functional criterion, each requirement is matched against a sequence of events (criteria chain) agreed to with the customer, such that occurrence of that sequence of events in an observed behavior means that the respective requirement is covered. The structural criterion requires that all user-specified paths in a requirements model are covered by the generated test suite. The tolerance range criterion holds that the customer specifies which concrete values of symbolic parameters in the generated symbolic scenarios should be substituted for the symbolic parameters to produce the tests in a test suite. These three criteria jointly ensure test coverage. We will illustrate the usage of these criteria, relying on the example of the VRS/TAT [4] requirements verification and test tools which apply a combination of model checking and deductive reasoning to the formalism of basic protocols and interacting agents.

The VRS/TAT tools formally represent system requirements as basic protocols [5]. A basic protocol (BP) is a minimally observable step of the system behavior and is expressed as a Hoare triple, i.e., a precondition, an observable action, and a postcondition. The pre- and postconditions describe the relevant subset of the of the system state (the set of system variables impacted by the observable action) before and after the indicated observable action has been performed. The BPs may contain symbolic parameters rather than concrete values and thus capture a range of equivalent system behaviors. Each BP should be related to one or more source requirements; some requirements may be expressed through several BPs, and one BP may also capture several requirements. Examples in this paper are taken from industrial projects which we formalized using the presented approach.

When formalizing system requirements, we chain BPs into requirements scenarios using the notation of use case maps (UCM, [6]). A use case map exhibits a causal sequence of events (termed "responsibilities") on a path from a start point to an end point. Each responsibility along a path on such map represents behavior the system performs and is expressed (following our methodology) by a BP such that the precondition of each BP must be derivable from the postcondition of a BP immediately preceding it in a map. Paths may branch into alternatives or concurrent paths, and may join again synchronized or unsynchronized.

Similarly, BPs may be chained into behavior traces, representing tests or observed system behaviors. When the BPs use symbolic parameters, these traces will be symbolic. Concrete tests may be derived from a symbolic trace by consistently substituting concrete values for symbolic parameters. The VRS/TAT tools are able to generate traces of observable events (either concrete events or symbolic events) implied by the formalized requirements.

The proposed criteria do not depend on the notion of a BP and its associated formalism. They are applicable to any requirements representation and testing technology, as long as the testing process supports a constructive procedure to verify that a given requirement holds. While the discussion below relies on the terminology of BP and UCM, we do so only for concreteness, and other suitable concepts may be substituted. Our approach was piloted in a number of industrial projects in the telecommunications domain; results obtained are summarized in the conclusion.

2 Functional Criterion

We associate with each requirement a constructive checking procedure (termed a "criteria chain"). A criteria chain is a series of observable events agreed to with the customer. When these events appear in an observed system trace in exactly the order given in the criteria chain, the respective requirement is said to be covered by this trace. (The checking procedure is constructive, as each of its steps is constructive in terms of conventional testing procedures: Each step involves checking that some event occurred. As each event is observable, the procedure is well defined and can be executed by a simple automaton.) After a set of criteria chains has been developed, an automated search through a set of test traces may either verify that the sequence of observable events expressed by the criteria chains are present in the test suite or establish that at least some of the chains are not present in the test suite. If a criteria chain is found in a trace, then the respective requirement is covered by this trace; otherwise the test suite does not cover this particular requirement and additional tests must be produced. Identifying and reviewing criteria chains constitutes the only manual effort following our approach; all other related testing activities are automated.

A data structure (traceability matrix) typically maps a source requirement into a criteria chain, see Fig. 1 (shown in columns "Requirements" and "Scenario of Requirements"). Every chain contains events which form the coverage criterion for this requirement. These events must occur in the same order in the formalized requirements [7].

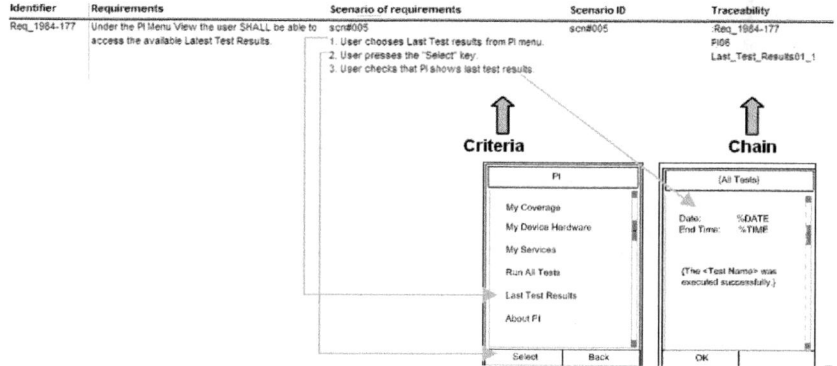

Fig. 1. Source textual requirement, criteria chain, and a reference to a BP which expresses this chain

The VRS/TAT tools generate test traces from the set of behaviors implied by the requirements in such a way that each criteria chain occurs in the set of test traces at least once, which entails complete coverage of the respective requirements.

The functional criterion is characterized by the percentage of the criteria chains covered by the given test suite which can be established straightforwardly. As the customer should approve the criteria chains, coverage of the chains by the test suite establishes a certain level of validity. The traceability matrix is an instrument for mapping the requirements (hence criteria chains and respective series of BPs) into test traces and for monitoring the level of requirements coverage during test generation.

3   Structural Criterion

This criterion refers to covering paths expressed in the requirements (here exhibited as UCM diagrams representing important behaviors) with the generated traces. We distinguish two different structural criteria: a criterion based on basic protocols and a criterion based on criteria chains.

With the BP structural criterion, the final set of test traces consists of traces which cover all basic protocols: Each BP developed during requirement formalization occurs at least once in the set of test traces. However, in spite of the fact that all BPs together cover all source requirements, this criterion is relatively weak. It is similar to the well-known C0 [8] criterion (substituting basic protocols for program operators) which requires that each operator of the program under test is covered at least once during execution of the test suite. This similarity allows us to consider the proposed BP structural criterion well-established. The BP structural criterion ensures test coverage of all functional requirements only when there is one-to-one correspondence between requirements and BPs. However, a single occurrence of a BP in a trace does not take into account the complete set of possible behaviors which include that BP. Consequently, test coverage of all relevant UCM paths is not ensured, and therefore, certain important behaviors may be missed by this criterion.

For example, to cover the requirement specified by element 7 in Fig. 2 using the BP structural criterion, it is irrelevant how this element 7 is reached during a test run. Therefore, any one of the three traces: 1-2-5-7, 1-3-5-7, and 1-4-5-7 may be used, while the two other traces will not be considered and the respective UCM paths will not be covered (hence, two possible behaviors will be omitted).

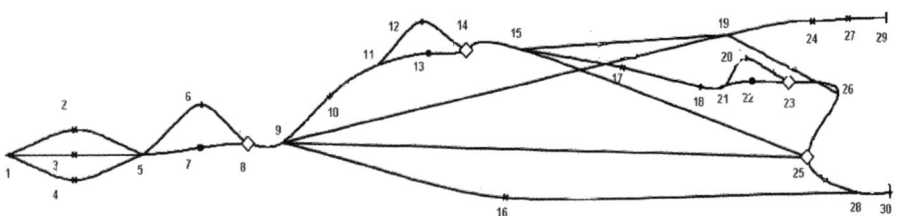

Fig. 2. Example of a high-level UCM (elements are numbered for discussion)

With the structural chain criterion, the final test suite consists of traces which cover all basic protocols referred to from the criteria chains for all requirements (and therefore all respective events) in the specified order. In this case the constraint of one-to-one correspondence between basic protocols and requirements is eliminated: Each requirement may be rendered with a chain of basic protocols considered as one unit. If all basic protocols and all respective events occur in the final trace in exactly the same order, then the requirement is covered. A customer can visualize the behavioral requirement on the UCM map and make appropriate corrections at a high level of abstraction. This criterion is similar to the well-known path criterion C2 ([8], all control flow paths shall be covered), where the set of paths includes designated important behaviors of the system under test. Without this constraint of one-to-one correspondence, the structural chain criterion becomes useless due to an exponential explosion of the number of paths to be covered for the criterion to be satisfied.

For example, traces 1-2-5-7-8-9-24-27-29, 1-3-5-7-8-9-24-27-29, and 1-4-5-7-8-9-24-27-29 constructed from the UCM map shown in Fig. 2 ensure complete coverage of the respective basic protocols. They also define traces where other important events occur which are necessary to cover the respective requirements, namely the stub 8, the selected branch 9, and two basic protocols: 24 and 27. If the chain for this requirement contains alternatives (e.g., 1-2-5, 1-3-5, 1-4-5 specified with 3 chains), then 3 traces need to be generated to cover the alternative chains.

If traces covering the alternative chains do not depend on this alternative, then the trace may be shortened for some tests by aborting tests with repeating behaviors. For example, the trace set 1-2-5-7-8-9-24-27-29, 1-3-5-7-8-9-24-27-29, and 1-4-5-7-8-9-24 may be replaced with the trace set 1-3-5-7-8-9-24-27-29, 1-2-5-8, and 1-4-5-8. In the two latter traces the test execution is aborted and the system under test is restarted to execute the next test in the given test suite.

If traces contain abstracted fragments of a common behavior, formalized with the stub element (e.g., element 8 in Fig. 3), then traces representing the behavior of such identified elements may be generated separately and can be substituted for this stub in the final, more detailed, symbolic trace.

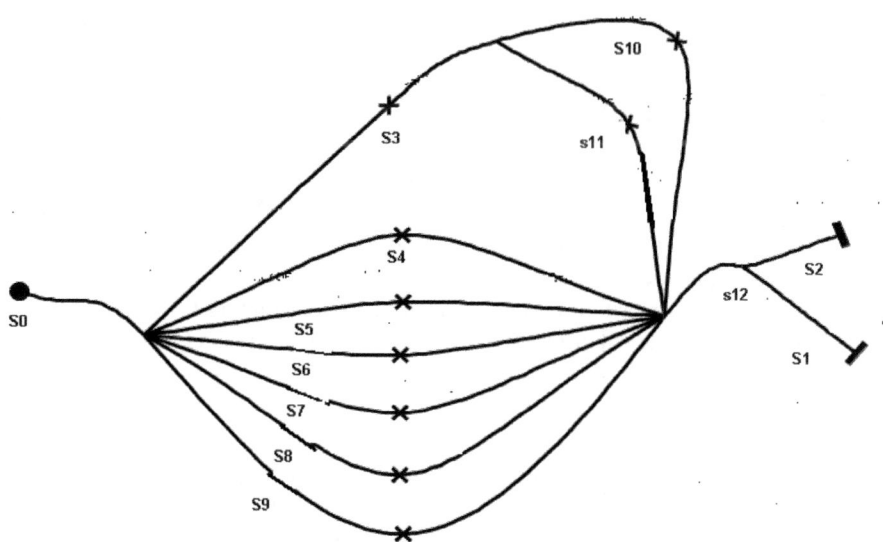

Fig. 3. UCM chart for stub 8 of Fig. 2

The structural chain criterion is relatively strong, because only those traces which contain the specified criteria chains of events and states in exactly the same order are selected from the set of all possible traces during test suite generation. As a result, this criterion may lead to an exponential explosion of the number of traces when generating and analyzing the symbolic traces.

Heuristics which use information beyond the criteria chains are employed to guide the process of trace generation in order to capture the specified chains and cope with the problem of exponential explosion. A heuristic consists of a list of responsibilities on a UCM map, which belong to a path that should be included in a test trace. These points are selected by the user and play the role of intermediate goals for the VRS trace generator, thus dramatically reducing the state space of possible traces to be explored in order to find a trace matching the desired path. As responsibilities are mapped onto BPs, the trace generator tries the respective BPs in the specified order first when constructing a trace through concatenation of appropriate BPs from the set of available BPs.

The resulting set of selected traces is minimized with respect to their total number and contains each chain at least once and covers all UCM paths, i.e., all paths through the system requirements. Minimization is performed by discarding traces which do not increase the current coverage rate with respect to the coverage criterion and thus may be considered redundant. If two traces are generated which contribute in the same manner to requirements coverage, then the shorter trace will be selected and the longer trace will be discarded.

However, it may happen that the user desires some particular traces (of relevance to the user) to be included in this minimal set. There are two reasons why these traces may not have been contained in the originally generated set of traces:

a)   A trace can be tracked to a path in the UCM specification but was discarded due to minimization. In this case, additional responsibilities should be added to force it to be included into the minimal set of traces.

b)   A trace cannot be tracked to a path because of undocumented requirements and therefore these additional requirements need to be formalized as paths in the UCM specification. Usually such additional paths contain responsibilities already encountered on the map, but with different preconditions (see Fig. 4).

Fig. 4 (left picture) contains a UCM map, which omits 3 alternatives handling a particular signal. In the right picture three responsibilities handling this signal have been added (see arrows).

The structural chain criterion together with heuristics guiding the trace generation process is the most efficient criterion to check requirements coverage by a test suite.

4   Tolerance Range Criterion

This criterion specifies how well the possible values for input parameters are captured in the test suite. The symbolic test traces contain symbolic variables rather than concrete values and it is possible to calculate the respective tolerance ranges for those variables during trace generation. Each symbolic trace represents an equivalence class of a number of concrete behavior scenarios, where concrete values from the evaluated tolerance ranges are substituted for the respective symbolic variables.

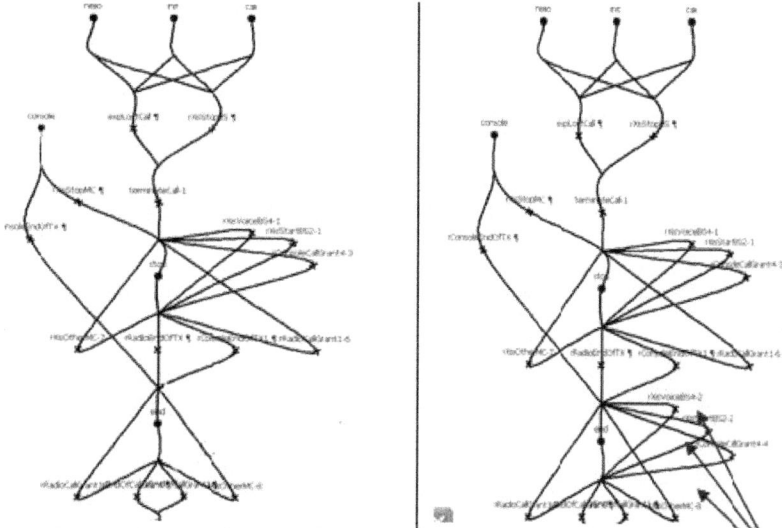

Fig. 4. Example of undocumented requirements

The tolerance range criterion answers the question: "How many different concrete values for particular input variables should be examined in order to ensure that all possible inputs are tested?" To try all possible values is infeasible; however, having identified equivalence classes for each input variable one can be sure that a test passed for one representative from a class would pass for any other representative of the same class. Therefore, it is sufficient to select just four concrete values for each input variable: some arbitrary value within the identified tolerance range, the lower and the upper limits of the range, and some value outside of the tolerance range. As the tolerance ranges for symbolic parameters are derived automatically, the particular choice of concrete values to be substituted into the test can be selected arbitrarily.

Automatic evaluation of tolerance ranges is feasible, subject to the following constraints [10]: a) the traces are finite; b) only linear arithmetic over integer and real numbers or enumerations is used in formulas; c) all loops are unrolled and bounded. Fortunately, these constraints are acceptable for many projects. Fig. 5 shows a trace fragment where tolerance ranges [32..34] and [0..∞] are defined for the symbolic variables _SequenceNumber_ and _TimeStamp_, respectively.

A complementary equivalence class consists of concrete scenarios where the concrete values of symbolic variables are out-of-range with respect to tolerance ranges discovered so far. Test suites with the middle, boundary, and out-of-range concrete values for input variables may be generated from each symbolic trace. Pass or failure of each such concrete test guarantees the same outcome for all other concrete tests from the same equivalence class or its complement.

It can be formally proven that if the input parameters are within their respective tolerance ranges at the initial step of a scenario, then the values of the output parameters (which are transformations of the input parameters performed by execution of this symbolic scenario) will be within the calculated tolerance ranges. If the input parameters are out of the expected tolerance range at run time, this may result in defects in the program behavior.

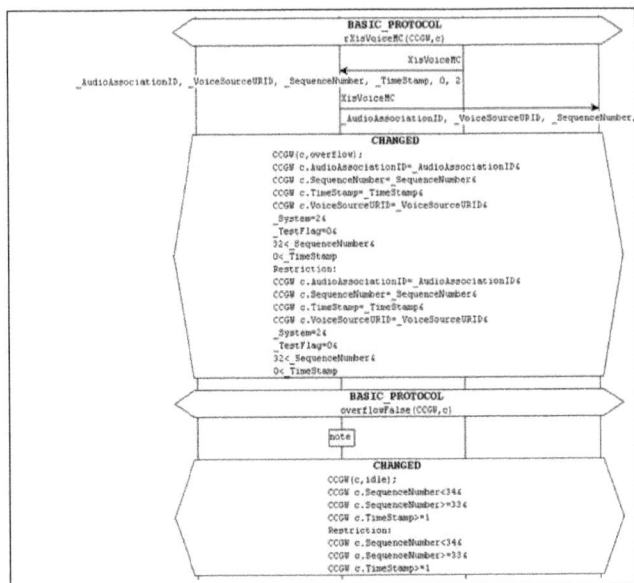

Fig. 5. Trace with tolerance ranges (for an enumeration type)

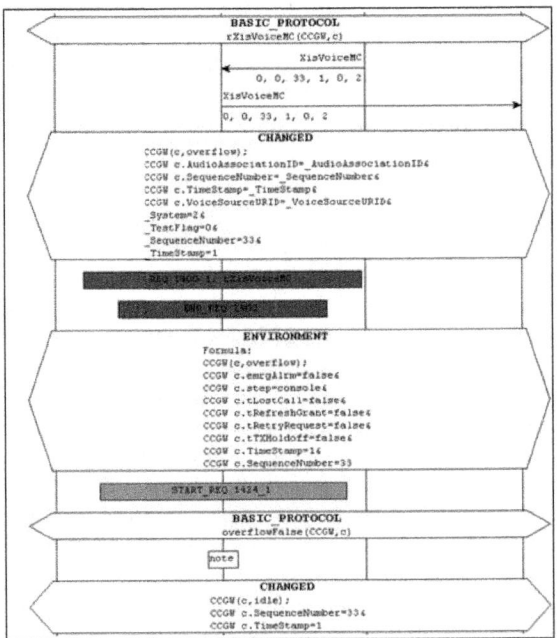

Fig. 6. A trace with substituted concrete values

Fig. 6 describes the assignment of values to the variables _SequenceNumber_ (33) and _TimeStamp_ (1) chosen from the identified tolerance ranges for these variables, [32..34] and [0..∞] respectively.

Experimental verification of the reachability of the goal state with all variables within their identified tolerance ranges, performed for all equivalence classes of behavior scenarios, guarantees the correct behavior of the system under test in all acceptable regimes of operation with respect to the specified correctness criteria. As all behaviors of the system belonging to the same equivalence class are equivalent, one needs to merely check the behavior of one arbitrary representative of the class to be able to validate the class, thus dramatically reducing the number of tests that need to be run in order to cover all behaviors specified by the requirements.

Successful testing confirms the correctness of the implemented system; however, it does not prevent usage of the system with violated constraints. It must be established that input and output communications between the system and its environment also satisfy the tolerance ranges, which can be achieved by tracking the tolerance ranges in the backward direction of the applied BP. Selecting correct and consistent tolerance ranges of input parameters to ensure acceptable ranges of the output parameters is a challenging engineering task which requires deep knowledge of the subject matter.

5   Conclusions

This paper formulates three coverage criteria for test suites derived from formalized specifications. The functional criterion is based on a user-specified constructive checking procedure for each functional requirement, and allows for identification of requirements covered by the given set of test traces. The structural chain criterion checks how many behaviors of the requirements specification are covered by the given test suite. Finally, the tolerance range criteria specifies what particular values from the identified tolerance range of each input variable must be selected for particular tests (e.g., a middle value, two boundary values, and one out-of-range value).

The combined use of the functional (covering all requirements), structural chain (optimal covering of all chains), and tolerance range criteria ensures the correspondence of an implementation with respect to its requirements. These coverage criteria allow the user to: (i) ensure reliable requirement coverage in accordance with the functional and structural chain criteria; and (ii) to control the impact of all input variables used in each behavioral trace, to calculate the respective tolerance ranges for the trace, and to derive concrete tests which cover the respective tolerance ranges. The table in Fig. 7 provides experimental data from industrial projects. In each of these projects, our approach to testing allowed us to reduce the overall project effort. For the considered projects (all projects have been taken from the telecommunications domain) an average gain in test productivity (including both test development and test execution, including analysis of test run results) is about 60%.

This study discussed an iterative process of achieving complete requirement coverage with the help of heuristics. It proves difficult to automate the generation of these heuristics for arbitrary domains without additional manual inputs. We therefore provided support for the user to directly specify navigation on the UCM paths which are not covered using the structural criterion.

While in [11] UCM is extended with temporal logic, our described approach uses the existing mechanism of UCM metadata to provide the necessary information and introduce new data types, thus allowing for a more detailed modeling of the system.

Our approach further copes with the exponential explosion of the number of tests by structuring and automation of test coverage on branches and paths. This differs from the approach in [12] which uses manually created test patterns.

An important feature of the described approach is a tight cooperation with the customer to define the "semantics of requirements" through a constructive checking procedure. After the customer agreed that observing a certain sequence of events in the SUT means that a particular requirement holds, then identifying such sequences in test logs and traces becomes a technical issue and generation of the respective test suite to cover the requirements can be automated.

The described approach was applied in a number of industrial projects using the VRS/TAT requirements verification and testing tools and demonstrated the above benefits along with reasonable efforts spent on formalization, test generation, and analysis of test runs.

Project	Number of requirements	Number of BPs	Staff-weeks for testing		% of effort reduction
			with VRS/TAT	Conventional	
# 1	107	163	1.8	5.9	69
# 2	148	205	2.2	5.7	61
# 3	51	283	2.1	6.3	67
# 4	57	497	2.8	7	60

Fig. 7. Sample industrial projects

References

1. Beizer, B.: Software Testing Techniques. ITP (1990)
2. Humphry, W.S.: Managing the Software Process. Addison-Wesley, Reading (1990)
3. Baranov, S.N., Drobintsev, P.D., Kotlyarov, V.P., Letichevsky, A.A.: The Technology of Automated Verification and Testing in Industrial Projects. In: Proc. IEEE Russia Northwest Section, 110 Anniversary of Radio Invention Conference, pp. 81–90. IEEE Press, St.Petersburg (2005)
4. Baranov, S., Kotlyarov, V., Letichevsky, A.: An Industrial Technology of Test Automation Based on Verified Behavioral Models of Requirement Specifications for Telecommunication Applications. In: Proc. Region 8 Eurocon 2009 Conference, pp. 122–129. IEEE Press, St.Petersburg (2009)
5. Baranov, S., Kapitonova, J., Letichevsky, A., Volkov, V., Weigert, T.: Basic Protocols, Message Sequence Charts, and Verification of Requirements Specifications. Computer Networks 49(5), 661–675 (2005)
6. Recommendation ITU-T Z.151 User requirements notation (URN) – Language Definition (2008)
7. Letichevsky, A.A., Kapitonova, J.V., Kotlyarov, V.P., Letichevsky, O.O., Volkov, V.V., Baranov, S.N., Weigert, T.: Basic Protocols, Message Sequence Charts, and the Verification of Requirements Specifications. In: Proc of ISSRE 2004 Workshop on Integrated Reliability Engineering (ISSRE 2004:WITUL), IRISA, Rennes France (2004)

8. Carel, M.: C0, C1 and C2 Coverage,
    `http://dev-logger.blogspot.com/2008/06/`
    `c0-c1-and-c2-coverage.html`
9. Nogueira, S., Sampaio, A., Mota, A.M.: Guided Test Generation from CSP Models.
    In: Fitzgerald, J.S., Haxthausen, A.E., Yenigun, H. (eds.) ICTAC 2008. LNCS, vol. 5160,
    pp. 258–273. Springer, Heidelberg (2008)
10. Potiyenko, S.V.: Methods of Direct and Reverse System Symbolic Modeling with Basic
    Protocols. Problems of Programming 4, 39–44 (2008) (in Russian)
11. Amyot, D., Weiss, M., Logrippo, L.: Generation of Test Purposes from Use Case Maps.
    Computer Networks 49(5), 643–660 (2005)
12. Hassine, J., Rilling, J., Dssouli, R.: Use Case Maps as a property specification language.
    Software and Systems Modeling 8(2), 205–220 (2009)

A New Approach in Model-Based Testing: Designing Test Models in TTCN-3

Antal Wu-Hen-Chang[2], Gusztáv Adamis[1], Levente Erős[1],
Gábor Kovács[1], and Tibor Csöndes[2]

[1] Department of Telecommunications and Media Informatics,
Budapest University of Technology and Economics,
Magyar tudósok körútja 2, H-1117, Budapest, Hungary
{adamis,eros,kovacsg}@tmit.bme.hu
[2] Ericsson Hungary
Irinyi J. u. 4-20, H-1117, Budapest, Hungary
{antal.wu-hen-chang,tibor.csondes}@ericsson.com

Abstract. Throughout the years, many model description languages have been used in different model-based testing tools, however, all these languages are quite unfamiliar to test engineers. In this paper, we propose TTCN-3 (Testing and Test Control Notation 3), the nowadays most popular and widely spread test definition language to be used for this purpose and give two alternative approaches how this could be carried out. TTCN-3 as modelling language can support test generation tools by means of the annotations we introduce in the paper.

Keywords: TTCN-3, extended finite state machine, model-based testing.

1 Introduction

When black box testing a communicating system, the test environment does not have any information about the internal structure of the System Under Test (SUT) and it can only investigate the SUT through the outputs it replies for different inputs. Nowadays, TTCN-3 (Testing and Test Control Notation 3) language is widely used for defining black-box tests [1], and many test designers have become familiar with TTCN-3.

Manual test design and testing however, has many drawbacks, since the whole testing process is carried out by humans. With the aim of getting rid of these problems, model-based testing, which is a partly automatic test generation method, has become popular in the last years. In the case of model-based testing, the test designer does not have to implement the test manually. Instead, he or she creates an abstract model of the SUT based on which, test cases are generated automatically, by a model-based testing tool. By transferring a part of the task of test generation from humans to automatic methods, model-based testing gains many advantages, as we will see in Section 2.

I. Ober and I. Ober (Eds.): SDL 2011, LNCS 7083, pp. 90–105, 2011.

In the last two decades, several model-based testing tools have been developed. Recently, three of the most promising tools are Conformiq Tool Suite, Elvior TestCast Generator , and SpecExplorer by Microsoft [2, 3, 4, 5]. These tools have different theoretical background and use different modelling languages for describing the abstract model of the SUT. In the case of Conformiq Tool Suite, the model of the SUT is described by UML (Unified Modeling Language) statecharts [6], and Java compatible source codes. Based on these inputs, Conformiq is capable of generating test scripts in various formats, like C/C++, Java, TTCN-3, etc. For Elvior TestCast Generator , the model of the SUT has to be described by UML state machines, and the tool generates TTCN-3 test cases as its output. SpecExplorer uses Abstract State Machine Language (AsmL) [7] and Spec# [8] for modelling, and as its output, it generates a data structure called a transition system, which can be converted to a C# code for running the test.

Besides the above, several other tools, languages and modelling techniques have been used for model-based testing. Tools Lutess [9], Lurette [10], and GA-TeL [11] use Lustre [12] as the language for modelling the SUT. Lustre is a declarative, synchronous dataflow language. In the case of Conformance Kit developed at KPN Research and PHACT developed at Philips, the model of the SUT is specified by an Extended Finite State Machine [13] (see in Section 2). TVEDA [14] and AutoLink [15] use SDL (Specification and Description Language) [16] for modelling the SUT, while in the case of TVEDA, Estelle [17] can be used as the modelling language as well. Cooper [18] uses LOTOS (Language of Temporal Ordering Specifications) [19, 20] as its input language, while in the case of TorX [21], the SUT can be modeled by LOTOS, Promela [22], and FSP (Finite State Process) [23].

These tools use different test derivation methods for generating test cases from the abstract model of the SUT. GATeL uses constraint logic programming (CLP) for generating test cases from the model [24]. Conformiq Tool Suite, Elvior, Conformance Kit, PHACT, AutoLink and TVEDA generate the necessary test cases based on finite state machines (FSM) [13].SpecExplorer, Cooper, and TorX use Labeled Transition Systems (LTS) [25] based theory for test case generation.

This paper investigates whether it is possible and practical to use TTCN-3 as modelling language and as the foundation for model-based testing. The rationale of adapting TTCN-3 relies on the following facts. It is a popular test definition language with tool and compiler support, and for many test engineers this is the only language they use on an everyday basis. Therefore, test designers who have skills in TTCN-3 do not need to learn a new formal description technique or language. TTCN-3 developers are likely to have designed many TTCN-3 test data structures of protocols, which exist in a data structure library and are ready to be used in test generation tools as well. This paper thus attempts to merge the advantages of the popularity of both TTCN-3 and model-based testing, by proposing, investigating, and comparing different approaches of utilizing TTCN-3 for describing the abstract model of the SUT. When defining the abstract formal model to TTCN-3 mappings, we took the experience of other existing formal description techniques and model-based testing approaches into account.

Partial TTCN-3 support has been alraeady available for modelling purposes in Elvior TestCast Generator and Conformiq Tool Suite. The former has native TTCN-3 support for data type and template type definitions, moreover, it has a feature that allows referring TTCN-3 functions in the UML model. The latter provides a TTCN-3 type definition import feature. This paper goes beyond this level of integration, and regards TTCN-3 as an exclusive modelling language.

The rest of the paper is organized as follows. In Section 2, we review the goals and basic concept of model-based testing. Section 3 presents our approaches for creating Extended Finite State Machine (EFSM) models and illustrates those through the example of the Alternating Bit Protocol. Section 4 takes a look at the advantages and disadvantages of the methods. An annotation-based extension of the TTCN-3 language is given in Section 5 that can make test generation based on TTCN-3 models more effective. Finally, a brief summary is given.

2   Model-Based Testing

There are multiple ways of black box testing communicating systems. In this section, we are going to present the partly or fully manual ways of test generation methodologies, the problems they raise [26], and the ways in which model-based testing attempts to solve these problems [26, 27].

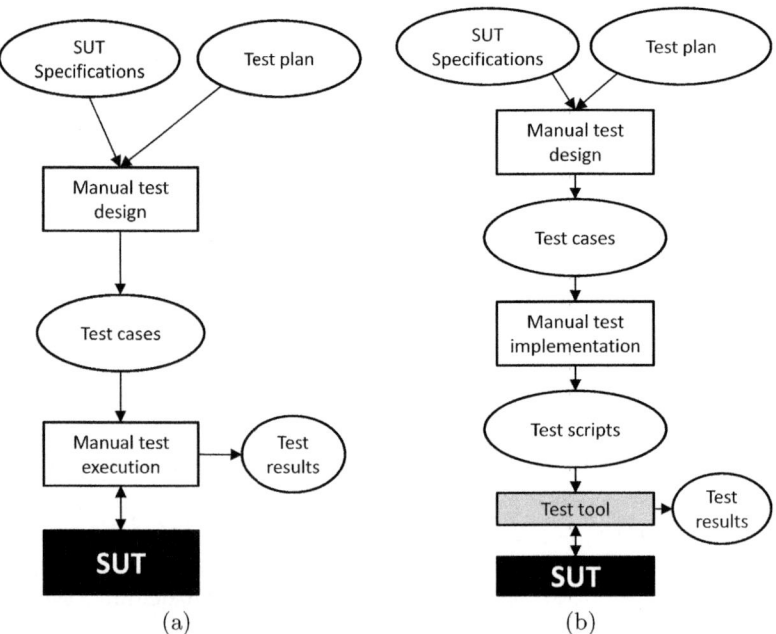

Fig. 1. Manual (a), and script based (b) test design

Figure 1(a) shows the steps of manual testing. When manually developing test cases, the test designer uses as input the written, informal or formal specifications of the SUT, and a test plan, which includes the purposes or goals of the test. Based on these inputs, the test designer develops the test cases manually on a high level of abstraction. The test cases created are then passed from the test designer to the tester. Following the steps described in the test cases, the tester executes the test manually by interacting with the SUT, and records the outputs the SUT returns for the inputs of the test case.

The so-called script based tests speed up the process of testing by automating the test execution phase. As in Figure 1(b), the test designer does the same job as in the manual case that is, designs the necessary test cases based on system requirements and the test plan. The tester on the other hand, rather than manually executing the test based on the high-level test cases, implements a test script. The created test script that interacts with the SUT, that is, it sends different inputs to the SUT, and observes the outputs sent by the SUT. Based on these observations, the script generates a test verdict as its output.

Although script based testing makes test execution a lot easier than in the case of fully manual testing, it is unable to solve the further problems raised by manual testing. Thus, tests remain unstructured, their coverage is incomplete, the number of necessary test cases can be huge, and thus, they are hard to maintain. In other words, the test is designed in an ad-hoc way, the quality

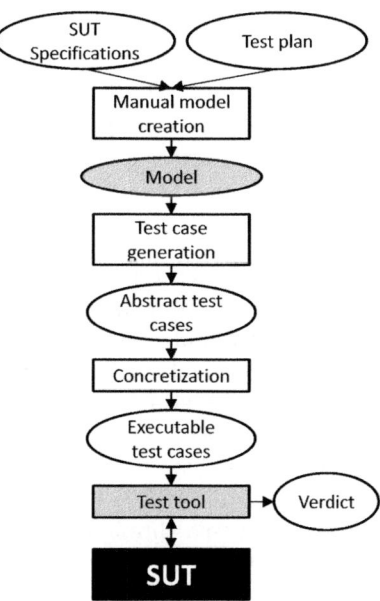

Fig. 2. Model based test design

of test depends on the expertise of the test designer. Besides, the design and maintenance of test cases is time consuming and costly.

The main goal of model based testing is to eliminate the problems mentioned above by partly automating test case generation. As Figure 2 shows, in model based testing instead of explicitly designing the different test cases to be run on the SUT, the test designer creates a *model* of the SUT. This model is written on an abstract level omitting some details of the behaviour of a valid SUT.

This paper focuses on finite state machine (FSM) based models, however, the model of the SUT can be given in a large variety of other formal modelling techniques. Finite state machines have been employed for modelling sequential circuits in hardware design, lexical analysis in compiler theory and pattern matching in artificial intelligence. Definition 1 gives a possible interpretation of the deterministic Mealy machine [13].

Definition 1. *An FSM is a quintuple:* $FSM = (I, O, S, \delta, \lambda)$, *where I and O are the finite sets of input and output symbols, respectively, S is the finite, nonempty set of states, $\delta : S \times I \to S$ is the state transition function, and $\lambda : S \times I \to O$ is the output function.*

Using an EFSM, defined in Definition 2, the values (state) of some variables are separated from the S control state set of the machine. Each EFSM can be unfolded to an FSM, but – depending on the size of the domain of variables – the number of states (elements of S) of the FSM can be by orders of magnitude larger than the number of states (elements of S) of the corresponding $EFSM$.

Definition 2. *An Extended Finite State Machine (EFSM) [13] is a quintuple $EFSM = (I, O, S, V, T)$, where I and O are the finite, nonempty sets of input and output symbols, respectively, S is the finite, nonempty set of states, V is the finite set of variables, and T is the finite set of transitions. Each transition $t \in T$ is a 6-tuple $t = (s_t, q_t, i_t, o_t, P_t, A_t)$, where $s_t \in S$ is the current state, $q_t \in S$ is the next state, $i_t \in I$ is the input, $o_t \in O$ is the output, $P_t(V)$ is a predicate on the current variable values, and $A_t(V)$ is an action on variable values.*

After designing the model, a test generator tool is used for automatically generating abstract test cases – traces – from the model. The test engineer usually has control over the testing efforts and number of test cases to be generated. This way, the theoretically infinite number of test cases can be limited.

The main benefits of model based testing are the following. The time and cost of test case generation is reduced, because the large number of necessary test cases is generated by the model based testing tool instead of a human. Also, the effect of human errors is reduced, since the test designer only creates a concise, abstract model, which is easier to see through than a manually written, long test code. Thus, model based test generation results in better test coverage and maintainability.

3   Designing Abstract Models in TTCN-3

This section takes a look at different approaches for defining – extended – finite state machine models in TTCN-3. In this paper, there are two alternative approaches, a functional one and a declarative one, considered that differ in the way of describing the behaviour, the system interface definition is the same in both cases. The functional approach defines the system behaviour as a large test case. The declarative approach defines a data structure that defines the constraints for maintaining the state of the EFSM and determining the appropriate transition function on an incoming event. The two approaches are illustrated on the example of the Alternative Bit Protocol.

3.1   Modelling System and Its Interfaces

First we introduce two refinements to the EFSM model given in Definition 2. The input set I and the output set O can contain huge numbers of events. To reduce their sizes, messages with similar structures are considered to be parameterized, we allow $i \in I$ and $o \in O$ be parameterized with a variable list $V' \subseteq V$ in our model, and denote them with $i(V)$ and $o(V)$. The second refinement is that we allow the input/output alphabet to be partitioned into finite number of sub-alphabets such that $I = I_1 \cup I_2 \cup \ldots \cup I_N \cup \iota$ and $O = O_1 \cup O_2 \cup \ldots \cup O_N$, where ι is an internal event, $1 \leq N < \infty$ and I_i and O_i may be empty.

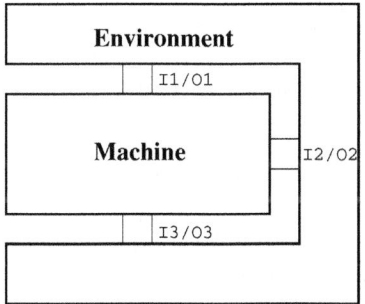

Fig. 3. EFSM interfaces

The abstract model of EFSM interfaces is shown in Figure 3. The model divides the domain into two parts, the machine itself and its environment. In the figure, the input and output sets of the machine are partitioned into three subsets, the communication between the machine and the environment takes place by message-based interaction through these ports.

An EFSM can be modelled with a TTCN-3 module. The module definition consists of two main parts, the interface definition part and the behaviour definition part. The interface definition contains optionally data type definitions and definitions of templates for output messages of the machine, at least one

port type definition, and the definitions component types of the machine called
SystemType and its environment called EnvironmentType.

For the parameters of each $i(V) \in I$ and $o(V) \in O$ a TTCN-3 data type
is defined if it does not yet exist. For each sub-alphabet $I_i/O_i, 1 \leq i \leq N$ a
message-based port type is defined such that for all $i_{ij}(v_j) \in I_i, 1 \leq j \leq |I_i|$
and $o_{ij}(v_j) \in O_i, 1 \leq j \leq |O_i|$ in port type i the type of v_j is declared as an
inout parameter. For each $o(v) \in O$ a parameterized template type is defined
with a format parameter of the type of v. For all $v \in V$, $i(v) \in I$ and $o(v) \in O$
a variable is declared in the component type of the system corresponding to
machine M, and a port of each port type is declared in both component types.
These mappings are summarized in Table 1.

Table 1. EFSM to TTCN-3 model – interface mappings concepts

EFSM element	TTCN-3 element
EFSM	Module, Component type definition
Set of variables	Data type definition
Input/Output message parameters	Data type definition
Input/Output set partition	Port definition
Output message	Parameterized template

Example. The interface definition of machine M is illustrated on the simple
Alternating Bit Protocol. The EFSM model of this protocol can be seen in Figure
4. The protocol provides the reliable transmission of user data to a peer entity.
The receipt of user data is guarded by a one-bit sequence number that alters
on each successful transmission. In the current example user data is considered
to be an integer value, and ports are named after the input or output messages
received or sent through them. The example is taken from [28].

The protocol has two control states ($Idle$ and $Wait\_Ack$) and four transitions. The system is initially in the $Idle$ state. On input of user data on the usr
port of the system in the $Idle$ state, the user data is coupled with the current
value of the one bit sequence number and transmitted via the snd port, and the
state machine begins to wait for an acknowledgement. In the $Wait\_Ack$ state,
three transitions are possible. On no input message on the rcv port of the system
a timeout event (ι) occurs resulting in the retransmission of the previous user
data value coupled with the current sequence number. If a sequence number is
received on the rcv port, it is compared to the current sequence number value.
If the two are the same, the system remains in the $Wait\_Ack$ state. If different,
the current value of the sequence number is inverted, and the state machine is
brought back to the $Idle$ state.

Formally, the elements of the EFSM tuple are the following. The set of states S
is $\{Idle, Wait\_Ack\}$. The set of variables V has two element NS and $userData$.
The input and output alphabets are $I = \{usr, rcv, \iota\}$ and $O = \{snd\}$ respectively. I is partitioned into $\{usr\} \cup \{rcv\}$. The usr input message has an integer
parameter, the rcv input message a Boolean parameter and the parameter of

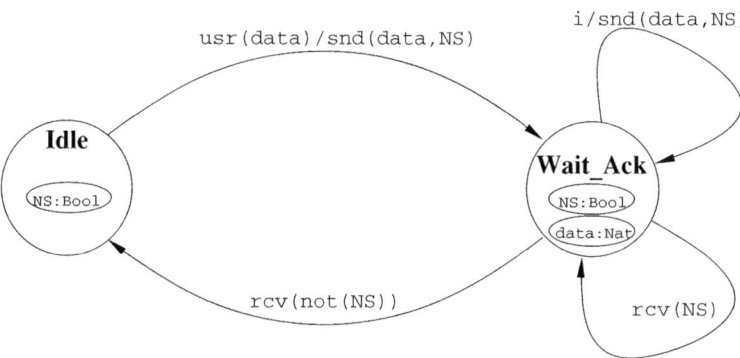

Fig. 4. EFSM of the Alternating Bit Protocol [28]

the *snd* output message is a record composed of an integer value and a Boolean value. There is an internal message ι to the system itself, this message models a timeout event.

The format of each message in the input/output alphabet is defined by a data type. The data types used in our example are shown in the listing below. The `AlternatingBit` is a `bitstring` limited to two possible values. The `DataFrameType` is a record composed of an `AlternatingBit` value representing the counter and and `integer` value representing the user data. As user data are considered to be `integer` values there is no need to define a new type for that.

```
type bitstring AlternatingBit ('0'B, '1'B);
type record DataFrameType {
   integer data,
   AlternatingBit counter
}
```

Output messages are represented with parameterized templates. The role of the template is to construct the data structure from its fields and initialize optional fields. In case of the Alternating Bit Protocol, there is only one outgoing message, the data frame sent via the `snd` port. The data record of that message has two fields, so the template must have two parameters, one of `integer` type, the other of `AlternatingBit` type.

```
template DataFrameType tDataFrame (integer pl_d,
    AlternatingBit pl_b) :={
   data:=pl_d,
   counter :=pl_b
}
```

The EFSM model of the Alternating Bit Protocol defines three ports for communicating with the environment: the `usr` port towards the user of this protocol entity, the `snd` port for sending data to the peer entity, and the `rcv` port for receiving acknowledgements for messages sent from the peer entity. As these ports are shared by the system and the environment, the values that can be offered through them are declared as inout parameters.

```
type port USRPortType message {
   inout integer;
}
type port SNDPortType message {
   inout DataFrameType;
}
type port RCVPortType message {
   inout AlternatingBit;
}
```

The TTCN-3 module representing the EFSM model has two component types: the system itself and its environment as shown in Figure 5.

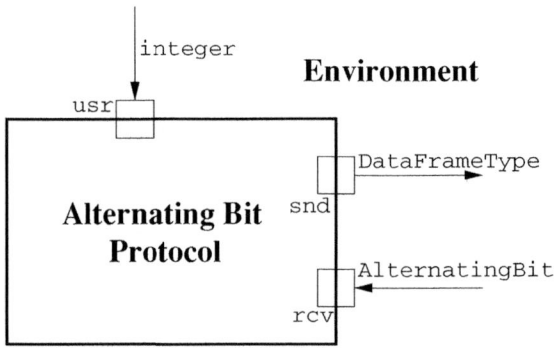

Fig. 5. Ports of the Alternating Bit Protocol

The component type of the system must declare besides the port definitions a variable for each element of the V set of the EFSM and each outgoing message parameter value. For each timeout event in I a timer is declared, in the code below the timer called T_retransmission corresponds to the inobservable input event ι.

```
type component SystemType {
   var AlternatingBit v_counter;
   var AlternatingBit v_received;
   var integer v_userData;
   timer T_retransmission := 5.0;
   port USRPortType usr_PT;
   port SNDPortType snd_PT;
   port RCVPortType rcv_PT;
}
```

The component type of the environment contains only the port definitions as shown below.

```
type  component  EnvironmentType {
    port  USRPortType  usr_PT;
    port  SNDPortType  snd_PT;
    port  RCVPortType  rcv_PT;
}
```

3.2   Functional Approach for Modelling Behaviour in TTCN-3

The behaviour of the EFSM is determined by the transition function according to Definition 2. This means formally that the elements of the $T \subseteq (S \times V) \times (I \times P(V)) \times (A(V) \times O) \times (S \times V)$ product.

The TTCN-3 language elements that can take part in the behaviour modelling are `control`, `testcase`, `if..else`, `alt`. The role of `control` is to execute the single `testcase` of the module. The role of the `testcase` is to implement the behaviour. This `testcase` is however turned inside out, it runs on the `SystemType` component type and its `system` is the environment.

A state $s \in S$ represents an execution point in the body of the `testcase` that can be represented with a `label`, a `function` name or an `altstep` name. In most cases the `testcase` contains an infinite loop that iterates over these points. The set of variables V is inherited from the component type the testcase runs on.

A transition is triggered by an $i \in I$ input event and selected by the $P_i(V) \subseteq P(V)$ set of conditions. At each execution point denoted as state all input events of I are allowed to be received and can be selected with an `alt` statement. The enabling conditions of the transition are checked with a set of `if..else` constructs.

The result of the transition is a set of outputs $O_i \subseteq O$ and a set of changes in the variable set V defined by $A_i(V) \subseteq A(V)$. An output event o_i is mapped to a `send` statement that takes a template parameterized with $V_i \subseteq V$ as argument. The variable set V is changed once by the parameters of the input event and updated with the `values` construct, and updated with the actions $A_i(V) \subseteq A$ during the transition by means of assignments.

The next state is set at the end of the executing transition by means of a `goto` if states are represented with labels, or setting the name of the next function or altstep to be executed in the body of the test case by means of a function reference.

The behaviour of the test case can be further decomposed into functions or altsteps, which can be parameterized with a subset of the ports and variables of the system and can therefore be used for introducing hierarchical considerations in the model.

Table 2 summarizes the functional approach for mapping EFSM transitions to TTCN-3 language elements.

Example. The mapping of the functional approach is illustrated on the example of the Alternating Bit Protocol introduced in the previous section.

Table 2. EFSM to TTCN-3 model – Functional approach for mapping behaviour

EFSM element	TTCN-3 element
State	label or function name or altstep name
Input	alt and receive and values
Predicate	if..else construct
Output	send using a parameterized template
Action	assingment
Next state	goto or function reference

```
control {
  execute (tc_Behaviour());
}
```

In the test case that is executed the modelled system type is declared as
mtc and the environment type is declared as system, this means that these
are swapped compared to real test cases. The ports of the mtc and system
are connected as in test cases, and since all ports declare one inout value, the
mapping is symmetric. The behaviour is specified in an infinite loop.

```
testcase tc_Behaviour (AlternatingBit pl_c := '1'B)
      runs on SystemType system EnvironmentType {
  v_counter := pl_c;
  map (mtc:usr_PT, system:usr_PT);
  map (mtc:rcv_PT, system:rcv_PT);
  map (mtc:snd_PT, system:snd_PT);
  var boolean v_r := true;
  while (v_r) {
    label idle;
    usr_PT.receive (integer:?) -> value v_userData;
    snd_PT.send (tDataFrame(v_userData, v_counter));
    T_retransmission.start
    goto waitAck;
    label waitAck;
    alt {
      [] T_retransmission.timeout {
        snd_PT.send(tDataFrame(v_userData, v_counter));
        T_retransmission.start
        goto waitAck
      }
      [] rcv_PT.receive(AlternatingBit:?) -> value v_received
         {
        if (v_received==v_counter) {
          repeat;
        }
        else {
            T_retransmission.stop;
            goto idle;
```

```
                  }
               }
            }
         }
      stop
   }
```

3.3   Modelling Behaviour with State Transition Tables

Alternatively, EFSM behaviour can be described in a declarative way as well. Just like in the case of the functional approach the control executes the single testcase of the module that runs on the System component type as mtc and the enviroment as system.

The mapping in this case is done by introducing data types for storing states, inputs, transition events and next states of the machine. A map data type with the key of state name and input event name pair and the value of function names defines the set of transition functions. Formally $I \times S \to F$ is used, which means that the name of a state and the input event serve as a key to select the appropriate TTCN-3 function to be called with a function reference.

Example. The code below shows a piece (the transition triggered by the internal event that retransmits the user data) of the data structure of a set of state machines that implements the Alternating Bit Protocol. Variable state is the current state of a machine, and the events structure defines the state transition table. The eventId field represents an incoming event, and the stateId field of the states record represents a state. The actions field is a list of identifiers referring to functions to be called on the incoming c_event_T_retransmission event, if the machine is in the c_state_waitAck state.

```
v_fsms := { {
   state := c_state_idle ,
   events := { {
      eventId := c_event_T_retransmission ,
      states := { {
         stateId := c_state_waitAck ,
         actions := {
            f_trans_fromWaitAck_toWaitAck_T_retransmission}
         }, ...
      }
   }, ...
   }
} }
```

The TTCN-3 function $f \in F$ associated with s and i implements $P(V) \times A(V) \times O \times S$ part of the transition, that is, it contains if..else constucts, assignments, send events and the setting of the next state name key. The code below shows the function that implements the transition selected in the example above.

```
function  f_trans_fromWaitAck_toWaitAck_T_retransmission(
    in  integer  fsmId ,  in  integer  eventId ,  in  integer  stateId )
    runs on SystemType {
    snd_PT.send(tDataFrame(v_userData[fsmId] ,  v_counter[fsmId])
        );
    T_retransmission.start
    v_fsms[fsmId].state  :=  c_state_waitAck ;
}
```

The name of the current state $s \in S$ is maintained in a variable of the component and the input event $i \in I$ is selected in the infinite loop in the body of the test case that listens for all possible events in an `alt` statement.

4   Analysis of Mapping Alternatives

The functional approach suits well to the concept of TTCN-3, it is easy to overview the code and therefore this method is practical for test developers. If components are implemented with processes or threads, the operating system could struggle with the large number of instances because of the frequent context switching. Between different instances only message-based communication is possible as internals a hidden from each other.

The advantage of the declarative approach is that the same behaviour can be instantiated multiple times making this approach suitable for performance testing. The number of instances is limited by the available memory. The instances run on the same component and can therefore share global variables. The disadvantage of this method is that it is difficult to define the data structure programmatically.

Table 3 compares the functional and the declarative approaches from several aspects. The declarative approach may have a better performance when dealing with multiple instances of the same behaviour at the cost of more difficult maintenance and a somewhat limited TTCN-3 language. Both approaches can support non-determinism by means of random number based – guarding – conditions. The TTCN-3 code used in both approaches is not only syntactically, but semantically valid.

Table 3. Comparison of the mapping approaches

	Functional	Declarative
Performance testing	no	yes
Maintenance	easy	hard
Expression Power	complete TTCN-3	limited TTCN-3
Non-determinism support	yes	yes
TTCN-3 code validity	semantic	semantic

5   Propositions

In order to produce the necessary test cases, beyond defining the abstract model of the SUT, the test designer has to provide the testing tool with some additional settings and parameters for the compiler. This can be done in configuration files, however, some parameters are model specific, so should be included in the model. While for instance, state space exploration depth should remain in the configuration file, the racing condition between two events is a vital part of the model. When such a consideration is used, test cases may become capable of handling racing conditions, so it can be possible to consider any order of reception of multiple messages sent by the SUT.

A possible way for adding such notations to the TTCN-3 code is the TTCN-3 Documentation [29]. However, we found the specialization of test cases beyond its capabilities. Thus, this section proposes annotation techniques for controlling racing conditions and test data selection.

To support test data generation, the possible values for the fields of templates considered during test generation may be given. The test designer should be able to define the minimum (min) and maximum (max) values of each template field, together with a step value to guide the equivalent partitioning technique. In this case, the test generator tool generates one template in which the value of that field is min, another template in which, the value of that field is max, and templates in which, the value of that field is $min + k * step$, where $k = 1, \ldots, \lfloor \frac{max-min}{step} \rfloor$. Furthermore, the test designer can define values (forced_value) that appear as field values in the generated templates. In our notation, forced values appear in curly brackets after an @ symbol followed by the corresponding keyword in a comment that is placed in the line of the field value of the corresponding incoming template definition as the following example shows:

```
template  OutputTemplateType  output1  (integer  a,  charstring  b)
    := {
    field1  :=  a  //@min{15}  @max{30}  @step{10}
    field2  :=  b  //@forced_value{"foo","bar"}
}
```

A racing condition can arise when the SUT sends multiple messages to the test environment sequentially via different ports, and the order in which the these messages are observed in the environment is not necessarily the same in all executions. Thus, the model based testing tool generates all possible orderings in interleave statement when this annotation is found. The test designer should inform the test generator tool about which messages of the SUT race with each other by labelling them. In our notation, each racing message m is labelled in curly brackets after an @ symbol and a race_label keyword in a comment placed in the line of the send statement. The messages that race with that m message are referred to by their labels listed in curly brackets after an @ symbol and a races_with statement placed in a comment in the line of the send statement. This is shown in the following example:

```
P1.send(output1); //@race_label R1 @races_with{R2,R3}
P2.send(output2); //@race_label R2 @races_with{R1,R3}
P3.send(output3); //@race_label R3 @races_with{R1,R2}
```

6   Conclusions

This paper proposed to use TTCN-3 as modelling language in model based test generation tools. This way test engineers would not need to learn a new notation for creating models beside the language they use every day in their work. Another benefit is that the valuable data structure libraries developed throughout the years in testing departments can be reused for modelling purposes. This way the time requirement and cost of model design could be significantly reduced and the quality of the model could be improved.

In this paper we suggested two alternative ways for designing abstract models of the SUT in TTCN-3. The functional approach follows the concepts of the TTCN-3 language and is practical for test developers. Though the declarative approach that stores the FSM transitions in a data structure is more difficult to maintain, it is suitable for performance testing as well. We proposed a syntax to guide model based test generation tools to be able to create more elaborated test cases that take for instance racing conditions and test data selection into account.

In the future we are going to extend our work on the annotation of TTCN-3 data structures with regard to functional dependencies between data structure fields. The work on TTCN-3 as modelling language can be further extended with hierarchical design and using parallel components within the model itself and a more sophisticated non-determinism support.

References

1. ETSI: ETSI ES 201 873-1 V4.2.1: Methods for Testing and Specification (MTS), The Testing and Test Control Notation version 3, Part 1: TTCN-3 Core Language (2010)
2. Conformiq: Tool suite, http://www.conformiq.com/
3. Huima, A.: Implementing Conformiq Qtronic. In: Petrenko, A., Veanes, M., Tretmans, J., Grieskamp, W. (eds.) TestCom/FATES 2007. LNCS, vol. 4581, pp. 1–12. Springer, Heidelberg (2007)
4. Elvior: TestCast Generator, http://www.elvior.ee/motes/
5. Microsoft: Specexplorer,
   http://research.microsoft.com/en-us/projects/SpecExplorer/
6. Group, O.M.: Unified modeling language, http://www.uml.org
7. Microsoft: Abstract state machine language,
   http://research.microsoft.com/en-us/projects/asml/
8. Microsoft: Spec#,
   http://research.microsoft.com/en-us/projects/specsharp/
9. du Bousquet, L., Zuanon, N.: An overview of lutess - a specification-based tool for testing synchronous software. In: Proc. 14th IEEE Intl. Conf. on Automated SW Engineering, pp. 208–215 (1999)

10. Raymond, P., Nicollin, X., Halbwachs, N., Weber, D.: Automatic testing of reactive systems. In: Proceedings of the IEEE Real-Time Systems Symposium, RTSS 1998, p. 200. IEEE Computer Society, Washington, DC (1998)
11. Marre, B., Arnould, A.: Test sequences generation from LUSTRE descriptions: GATEL. In: Proceedings of the 15th IEEE International Conference on Automated Software Engineering, p. 229. IEEE Computer Society, Washington, DC (2000)
12. Halbwachs, N., Caspi, P., Raymond, P., Pilaud, D.: The synchronous dataflow programming language LUSTRE. Proceedings of the IEEE, 1305–1320 (1991)
13. Lee, D., Yiannakakis, M.: Principles and methods of testing finite state machines – a survey. Proceedings of the IEEE 84(8), 1090–1123 (1996)
14. Clatin, M., Groz, R., Phalippou, M., Thummel, R.: Two approaches linking test generation with verification techniques. In: Proceedings of the 8th International Workshop on Protocol Test Systems, IWPTS 1996 (1996)
15. Koch, B., Grabowski, J., Hogrefe, D., Schmitt, M.: Autolink- A Tool for Automatic Test Generation from SDL Specifications. In: Proceedings of Workshop on Industrial Strength Formal Specication Techniques (WIFT 1998), Boca, October 21-23, pp. 21–23 (1998)
16. ITU-T: Recommendation Z.100: Specification and Description Language (2000)
17. 9074, I.: Information processing systems – Open Systems Interconnection – Estelle: A formal description technique based on an extended state transition model (1989)
18. Alderden, R.: COOPER - The Compositional Construction of a Canonical Tester. In: Proceedings of the IFIP TC/WG6.1 Second International Conference on Formal Description Techniques for Distributed Systems and Communication Protocols, pp. 13–17. North-Holland Publishing Co., Amsterdam (1990)
19. ISO/IEC: ISO-880: LOTOS – A Formal Description Technique Based on the Temporal Ordering of Observational Behavior (1989)
20. van Eijk, P.H.J., Vissers, C.A., Diaz, M. (eds.): The Formal Description Technique LOTOS. Elsevier Science Publishers B.V., Amsterdam (1989)
21. Tretmans, J., Brinksma, E.: Côte de resyste: Automated model based testing. In: Schweizer, M. (ed.) 3rd PROGRESS Workshop on Embedded Systems, pp. 246–255. STW Technology Foundation, Utrecht (2002)
22. Holzmann, G.J.: Tutorial: Design and validation of protocols. Tutorial Computer Networks and ISDN Systems 25, 981–1017 (1991)
23. Magee, J., Kramer, J.: Concurrency: state models & Java programs. John Wiley & Sons, Inc., New York (1999)
24. Apt, K.: Principles of Constraint Programming. Cambridge University Press, New York (2003)
25. Tretmans, J.: Specification based testing with formal methods: A theory. In: Fantechi, A. (ed.) FORTE/PSTV 2000 Tutorial Notes, Pisa, Italy, October 10 (2000)
26. Utting, M., Legeard, B.: Practical Model-Based Testing: A Tools Approach, 1st edn. Morgan Kaufmann, San Francisco (2007)
27. Pretschner, A., Philipps, J.: Methodological issues in model-based testing. In: Broy, M., Jonsson, B., Katoen, J.-P., Leucker, M., Pretschner, A. (eds.) Model-Based Testing of Reactive Systems. LNCS, vol. 3472, pp. 281–291. Springer, Heidelberg (2005)
28. Saloña, A.A., Vives, J.Q., Gómez, S.P.: An introduction to LOTOS (1993), http://www2.cs.uregina.ca/~sadaouis/CS872/lotos_language_tutorial.ps
29. ETSI: ETSI ES 201 873-10 V4.2.1: Methods for Testing and Specification (MTS), The Testing and Test Control Notation version 3, Part 10: TTCN-3 Documentation Comment Specification (2010)

Towards a Model Based Approach for Integration Testing

Mohamed Mussa and Ferhat Khendek

Department of Electrical and Computer Engineering,
Concordia University,
1515 St.Catherine West, S-EV005.139,
Montréal, QC, Canada H3G 2W1
{mm_abdal,khendek}@ece.concordia.ca

Abstract. In this paper, we introduce a model based approach for integration test cases generation. The approach is based on UML 2 Testing Profile and follows the Mode-Driven Architecture for generating integration test cases from unit test models. The generated test models can be exported to test execution environments such as JUnit and TTCN-3 for execution and evaluation.

Keywords: Model Based Testing, UTP, Integration Testing, Test Cases Generation.

1 Introduction

The development of test artifacts goes through several stages in parallel with the software development process. Important stages include unit-level, integration-level and acceptance-level testing. Unit-level testing is applied to components and targets frequent developers' bugs. Integration-level testing is used to check compatibility, interoperability and the consistency among the integrated components. Acceptance-level testing aims at validating the system against user requirements.

To master and overcome the increasing complexity of software systems, new development and testing techniques need to be developed. The Unified Modeling Language (UML) [28] is nowadays a widely accepted modeling language. The Model-Driven Engineering (MDE) paradigm [23] aims at increasing the level of abstraction in the early stages of the software development process and eliminate barriers between modeling (documentation) and implementation (code). Model Driven Architecture (MDA) [25] is the most widely known initiative of MDE. On the other hand, Model-Based Testing (MBT) [29] was introduced to cope with model development techniques, involve and enforce test planning in the early stages of the software lifecycle. Test models can be shared among stakeholders and enable mutual understanding. MBT approaches based on UML have been proposed for different testing phases; see for instance [1, 5, 11, 20]. Moreover, several domains have been targeted including automotive and telecommunications [7, 19, 24].

UML Testing Profile (UTP) [27] extends UML to support testing activities and artifacts. Section 2 introduces the main concepts in UTP. There have been a number of

I. Ober and I. Ober (Eds.): SDL 2011, LNCS 7083, pp. 106–121, 2011.
© Springer-Verlag Berlin Heidelberg 2011

research investigations based on UTP, see for instance [16, 17, 19, 20]. However, most of these studies focus on one phase of the testing process, mainly unit-level or system level testing. In our research project, we aim at covering the integration and acceptance testing starting from available unit testing artifacts. We focus on an MDA conform approach to generate integration UTP models from unit UTP models. In this approach, components are integrated into system context in a recursive manner. A component and a context test models are merged to generate an integration test model, which will form the context test model for the next integration step. Test cases with interactions involving the component and the context are selected and merged to build the integration test model. Unit test stubs and drivers are reused in the integration test model. Our approach is illustrated throughout the paper.

The rest of this paper is structured as follows. Section 2 introduces briefly UTP for setting up the context. We introduce our approach for integration test models generation in Section 3. In Section 4, we discuss related work and we finally conclude in Section 5.

2   UML Testing Profile (UTP)

UTP [27] extends UML to support testing activities and artifacts by introducing concepts, such as data representation, time concepts and evaluation mechanisms. UTP defines several test concepts to enable the building of precise test models in a systematic manner [1]. A UTP test model may consist of several diagrams. The most significant ones are the test-architecture diagram, the test-context diagram, the test-configuration diagram and the test-case diagram.

The test-architecture diagram defines the overall structure of the test model (see Figure 1). The UML package diagram is used to describe the test-architecture. It consists of the test package, which imports all required packages to realize the test. The test package contains the test control and test cases, which are described in more details in the other three UTP diagrams. In addition to the test package, two packages are mandatory: the UTP and the System Under Test (SUT). Optionally, other stub and dummy packages may be imported to describe some environment functionalities, such as operating system APIs, which are not accessible during test execution.

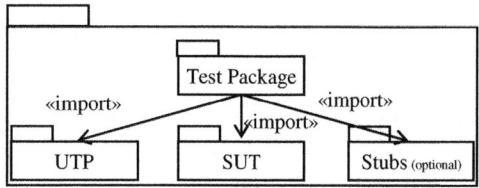

Fig. 1. UTP test-architecture

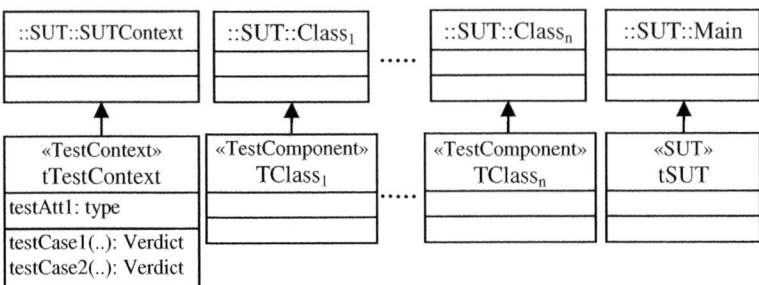

Fig. 2. UTP test-context

A test-context diagram (see Figure 2) defines the test suite and the required test components which support the test realization. UML class diagrams are used to represent the test-context and test components. These classes are identified by special stereotypes defined in UTP. The TestContext stereotyped class is the main instantiated class in the diagram and it defines test cases as methods. It is also responsible for controlling test cases and defines their execution order [1]. Optionally, other classes can be instantiated from the SUT or stubs, which are defined in the test-architecture diagram. The TestComponent stereotype is used to identify these classes, which are defined by Baker as "objects within the test system that can communicate with the SUT or other components to realize the test behavior." [1]. Test stimulus can be defined here as UTP data pool and UTP data partition.

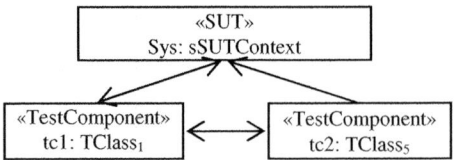

Fig. 3. UTP test-configuration

A test-configuration diagram (see Figure 3) describes the relationships between the test components and between the SUT and the test components [1]. The UML composite diagram of the TestContext class is used for the test-configuration diagram. Different test-configuration diagrams may be built to represent different test setups. Each test case, or set of test cases, is associated with a specific test-configuration diagram.

Behavioral UML diagrams (sequence, activity and state machine diagrams) are used to express test behavior; Figure 4 shows a UML sequence diagram. Each test case, defined in the TestContext as a method, is associated with a behavioral UML diagram. UTP concepts are used to enrich these diagrams with the necessary test specification.

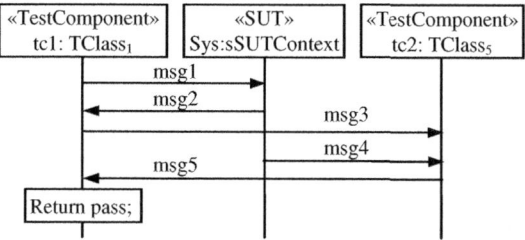

Fig. 4. UTP test case

In addition to the aforementioned concepts, there are several others that can be used to model concise test specifications. For example, testers can use time concepts to define shared time zone among group of test components, use data concepts to define wild cards for ignoring unimportant data in the test model, or use test arbiters to evaluate the test case verdict. A UTP test model can be mapped to a test execution environment such as JUnit [12] or TTCN-3 [26] to execute the test cases and analyze the results [1].

3 UTP Based Integration Testing Approach

3.1 Overall Approach

Software systems go through three major testing phases. In the first phase, unit tests are applied on individual components to detect potential bugs. Components are then integrated and tested to check their interoperability and interactions. System acceptance testing is the final testing activity performed on the product to validate it against user requirements.

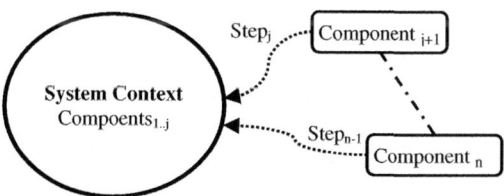

Fig. 5. Component integration process

Integration process can follow one of several well known strategies: bottom-up, top-down, big-bang or ad-hoc [1]. Our approach adopts an ad-hoc strategy for integration testing. In general, components are developed and finalized independently from each other. Components, which have passed the unit-test, are integrated in sequence as show in Figure 5. The required drivers and stubs have already been built during unit-level testing. They are reused after eliminating redundancies. Testers gradually select the next available component, merge it with the context and generate integration UTP model which will be eventually executed.

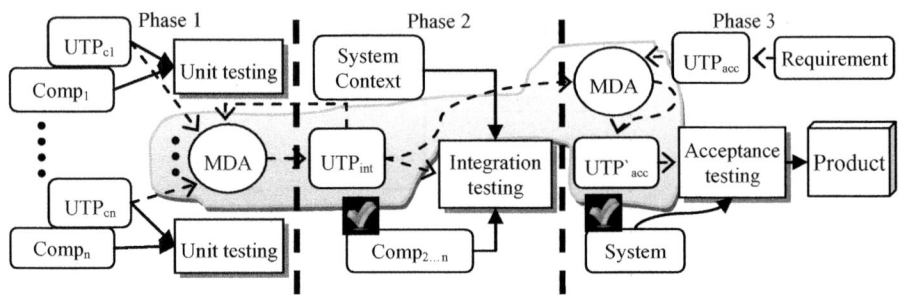

Fig. 6. Framework overview

Our overall framework for software testing (see Figure 6) starts from unit testing through integration testing to acceptance testing. MDA is applied to generate UTP models throughout the testing process. The shadowed area in Figure 6 represents the contributions in this paper focusing on integration testing. Unit UTP model are built manually or automatically using existing approaches [1, 16-20]. The framework consists of the following phases:

1. Unit testing phase
   (a) Unit testing is performed on each developed component,
   (b) Components that pass the unit test are submitted to Phase 2.
2. Integration testing phase (as detailed in Figure 7)
   (a) Initially, two unit UTP models (UTP_{c1} & UTP_{c2}) are supplied to the transformation engine to generate the first integration UTP model (UTP_{int}).
       (i) Integration testing is applied to the sub-system (Context) consisting of the two components ($comp_1$, $comp_2$).
       (ii) Once completed, the integration UTP model (UTP_{int}) becomes the context UTP model ($UTP`_{int}$), and the integrated components ($comp_1$, $comp_2$) will become the system context (Context) for the next step.
   (b) The context UTP model ($UTP`_{int}$) along with the next unit UTP model ($UTP_{c3...cn}$) is supplied to the transformation engine to generate the next integration UTP model (UTP_{int}).
       (i) Integration testing is applied to the Context and the Component (Context and $comp_{3...n}$).
       (ii) After completion, the integration UTP model (UTP_{int}) will become the next context UTP model ($UTP`_{int}$), and the integrated sub-system (Context`) will become the next system context (Context). The previous integration UTP model is kept in a test repository for later usage.
       (iii) Step 2.b is repeated for subsequent components integration.
3. Acceptance testing phase
   (a) Independently, the acceptance UTP model is generated from the user requirements.
   (b) After integration testing, the acceptance UTP model is supplied to the transformation engine along with all generated UTP models in the previous phase to optimize/eliminate from the acceptance UTP model test cases that have been performed in the previous phase.

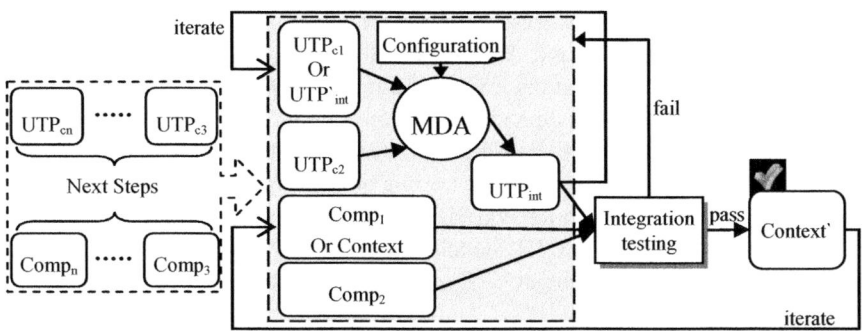

Fig. 7. UTP based integration testing

The framework is based on standards where test models are built and generated based on UTP and the transformations using QVT (Query, View and Transformation) [21]. Reusability is a central asset in the framework where unit UTP models are reused to generate the integration UTP model and test case merger is used to produce an optimized UTP model.

3.2   Test Model Generation

Unit UTP Model Generation. Concurrently to component development, unit UTP models are generated using existing approaches [1, 16-18, 20]. Unit-testing is applied to completed components. These components are submitted to test execution environments, such as JUnit [12], along with their unit UTP models. During this phase, any detected bug is fixed and tests repeated until component passes the unit- tests. Such components are then submitted for integration. Our approach relies on the unit UTP models for generating integration UTP models. We assume the unit test cases cover all the component interface ports that connect the component with its environment.

Integration UTP Model Generation. This algorithm takes two UTP models (for the Context and a new Component) as input and produces an integration UTP model through transformation rules. The transformation rules select and merge only test cases that are related to the current integration step, and are described in QVT. The algorithm consists of three phases: UTP test-cases generation, UTP test-context generation and UTP test-architecture generation.

Phase I: UTP Test Cases Generation. This phase concerns the generation of integration test cases by first selecting test cases from the Context and the Component test cases. The selected test cases reflect the interaction between the Context and the Component. Next, the selected test cases are compared against each other to remove redundancies. Finally, test cases with "shared" behavior are merged.

Step 1: Selecting test cases with interactions between the Context and the Component. Finding interaction test cases between the two SUTs (the Context and the Component) is not an easy task. An instance of the two SUTs must be present in the selected test case with at least one exchanged message. This interaction can be direct or indirect. The interaction is direct when one or each SUT is present in the other UTP model as a TestComponent (stub or driver). Interactions are called indirect when there is a shared UTP test-component in the two input UTP models. The shared UTP test-component must interact with the two SUTs with complementary messages in one test case at least in each input UTP model. The following algorithm uses UTP Test-context Diagrams of the two input UTP models to locate the interaction objects.

```
// Identify the SUTs from the two UTP test-contexts
contextSUT = CONTEXT!SUT->allInstances();
componentSUT = COMPONENT!SUT->allInstances();
// identify the component SUT (if it exists) in the Con-
text's UTP test-context
contextCOMP = null;
for(tc in CONTEXT!TestComponent->allInstances()) {
   if(componentSUT->select(e|e.name=tc.name)->notEmpty())
      contextCOMP = contextCOMP-> append(tc);
}
// identify the context SUT (if it exists) in the Compo-
nent Test-context
componentCONT = null;
for(tc in COMPONENT!TestComponent->allInstances()) {
  if(contextSUT->select(e|e.name=tc.name)->notEmpty())
     componentCONT = componentCONT-> append(tc);
}
// identify the shared test components (if it exists) in
the two test-contexts
SharedCOMP = null;
for(tc in CONTEXT!TestComponent->allInstances()) {
   if( COMPONENT!TestComponent->
       select(e | e.name = tc.name)->notEmpty())
      SharedCOMP = SharedCOMP-> append(tc);
}
```

The algorithm starts by indentifying each SUT in the other UTP model. The UTP test-context diagram is used for fulfilling this task through the UTP meta-model. The Context SUT object is compared to the UTP test-components in the test-context of the Component UTP model. This comparison can be done either by using a special stereotype or by using the object names. The second method is applied in this approach since it gives more flexibility for the UTP modeling and does not require any change to the UTP specification. Similarly, the component SUT object is compared to the UTP test-components in the test-context of the Context UTP model. In addition to the identification of each SUT in the other UTP model, the algorithm looks for the existence of any shared UTP test-components defined in the two UTP models. This task is accomplished by comparing each UTP test-component in the Context test-context diagram against the UTP test-components in the Component test-context diagram.

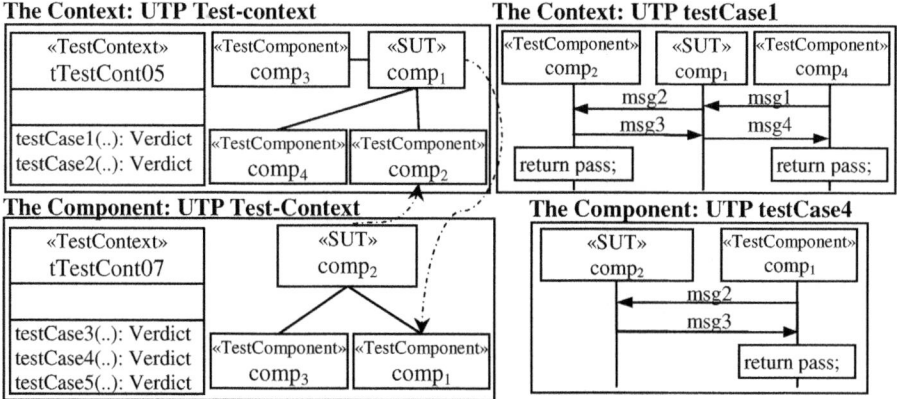

Fig. 8. Direct interaction between Context and Component

Figure 8 illustrates a direct interaction scenario. From the two UTP Test-contexts, the Context SUT (comp$_1$) is represented in the Component UTP model as a TestComponent and the Component SUT (comp$_2$) is represented in the Context UTP model as a TestComponent. By searching test cases (testCase1, testCase2, testCase3, testCase4 and testCase5), test cases with comp$_1$ and comp$_2$ present in their diagram are selected (testCase1 and testCase4). The flow of the received/sent messages of the two objects is examined in each selected test case. The existence of direct or indirect messaging between the two objects moves the selected test cases to the next step.

The following algorithm searches for the existence of the two SUTs in the test cases. It consists of two rounds. The first round is executed when the Component SUT is identified in Context UTP model. It searches through the meta-model of the Context UTP model for the declared test cases in the test-context class. The Context UTP test-components of each test case are compared to the Context UTP test-component which represents the Component SUT. If there is a match then this test case is added to the selected test cases list. The second round is executed only if the Context SUT is identified in Component UTP model. It searches through the meta-model of the Component UTP model for the declared test cases in the test-context class. The Component UTP test-components of each test case are compared to the Component UTP test-component which represents the Context SUT. If there is a match then this test case is added to the selected test cases list.

```
intTestCases = null;//holder for the selected test cases
// *****   Phase I   *****
// select test cases that consist both SUTs from the Con-
text UTP model
If (contextCOMP != null) {
    for(tc in CONTEXT!TestContext->collect(e|e.TestCase)){
       if(contextCOMP->select(e|e.name=tc->one(a|a.Behavior)
          ->one(b|b.TestComponent).name)->notEmpty())
       ...
       intTestCases = intTestCases-> append(tc);
   }
}

// select test cases that consist both SUTs from the
Component UTP model
If (componentCONT!= null) {
  for(tc in COMPONENT!TestContext->collect(e|e.TestCase)){
   if(componentCONT->select(e|e.name=tc->one(a|a.Behavior)
      ->one(b|b.TestComponent).name)->notEmpty())
      ...
      intTestCases = intTestCases-> append(tc);
   }
}
```

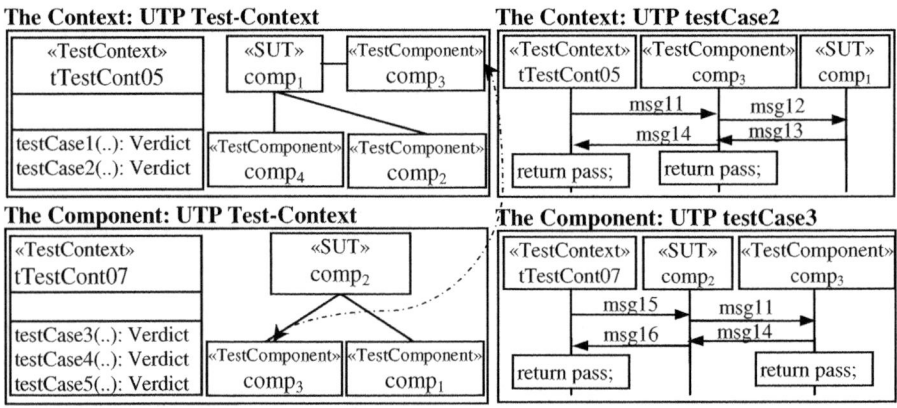

Fig. 9. Indirect interaction between Context and Component

Figure 9 illustrates an indirect interaction scenario. The TestComponent (comp$_3$) exists in the two input UTP models (the Context and the Component). By searching remaining test cases (testCase2, testCase3 and testCase5) for the existence of the shared TestComponent (comp$_3$) in their diagram. If there is at least one test case from each UTP model with the shared TestComponent (comp$_3$) in their diagram, these test cases are selected. Messages of the shared TestComponent (comp$_3$) in each selected test case of the Context are mapped against messages of the shared TestComponent (comp$_3$) in selected test case of the Component. Test cases with complementary messages (testCase2 and testCase3) are selected for Step 3.

Step 2: Comparing the selected test cases. Test cases in each input UTP models are assumed to be unique. Each selected test case from the Context UTP model is mapped against the selected test cases of the Component UTP model. Test cases which are included in other test cases are removed. For illustration purpose, testCase4 in Figure 8 is removed since it is included in testCase1. Test cases with same set of messages exchanged between the two SUTs are selected to the next step.

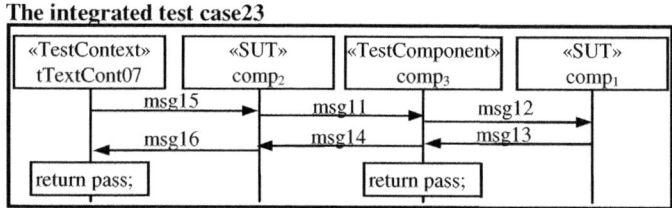

Fig. 10. Merging complementary test cases

Step 3: Merging the selected test cases. In this step, complementary test cases among the selected test cases are merged. Messages of the merged objects are ordered to preserve their order according to the specification of the two test cases. TestContext which represents the test-environment is replaced with the actual TestComponent or SUT when applicable. For instance, test cases (testCase2 and testCase3) in Figure 9 are merged to produce one test case (testCase23) shown in Figure 10. Test-component (comp$_3$) is the shared UTP test-component. Messages (msg11 and msg14) are identified in the two test cases. The TestContext (tTestCont05), which represents the test-environment in the first test case (testCase2), is substituted by the Component SUT (comp$_2$). The two test cases are mapped with reference to the shared (comp$_3$). Messages of the shared component (comp$_3$) in the two test cases (testCase2 and testCase3) are merged with order preservation.

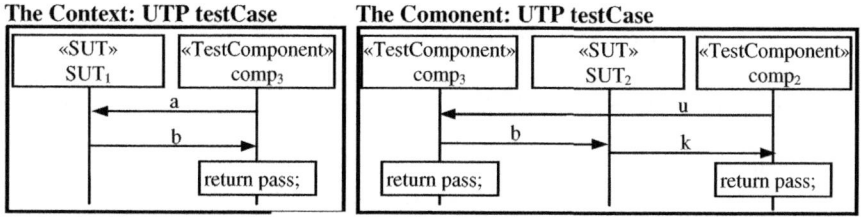

Fig. 11. Test cases merging issues

It is well known that merging sequence diagrams is not always straightforward [2, 10, 15]. Each test case captures only a portion of the system behavior, with a partial view. Merging two partial views and ordering the events/messages is a challenging problem as discussed thoroughly in [10, 13, 14]. For instance, in Figure 11 we have two test cases with a shared UTP test component (comp$_3$) that acts as a medium between the Context SUT (SUT$_1$) and the Component SUT (SUT$_2$) by passing messages (b in this case). To merge these test cases, events of the shared UTP test component (comp$_3$) have to be ordered. However, from the given diagrams, one cannot order of sending of **a** and the reception of **u**. Does the test component (comp$_3$) consume message **u** then produce message **a** or vice versa? This case and several other issues have been discussed in [2, 15], and some merging algorithms have been developed [10, 13, 14, 22]. We adopt the merging technique proposed by Hélouët et al. [10].

The integrated testCase1

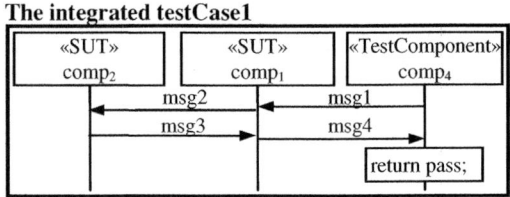

Fig. 12. Updated test case

As a result of the three steps, two test cases are selected. testCase1 is updated (see Figure 12) to reflect the new relations by replacing the stub TestComponent (comp$_2$) with the Component SUT (comp$_2$), and testCase23 (see Figure 10) is created from the merging of testCase2 and testCase3. These two test cases are selected to the generated UTP model.

Phase II: UTP Test-context Generation. The second phase targets the construction of the test-context diagram of the integration UTP model. Since the UTP test-context represents the structural part of the UTP model, the two input test-contexts share most of their components. Our approach generates the integration test-context by updating the Context test-context from the Component test-context using the following transformation rules:

- A copy of the Context test-context diagram builds the initial integration test-context diagram.
- The methods (test cases) of TestContext class are examined against the selected test cases from the previous phase. Only methods related to the selected test cases are kept in the integration TestContext.
- The Component SUT is copied to the generated test-context diagram, and any TestComponent representing the Component SUT is removed from the generated test-context diagram.
- The methods (test cases) of the Component TestContext class are examined against the selected test cases from the previous phase. Only methods related to the selected test cases are added to the integration TestContext.
- The new test cases which were produced from the merging process are added to the generated test-context methods.

- The Component TestComponent classes that are present in the selected test cases and which do not exist in the Context test-context diagram are added to the integration test-context diagram.
- Associations among test-components, SUTs and the integration TestContext are reorganized according to their behavior on the selected test cases.
- All data representations, e.g. data partitions, are optimized to reflect only data used by the selected test cases.

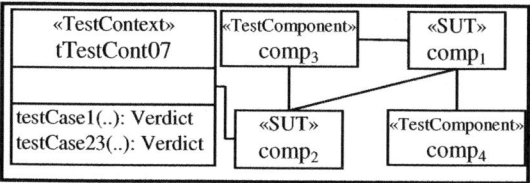

Fig. 13. Integration UTP test context diagram

Figure 13 shows the generated test-context diagram. The test-context class is updated to reflect the merging of the two input test-contexts (tTestCont05 and tTest-Cont07), and only the two selected test cases (testCase1 and testCase23) are set as methods in the generated test-context class. The Component SUT (comp$_2$) is added to test-context and the TestComponent (comp$_2$) is removed. There is no need for adding the Component test-components or methods. Association among the classes is rebuilt according to their relations in the selected test cases.

Phase III: UTP Test-Architecture Generation. The test-architecture diagram represents the infrastructure of the UTP model which it is the same infrastructure for the Context and the Component since they represent different parts of the same system. In our approach, the Context test-architecture is updated from the Component test-architecture to build the generated test-architecture. The following transformation rules are applied:

- If a Context stub (or driver) which represents the Component SUT exists, it is replaced with the Component SUT package from the Component test-architecture. Otherwise, the Component SUT package is copied to the generated test-architecture.
- Component stubs (dummies, drivers, emulators, or actual libraries) which are realized in the generated test-context and which do not already exist in the Context test-architecture are copied to the generated test-architecture.

Figure 14 shows the two input test-architectures and the generated one. The generated UTP model (see Figure 10, 12, 13, 14) is submitted to the test execution environment for testing the implementation. After passing the test, the generated UTP model is optimized for the next integration to become the next Context UTP model as shown in Figure 15. The two SUTs are merged, and all internal messaging is removed.

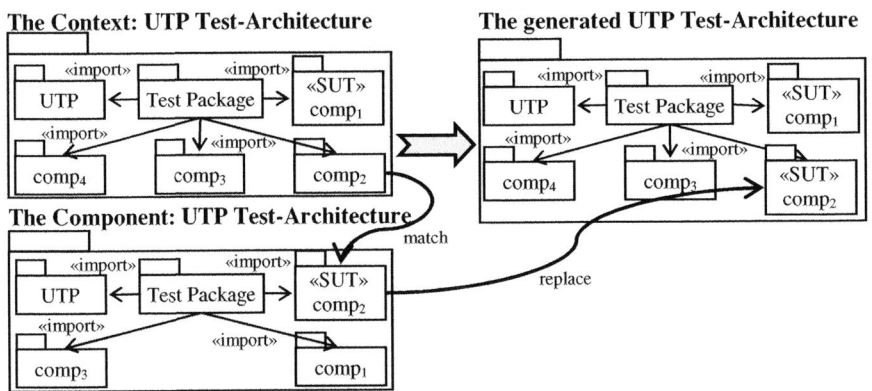

Fig. 14. Generating the test-architecture

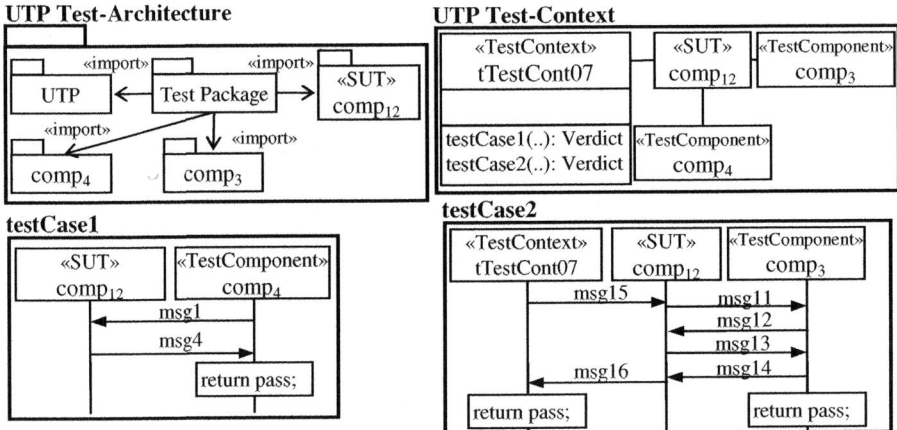

Fig. 15. The next context-test model

4   Related Work

UTP has been adopted recently, thus there is a limited work related to its usage in the literature.   Busch et al. [6] present an MDA approach for generating UTP models from design models. Platform independent models (PIMs) are transformed into platform independent UTP models (PITs). Platform specific models (PSMs) are transformed into Platform specific UTP models (PSTs), and finally   PITs are transformed into PSTs. Both PIT and PST are based on UTP. The approach focuses only on system testing; while our approach focuses on integration testing. In this approach, system testing is applied after integration testing and prior to acceptance testing, and it is intended to demonstrate that the system behaves as designed/specified. Lamancha et al. [16] propose an MDA approach to generate UTP models from the system design models. UTP models are built from UML use cases and sequence diagrams.

The authors in [16] focus only on system testing. Liang and Xu [17] present Test Driven Development (TDD) for component integration based on UML 2.0 Testing and Monitoring Profile (U2TMP) [17], which is an extension to UTP to enable monitoring. The generated test cases allow for building glue code between the integrated components.

Other existing integration testing approaches [3, 8, 9, 31] use state based models such as Finite State Machines (FSMs) [4]. The components are modeled with FSMs and test cases are generated from this model. For integration testing, a system model consists of the composition of the models of the integrated components. However, this leads to the well know problem of state space explosion [30]. New methods for avoiding this state space explosion and reducing the final number of test cases, such as C-Method [9], have been proposed. Such methods can be integrated into our framework in the future.

The main characteristics that differentiate our approach from existing work are reusability, optimization and at the same time conformance to MDA. Test artifacts are reused from a testing phase to the next. They are optimized and described with a standard notation.

5 Conclusion

In this paper, an approach for building integration test models using UTP has been presented. Integration UTP models are constructed recursively from unit UTP models. Notice that this integration can be done, and repeated, at different levels depending on the level of granularity of the units.   Our work is still in progress and a full framework is under investigation.

We are currently finalizing the approach and investigating QVT tools for the implementation. Future work includes:

- Finalize the approach for integration testing and implement it,
- Developed the framework further to handle acceptance testing,
- Include other UTP constructs such as test configuration diagrams to the generated UTP models,
- Build traceability mechanism among UTP models through the test process,
- Considering UML state machine diagrams as test case construct in addition to the UML sequence diagrams,
- Integrate existing FSM based approaches into the framework.

Acknowledgments. This work has been partially supported by the Natural Sciences and Engineering Research Council of Canada (NSERC).

References

1. Baker, P.: Model-Driven Testing: Using the UML Testing Profile. Springer, New York (2008)
2. Ben-Abdallah, H., Leue, S.: Syntactic detection of process divergence and non-local choice in message sequence charts. In: Brinksma, E. (ed.) TACAS 1997. LNCS, vol. 1217, pp. 259–274. Springer, Heidelberg (1997)

3. Berrada, I., Castanet, R., Félix, P.: Testing communicating systems: A model, a methodology, and a tool. In: Khendek, F., Dssouli, R. (eds.) TestCom 2005. LNCS, vol. 3502, pp. 111–128. Springer, Heidelberg (2005)
4. Bogdanov, K., Holcombe, M.: Refinement in statechart testing. Software Testing Verification and Reliability, 189–211 (2004)
5. Bouquet, F., et al.: A subset of precise UML for model-based testing. In: Proceedings of the 3rd International Workshop on Advances in Model-Based Testing, London, United Kingdom, pp. 95–104 (2007)
6. Busch, M., et al.: Model transformers for test generation from system models. In: Proceedings of Conquest 2006, 10th International Conference on Quality Engineering in Software Technology, Berlin, Germany (2006)
7. Cartaxo, E.G., et al.: LTS-BT: A tool to generate and select functional test cases for embedded systems. In: 23rd Annual ACM Symposium on Applied Computing, SAC 2008, pp. 1540–1544 (2008)
8. Dong, W., Wang, J., Qi, Z., Rong, N.: Compositional verification of UML dynamic models. In: 14th Asia Pacific Software Engineering Conference, ASPCE 2007, pp. 286–293 (2007)
9. Gotzhein, R., Khendek, F.: Compositional testing of communication systems. In: Uyar, M.Ü., Duale, A.Y., Fecko, M.A. (eds.) TestCom 2006. LNCS, vol. 3964, pp. 227–244. Springer, Heidelberg (2006)
10. Hélouët, L., Hénin, T., Chevrier, C.: Automating scenario merging. In: Gotzhein, R., Reed, R. (eds.) SAM 2006. LNCS, vol. 4320, pp. 64–81. Springer, Heidelberg (2006)
11. Javed, A.Z., Strooper, P.A., Watson, G.N.: Automated generation of test cases using model-driven architecture. In: Proceedings of the Second International Workshop on Automation of Software Test, vol. 3 (2007)
12. JUnit, http://www.junit.org
13. Khendek, F., Bochmann, G.V.: Merging behavior specifications. Formal Methods Syst. Des., 259–293 (1995)
14. Klein, J., Caillaud, B., Helouet, L.: Merging scenarios. In: Proceedings of the Ninth International Workshop on Formal Methods for Industrial Critical Systems (FMICS 2004), pp. 193–215 (2005)
15. Ladkin, P.B., Leue, S.: Four issues concerning the semantics of message flow graphs. In: Proceedings of the 7th IFIP WG6.1 International Conference on Formal Description Techniques VII, pp. 355–369 (1995)
16. Lamancha, B.P., Mateo, P.R., de Guzm'an, I.R., Usaola, M.P., Velthius, M.P.: Automated model-based testing using the UML testing profile and QVT. In: Proceedings of the 6th International Workshop on Model-Driven Engineering, Verification and Validation, Denver, Colorado, pp. 6:1-6:10 (2009)
17. Liang, D., Xu, K.: Test-driven component integration with UML 2.0 testing and monitoring profile. In: 7th International Conference on Quality Software, QSIC 2007, pp. 32–39 (2007)
18. Mlynarski, M., Güldali, B., Späth, M., Engels, G.: From design models to test models by means of test ideas. In: Proceedings of the 6th International Workshop on Model-Driven Engineering, Verification and Validation, pp. 7:1-7:10 (2009)
19. Pietsch, S., Stanca-Kaposta, B.: Model-based testing with UTP and TTCN-3 and its application to HL7. In: Testing Technologies IST GmbH, Germany (2008)
20. Yuan, Q., Wu, J., Liu, C., Zhang, L.: A model driven approach toward business process test case generation. In: 10th International Symposium Web Site Evolution, WSE 2008, pp. 41–44 (2008)

21. QVT, http://www.omg.org/spec/QVT
22. Sadaoui, S.: Composition of Structured Process Specifications. Electronic Notes in Theoretical Computer Science, 132–143 (2003)
23. Schmidt, D.C.: Guest Editor's Introduction: Model-Driven Engineering. Computer, 25–31 (2006)
24. Suss, J.G., Pop, A., Fritzson, P., Wildman, L.: Towards integrated model-driven testing of SCADA systems using the eclipse modeling framework and modelica. In: 19th Australian Conference Software Engineering, ASWEC 2008, pp. 149–159 (2008)
25. The Architecture of Choice for a Changing World, http://www.omg.org/mda
26. TTCN-3, http://www.ttcn-3.org
27. UML Testing Profile, http://utp.omg.org
28. Unified Modeling Language, http://www.uml.org
29. Utting, M., Legeard, B.: Practical Model-Based Testing: A Tools Approach. Morgan Kaufmann Publishers, Boston (2007)
30. Valmari, A.: The state explosion problem. Advances in Petri Nets, 429–528 (1998)
31. Xie, G., Dang, Z.: Testing systems of concurrent black-Boxes—An automata-theoretic and decompositional approach. In: Grieskamp, W., Weise, C. (eds.) FATES 2005. LNCS, vol. 3997, pp. 170–186. Springer, Heidelberg (2006)

Session Initiation as a Service

Urooj Fatima[1], Rolv Bræk[1], and Humberto Nicolás Castejón[2]

[1] Department of Telematics, Norwegian University of Science and Technology (NTNU),
Trondheim, Norway
{urooj,rolv.braek}@item.ntnu.no
[2] Telenor Corporate Development, N-7004, Trondheim, Norway
Humberto.Castejon@telenor.com

Abstract. The main focus of this paper is on services involving sessions among dynamically linked objects. It is argued that session initiation in many cases can be generalized and separated from session behaviour. In general, session initiation depends on the state of the actor that is requested to participate in a session. If the actor can handle the requested session in its current state, then it may be initiated. If not, the request may be rejected, queued, forwarded or given other treatment depending on the preferences of the actor. We demonstrate that session initiation and session behaviour can be modeled as separate services using UML collaborations and activity diagrams, and then composed in different ways into complete composite services with dynamic session initiation. Possible solutions for composition of session initiation with service sessions are proposed and discussed.

Keywords: Session initiation, choreography, role binding, service composition.

1 Introduction

Reactive systems are "the systems that engage in continuous stimulus-response behaviour with their environment" [6]. Therefore, they must be designed from the structure of the environment. When these reactive systems are distributed, "they consist of separated autonomous components that may take independent initiatives, operate concurrently and interact with each other and the environment in order to provide services" [5].

The concept of "service" is widely used and many informal definitions pertaining to different domains can be found, for example in [1-3]. The definition of service is elaborated in [4] by identifying the following properties:

- Services are functionalities; they are behaviors performed by entities.
- Services imply collaborations; it makes no sense to talk about a service unless at least two entities collaborate.
- Service behavior is cross-cutting; it involves coordination of two or more entity behaviors to fulfill a certain task.
- Service behavior is partial; it is to be composed with all the other services provided by the system to obtain a complete behaviour of the system.

I. Ober and I. Ober (Eds.): SDL 2011, LNCS 7083, pp. 122–137, 2011.

Generally, the behaviour of services is composed from partial actor behaviours, while actor behaviour is composed from partial service behaviours as already recognized by [4], [7]. According to [5], separation between services and actors can be obtained by using the concept of *service role* i.e. the part a system component/actor plays in a service. Therefore, the final definition of service which we will use in this paper is:

"A service is an identified functionality with value for the service users, which is provided in a collaboration among service roles played by actors or service users" [5].

Since there is not a one-to-one relationship between actors and services, the joint behaviour of several actors must be considered in order to understand how service works. In order to describe complete service behaviour there is a need to understand collaborative behaviour and to model services independently of particular system designs or implementations. For this, we will use the service-engineering approach proposed in [5]. In this approach, the services of a distributed reactive system are modeled in two steps. First, service structure is modeled using UML 2 collaborations defining roles and collaboration uses representing sub-services and interfaces. Thereafter, global service behaviour is modeled as a *choreography* of the service collaborations or sub-services referenced by collaboration uses in the main service collaboration structure, using UML 2 activity diagrams. Sequence diagrams can be used to describe the behaviour of *elementary collaborations* i.e. collaborations that are not further decomposed into collaboration uses.

According to the above service engineering approach, the behaviour of each actor is designed as a composition of the roles played by that actor in different services. These roles are bound either statically or dynamically. In static role binding, the roles are bound to the actor during service development. However, generally the structure of collaborating actors is dynamic. Links between actors are created and deleted dynamically, and many services depend on whether the link can be established or not [12]. Actors must be able to execute the appropriate roles in each service collaboration, avoiding undesirable interactions with other roles. Therefore, it is necessary to consider how to dynamically bind roles to actors during service execution i.e. the process of dynamic role binding. In the simplest case of dynamic role binding, the actor is always able to play a role, hence the dynamic role binding is just a matter of invoking the role on the right actor. In many cases, however, the role binding is conditional on the current state of the actor in terms of other active roles and its availability. In this situation, extra coordination functionality is needed before a service session can be initiated. Traditionally, such session initiation behaviour has been bundled with service session behaviour. Here we propose to factor out session initiation and to model it as a service (using the same general approach as for services) that can be composed with session behaviour and hence can be reused in combination with different session behaviours. In this paper, we utilize activity

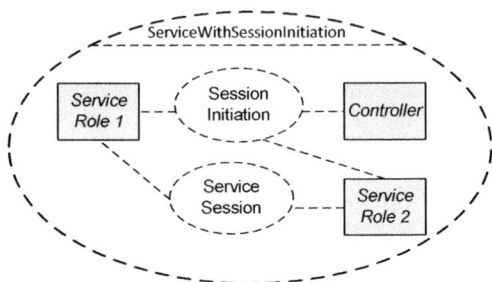

Fig. 1. UML 2 collaboration representing a service utilizing the session initiation functionality

diagrams to model service initiation behaviour as a choreography of collaboration uses (i.e. sub-services). By using activity diagrams rather than sequence diagrams, we are able to completely define the global session initiation behaviour.

In Section 2, we present our approach for modeling session initiation behaviour. A case for dynamic session initiation is presented with the help of a *SimplePhoneCall*. Some variants of the session initiation behaviour have been identified. Section 3 explains some of the possible system designs with incorporation of session initiation functionality. In Section 4, we discuss how a service and a session initiation behavior can be composed and re-used. Finally, we conclude in section 5.

2   The Case for Dynamic Session Initiation

In a system, multiple occurrences of the same service may co-exist. In service modeling, one isolated occurrence of a service is considered because the focus is on specifying the service behaviour [5]. But during the system design process, we have to deal with the composition of services and the possibility of having multiple concurrent occurrences of the service running in the system where roles played by an actor may interact in undesired ways if executed concurrently. It is therefore important that only roles that can execute together are invoked for concurrent execution. Depending on its current situation, an actor needs to decide whether a request to play a service role can be accepted or not.

An actor (e.g. a *UserAgent*) may be requested to participate in a service session when it is already participating in another session of that service. If there are restrictions on the number of simultaneous service sessions handled by an actor, the session initiations must be coordinated. This coordination functionality can be separated from the session behaviour by defining it as a separate service involving a coordinator role, which is external to the coordinated service roles. This is illustrated by the UML 2 collaboration in Fig. 1, where the *Controller* role performs the coordination.

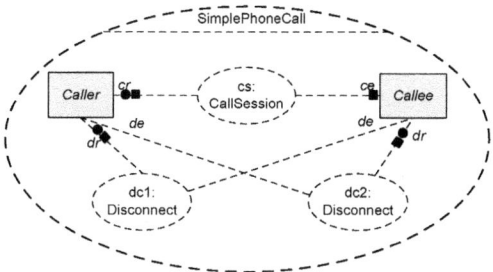

Fig. 2. a *SimplePhoneCall* collaboration

2.1 Example Service (*SimplePhoneCall*)

In this section, we introduce a *SimplePhoneCall* service that will be used as a running example throughout the paper.

The structure of this service can be modeled as a UML 2 collaboration. For this, we first identify the roles needed to provide the service. Each role should specify the properties and behavior that an actor should have in order to participate in one single occurrence of the service. Thereafter, the service behaviour is decomposed into more manageable collaboration uses, which normally correspond to phases of the service. Fig. 2 shows a UML 2 collaboration describing the structure of the *SimplePhoneCall* service[1]. Two roles have been identified for this service: the *Caller* and *Callee*. An actor (e.g. a *UserAgent*) playing the *Caller* role can initiate call sessions, an actor playing the *Callee* role can receive calls, and an actor playing both roles can initiate call sessions and receive calls. Three collaboration uses have also been identified, which correspond to two different phases of the *SimplePhoneCall* service:

- *Call Session*[2]: The session negotiates and controls the streaming voice connection between the *Caller* and *Callee*.
- *Disconnect*: The call session will be ended if either the *Caller* or the *Callee* disconnects.

Each collaboration, referred in a collaboration use, can be completely described separately using activity diagrams or sequence diagrams.

At this point, we know the collaboration uses in which the service roles participate in order to provide the service. Assuming that their behaviour has been described separately (not shown here), we need to specify the order in which those collaboration uses should be executed, so that their global, joint behaviour matches the intended

---

[1] Filled circles and filled squares have been used to identify the initiating and terminating roles of each collaboration use, respectively. That is, the roles performing the first and last actions of each collaboration use. We note this notation is not standard UML, but can be added by means of a profile.

[2] It is assumed that the *Callee* role exists and can be addressed in the call session i.e. the role has already been bound to the actor.

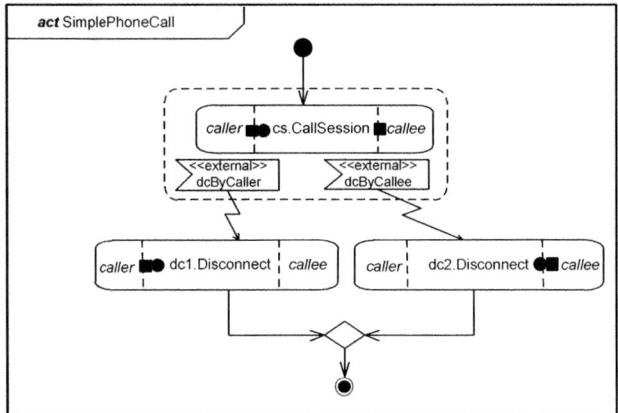

Fig. 3. Choreography for the *SimplePhoneCall* Collaboration

behaviour for the *SimplePhoneCall* service collaboration. This global behaviour can be defined as a choreography of the collaboration uses [5], also called 'flow-global choreography' in [14]. For this, UML 2 activity diagrams can be used, as shown in Fig. 3 for the *SimplePhoneCall* service.

The activity nodes are *CallBehaviourActions* that invoke the behaviour associated with the collaboration uses. An interruptible activity region is shown as a dashed rectangle. The occurrence of any of the interrupting event triggers (*dcByCaller* and *dcByCallee*), which are external events coming from the environment, causes the activity in the interruptible region to terminate and the control is transferred to the target activity node outside the region. The UML concept of *partition* is utilized to represent the role participation in collaborations.

2.2   The Session Initiation Functionality

In the *SimplePhoneCall* example, a *Caller* requests a *UserAgent* to play a *Callee* role in a call. The request is for a specific identified *UserAgent* i.e. it is a direct request, as we want in phone calls. If the called *UserAgent* is not busy with other calls, it will accept the request. If it is busy, then it may invoke busy handling behaviour, which in the simplest case can be just 'rejection'. In other cases, it may involve a queuing or forwarding. Thus, there is a session initiation behaviour associated with the request that controls the invocation of subsequent service behaviour. In general, such session initiation behaviour is needed whenever service sessions and service roles are dynamically invoked, and can be modeled as a UML collaboration involving a new role, a *Controller*.

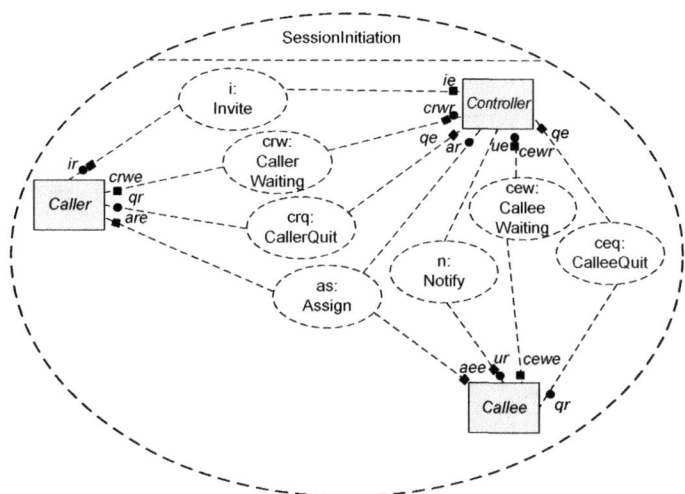

Fig. 4. UML collaboration of the *SessionInitiation* service

In our example service, the *Controller* will act as a coordinator between the *Caller* and *Callee* roles and their respective actors. Since the *Controller* is coordinating among roles played either by one actor or by different actors, it must have some basic knowledge about the actors and their preferences, for instance, whether an actor may have one instance of a particular role or many. The responsibility of the *Controller* can be seen as:

- keeping an overview of the actor situation i.e. its active roles (either by polling or notification).
- handling role requests (e.g. *invite*) and deciding if the requested role can be assigned.
- busy handling, in the case when the requested role cannot be invoked (either by rejecting the role request or providing alternative functionality such as queuing or forwarding).

We now introduce a general form of session initiation where requests are queued when the requested role is not available. The case where requests are not queued, but rejected, can be seen as a simplification of this. The collaboration is given in Fig. 4. We assume that the *Controller* keeps track of the availability of the *Callee* roles, by receiving notifications whenever the *Callee* role becomes available (*Notify* collaboration use). The *Caller* sends an invitation request to the *Controller* (*Invite* collaboration use). On receiving the request, the *Controller* assigns the requested role (*Callee*) to the requested actor and notifies the *Caller* if the *Callee* is available (*Assign* collaboration use). If the *Callee* is busy, the *Controller* puts the *Caller* reference on waiting (*CallerWaiting* collaboration use).

In Fig. 5, the corresponding choreography graph is shown. For simplicity, we formally represent only one instance of the *Caller* and *Callee* in the choreography, but

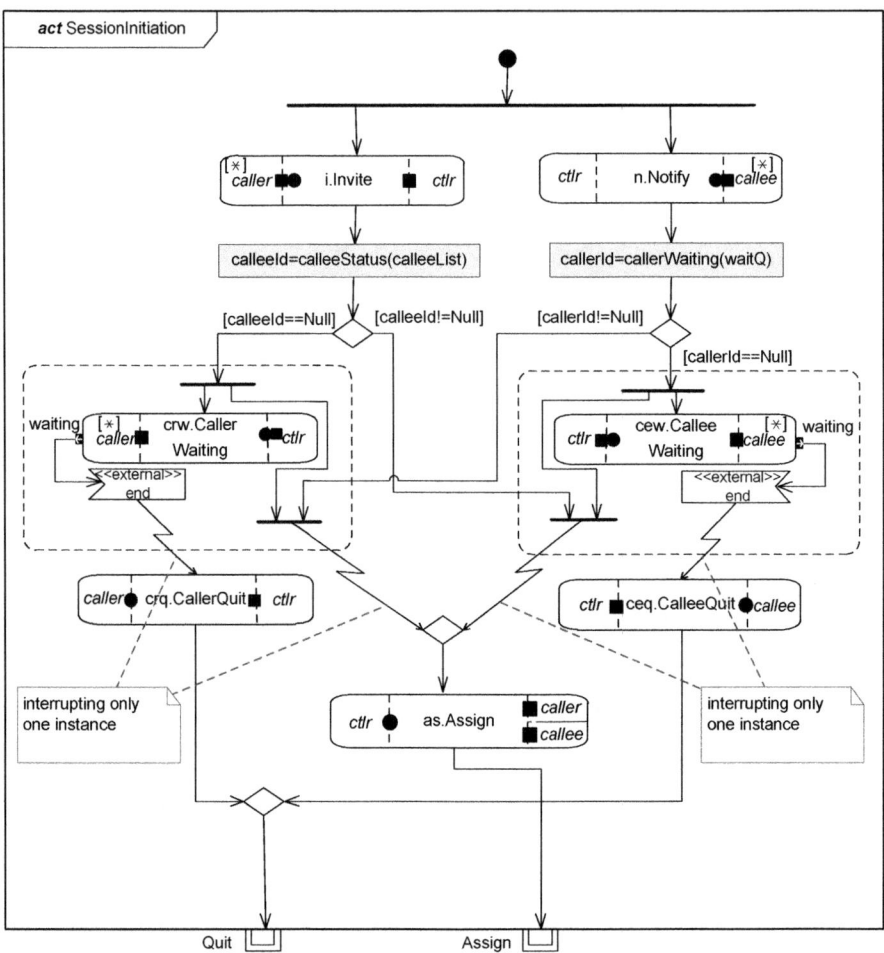

Fig. 5. Choreography for the *SessionInitiation* service

we take into account the possibility that there may be many instances. The *Controller* maintains a *calleeList* of references to available *Callee* roles. When the *Caller* sends an invitation request, the *Controller* checks this list. This function is performed by the operation *calleeId=calleeStatus(calleeList)* shown in the choreography graph in Fig. 5. If the list is empty (*calleeId==null*), the *Controller* inserts the *Caller* reference into a waiting queue (*waitQ*) and communicates to the *Caller* its current position in the queue in the *CallerWaiting* collaboration use. The *Caller* can opt to quit the waiting option (*CallerQuit* collaboration use). In that case, the *Caller* reference will be deleted from the waiting queue by the *Controller*. Whenever a *Caller* leaves the queue, either because it decided not to wait any more, or because it was assigned to a *Callee* that became available, the *Controller* updates the position of the other callers in the queue, and informs them about their new position via the *CallerWaiting* collaboration use. To avoid complexity in the choreography graph (Fig. 5), the queue

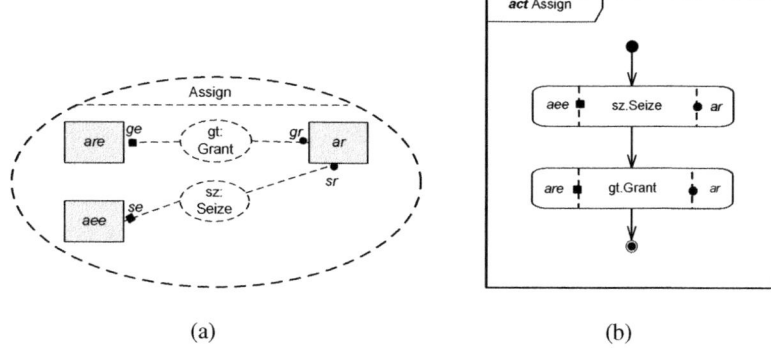

Fig. 6. (a) UML Collaboration of *Assign* (b) Choreography of the *Assign* Collaboration

operations are kept hidden in the *CallerWaiting* and *CallerQuit* collaboration uses, but of course they may be moved outside to show this explicitly.

If there is no *Caller* waiting in the queue when a notification is received from a *Callee*, i.e. *waitQ* is empty (revealed by the operation *callerId=callerWaiting(waitQ)* in the choreography graph Fig. 5), then the *Controller* inserts the *Callee* reference in the *calleeList* and requires the *Callee* to wait (*CalleeWaiting* collaboration use). While in the *CalleeWaiting* collaboration use, the *Callee* can opt to quit waiting (*CalleeQuit* collaboration use). If the *Callee* continues to wait, then whenever a *Caller* sends an invitation request, the *CalleeWaiting* collaboration use will be interrupted and a *Callee* will be assigned to the *Caller* by the *Controller* using the *Assign* collaboration use. In both the cases, the *Callee* reference will be deleted from the *calleeList* of available callees by the *Controller*.

The *Assign* collaboration use is further composed of two collaboration uses; *Seize* and *Grant*, as shown by the UML collaboration of *Assign* in Fig. 6(a). The available *Callee* is seized for the *Caller* and then granted to the *Caller* in *Seize* and *Grant* collaboration uses respectively. The choreography of *Assign* is shown in Fig. 6(b). After the assignment of the *Callee* to the *Caller*, the *CallSession* can be initiated by the *Caller*.

The choreography in Fig. 5 may seem complicated at first but a closer study reveals that the complexity is due to the problem at hand, which is reflected quite directly and to the point. As shown in Fig. 5, the session initiation behaviour can be completely specified on a global level. The use of interrupting flows and interruptible regions helps to describe the intended behaviour without dealing with the detailed coordination needed in a distributed realization, for instance to handle mixed/colliding events. Describing this kind of behaviour completely using sequence diagrams and Interaction Overview Diagrams (which do not support interruption) will lead to a more complex diagram if at all possible.

The initiation service, we just discussed, is not the only solution to the problem. The initiation service in Fig. 5 can be classified as 'Assign role or Queue request – via

Notification' (AQ-N). Other disciplines can be used as well if the requested role cannot be assigned (i.e. busy). For instance, rejection of the role request can be used when queuing is not needed. In that case, the activity node representing the *CallerWaiting* collaboration use (Fig. 5) needs to be replaced with a *Reject* collaboration use. The interruptible region and the *CallerQuit* collaboration uses will be removed (static editing). The basic structure of the initiation service will remain the same as shown in Fig. 5. Hence, the representation of the session initiation service using choreography graphs offers a flexible approach to apply modifications during service development, according to the service requirements. Other disciplines[3] are:

1. **A**ssign role or **R**eject request – via **P**olling (AR-P)
2. **A**ssign role or **R**eject request – via **N**otification (AR-N)
3. **A**ssign role or **F**orward request – via **N**otification (AF-N)

Note that the initiation services are quite independent of the service session behaviours.

We have found that the number of different session initiation behaviours is quite limited and therefore reusable. They can be deployed in a library to make them available for re-use. If we have *n* different initiation services in the library and *m* different service sessions, then there are *nxm* different ways of composing the initiation services with the service sessions.

3   System Design (with Controller Role)

A system is essentially modeled as a UML structured class. In system design we must consider the multiplicity of actors and the localization of the *Controller* role. There can be two options for localization of the *Controller* role for a system consisting of multiple *UserAgents: Controller* role localized within one *UserAgent; Controller* role bound to an external actor, managing a pool of agents.

Depending upon the service requirements, the *Controller* role can perform the coordination functionality for different types of *UserAgents*. In a *TaxiSystem,* for example, customers can book taxis by placing calls to the taxi system. There are a number of operators that answer calls and receive taxi bookings. After receiving a booking, the operators send the tour orders with the pickup location to the *TaxiController*. The *TaxiController* keeps an overview of available taxis and assigns taxis to customers as fairly as possible. Once the taxi is assigned to the customer, it can contact the customer via phone call. The system diagram for this *TaxiSystem* is depicted in Fig. 7 showing three different agents, namely *UserAgent, OpAgent,* and *TaxiAgent*. The *SimplePhoneCall* service, for incoming calls towards operators, can use the session initiation with queues (AQ-N) described in Fig. 5. The *SimplePhoneCall* service between taxi agents and user agents can use a simple variant of session initiation without queues (i.e. AR-N, described in section 2). Note that, the

---

[3] For the details of these disciplines, the reader is referred to [13].

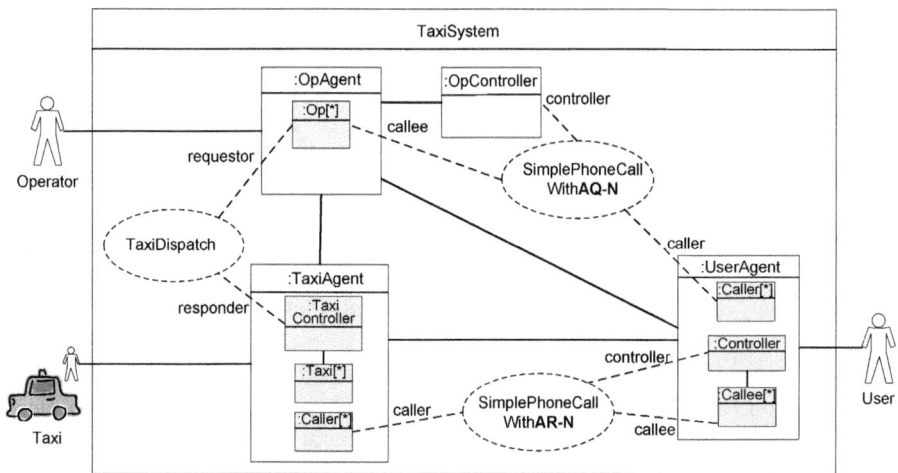

Fig. 7. System Diagram of *TaxiSystem*; AQ-N and AR-N are explained in section 2

Controller role of *OpAgent* is bound to an external actor *OpController* because it handles a pool of operators. The *Controller* role of *UserAgent* is localized within the *UserAgent* because it handles just one user. The *TaxiAgent* uses a *TaxiController* which assigns the available resource (taxi) by taking into account not only the information of availability of taxis but also their location. Hence, the *TaxiDispatch* behaviour is very similar to the session initiation behaviour.

4   Composition of Session Initiation and Service Sessions

In the *SimplePhoneCall* example, The *Controller* role is involved in the session initiation service until the *Callee* is invoked (*Assign* collaboration use), or in other words, until the 'actual' service session starts between the two parties. The *SessionInitiation,* discussed in previous sections, is service independent and generic for a broad range of services. To keep the essence of generality, the *Caller* and *Callee* roles (from Fig. 4) can be renamed as *Requestor* and *Responder* respectively. The collaboration uses can be renamed accordingly.

The next question is "how the session initiation service can be composed with particular service sessions to provide coordination". We discuss in the following two alternatives to achieve that, namely the UML 2 generalization relationship and the UML templates concept.

Generalization. In [8] generalization is defined as "*a taxonomic relationship between a more general classifier and a more specific classifier. Each instance of the specific classifier is also an indirect instance of the general classifier. Thus, the specific classifier inherits the features of the more general classifier*" .

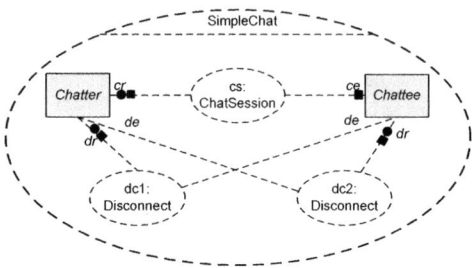

Fig. 8. UML collaboration of *SimpleChat* service

In order to compose the session initiation service with a service session using the generalization relationship, the service model should specialize an initiation service, for instance the AQ-N. By specializing a general classifier, all the properties of the general classifier are inherited by the specialization and any redefinable element of the general classifier (declared as **{redefined}** in the specialization) may be either replaced or extended [9]. An entity that cannot be redefined in specializations is declared as **{final}** in the general classifier [8]. Now let us see how we can use the UML 2 generalization relationship to reuse our session initiation service in service models.

Consider for example a *SimpleChat* service (shown in Fig. 8). In this service, messages are exchanged in a sequence. If the *SimpleChat* service needs to have the session initiation functionality of the AQ-N service, we can create a new *SimpleChatwithAQ-N* collaboration that specializes the AQ-N initiation service and extends it with the functionality of *SimpleChat*. For this, we redefine the *Requestor* and *Responder* roles and extend them with the behaviour defined by the *Chatter* and *Chattee* roles. Because, we do not want the *Controller* to be redefined, it is declared as **{final}** in the AQ-N initiation service (see Fig. 9). The inherited aspects are represented by dashed lines which differentiate them from the extension added in the classifier [9]. Since, dashed lines are also used to represent the ellipse of UML 2 collaborations, we use a double dashed line (shown in Fig. 9) to represent the inherited collaboration. The specialized *SimpleChatwithAQ-N* service is shown in Fig. 9. It can be seen that the *Requestor* and *Responder* roles are *redefined* in *SimpleChatwithAQ-N*. This redefinition means that the behaviour of the *Chatter* and *Chattee* roles in *SimpleChat* is added to the behaviour of the *Requestor* and *Responder* in AQ-N according to the ordering of actions defined in the choreography shown in Fig. 10. They will run in sequence with AQ-N as illustrated in the choreography. Inheritance is not defined in UML for activity diagrams, however it is defined for state machines (which are also used to model behaviour). We have worked out a way to define inheritance for activity diagrams. In order to represent the elements that are inherited in activity diagrams, we used dashed lines in combination with solid lines such that dashed lines appear outside solid lines (see Fig. 10). We avoid using *only* dashed lines because they are used to represent interruptible regions in activity diagrams. It can be seen in Fig. 10 that the *Requestor* and *Responder* roles are *redefined* only for the *SimpleChat* collaboration.

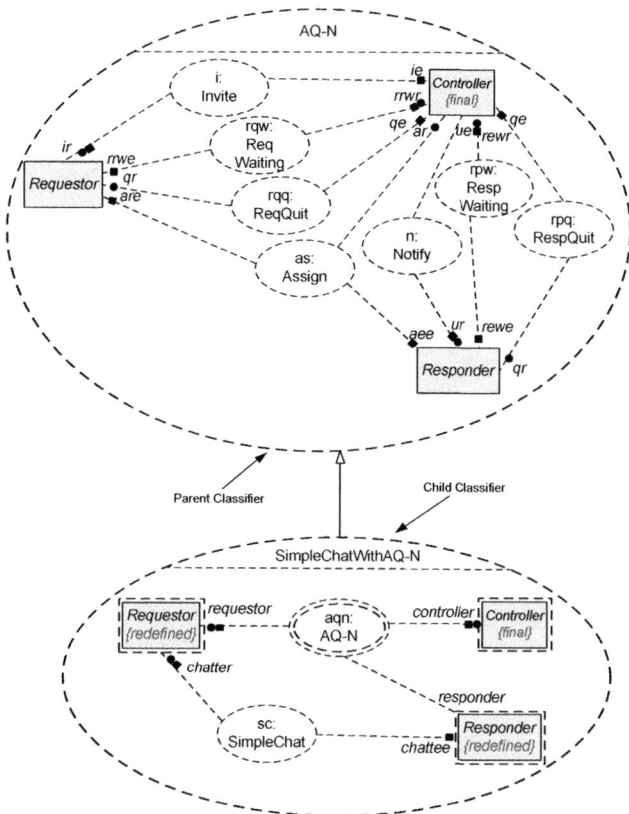

Fig. 9. UML 2 Generalization relationship: *SimpleChatwithAQ-N* collaboration is specialized from general AQ-N collaboration

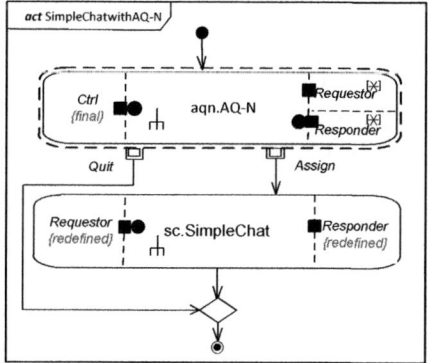

Fig. 10. Choreography for *SimpleChatwithAQ-N* collaboration: The symbol ⊓ represents a complex activity

When specializing a general classifier, we can add new properties and can also redefine the existing ones. The redefinable element of the general classifier can be extended or replaced [10]. The replacement does not serve our purpose. Therefore, redefinition of elements is advantageous if the properties are added, but if the existing behaviour of the *Requestor* and *Responder* role is replaced then it will be disadvantageous. So additional constraints are required which ensure that the redefinition will result in the extension of properties and not in replacement. For this, it must be ensured that the *Controller* role is declared as **{final}**. In order to compose session initiation service with particular service sessions such as *SimpleChat,* the UML 2 generalization relationship does not provide a modular solution i.e. we have to modify the general model for additional functionalities. For example, the *Requestor* role of AQ-N should be modified in accordance with the behaviour defined by the *Chatter* role of *SimpleChat*. How to do this is open for further studies.

UML templates. UML templates provide another way to compose session initiation service with service sessions, keeping the essence of modularity. It allows us to provide abstractions. [10] defines a template as *"the descriptor of an element with one or more unbound parameters"*. Typically, the parameters are UML classifiers. The templates must be instantiated by binding the unbound parameters to actual values. To declare the AQ-N initiation service as a UML collaboration template, we have to introduce a collaboration use (say *UndefinedService*) as an unbound parameter between the *Requestor* and *Responder* roles. The *UndefinedService* unbound parameter will then be substituted by the *SimpleChat* collaboration. In UML templates, the binding of the role means complete substitution of the role. For example, if we declare *Requestor* role as an unbound parameter, then upon instantiation of the template, the *Requestor* role will be substituted by the actual *Chatter* role of *SimpleChat* service. As the *Requestor* role is completely replaced by the *Chatter* role, the derived service will discard the presence of the *Controller* and that will result in the original *SimpleChat* service without session initiation. In our example, the *Requestor* role cannot be declared as an unbound parameter because it is already bound in collaboration uses of AQ-N.

The two solutions proposed for the composition of session initiation behaviour with particular service sessions have both pros and cons, and are not hundred percent modular. Nonetheless, we believe the UML generalization relationship has some advantages over UML 2 templates:

1. By specializing a general classifier, we can add new properties and can also redefine the existing ones.
2. Unlike UML 2 templates, we do not need to introduce an *UndefinedService* parameter.

We note that another solution to this problem is the 'Service Composition' approach proposed in [11]. This approach always works and is directly supported. It is less elegant but still powerful.

5 Discussion and Related Work

We have discussed session initiation functionality as a general requirement for dynamic role binding before a service session can be initiated. This functionality has been traditionally designed using state machines and sequence diagrams as part of service session behaviour. Here we have shown how it can be factored out as a general service in its own right. Modeling of session initiation separately as a service enables us to compose it with session behaviour to realize a complete coordinated session. Session initiation behaviour and session behaviour are modeled in the same way using UML 2 collaboration and activity diagrams. As compared to using sequence diagrams or interaction overview diagrams, activity diagrams help to specify the session initiation behaviour completely on a global level. This is due to the token flow semantics and the use of interrupting flows. The absence of interruptible regions will lead to a more complex diagram. The use of choreography (utilizing activity diagrams) provides an easier and flexible way to define various disciplines of session initiation behaviour.

The *Controller* role is the core of the session initiation. It has been designed to keep track of the actor status and handles role requests with assignment and busy handling behaviour. Two major possibilities are discussed for busy handling: either to reject the request; or to put the *Requestor* in waiting queue. The possibility to reject the request is one of the simplest busy handling behaviours. It is not elegant but serves at least the purpose of handling the requests in a simple way when the resource is busy. As compared to this, the second possibility, which is to put the *Requestor* on a waiting queue, is a better approach to handle busy resources. The *Requestor* is not forced to wait once it has sent the role request. It can opt to quit the waiting queue anytime. We have proposed *polling* as one of the options for the *Controller* to keep the track of the actor situation but it is normally better to use *notification*.

The session initiation behaviour discussed may some times be limited to be applicable for particular situations only. For instance, in the *TaxiSystem*, the decision to assign an available taxi is not only dependent on the availability of the resource (taxi) but also the location of the taxi. The latter possibility is not considered in the design of the *Controller* but may easily be added by modifying the search criteria for the list of available resources. The choreography graphs provide a flexible way to alter the session initiation behaviour during service development. Looking into the design of the *Controller* with different decision policies would be interesting. The basic structure of the behaviour will remain the same in most cases. We have found that the number of different session initiation behaviours is limited and therefore can be deployed in a library for re-use.

The session initiation behaviour is service independent. Given a service and session initiation behaviour, we have next proposed some solutions for how they can be composed and re-used. The UML generalization relationship might be used as outlined, but currently there is no definition of this for activity diagrams. One of the approaches that always work is to simply compose services with session initiation. The composite session and session initiation behaviour can subsequently be re-used as service building blocks (as demonstrated in the taxi example).

The idea behind the *Controller* originates from the concepts of semaphores and monitors used in operating systems [16], [17], and the resource allocators recommended in [18]. Related work on dynamic role binding has been done in [12], which presents a service architecture where dynamic linking is supported by means of roles and general platform mechanisms. In contrast to this, we model role binding as a service, and we use activity diagrams for both sessions and role binding. The work in [11] is focused on coordinated policy making and negotiations for dynamic composition of services. The concept of a policy enforcement state machine (PESM) diagram is used. Our focus is on session initiation behaviour and to model it on a global level using standard activity diagrams. The Session Initiation Protocol (SIP) is used for controlling multimedia communication sessions. However, it seems to bundle the session initiation behaviour and the service behaviour. It is a protocol and not a modeling approach. We isolated the session initiation behaviour and modeled it as a service. Modeling session initiation in the same way as services allows a more explicit modeling of complete service behaviour within the same framework. Transformation to orchestrations and implementations follows the same approach for both service initiation and service sessions. We do not rely on special platform support such as the role request protocol in ActorFrame [15]. In [19], design patterns for a protocol system architecture are presented by identifying the common general parts and relations in different protocols. The UML pattern notation and class diagram are used to represent the patterns. We did not follow any particular pattern schema for defining the variants of the initiation service and we used UML activity diagrams to represent them. Our initiation service variants addresses a single domain i.e. session initiation. Whereas the patterns identified in [19] addresses different problem domains of a protocol system i.e. one pattern for each domain. The work in [20] is based on a specialization of concept of design patterns to communication protocols. The authors used SDL-92 and MSCs to specify these patterns and to define the rules to instantiate and compose them. Our focus is on generalization as well as separation of session initiation service from service behaviour for which we have utilized activity diagrams.

References

1. Mierop, J., Lax, S., Janmaat, R.: Service Interaction in an Object-Oriented Environment. IEEE Communications Magazine (1993)
2. Broy, M., Krüger, I.H., Meisinger, M.: A formal model of services. ACM Transactions on Software Engineering and Methodology 16(1), 5 (2007)
3. Keck, D.O., Kuehn, P.J.: The Feature and Service Interaction Problem in Telecommunications Systems: A Survey. IEEE Transactions on Software Engineering 24 (1998)
4. Kræmer, F.A., Bræk, R., Hermann, P.: Compositional Service Engineering with Arctis. Telektronikk 1 (2009)
5. Castejón, H.N.: Collaborations in Service Engineering: Modeling, Analysis and Execution. PhD thesis, Department of Telematics, Norwegian University of Science and Technology (2008)
6. Wieringa, R.J.: Design Methods for Reactive Systems: Yourdon, Statemate, and the UML. Morgan Kaufmann, San Francisco (2003)

7. Castejón, H.N., Bochmann, G.V., Bræk, R.: Using Collaborations in the Development of Distributed Services. In: 14th Asia-Pacific Soft. Eng. Conf. (APSEC 2007), pp. 73–80. IEEE Computer Society Press, Los Alamitos (2007)
8. Unified Modeling Language 2.1.2 Specification (superstructure 09-02-02) (2009), http://www.omg.org
9. Haugen, O., Moller-Pedersen, B., Weigert, T.: UML for real: design of embedded real-time systems, pp. 53–76. Kluwer Academic, Dordrecht (2003)
10. Rumbaugh, J., Jacobson, I., Booch, G.: The Unified Modeling Language Reference Manual. Addison-Wesley, Reading (2005)
11. Rossebø, J.E.Y.: Dynamic Composition of Services – a Model – Based Approach. PhD thesis, Department of Telematics, Norwegian University of Science and Technology (2009)
12. Castejón, H.N., Bræk, R.: Dynamic Role Binding in a Service Oriented Architecture. In: Glitho, R., Karmouch, A., Pierre, S. (eds.) Intelligence in Communication Systems 2005. IFIP, vol. 190, pp. 109–122. Springer, New York (2005)
13. Fatima, U.: Coordination Patterns for Reactive Services. Master's thesis, Department of Telematics, Norwegian University of Science and Technology (2010)
14. Kathayat, S.B., Bræk, R.: From Flow-Global Choreography to Component Types. In: Kraemer, F.A., Herrmann, P. (eds.) SAM 2010. LNCS, vol. 6598, pp. 36–55. Springer, Heidelberg (2011)
15. Programming ActorFrame Plugins, http://telenorobjects.onjira.com/wiki/display/coos/Programming+ActorFrame+Plugins
16. Dijkstra, E.W.: Cooperating Sequential Processes. In: Genuys, F. (ed.) Programming Languages, Academic Press, New York (1968)
17. Hansen, P.B.: Operating System Principles. Prentice Hall, Englewood Cliffs (1973)
18. Bræk, R., Haugen, Ø.: Engineering Real Time Systems: An object-oriented methodology using SDL. Prentice Hall, Englewood Cliffs (1993)
19. Pärssinen, J., Turunen, M.: Patterns for Protocol System Architecture. In: 7th Conference on Pattern Languages of Programs (PLoP 2000), Monticello, Illinois, USA (2000)
20. Geppert, B., Rößler, F.: Pattern-based Configuring of a Customized Resource Reservation Protocol with SDL. SFB 501 Report 19/96, Computer Science Department, University of Kaiserslautern, Germany (1996)

PMG-Pro: A Model-Driven Development Method of Service-Based Applications

Selo Sulistyo and Andreas Prinz

Faculty of Engineering and Science, University of Agder,
Jon Lilletuns vei 9, N-4879 Grimstad, Norway
{selos,andreas.prinz}@uia.no

Abstract. In the Internet of Things, billions of networked and software-driven devices will be connected to the Internet. They can communicate and cooperate with each other to form a composite system. In this paper, we propose PMG-pro (present, model, generate and provide), a language independent, bottom-up and model-driven method for the development of such composite system. We envision that all devices in the Internet of Things provide their functionalities as services. From a service description, a service presenter generates source code (i.e., for the service invocations) and uses an abstract graphical representation to represent a service. The code is connected to the abstract graphical service representation. A service abstractor constructs the abstract graphical representations even more abstract in hierarchical service taxonomy. Software developers use the abstract graphical service presentations to specify new service-based applications, while the source code is used for the automation of code generation.

1 Introduction

Today's Internet technology is mainly built for information sharing. Information providers, which typically are implemented as servers, provide information in the form of web pages that can be accessed by internet clients. In the *Future Internet* [19], various independent networked computing devices from small devices (mobile devices, embedded systems, etc) to powerful devices (desktops and servers) may be easily connected to the Internet, in a plug and play manner. These devices can communicate and cooperate with each other. The Internet of Things is one of the popular terms illustrating the *Future Internet*.

From the software developer's point of view, the 'Thing' in the Internet of Things can be seen as all kinds of networked devices that are driven and delivered by (embedded) software. Considering that the device's functionalities are provided as services, we will have billions of services in the Future Internet. Composing these services is a challenge for the development of service-based applications. Unfortunately, traditional software engineering approaches are not fully appropriate for the development of service-based applications. There is an urgent need for developing comprehensive engineering principles, methodologies and tools support for the entire software development lifecycle of service-based

I. Ober and I. Ober (Eds.): SDL 2011, LNCS 7083, pp. 138–153, 2011.

applications [24]. Within the European Community, composing services in the Internet of Things has been proposed as one of the research agendas during 2010-2015 [1].

Model-driven development (MDD) is considered as a promising approach for the development of software systems. With this approach, models are used to specify, design, analyze, and verify software. It is expected that running systems can be obtained from executable models. One approach is to transform models into source code conforming to existing programming languages, such as Java and C++ (i.e., code generation). A more distinct approach is model interpretation. The transformation approach has several benefits, because the resulting code can be easily inspected, debugged, optimized and becomes more efficient. In addition, the generated implementation is easier to understand and can be checked by the compiler.

However, fully-automated code generation is a difficult task. In the context of the Model-driven Architecture (MDA) [16], unclear definitions of platform models and also a big variability of device capabilities and configurations are two reasons why it is difficult. If a fully-automated code generation can be achieved, it is restricted only to a specific domain in the context of domain-specific modeling (DSM). The automation in the DSM is possible because of domain-specificity where both the modeling languages and code generators fit to the requirements of a narrowly defined domain. In this paper we propose PMG-pro, a language-independent, bottom-up and model-driven development method of service-based applications. To achieve a fully-automated code generation, we adapt the DSM concepts, where we construct models as a representation of real things.

The remainder of the paper is organized as follows: In Section 2 we present a development scenario of a service-based application. Then, in Section 3 we present the PMG-pro method. Based on the scenario, we illustrate the use of PMG-pro. Section 4 is devoted to related work. Finally, we draw our conclusions in Section 5.

2   Service-Based Applications: *A Scenario*

A typical example of an environment containing embedded services is a smart home where a residential gateway is controlling and managing home devices with embedded services. A smart home example was also used in [25] and [5]. In this type of dwelling, it is possible to maintain control of doors and window shutters, valves, security and surveillance systems, etc. It also includes the control of multimedia devices that are parts of home entertainment systems. In this scenario, the smart home is containing the following devices:

1. WeatherModules that provide different data collection services (i.e., air temperature, solar radiation, wind speed, and humidity sensors).
2. Lamps that provide on-off and dimmer services.
3. Media Renderers that provide playing of multimedia services.
4. Virtual devices that provide sending e-mail services.

We consider that all the devices have been implemented their functionalities as embedded services. Different open and standardized languages and technologies may have been used to describe the services. For example, Universal Plug and Play (UPnP) is one of the popular standards for describing embedded services of home entertainment devices (e.g., media renderer). Other examples are Web Services Description Language (WSDL) and Device Profile for Web Services (DPWS). Based on these different embedded services, new applications can be promoted. In this scenario, a new application is promoted with the following new functionalities:

- the application is able to send notifications (e-mail) when the air temperature from the WeatherModule is greater than 50°C,
- it will play music/songs on the Media renderer when the light is turned on and the solar radiation is below than 10, and
- the application provides two new UPnP services. The first service is to enable a user to configure the song to be played for a specific weather condition, while the second service is to get the configuration information.

3   The PMG-Pro Method

Different approaches can be used for developing the application scenario mentioned above, for example bottom-up and top-down development. Since embedded services can be abstract (i.e., models) or concrete (i.e., real implementations at run-time), the development of service-based applications can use both approaches. Bottom-up development approaches assume that all abstract services have concrete services, while in top-down approaches abstract services may be services that will be implemented in the future. Since we will use existing (i.e., implemented) embedded services, we consider that the bottom-up development approaches are suitable for the development of service-based applications.

With regard to the software production, there are different approaches, which focus on how to specify, design, implement, test, and deploy software systems. They can be categorized as implementation- and model-oriented approaches. The implementation-oriented approach focuses on the implementation. Although there may exist design descriptions and models, they are not formal and are often incomplete. In contrast, the model-oriented approach focuses on the descriptions of the functionality or the properties of the system. These descriptions constitute more or less formal models of the system and they can be verified, analyzed, and understood independently of the implementation of the system.

PMG-pro combines bottom-up and model-driven development approaches to promote a rapid and automatic development of service-based applications. As it is indicated by the name, PMG-pro (Present, Model, Generate, and provide) has four steps (i.e., presenting, modeling, generating, and providing). PMG-pro combines the generating and providing as one step.

The PMG-pro architecture (see Fig. 1) consists of three main parts: the presenter/abstractor that is used at the presenting step, the modeling editor that

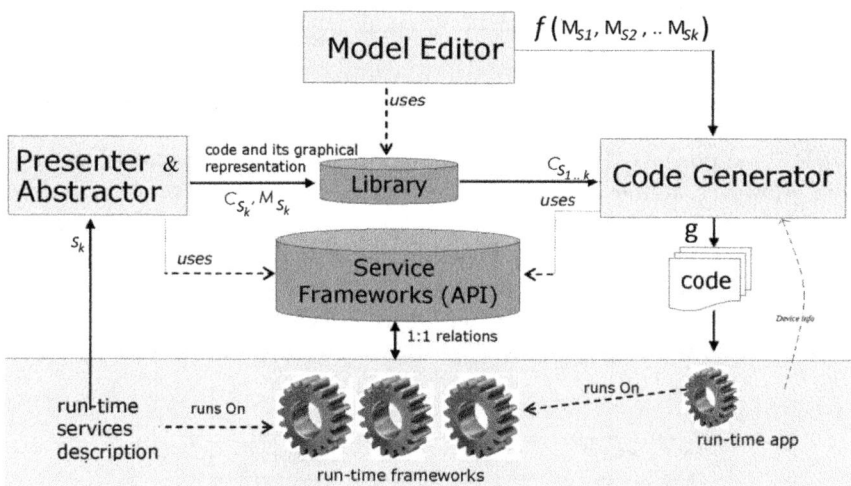

Fig. 1. The PMG-pro Architecture

is used at the modeling step, and the code generator/provider that is used at the generating/providing step. There is also a library that is used to store the generated source code and service models at the presenting step. Each service model (abstract) stored in the library binds to source code (concrete). Within the DSM context, the generated service model represents a real thing as it has been implemented (i.e., embedded services). At the modeling step, based on the stored service models, developers can specify (i.e., produce) new models of service-based applications using selected the modeling editor. At the generating step, referring to the library the models of a service-based application is transformed to source code.

3.1   The Presenting Step

Specifying models of a service-based application is only possible if the models of the included (i.e., existing) services are in place. The presentation step consists of a transformation mechanism of service descriptions into graphical representations and source code. It involves re-engineering or reverse engineering processes. For example, in the context of Web services, we can use WSDL2Java [8] to re-engineer (WSDL) service descriptions into source code. The source code is used as a proxy for service invocations to the concrete services that reside in service providers. The graphical representation will be used by the developers in order to be able to work in a model-driven fashion.

From a service description (s), the abstractor/presenter generates a graphical service model ($\mathbf{M}_s$) conforming to a selected modeling language and source code ($\mathbf{C}_s$) conforming to a selected programming language. To automate the transformation process, existing service frameworks and APIs (e.g., the Web Service framework and API) are used. PMG-pro uses `Cyberlink for Java` for

142   S. Sulistyo and A. Prinz

the UPnP services [12], WS4d [6] for the DPWS services, and WSDL2Java(Axis) [8] for the Web services. Obviously, this can be extended for other service frameworks and APIs.

Depending on the selected modeling language, different graphical representations (i.e., notations) can be used to represent the existing services. UML classes, CORBA components, Participants in SoaML, or SCA components are among them. However, it must be noted that within the context of domain-specific modeling (DSM), a graphical representation must relate to a real thing which in this case is the implementation of the service. Therefore, it is important to keep the relation (bindings) between graphical representations (i.e. service models) and source code (i.e. implementation for the service invocations). Fig. 2 shows the relation between a service description, its model, and source code.

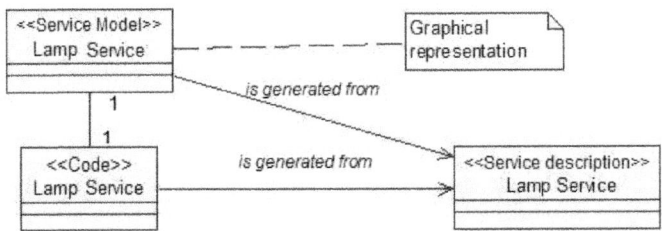

Fig. 2. The relation between a service description, its model and source code

Different service frameworks and APIs have been developed using different programming languages and run on different platforms, helping developers to implement services. For example, in the Web services context there are Apache Axis (Java and C++), appRain (PHP), .NET Framework (C#, VB and .NET), etc. Therefore, a graphical representation of a service may have several implementations (i.e., source code). This source code may also use different programming languages and may run on different platforms. Thus, the 1..1 relation (model-source code) in Fig. 2 can be a 1..* relation.

A Common Service Model. Different standards and technologies may be used to describe services, although they have similar functionalities. In PMGpro, from a service description pair of source code and graphical representation is generated. For similar services, there will be a common service model. An example of a common service model is shown in Fig. 3. The figure shows three different services that provide similar functionalities, but they use different standards and technologies for describing their services. The UPnP_Lamp service and the UPnP_Light use UPnP schema to describe services while the DPWS_Lamp uses DPWS to describe the service. However, all lamp services provide functionalities to switch ON-OFF the light even though they use different operation names. From these different service models a common model for the Lamp services which has ON and OFF functionalities can be constructed.

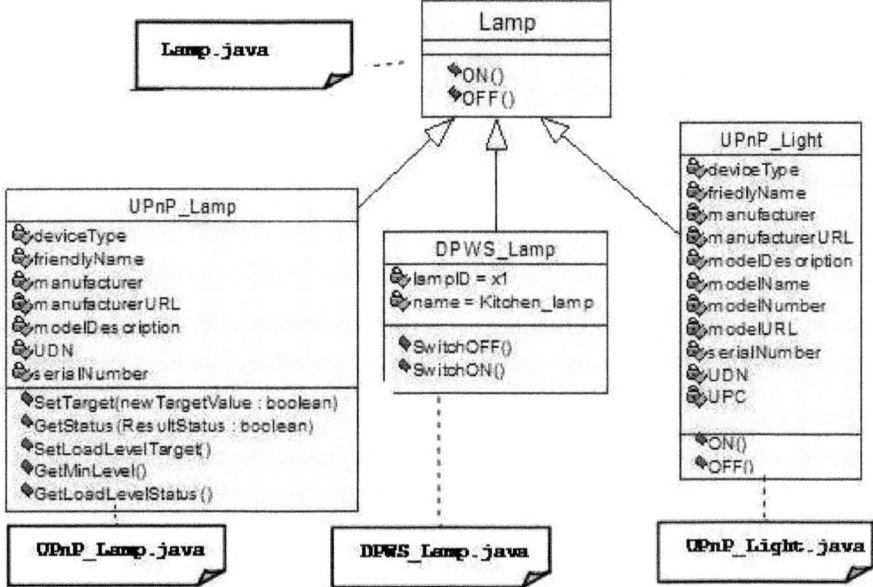

Fig. 3. A platform independent service models and its code

Listing 1.1. Lamp Code

```
public class Lamp {
...
public void Lamp(){
UPnP_Lamp upnp_lamp= new UPnP_Lamp();
UPnP_Light upnp_light=new UPnP_Light();
DPWS_Lamp dpws_lamp = new DPWS_Lamp();
}

public void ON (String selectedService){
   if (selectedService.equalsIgnoreCase("UPnP_Lamp")) {
        upnp_lamp.SetTarget(true);
   } else if (selectedService.equalsIgnoreCase("UPnP_Light")) {
        upnp_light.ON();
   } else if (selectedService.equalsIgnoreCase("DPWS_Lamp")) {
        dpws_lamp.SwitchON();
   }

public void OFF (String selectedService){
   if (selectedService.equalsIgnoreCase("UPnP_Lamp")) {
        upnp_lamp.setTarget(false);

.........
}
```

A common service model can be seen as a platform-independent model. In PMG-pro, a common service model binds also to source code or a script. The script provides information about what possible source code can be used at the code generation step. Listing 1.1 code above illustrates an example of source code of the common service model for the Lamp service. This is just an example to illustrate the idea of platform-independent service models. The use of scripts will facilitate the realization of the idea. Moreover, at the moment, the example is a manual implementation of an old feature provided by object languages, the polymorphism.

Service Taxonomy and Ontology. In general, taxonomy can be defined as a classification of things, as well as the principles underlying such a classification. A hierarchical taxonomy is a tree structure of classifications for a given set of things. On the other hand, ontology is a data model that represents a set of concepts within a domain and the relationships among the concepts. A common service ontology and taxonomy enables us to identify the common characteristics of services that fall into a particular category. In the context of service-oriented architectures (SOA), the service taxonomy introduced in [4] is an example service categorization. In [4], services are categorized as *Bus Services* (Communication Services and Utility Services) and *Application Services* (Entity Services, Capability Services and Activity Services, and Process Services).

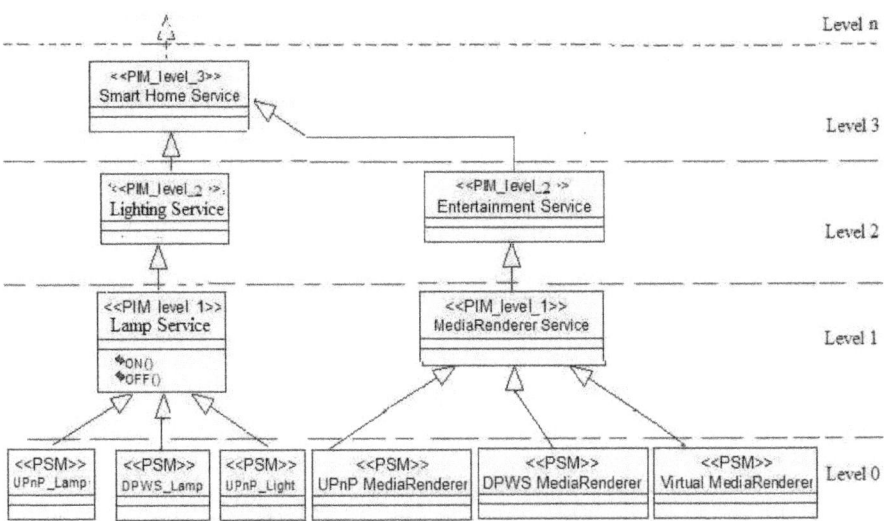

Fig. 4. Taxonomy of service models

In PMG-pro, the hierarchy of service models is stored (at the moment manually) in the service library. For automatic generation of the hierarchy the service description must contain enough information for the service categorization.

Categorization enables with the manageability of services, which can help with the discoverability for code generation.

Fig. 4 shows an example of service taxonomy in a smart home domain, where different implementations of `MediaRenderer services` (e.g. UPnP and DPWS) are categorized under the `MediaRenderer services`, `Entertainment Services`, and `Smart home services`, respectively. All `MediaRenderer` services at level 0 of the hierarchy have graphical representation (with `<<PSM>>` stereotype) and source code (with `<<code>>` stereotype). MediaRenderer services at level 1 of the hierarchy are defined as a common model to represent all media renderer services at level 0. Accordingly, the `Lamp services` have a similar hierarchy. It should be noted that all the service models at any level of the hierarchy finally relate to source code.

At level 1 and above, there is a similar relation between model and code. The service models at level 1 and above are platform-independent models and denoted with `<<PIM_level_n>>`. At a very high level of the hierarchy it would be kind of a script that contains information about possible target platforms that can be used in the code generation step.

An Example: *Arctis Building Blocks*. In this case study we use Arctis. Arctis [13] is a modeling editor that uses a building block as a basic entity. Obviously, different modeling editor and tools can be used. For this purpose, we have developed a service abstractor/presenter that is able to transform UPnP service descriptions into Arctis building blocks and its connected source code (Java class). An Arctis building block is considered as an encapsulation of activities which can be accessed through its ports. In this case, one building block can be used to represents several services.

Table 1. Transformation rules between UPnP and Arctis Building Block

UPnP	Arctis Building Block
Device name	Building block name
Action	Parameter input
Action argument	Parameter type (input)
State variable	Parameter output
Type of state variable	Parameter type

A UPnP device has two kinds of descriptions; device description and service description. A UPnP device can have several services that are in a UPnP service description called Actions. To automate this step we use transformation rules. Table 1 shows transformation rules to transform different properties in a UPnP service description into properties in an Arctis building block. To construct the transformation rules, both Arctis and UPnP meta-models are required. However, the rules are very simple. For example, to present the name of the building block, we use the name of the UPnP device. Obviously, other XML-based service descriptions (e.g., WSDL, DPWS) will use a similar process.

In Fig. 5, three building blocks (i.e., WeatherModule, Lamp and MediaRenderer) representing services are shown. Each of these building blocks has source code (a Java class for service invocations). Obviously, other programming languages can also be used. After all service descriptions are transformed into graphical service models the modeling step can be started.

3.2   The Modeling Step

In software development, models are used to describe the structures and the behaviors of the software systems. The structure specifies what the instances of the model are; it identifies the meaningful components of the model construct and relates them to each other. The behavioral model emphasizes the dynamic behavior of a system, which can essentially be expressed in three different types of behavioral models; interaction diagrams, activity diagrams, and state machine diagrams. We use interaction diagrams to specify in which manner the instances of model elements interact with each other(roles).

Even though for model-driven development, state-machine diagrams are considered as the most executable models, we are still interested in using UML activity diagram and collaboration diagram. The reason is that from activity diagrams we can generate state machine diagrams [14]. The UML activity diagrams are used mostly to model data/object flow systems that are a common pattern in models. The activity diagram is also good to model the behavior of systems which do not heavily depend on external events.

PMG-pro is a language-independent method. It is possible to use different existing modeling languages and different modeling editors. This is done by developing and implementing different service abstractors/presenters. The requirement is that the presenter must generate notations (i.e., abstract service models) that conform to the chosen modeling languages. Using the abstract service models $(\mathbf{M}_{s1}, \mathbf{M}_{s2}, ..., \mathbf{M}_{sk})$, a service-based application can be expressed in a composition function $f\{\mathbf{M}_{s1}, \mathbf{M}_{s2}, ..., \mathbf{M}_{sk}\}$, where $s1..sk$ are the included services in the service-based application.

To demostrate the language-independent feature, we have developed prototypes (i.e., service abstractor/presenter) that supports Arctis [13] and Rational Rose [20]. Using Arctis, behaviors of a service-based application are modeled using collaboration activity diagrams while using UML (Rational Rose), the behaviors are modeled using sequence diagrams. Obviously, the semantics of the language follows the chosen modeling languages.

An Example: *Collaboration Activities in Arctis*. Using the service taxonomy (see Fig. 4), it would be possible for the modelers to model new service-based applications using service models at any level of hierarchy. The higher the level of hierarchy the more platform-independent the models would be. By high-level models, we mean models of service-based applications that are built using platform-independent service models at level 1 and above of the hierarchy in the service taxonomy. From high-level models of service-based applications different source code can be generated. Obviously, it will be limited by the number of source code binds to the service models that are stored in the service library.

Using Arctis, a service-based application can be specified as a building block diagram. The behavior of the new service-based application is defined by interactions between building blocks, which are in this case defined using activity nodes defined in UML 2.0. Accordingly, the semantic follows the semantic of UML 2.0 activity diagrams. Fig. 5 shows an Arctis model of the service-based application defined in the scenario. There are four building blocks that represent different existing services mentioned in the scenario. In this model, the service models are taken from the level 1 of the service hierarchy (see Fig. 4). This means that they may have several different implementations.

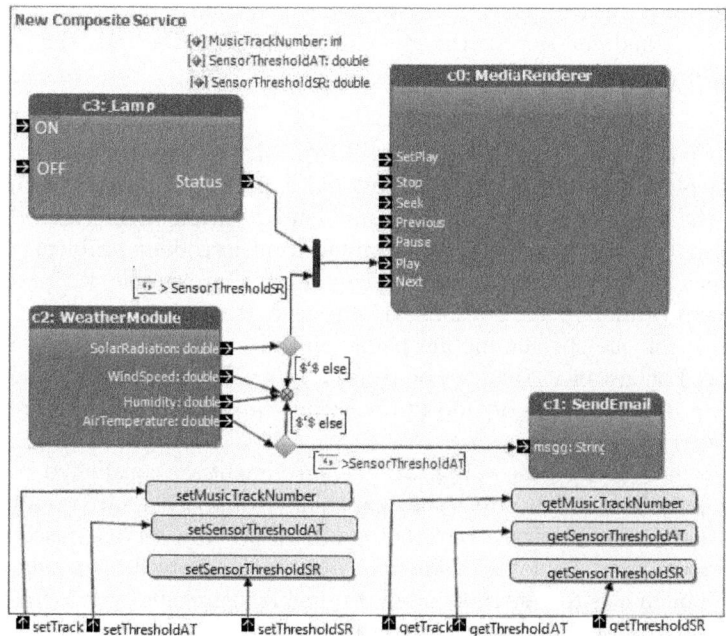

Fig. 5. The Arctis model of the new application

In Arctis, a service-based application can be, again, encapsulated and presented as a new building block. This allows us to model the new provided services defined in the scenario. As defined in the scenario the new service-based application will provide two new services (i.e., SettingService and GetConfiguration Service). In Arctis, this can be specified by defining new parameters (i.e., ports). Obviously, this new building block can be used to build a new building block diagram as new specification of a software system. This is the way how an incremental development of a large application can be done in Arctis.

3.3   The Automated Code Generation Step

For model execution, we use code generation approaches instead of model interpretations. For this, we did not use any transformation language to generate code, but a Java program to transform models into texts (i.e., source code). At the moment, the program can only read collaboration activity diagrams (i.e., Arctis diagrams) and sequence diagrams (i.e., UML sequence diagrams). The potential code generation from activity diagrams was studied in [3] and [7]. For a tool, Enterprise Architect from Sparx Systems [21] is an example for modeling tools that support code generation from activity diagrams.

The code generation process of a service-based application can be expressed as a generation function $g[f\{\mathbf{M}_{s1}, \mathbf{M}_{s2}, .., \mathbf{M}_{sk}\}, \mathbf{C}_{s1..sk}, dev\_info] \Rightarrow code$, where $f\{\mathbf{M}_{s1}, \mathbf{M}_{s2}, .., \mathbf{M}_{sk}\}$ is the model of the service-based application, $s1, s2 .. sk$ are the included services, $\mathbf{C}_{s1..sk}$ are the connected code of the used service models ($\mathbf{M}_{s1..sk}$), and dev_info is the given device information (i.e., the capability and configuration information).

Configuration and Capability Matching. In the context of MDA, different target platforms require different tailored code. In the context of embedded systems, the terms of device capability and configuration are often used instead of platforms. Device capability and configuration introduce problems for code generation even within the same device capability. For example, it can occur the development of mobile applications. In this case, it can happen that a working source code for one specific mobile phone will not work on another one of the same type. For instance, this can be caused by a difference in the user configurations (e.g. memory size) or/and in the device capabilities (e.g., the resolution of camera).

Services in a service-based application environment are considered being provided by third parties; therefore they can easily come and go. It would be very possible that included services are not available when a service-based application is implemented, deployed, and run. To solve the problem, two solutions are possible. The first is to generate code for possible aggregated services in the ontology. All possible device configurations would also support run-time adaptation in case of services are removed or new services appear.

The second possible solution is to generate code only for the present (specific) services. This solution requires information about what devices are available at runtime. This means code cannot be generated before the platform is used, which essentially means on-demand code generation.

An Example: *From Arctis models to Code.* To illustrate the code generation in PMG-pro, we use the Java programming language. To generate code from the structure the block diagram and building blocks are used. From a building block diagram the main application (class) is generated. The name of the class is defined using the name of the building block diagram.

From each building block, one object is instantiated. Since the building blocks in this scenario are platform independent, the objects to be instantiated are depending on the platform selection. Listing 1.2 shows an example of the generated code when the UPnP platform is selected at the generating step. Only classes that implement UPnP services are instantiated. Get and Set methods are generated for all the introduced variables.

Listing 1.2. New Composite Service

```
public class New_Composite_Service {

private UPnP_MediaRenderer c0;
private SendMail c1;
private UPnPWeatherModule c2;
private UPnP_Lamp c3;
MusicTrackNumber int;
SensorTresholdAT double;
SensorTresholdSR double;

public New_Composite_Service() {
    // main behavior
}

public void setMusicTrackNumber (int number){
    this.MusicTrackNumber=number;
}

public void setSensorTresholdAT(double sensorTresholdAT){
    this.SensorTresholdAT=sensorTresholdAT;
}

public void setSensorTresholdSR (double sensorTresholdSR){
    this.SensorTresholdSR=sensorTresholdSR;
}

public int getMusicTrackNumber (){
return this.MusicTrackNumber;
}

.....

public static void main(String [] orgs){
  new New_Composite_Service();
}
}
```

Code from the behavior parts is taken from the activity nodes. For this we adapt the generation method presented in [3]. With regard to their method, an Arctis building block can be considered as an entity that executes an external action. For example, for the decision node (i.e., the decision node with the airtemperature input) the following code is produces.

Listing 1.3. An example of code for the behavior part

```
if (c2.airtemperature >= SensorTresholdAT) {
    c2.msgg=SetMessage();
}
else
    break;
```

For the scenario example, two new services are provided as UPnP services. For this, UPnP code must be added. We have implemented a code generator to generate code for the application scenario. Fig. 6 is a screenshot of the running UPnP services. We use deviceSpy software provided by Intel Tool for UPnP technology [11]. It can be seen that the new application (composite service) provides two UPnP services: `GetConfiguration()` and `SettingService()`.

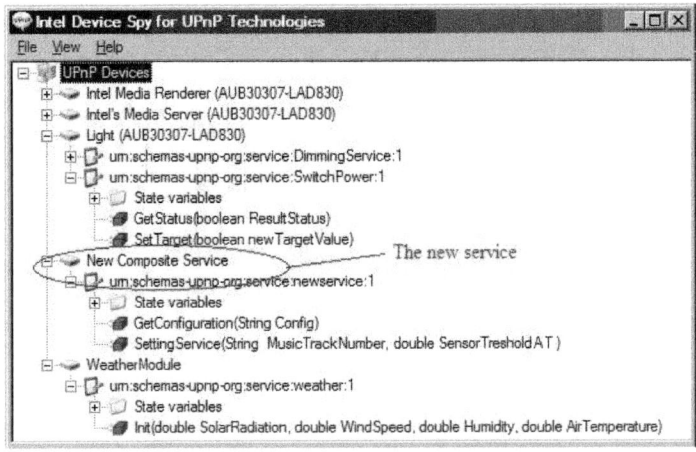

Fig. 6. The new composite service at run-time

4   Related Work

Service composition is gaining importance, as it can produce composite services with features not present in the individual basic services. Several research projects for promoting tools and methods have been conducted, for example the SeCSE project [22]. One of the SeCSE goals is to create methods, tools, and techniques to enable service integrators to develop service-centric applications. The SODIUM [23] project focuses on the need for standards-based integration of heterogeneous services. One thing that makes PMG-pro different from the projects mentioned above is that, while they proposed new modeling languages for the development of service-based applications, PMG-pro uses existing technologies (e.g., modeling languages). PMG-pro focuses on an automated abstraction/presentation of existing services. Depending on the abstractor/presenter, any graphical presentation conforming to a modeling language can be used to present a service. We construct platform information by maintaining the relation between service models and their code (i.e., their real implementations).

The fact that different perspectives may have different definitions of a service, the definition of service composition may also be different. PMG-pro considers that a service is just a kind of software component model that has evolved from the older software component models (i.e., modules, objects, and components). Here, we use a definition of software component models, which is different from the definition of standardized component models such as CORBA and DCOM. With this definition, a services composition can be done in a similar way as a composition of software units that normally is done at design-time using bottom-up approaches. Thus, PMG-pro focuses on design-time compositions. However, the PMG-pro method can be extended to support run-time compositions. Using the PMG-pro method it would be possible to generate graphical service representation that can be used by end-users (i.e., run-time composition). In the ISIS project for example [26], ICE, an end-user composition, has been developed. A service in ICE is presented as a puzzle with either one input (trigger) or one output (action). By developing a service abstractor/presenter, ICE puzzles for end-users and source code for implementing service invocations can be generated. The ICE puzzles then can be used by end-users to model the composition (at run-time) while the source code is used by ICE to execute the composition.

For the composition of service component models (i.e., software units), composition techniques, and composition languages are required [2]. For the composition languages, there is no particular language that is supposed to be a language for the service compositions. In Web service context, the Web Service Business Process Execution Language (WS-BPEL) [18] and the Web Services Choreography Description Language (WS-CDL) [9] can be considered as a composition language. Within the OMG context, the Service-oriented architecture Modeling Language (SoaML) [17] is another example of composition languages. Also in the Web services context, services orchestration and choreography are well-known service composition techniques. In the context of Service Component Architecture (SCA) [10], wiring can also be considered as a type of composition techniques. For this reason, PMG-pro is language-independent. To show this feature, we support Arctis [13] by developing a presenter to present sevices using building blocks. We also have developed a service presenter to present sevices using UML classes in Rational Rose 2000.

Presenting software functionality into abstract graphical representation has also been studied by other researchers. For example, in [15] UML is used to model Web services. The main contributions of their method are conversion rules between UML and web services described by WSDL. However, their work focused only on Web services and did not think about how automated code generation can be achieved. In [27], software components are visualized using graphical notations that developers can easily understand. They use a picture of a real device to present a software component. The integration is done by simply connecting components graphically. Obviously, the approach is only applicable for a specific domain. In contrast, PMG-pro is domain-independent.

5 Conclusion

In this paper, we propose PMG-pro, a language independent, bottom-up, and model-driven method for the development of service-based applications. To enable the auotmation, the method adapts the concept of domain-specific languages. Based on the existing service frameworks, APIs, and service descriptions, a service presenter and service abstractor captures platform knowledge statically and presents services using abstract graphical representations. Different notations conforming to modeling languages can be used to represent the services. Each of the generated abstract service model is connected to the code for the service invocations. We use these pairs of code - abstract graphical as a platform-specific model. Ontology is used to construct more abstract the platform models. Service developers can use the abstract graphical service representation to model new service-based applications.

For the code generation, information about the actual targeted platform is required. We have shown two ways of using the constructed platform models. Firstly, based on the information of the targeted platform, the code generator uses the platform models to generate code tailored for the selected target platform. Alternatively, the generated code includes code that contains a detection mechanism to do necessary adaption at run-time. The fully automated code generation is possible, since the service models are connected to code for implementing the service invocations. Just like in domain-specific languages (DSM), the service models are constructed using concepts that represent real things in the application domain.

References

1. Rezafard, A., Vilmos, A., et al.: Internet of things: Strategic research roadmap (2009)
2. Assmann, U.: Invasive software composition. Springer, Heidelberg (2003)
3. Bhattacharjee, A.K., Shyamasundar, R.K.: Validated code generation for activity diagrams. In: Chakraborty, G. (ed.) ICDCIT 2005. LNCS, vol. 3816, pp. 508–521. Springer, Heidelberg (2005)
4. Cohen, S.: Ontology and taxonomy of services in a service-oriented architecture. MSDN Libary Infrastructure Architectures 11(11) (2007)
5. Coyle, L., Neely, S., Stevenson, G., Sullivan, M., Dobson, S., Nixon, P.: Sensor fusion-based middleware for smart homes. International Journal of Assistive Robotics and Mechatronics 8(2), 53–60 (2007)
6. Zeeb, E., Bobek, A., et al.: WS4D: SOA-Toolkits making embedded systems ready for web services. In: Proceedings of Second International Workshop on Open Source Software and Product Lines. ITEA, Limerick (2007)

7. Eshuis, R., Wieringa, R.: A formal semantics for uml activity diagrams - formalising workflow models (2001)
8. Goodwill, J.: Apache Axis Live: A Web Services Tutorial, Sourcebeat (December 2004)
9. Diaz, G., Pardo, J.-J., Cambronero, M.-E., Valero, V., Cuartero, F.: Automatic translation of ws-cdl choreographies to timed automata. In: Bravetti, M., Kloul, L., Tennenholtz, M. (eds.) EPEW/WS-EM 2005. LNCS, vol. 3670, pp. 230–242. Springer, Heidelberg (2005)
10. IBM. Service component architecture (November 2006), http://www.ibm.com/developerworks/library/specification/ws-sca/
11. Jeronimo, M., Weast, J.: UPnP Design by Example: A Software Developer's Guide to Universal Plug and Play. Intel Press, Hillsboro (2003)
12. Konno, S.: Cyberlink for java programming guide v.1.3 (2005)
13. Kræmer, F.A.: Arctis and Ramses: Tool suites for rapid service engineering. In: Proceedings of NIK 2007 (Norsk informatikkonferanse). Tapir Akademisk Forlag, Oslo (2007)
14. Kræmer, F.A.: Engineering Reactive Systems: A Compositional and Model-Driven Method Based on Collaborative Building Blocks. PhD thesis, Norwegian University of Science and Technology, Trondheim (August 2008)
15. Grønmo, R., Skogan, D., Solheim, I., Oldevik, J.: Model-Driven web services development. In: Proceedings of International Conference on e-Technology, e-Commerce, and e-Services, pp. 42–45. IEEE Computer Society, USA (2004)
16. OMG. Model driven architecture guide, version 1.0.1, omg/03-06-01 (June 2003)
17. OMG. Service oriented architecture modeling language (SoaML): Specification for the UML profile and metamodel for services, UPMS (2009)
18. Ouyang, C., Verbeek, E., van der Aalst, W.M.P., Breutel, S., Dumas, M., ter Hofstede, A.H.M.: Formal semantics and analysis of control flow in WS-BPEL. Science of Computer Programming 67(2-3), 162–198 (2007)
19. Papadimitriou, D.: Future internet: The cross-etp vision document. Technical Report Version 1.0, European Future Internet Assembly, FIA (2009)
20. Quatrani, T.: Visual modeling with Rational Rose 2000 and UML, 2nd edn. Addison-Wesley Longman Ltd., Essex (2000)
21. Sparx Systems. Enterprise architect, http://www.sparxsystems.com/products/ea/index.html
22. The SeCSE Team: Designing and deploying service-centric systems: the secse way. In: Proceedings of the Service Oriented Computing: a look at the Inside (SOC @Inside 20 (2007)
23. Topouzidou, S.: Service oriented development in a unified framework (sodium). Deliverable CD-JRA-1.1.2, SODIUM Consortium (May 2007)
24. van den Heuvel, W.-J., Zimmermann, O., et al.: Software service engineering: Tenets and challenges. In: Proceedings of the 2009 ICSE Workshop on Principles of Engineering Service Oriented Systems, PESOS 2009, pp. 26–33. IEEE Computer Society, Washington, DC (2009)
25. Wu, C.-L., Liao, C.-F., Fu, L.-C.: Service-oriented smart-home architecture based on OSGi and mobile-agent technology. IEEE Transactions on Systems, Man, and Cybernetics, Part C: Applications and Reviews, 193–205 (2007)
26. Su, X., Svendsen, R., et al.: Description of the ISIS Ecosystem Towards an Integrated Solution to Internet of Things. Telenor Group Corporate Development (2010)
27. Yermashov, K.: Software Composition with Templates. PhD Thesis, De Montfort University, UK (2008)

A Model-Driven Framework for Component-Based Development

Surya Bahadur Kathayat, Hien Nam Le, and Rolv Bræk

Department of Telematics, Norwegian University of Science and Technology,
NO 7491, Trondheim, Norway
{surya,hiennam,rolv.braek}@item.ntnu.no

Abstract. This paper presents a Model-Driven framework to support component-based development. The framework addresses the following important issues: (1) how to reduce the cost of making component reusable, (2) how to efficiently ensure compatibility among components in a composition, (3) how to relate service composition to system composition. The framework supports three kinds of reusable building blocks: (1) collaborations for global cross-cutting behaviors including services and interfaces; (2) roles or partial components for component compositions; and (3) components for system compositions.

1 Introduction

Component-based development has a potential to reduce cost and time to market, but there is additional cost associated with making components reusable that must be justified by cost reductions in later re-use. This cost and delayed return of investment is a key obstacle for component-based development. Therefore it is essential to (1) reduce the cost of making building blocks reusable, (2) identify building blocks with a high potential for reuse, and (3) increase the benefits of reuse in terms of quality gains and cost savings. In the following we use the term "building block" for reusable entities in general. They may be traditional components used to build systems or they may be cross-cutting collaborations representing services or interfaces. Central issues are the nature and granularity of building blocks, how to efficiently define interfaces so that building blocks can be connected together, and how to specify the behaviors of composite components and interfaces [3,4].

This paper presents a service-oriented development approach leading to reusable building blocks derived directly from service models, at little or no extra additional costs. The approach helps to overcome some serious problems that have plagued component oriented development by:

- Reducing the cost of developing component interfaces for reuse.
- Improving the quality of interfaces by including a precise description of interface behaviors.
- Defining interfaces as reusable entities (contracts) that can be validated separately.
- Reducing compatibility checks on links between components to static contract checks.

I. Ober and I. Ober (Eds.): SDL 2011, LNCS 7083, pp. 154–167, 2011.

- Supporting a granularity of components ranging from a few actions to complex sub-systems.
- Supporting service composition as well as component and system composition.

The approach is based on collaborative services [8]. The term *service* is used here to denote a partial system functionality where two or more entities collaborate to achieve some goal [11]. A component may participate in several services and a service can involve roles played by different components. Thus there is a need for composition both in the service dimension and in the system dimension. The development approach leads to components with interfaces suitable for composition in both dimensions.

The rest of the paper is as following. Section 2 presents the Model-Driven framework for component-based development illustrated by a Train Control System (ERTMS) [10]. Section 3 discusses the composition of components. How a system is developed by composing components is discussed in Section 4. Section 5 discusses related work. Conclusions are is given in Section 6.

2   The Model-Driven Framework for Component-Based Development

The model-driven framework is shown in Figure 1 and has three main models: (1) Service Models for specifying the structure and behavior of cross-cutting services and interfaces; (2) Component Models for specifying the interfaces and local behaviors of both elementary and composite components; and (3) System Design for developing systems by composing components. The details of the framework are described below and illustrated by a Train Control System - based on the new European Rail Traffic Management System (ERTMS) [7,10].

2.1   Service Models

We distinguish between elementary services and composite services. Elementary services can not be decomposed further into sub-services while composite service is composed from smaller services. We use UML 2.x collaborations to specify the structure of collaborating entities in a service and activity diagrams to specify their behavior. Figure 2 defines the structure of the Train Control System (ERTMS) using UML 2.x collaborations.

While moving in a physical geographical region, a Train must always be supervised by a Radio Block Center (RBC) whose responsibility is to monitor and control all train movements within its region. The Train Control System is decomposed into three collaboration uses that refer to separately defined collaborations each having an associated activity diagram:

- *Movement supervision:* this composite collaboration monitors the location of the Train via the *PositionReport* service, and controls the safe traveling distance of the Train via the *MoveAuthority* service.

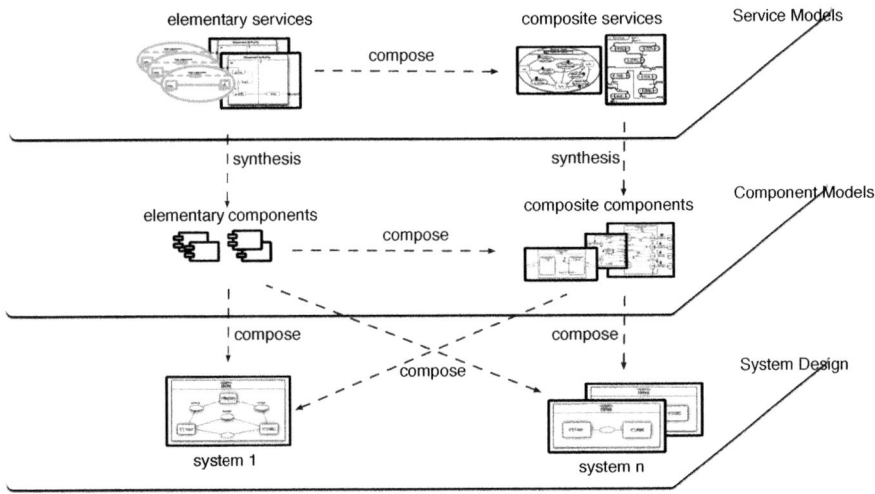

Fig. 1. The Collaboration Based Framework

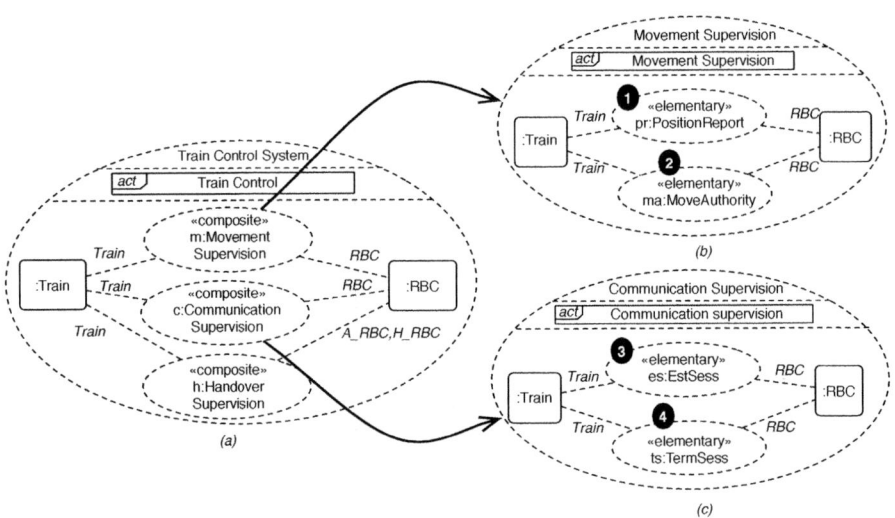

Fig. 2. Structural Model of Train Control System

– *Communication Supervision:* this collaboration monitors and manages the communication between the Train and the RBC. The *Communication Supervision* is a composite service which is composed from collaboration uses referring to smaller collaborations that are defined separately, i.e., the elementary services *EstSess* and *TermSess*, which represents the establishment and termination of communication sessions between a Train and a RBC, respectively. The roles of the collaboration uses are bound to the roles of the enclosing collaborations. For example the roles *Train*, and *RBC* of the *EstSess* collaboration are bound to the roles *Train* and *RBC* of the *Communication Supervision* collaboration which in turn are bound to the roles *Train* and *RBC* of the Train Control System.[1] Note that the numeric identifiers associated with collaborations uses are used just for ease of referencing within this paper.

– *Handover supervision:* during its journey, the Train may travel across more than one geographical region; this means the supervision of the Train movement is handled by more than one RBC. The handover is performed by the collaborative activity *HandoverSupervision*. When the handover supervision is completed, the Train will switch back to normal movement supervision (i.e., the Train will now be under supervised by the new RBC). During the handover process, the current RBC plays a handing over role (H_RBC) and the neighbor RBC where the train is approaching plays an accepting role (A_RBC).

The behavior of collaborations and roles can be specified using the token flow semantics of UML activity diagrams, for example using the swim-lane notation of [5]. In this paper, it is assumed that elementary services are available in a repository as building blocks that can be reused in the behavior specification (called *choreography*) of a composite service.

For composite services, the choreography is very useful for discussion with end-users and to capture requirements in a very abstract way and to specify the intended global behavior [7,8]. The choreography of a collaboration is specified using UML activity diagrams as illustrated in Figure 3 for the collaborations represented in Figure 2. One can see that the choreography of a composite service specifies an ordering of the actions representing behaviors defined for the collaborations referenced by the corresponding collaboration uses. Note that the sub-collaborations in *Handover Supervision* referenced in Figure 3(c) are composite collaborations with choreography defined in Figure 4. The choreography models specify the following aspects:

– *Participating roles.* The participating roles are represented as partitions of collaborative actions.
– *Initiation and termination.* The initiating and terminating roles in a collaboration are indicated by black filled circle and square boxes respectively. Note that this notation is not the part of standard UML, but needed for analysis on the level of choreography and may be provided by additional profiling. For example, in Figure 3(a), the *Train* will initiate and terminate the *Communication Supervision* collaboration

---

[1] Note that the roles of a collaboration use need not have the same name as the roles of the collaboration they are bound to.

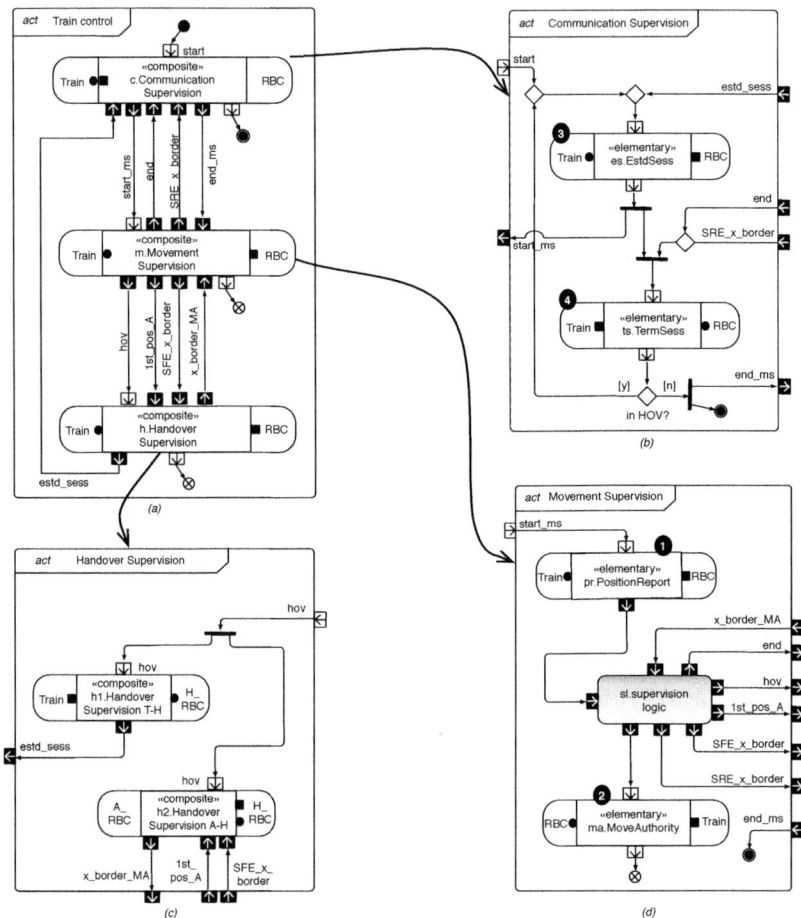

Fig. 3. Choreography of the Train Control System

with the *RBC*, while in the *Movement Supervision* collaboration, the initiating role is the *Train* and the terminating role is the *RBC*.

- *Execution order of collaborations.* As shown in Figure 3(a), the *Movement Supervision* is only started when the communication between the *Train* and the *RBC* has been established and a token is emitted on the *start_ms* pin.
- *Collaboration interactions.* The choreography model also has the capacity to specify how collaboration activities interact while they are active by means of streaming pins. For example when the *Train* reaches the region border, the movement supervision will issue a token via the *end* streaming output pin to the communication supervision to terminate the communication session.
- *Local actions.* As shown in Figure 3(d), the interaction between collaborations *PositionReport* and *MoveAuthority* can involve local actions like the *supervisionlogic* performed by the *RBC*.

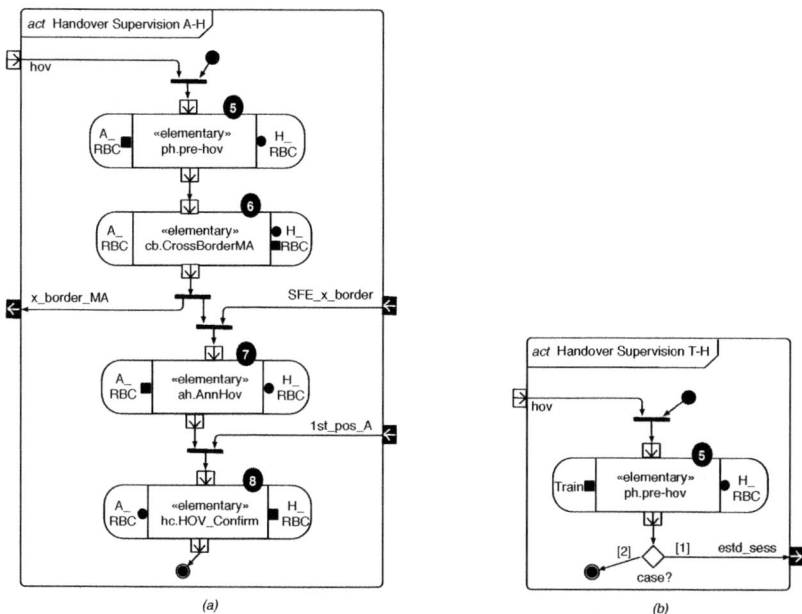

Fig. 4. Choreography of the Handover Supervision Collaboration in the Train Control System

The choreography model does not explicitly specify the behavior of individual components, for example, the *Train* or *RBC*. However, based on this level of specification, the behavior of components as well as their interfaces can be synthesized using a projection technique as explained in [7,8,11]. Elementary services result in elementary components performing a single role while composite service models result in composite components performing several roles. The next section explains the resulting component models.

2.2 Component Models

Figure 5 shows the communication supervision component *rbc_cs* for the *RBC* role derived from the choreography. Another component the *train_cs* for the *Train* role is shown in Figure 6. These component models specify the following aspects:

- *Interfaces:* Components have two types of interfaces: (1) semantic interfaces for inter-component interaction and, (2) local pins for intra-component interactions. Note that we use the term "semantic interface" differently from [2,15] where semantic interfaces have been defined using state-machines defining the observable behavior at the service interface. A novelty introduced here is to directly use the collaboration and activity diagram to define the semantic interfaces both statically and dynamically. In this way, the semantic interfaces become reusable building blocks with pins for local composition. For example, in Figure 5(a), the *rbc_cs* component has two semantic interfaces defined by the collaborations *EstSess* and *TermSess* responsible for establishing and terminating communication session with the *Train*.

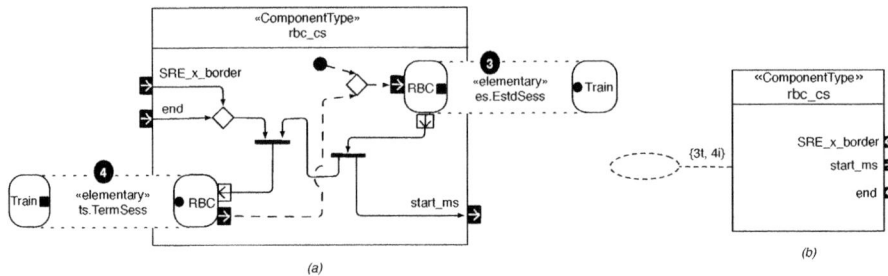

Fig. 5. The RBC Component in Communication Supervision Service

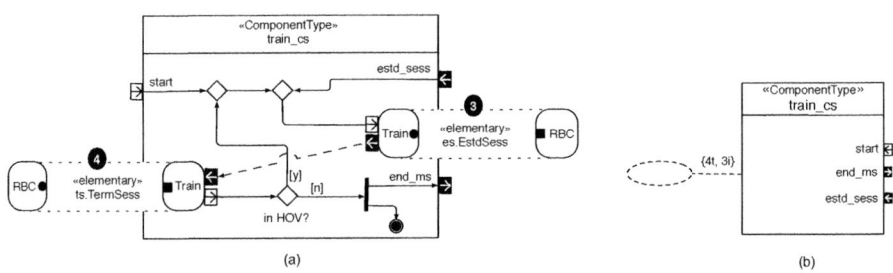

Fig. 6. The Train Component in the Communication Supervision Service

While monitoring the communication session, the *rbc_cs* component may interact with other local components using the streaming pins. The *rbc_cs* component has two input streaming pins *SRE_x_border* and *end*; and one output pin *start_ms*.

- *Internal behavior:* The internal behavior of a component is represented by the flows which link actions performed by the component. There are two different types of flows: initiating flows and responding flows. Initiating flows in Figure 5(a) are directly projected from the choreography models shown in Figure 3(b) using techniques presented in [7,8]. The responding flows capture the global flows that are external to the component (c.f [7] for details). Responding flows in a component specify when a particular role should be ready to respond to the external initiating role in a particular collaboration. Responding flows are represented by dashed lines. In Figure 5(a), there is a responding flow from the service role *RBC* in *ts.TermSess* to the role *RBC* in *es.EstdSess* to represent that when the *rbc_cs* component is finished playing its role in *ts.TermSess* service, it should be ready to respond in the *es.EstdSess* service in order to be ready to handle the handover activity.

Such component models can be represented externally as black boxes by hiding the internal details and showing just the information about interfaces as in Figure 5(b) and 6(b). The name and type of the pins corresponding to local interfaces is retained. The semantic interfaces are abstractly represented by a set $\{ns\}$ where n is a reference[2]

---

[2] In this paper we simply use numeric references.

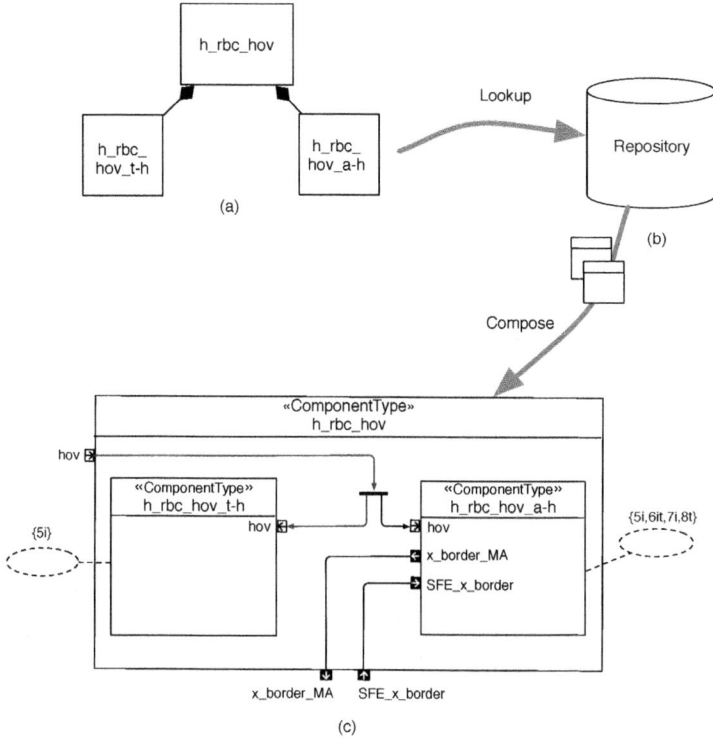

Fig. 7. Handingover RBC Component

to an interface and s is a character having values of (1) i representing that component plays initiating role; (2) t representing that component plays a terminating role; and (3) p representing that the component plays a participating role in a collaboration.

Semantic Interfaces of a component define virtual sockets, plugs and cables for wiring components together. As long as the plugs and sockets of a cable are compatible with the plugs and sockets of the components it links, we can rest assured that the wiring is valid.

3   Component Composition

This section discusses how to compose a component from smaller components. For illustration purposes, we select a *RBC* component from the Train Control System [10]. We assume that the inner parts of a composite component are in a repository and can be connected together via pins (as local interfaces) at their boundary. A component composition involves the following steps:

– *Specify the roles to be provided.* For example, the roles to be provided by the handing over *RBC* component *h_rbc_hov* in the Train Control System can be specified as in Figure 7(a) to consist of two elementary roles representing handover interactions with the Train (*h_rbc_hov_t-h*) and the accepting RBC (*h_rbc_hov_a-h*).

- *Find components providing the roles* in a component library, Figure 7(b). This can be done manually by the composer based on the requirements at hand or recommended/selected based on the information available in the service choreography models from which the roles (or components) have been synthesized.

- *Compose the selected components together* using the pins at the boundary of the selected components. The composition can be done manually by the composer or based on the information available in the service choreography. Pins may also be connected based on the data types that they use. Pins that are not connected to any other pins are made available at the boundary of a composite component. For example the composition of inner components in *h_rbc_hov*, shown in Figure 7(c), is done according to the choreography model of the handover supervision service in Figure 3(c). Note that pins *x_border_MA* and *SFE_x_border* are made available to the component (*h_rbc_hov*) boundary as local interfaces.

In similar way as the *h_rbc_hov*, a *RBC* component can be composed as shown in Figure 8. The role structure is shown in Figure 8(a). Note that inner roles of a component may be composite, i.e. they may be composed from inner roles. For example the *h_rbc_hov* and *a_rbc_hov* roles of the handing over RBC component are composed together to make a composite handing over RBC role (*rbc_hov*). Finally the *rbc_hov*, *rbc_cs* and *rbc_ms* are composed together to make a composite *RBC* component, as shown in Figure 8(c).

In a similar way, the components of the *Train* in a Train Control System can be composed. Note that the composed components can be placed back into the repository so that they can be reused in other compositions.

4   System Composition

This is the last composition step where system level components (i.e. not the inner roles of a component) are composed together in order to make a system. In this step, components are composed together mainly using semantic interfaces.

Figure 9 shows a system design model for the Train Control System. Note that the *Train* and *RBC* component types interact via collaborations (indicated by the dotted ellipse symbols referring to semantic interfaces) and send-receive message events (shown by solid line connecting local interface pins). In the cases where collaborating components have pins at the interfaces, such pins will be replaced by send and receive events. For example in Figure 9, there will be a *start-ms* sending event at the *RBC* component and corresponding receive event at the *Train* component.

Compatibility among components across semantic interfaces are ensured by the following steps:

- Each semantic interface is analyzed separately for internal consistency.
- Each component is analyzed separately to make sure it is consistent with all its semantic interfaces.

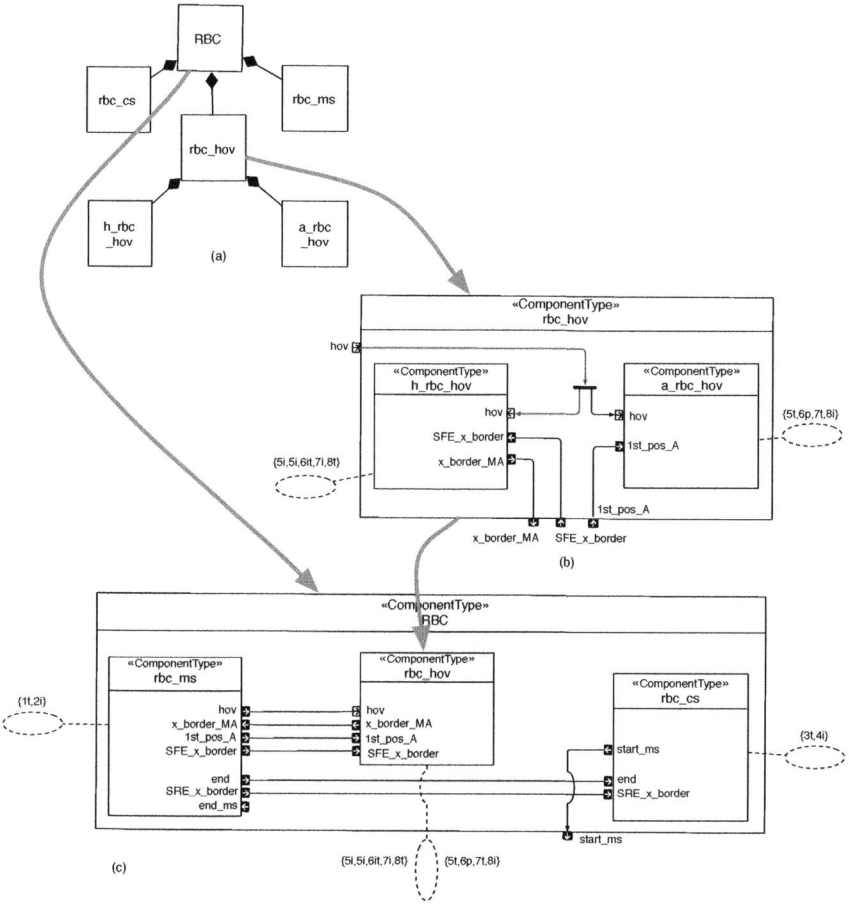

Fig. 8. Composition of a RBC Component

- When two components are linked we check that the linked roles are complementing roles of the same semantic interface; this assures that the link is consistent, but not that the ordering of roles using different links are compatible.
- We ensure compatibility in the ordering of roles by considering either the local ordering within each component against a global choreography, or by considering the responding flows of a component against the initiating flows of linked components.

The local interfaces are currently represented just as pins, and thus as a kind of static interface. The concept of external state machine, *esm*, used in the Arctis tool [19] may be used to define the external behavior across local interfaces, but this has not been elaborated here.

In a system, there may be many instances of the same service running concurrently with roles assigned to different system components. Each system component may play

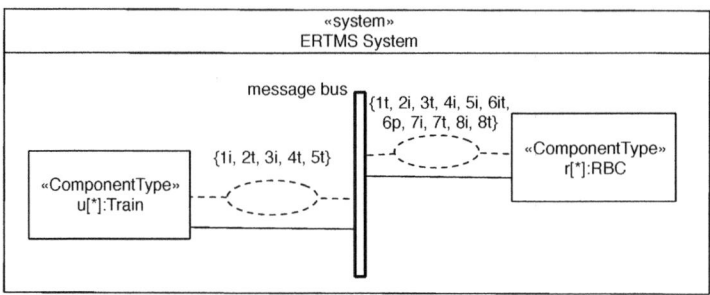

Fig. 9. System Design Model for Train Control System

roles in different services, and different components may be able to play different combinations of the roles. This variability is provided through the component and system composition steps.

5   Related Work

Traditionally component-based development is considered as an approach for software development in which software solutions are developed by assembling software parts defined as reusable components such that the desired system behavior is achieved through the collaboration of those parts [1,3,6]. However, there are many different definitions of what a component is depending on the context in which a component performs. For example, [1] defines a software component as a unit of composition with contractually specified interfaces and explicit context dependencies that can be deployed independently and be composed by third parties. In [14], a component is defined as a run-time software component which is a dynamically bindable package of one or more programs managed as a unit and accessed through documented interfaces that can be discovered at run-time. These definitions focus on the development or the execution of individual component without detailing how components are combined with others [3]. In general, software components can be defined as reusable and composable software units which can be composed together with other software components to form new, more composite structures [1,6].

A large body of work on component based development is based on the approach that first components (and their internal details) are designed and then static interfaces are defined. For example IDL based interfaces in CORBA and WSDL based interfaces in web-services. This means that additional work is needed to make interfaces to the components. In these approaches, existing components are usually assumed to be compatible and connectable as long as their static interfaces match. But in order to ensure that dynamic problems will never happen, it is also necessary to define and analyze interface behavior. However there is no standard way of defining interface behavior, but there are several proposals [21,22,23]. Most of these require additional efforts both to define the interfaces and to ensure that interfaces are consistent with component behavior, whereas we derive semantic interfaces as an integral part of the approach. The concept of semantic interfaces have previously been used in [2,15]. The role behaviors in that approach are projections of component behaviors, and not easily composed. In the work presented here, role behaviors are entities with interfaces suitable for composition.

In our approach, we start from the collaborative service models and derive components as well as interface contracts. Since we produce interface contracts and components from the same source, the additional cost of making components reusable is very low. Moreover the interface contracts are themselves reusable building blocks with behaviors that can be validated once and for all without considering particular components. Given the validated interfaces, checking the consistency of links among components is simply a matter of static matching.

Much related work focus on component composition [6,12,13]. For example, in [6], composite components are created by connecting existing components via a connector. In their approach, existing components, which are assumed to be compatible, are connected together either in sequential or parallel patterns. Our approach allows any pattern of composition as long as the interfaces are respected. We provide two types of interfaces to a component: local interfaces for local composition and semantic interfaces for system composition.

In our approach, components along with their interfaces may be automatically synthesized from service models [7,8,9]. External dependencies to a component are maintained by a special kind of flows called *responding flows* [8]. The responding flows are also useful to detect any problems with emergent behavior, also called realizability problems, as briefly described in [8].

Several approaches use a similar projection technique as we do, but without mapping external flows to responding flows within the components. The idea to keep collaborations as interface contracts is believed to be original in our approach, although SOA-ML[20] also uses collaboration for contracts.

6   Concluding Remarks

In this paper, we have presented and discussed a Model-Driven framework, which is based on the concept of collaborative services, to support component-based development. UML collaborations are used to model the structure of collaborating entities in a service. Global behavior, called choreography, is specified using UML activity diagrams. From collaborations with choreography we derive semantic interfaces that are building blocks and can be put into a library for reuse. We also synthesize reusable components of variable granularity equipped with semantic interfaces ready to be put into a repository. Given a library of semantic interfaces and components one can design new components and eventually a system, according to the requirements at hand, by composing existing components together effectively ensuring compatibility. We are not aware of other approaches that can support both traditional component composition and cross-cutting service composition in a similar way.

References

1. Szyperski, C.: Component Software: Beyond Object-Oriented Programming. Addison-Wesley Longman Publishing Co., Inc., Boston (2002)
2. Bræk, R., Floch, J.: ICT convergence: Modeling Issues. In: Amyot, D., Williams, A.W. (eds.) SAM 2004. LNCS, vol. 3319, pp. 237–256. Springer, Heidelberg (2005)
3. Crnkovic, I., Larsson, S., Chaudron, M.R.V.: Component-Based Development Process and Component Lifecycle. CIT 13(4), 321–327 (2005)
4. Jisa, Laurentiu, D.: Component Based Development Methods: Comparison, Computer Systems and Technologies, pp. 1–6 (2004)
5. Kraemer, F.A., Kathayat, S.B., Bræk, R.: Unified Modeling of Service Logic with User Interfaces. International Journal of Cooperative Information Systems (IJCIS) 20(2), 177–200 (2011)
6. Lau, K.-K., Wang, Z.: Software Component Models. IEEE Transactions on Software Engineering 33(10), 709–724 (2007)
7. Kathayat, S.B., Bræk, R., Le, H.N.: Automatic Derivation of Components from Choreographies - A Case Study. In: International Conference on Software Engineering, Phuket, Thailand (2010)
8. Kathayat, S.B., Bræk, R.: From Flow- Global Choreography to Component types. In: Kraemer, F.A., Herrmann, P. (eds.) SAM 2010. LNCS, vol. 6598, pp. 36–55. Springer, Heidelberg (2011)
9. Le, H., Kathayat, S.B.: A Framework to Support the Development of Collaborative Components. In: 9th Workshop on System/Software Architectures. LNBIP, vol. 83, pp. 378–384. Springer, Heidelberg (2011)
10. FIS for the RBC/RBC Handover, http://www.era.europa.eu/Document-Register/Documents/SUBSET-039v2.3.0.pdf (accessed on April 2011)
11. Bræk, R., Castejon, H.N., Le, H.N., Rosseb, J.E.Y.: Policy-Based Service Composition and Recommendation, Service Intelligence and Service Science: Evolutionary Technologies and Challenges. IGI Global (2010)
12. Almeida, J.P.A., Lacob, M.E., et al.: Model-Driven Development of Context-Aware Services. Distributed Applications and Interoperable Systems, 213–227 (2006)
13. Phung-Khac, A., Beugnard, A., Gilliot, J.-M., Segarra, M.-T.: Model-Driven Development of Component-Based Adaptive Distributed Applications. In: Proceedings of the 2008 ACM Symposium on Applied Computing, pp. 2186–2191. ACM, New York (2008)
14. de Cesare, S., Lycett, M., Macredie, R.D.: Development Of Component-based Information Systems (Advances in Management Information Systems). M. E. Sharpe Inc., USA (2005)
15. Jiang, S., Floch, J., Sanders, R.: Modeling and Validating Service Choreography with Semantic Interfaces and Goals. In: IEEE International Workshop on Service-Oriented System Engineering, pp. 73–78. IEEE Computer Society, Los Alamitos (2008)
16. Busi, N., Gorrieri, R., Guidi, C., Lucchi, R., Zavattaro, G.: Choreography and Orchestration Conformance for System Design. In: Ciancarini, P., Wiklicky, H. (eds.) COORDINATION 2006. LNCS, vol. 4038, pp. 63–81. Springer, Heidelberg (2006)
17. Qiu, Z., Zhao, X., Cai, C., Yang, H.: Towards the Theoretical Foundation of Choreography. In: Proceedings of the 16th International Conference on World Wide Web, pp. 973–982. ACM, New York (2007)
18. Salaün, G., Bultan, T.: Realizability of Choreographies Using Process Algebra Encodings. In: Leuschel, M., Wehrheim, H. (eds.) IFM 2009. LNCS, vol. 5423, pp. 167–182. Springer, Heidelberg (2009)

19. Kraemer, F.A., Slåtten, V., Herrmann, P.: Tool Support for the Rapid Composition, Analysis and Implementation of Reactive Services. Journal of Systems and Software 82, 2068–2080 (2009)
20. Object Management Group.: Service Oriented Architecture Modeling Language (SoaML) - Specification for the UML Profile and Metamodel for Services (November 2008)
21. Beyer, D., Chakrabarti, A., Henzinger, T.A.: An Interface Formalism for Web Services. In: Proceeding of the First International Workshop on Foundations of Interface Technologies (August 2005)
22. Beyer, D., Chakrabarti, A., Henzinger, T.A.: Web Service Interfaces. In: Proceedings of the 14th International Conference on World Wide Web, pp. 148–159. ACM, New York (2005)
23. Mencl, V.: Specifying Component Behavior with Port State Machines. Electronic Notes on Theoretical Computer Science 101C, 129–153 (2004)

Separation of Concerns with Transactional Regions

Thomas Cottenier[1], Aswin van den Berg[1], and Thomas Weigert[2]

[1] UniqueSoft LLC,
Palatine, IL, USA
{thomas.cottenier,aswin.vandenberg}@uniquesoft.com
[2] Dept. of Computer Science, Missouri University of Science and Technology,
Rolla, MO, USA
weigert@mst.edu

Abstract. Orthogonal regions allow a system represented as a state machine to be decomposed into a set of semi-independent modules. Regions of a state machine are usually not completely independent and interact through synchronization and communication primitives, causing coupling between the regions. As the number of regions in the system grows, these interactions become harder to maintain and the behavior of the system as a whole becomes harder to reason about. We introduce a transactional composition semantics, which overcomes these scalability limitations by implicitly and non-invasively capturing dependencies between regions. The approach is evaluated by comparing a monolithic legacy implementation of a telecommunication component to an implementation based on transactional region composition. Our results show that region-based modularization can achieve complete separation of concerns between the features of a non-trivial system and that the proposed transactional composition semantics enable region-based decomposition to be performed on a large scale.

Keywords: Language Constructs and Features – classes and objects, modules, packages.

1 Introduction

In the paper, we view orthogonal regions as a construct to decompose a system represented as a state machine into multiple dimensions of concern. Orthogonal regions were first introduced by Harel [1] as a method to overcome the state explosion problem in state machine representations of reactive systems. Orthogonal regions are typically used to encapsulate behaviors that are independent from each other. While the concept of orthogonal regions has been widely adopted in state machine based modeling formalisms such as the UML, it is mostly regarded as a concurrency concept, rather than a modularity construct.

A component that consists of a single region is structured according to a single dimension that is imposed by the states of that region. Behaviors that follow a different structure need to be projected on the transitions of the main decomposition, causing tangling and code replication. On the other hand, a component that consists of

I. Ober and I. Ober (Eds.): SDL 2011, LNCS 7083, pp. 168–185, 2011.
© Springer-Verlag Berlin Heidelberg 2011

multiple regions allows variables and methods associated with a feature of the system to be associated with their own decomposition into states and transitions.

Decomposition into multiple concerns requires a coordination mechanism to weave the independent behaviors into a coherent whole. The more there are concerns in the decomposition, the more complex the coordination of behaviors becomes.

In the case of regions, this coordination is performed using synchronization and communication primitives which group the transitions of different regions into execution steps. As the number of regions in the system grows, these interactions become harder to maintain. This is similar to the situation with aspect-oriented decompositions, where interactions and ordering relations between aspects are increasingly difficult to comprehend and maintain as the number of aspects increases.

As an example, we enhanced an industrial telecom component which had initially been developed as a monolithic state machine by a third party. This component went through several refactoring phases where behaviors were successively pulled out of the main state machine and modularized into their own region. We delivered the results of our experiments to our project manager in the form of printouts of the state diagrams of each region. He immediately acknowledged the improved structure of the system and the increased understandability of the individual features of the system. Yet, as the number of regions increased, he started complaining that the overall behavior of the system was becoming more difficult to follow. He finally had to resort to using AA batteries placed on the current state of each state diagram to keep track of the complex coordinated transitions of the system.

As the number of regions in the system grows, the individual regions become easier to understand in isolation but the overall behavior of the system becomes harder to reason about. The state of the system is determined by the possible combinations between the states of each region and each region can respond independently to a given input, producing an explosion of possible state configurations. Hence, the number of synchronization constraints between regions grows quadratically with the number of regions, making the approach impractical on a large scale.

In this paper, we describe a region composition operator that uses transactional semantics to treat region coordination primitives in one logical step of execution. This operator can implicitly and non-invasively capture complex interactions between regions, making the approach scalable over a large number of regions and hence, allowing a more complete modularization of the system.

The approach is evaluated by comparing size, coupling, and separation of concerns metrics for different versions of the telecom component mentioned above.

The paper is organized as follows. Section 2 discusses orthogonal regions as a modularization construct. Section 3 introduces transactional regions. Section 4 presents our case study and the experiment setting. Section 5 discusses the metrics used to evaluate the approach and summarizes the results of our study, discussing the advantages and drawbacks of the proposed approach in terms of size, coupling and separation of concerns. Section 6 reviews related work.

2   Regions as Modular Units

2.1   Orthogonal Regions

State machine representations of software are used for the development of embedded and real-time software systems in application domains such as telecom or avionics, where components interact according to protocols. Orthogonal regions are used to structure a state machine representation of a system into independent parts that encapsulate a sub-feature of the state machine.

Listing 1 presents an example of two regions that interact to implement a protocol. The regions are represented using a textual modeling language. Regions are defined in the context of a state machine which captures the behavior of a class. Each region encapsulates a set of states, transitions, attributes, and operations that are specific to the perspective or feature implemented by the region. The regions respond to a set of external signals defined by the ports of the class. In the example, regions *R1* and *R2* respond to the external signals *s, t, u* as defined by the *env* port of class *C*. In response to these inputs, region *R1* calls methods *f, g,* and *h* and region *R2* calls methods *m,* and *n*.

From the perspective of region *R1*, the protocol accepts the inputs $((s \cdot u) \mid (s \cdot i \cdot u))^*$. From the perspective of region *R2*, the protocol accepts the sequences of inputs $(t)^*$ or $(t \cdot u)^*$ depending on the value of the conditional at line 10 in region *R2*.

A state machine that consists of multiple regions executes according to steps between state configurations.

A state configuration is a reachable combination of the states of each region. In the example of Listing 1, the reachable configurations are *(A,X), (A,Y), (B,X), (B, Y)*, and *(C,Y)*.

An execution step is the response of the state machine to an external signal. In includes the behavior executed by all the regions in response to the signal.

```
     class C {
         port env in with s, t, u;
         statemachine sm () {
 1.      region R1 {                      region R2 {
 2.          operation f() void;              attr Boolean c = 1;
 3.          operation g() void;              operation m() void;
 4.          operation h() void;              operation n() void;
 5.          start { nextstate A; }          start { nextstate X; }
 8.      forstate A {                        forstate X {
 9.          input s() {                         input t() {
10.              f();                                if (c) {
11.              nextstate B;                            gen i();
12.          } }                                         m();
13.      forstate B {                                    nextstate Y;
14.          input i() {                             else {
15.              g();                                    n();
16.              nextstate C;                            nextstate X;
17.          } }                                     } } }
18.      forstate B, C {                     forstate Y {
19.          [R1::Y]input u(){                    input u() {
20.              h();                                 n();
21.              nextstate A;                         nextstate X;
22.          } } }                            } } } } }
```

Listing 1. Orthogonal composition of two regions

Listing 2 presents a state machine with a single region that is one possible implementation of the composition of region *R1* and *R2*. Listing 2 is more specific than Listing 1, as an arbitrary ordering was chosen between transitions executing in the same step.

The state machine of Listing 2 accepts the inputs $((s \cdot t \cdot u) / t)^*$ or $((s \cdot t \cdot u) / (t \cdot (u / s \cdot u))^*$ depending on the value of the conditional at lines 20 and 29.

```
1.  class C {                               27.        forstate B_X {
2.     port env in with s, t, u;           28.           input t() {
3.     statemachine sm () {                 29.              if(c) {
4.        region R1_R2 {                     30.                 m();
5.           attr Boolean c = 1;            31.                 g();
6.           operation f() void;            32.                 nextstate C_Y;
7.           operation g() void;            33.              } else {
8.           operation h() void;            34.                 n();
9.           operation m() void;            35.                 nextstate B_X;
10.          operation n() void;            36.           } } }
11.       start {                           37.        forstate A_Y {
12.             nextstate A_X;               38.           input u () {
13.       }                                  39.              n();
14.       forstate A_X {                     40.              nextstate A_X;
15.          input s() {                     41.           }
16.             f();                         42.           input s() {
17.             nextstate B_X;               43.              f();
18.          }                               44.              nextstate B_Y;
19.          input t() {                     45.           } }
20.             if(c) {                      46.        forstate B_Y, C_Y {
21.                m();                       47.           input u() {
22.                nextstate A_Y;            48.              n();
23.             } else {                      49.              h();
24.                n();                       50.              nextstate A_X;
25.                nextstate A_X;            51.        } } } } }
26.             } } }
```

Listing 2. One possible implementation of Listing 1

Region *R1* and *R2* interact through 3 types of interactions:

1. **Common inputs:** Both regions respond to input *u*. When *u* is received in the state configuration *(B, Y)* or *(C, Y)*, both transitions *(B // C, u , A)* in region *R1* and *(Y, u, X)* execute in a single step. The semantics of region composition do not impose an order of execution between the transitions.

2. **Internal signals:** At line 11 of region *R2*, an internal signal *i* is generated using the gen keyword. The signal is consumed in *R1* at line 14. When input *t* is received in configuration *(B, X)*, both transitions *(X, t, Y)* and *(B, i, C)* are executed in a single step. The semantics of region composition do not impose an order of execution between the transitions.

3. **Guards:** The transition *(B // C, u , A)* in region *R1* is guarded by the state *Y* of region *R2*, meaning that the transition can only be triggered when region *R2* is in state *Y*. Guards are evaluated at the beginning of each step. If the guard evaluates to false, the input is discarded by the region.

These semantics are largely based on the step semantics of statecharts as presented in [1] and further discussed in [2][3]. In contrast with other approaches, we do not allow sharing of attributes or operations between regions. This choice eliminates a significant source of interaction between regions and greatly simplifies its semantics. The use of global variables leads either to non-determinism or to an inefficient implementation due to the need for double buffering between regions.

The implementation of region composition can be performed in two ways. The first approach consists in weaving the regions into a single region, as done in the example of Listing 2. This approach has the advantage of statically detecting leaf states and unreachable states by flattening the transitions for all the possible combinations of states of the state machine. This approach does not scale well for systems composed of a large number of regions. The second approach consists of building an execution engine that selects and executes the enabled transitions of the different regions given the current configuration. This approach is scalable, but cannot statically prevent deadlocks. We therefore implement a hybrid approach using a lightweight static checker to pre-compute the reachable configurations of states and other information, which is used by the execution engine.

2.2   Regions as Units of Modularity

Assuming the regions *R1* and *R2* correspond to separate features of the protocol, the state machine of Listing 1 is more modular than the state machine of Listing 2. The composition of the regions introduces tangling and crosscutting in the implementation of Listing 2. Replication of code appears at lines 19-24 and 28-34, lines 15-16 and 42-43 and lines 38-39 and 47-48. Tangling occurs between the features on the transitions *(B_X, t, C_Y)* and *(B_Y || C_Y, u, A_X)*.

Each region defines a set of states that correspond to the view of the protocol from the perspective of the feature. In order to produce a coherent whole, these perspectives are composed using common inputs, internal signals, and guards. Hence, the regions are not completely independent. In Listing 1, a transition of region *R1* is guarded by a state of region *R2* at line 19 and region R2 interacts with region R1 through an internal signal at line 11.

Maintenance and refinement of a region requires knowledge about the structure of the other regions it interacts with. In particular, the regions cannot be tested in isolation without simulating the other regions through stubs.

The dependencies between regions can be extracted from the region implementation using an aspect-oriented notation. The notation presented in Listing 3 captures synchronization between regions. The synch construct is used to generate internal signals at locations determined by a pointcut expression. The guard construct introduces guards in transitions matched by a pointcut expression. The synch construct allows the internal signal *i* generated at line 11 in the region *R2* of Listing 1 to be specified outside of region *R2*. The guard of Listing 3 captures the guard *R2::Y* at line 19 of region *R1*.

As with aspects, syntactically decoupling regions using synchs and guards does not make them completely independent. Modifying a region requires awareness about the synchs and the guards that are defined in terms of the states and transition of this region. Yet, it allows individual regions to be refined and tested independently.

```
synch i() when transition (forstate X input t() nextstate Y)  && within (R2);
guard transition (forstate B, C input u()) && within (R1) with R2::Y;
```

Listing 3. Aspect-oriented notation for internal signals (synchs) and guards

3 Transactional Regions

3.1 Motivation

When building complex systems with orthogonal regions, it is often the case that multiple regions interact to handle a single environment input. Transitions from multiple regions are executed in one execution step in response to an input.

Listing 4 presents an example of three regions that interact to handle an environment request and produce a response.

```
1. region R1 {               region R2 {               region R3 {
2.   attr req_t r;             attr req_t r;             attr req_t r;
3.   attr x_t x;               attr y_t y;               attr z_t z;
4.   forstate A {              forstate X {              forstate S {
5.     [R2::X && R3::S]          [R1::A && R3::S]          [R1::A && R2::X]
6.     input req (r) {          input req_2 (r) {         input req_3 (r) {
7.       if                       if                        if
validate_req1(r, x)){      (validate_req2(r, y)){    (validate_req3(r, z)){
8.       gen req_2(r);            gen req_3(r);             gen req_ok();
9.       nextstate B;            nextstate Y;              nextstate T;
10.    } else {                } else {                  } else {
11.       gen req_fail1();        gen req_fail2();          gen req_fail3();
12.       output rsp(FAIL);      nextstate Z; } }          nextstate U; } }
13.       nextstate C; }}}      [R1::A && R3::S]          [R1::A && R2::X]
14. forstate B {               input req_fail1 {         input       req_fail1,
15.   input req_fail2,           nextstate Z; } }        req_fail2 {
req_fail3 {                   forstate Y {                nextstate U; } } }
16.     output rsp(FAIL);        input req_fail3{
17.     nextstate C; }            nextstate Z; } } }
18.   input req_ok(){
19.     output rsp(OK);
20.     nextstate B; }}}
```

Listing 4. Transactional interaction pattern between regions

Each region contains its own data and operations, and performs validation of the environment request using its data. First, all regions also need to be ready to accept the request. This is expressed using the guards at line 5.

In order to produce a response, the regions need to agree on a common outcome. Each region needs to be informed of the result of the validation performed by the other regions.

In the implementation of Listing 4, an arbitrary order of execution between the different regions was chosen and region *R1* was selected to be responsible for sending a response back to the environment. Region *R1* first validates the request against its data, represented by the *x* attribute. If the request is valid from *R1*'s perspective, an internal signal *req_2* is generated, which triggers the validation of the request from *R2*'s perspective. If successful, the request is forwarded to *R3* using the *req_3* internal signal, which performs the final validation.

Region *R1* is notified of the final decision performed in region *R3* by the *req_ok* internal signal and sends the response back to the environment. In case the validation fails in one region the other regions need to be notified so they can step into the appropriate state.

Variants of this interaction pattern appear whenever multiple regions act together to produce a common result. The pattern requires choosing an arbitrary order of execution between the regions, and arbitrarily selecting a region to collect the result of the interaction. For an interaction between n regions, the pattern requires n-1 guards in each region, n-1 internal signals to forward the request, and n internal signals to propagate failures. Hence, the pattern involves $n \cdot (n-1)$ guards and n^2 transitions to handle the propagation of request failures.

In complex systems that consist of many regions, the number of guards and internal signals required to implement the interaction pattern rapidly becomes cumbersome and the system becomes hard to reason about and to maintain. The pattern also introduces high coupling between the regions, even if the guards and internal signals are extracted from the region implementation.

3.2 Transactional Composition

The interaction pattern of Listing 4 is clearly transactional: the regions perform handshaking to agree on a common outcome for the transition. The transaction composition notation allows this behavior to be specified without introducing coupling between the regions. We introduce syntax to capture the interaction pattern of Listing 4 explicitly without requiring the exchange of internal signals between regions.

Listing 5 expresses that regions *R1*, *R2* and *R3* engage in a transaction triggered by the *req* signal. The transaction is defined in terms of the exception type *InvalidRequest*. The source state of the transaction is a pre-condition expressed in terms of the states of the regions that participate in the transaction. The transaction steps into a result state that is a post-condition for the transaction, expressed as a logical expression over the resulting states of the regions. The transaction specification first propagates the request to the three regions using internal signals at line 4. If the transaction completes correctly a response is sent to the environment. If the *InvalidRequest* exception is raised during the transaction, the system responds by sending an error code.

Without transactions, exceptions are local to a region. An exception raised in one region does not propagate to other regions. Using transaction, an exception that is raised in one transition propagates to the transition of other regions that are executed during the same execution step.

Listing 6 presents three regions that implement the same interaction pattern as Listing 4 using transactional composition. The transitions *(A, req_1, B)*, *(X, req_2, Y)*, and *(S, req_3, T)* are executed during the same step because they are triggered by the internal signal generated at line 4 of Listing 6. The validation operations *validate_req1*, *validate_req2* and *validate_req3* have been modified to throw the *InvalidRequest* exception if the validation fails. The exception handlers at lines 9-10 handle a transactional exception. If the exception is raised in one region, the corresponding handlers are executed in all regions.

The transaction specification handles the interaction pattern of Listing 4 with minimal coupling between the regions. The regions do not explicitly refer to each other. The interaction occurs implicitly, through the sharing of the *InvalidRequest* exception type. The transaction specification handles the regions symmetrically, as opposed to the solution of Listing 4. We do not need to select an arbitrary execution order between the regions.

```
1.  transaction T {
2.    forstate R1::A && R2::X && R3::S {
3.      input req (r) {
4.        gen req_1(r), req_2(r), req_3(r);
5.        try {
6.          output rsp(OK);
7.          nextstate R1::B && R2::Y && R3::T;
8.        } catch InvalidRequest {
9.          output rsp(FAIL);
10.         nextstate R1::C && R2::Z && R3::U; } } }
```

Listing 5. Transaction specification

```
1.region R1 {            region R2 {              region R3 {
2. attr req_t r;           attr req_t r;            attr req_t r;
3. attr x_t x;             attr y_t y;              attr z_t z;
4. forstate A {            forstate X {             forstate S {
5.   input req_1 (r) {       input req_2 (r) {        input req_3 (r) {
6.     try {                  try {                    try {
7.       validate_req1(p,       validate_req2(p,         validate_req3(p,
x);                       y)){                     y)){
8.         nextstate B;           nextstate Y;             nextstate U;
9.       } catch                } catch                  } catch
InvalidRequest {          InvalidRequest {         InvalidRequest {
10.        nextstate C; }         nextstate Z; }           nextstate V; }
} } }                     } } }                    } } }
```

Listing 6. Transaction composition of regions

4 Case Study

We evaluate the approach by comparing two implementations of a telecommunication component using modularity metrics. The component used in the case study is a base station controller of a cellular network. Figure 1 presents a high level view of a typical cellular network. A mobile subscriber (MS) communicates with the network through a set of base stations (BS). Each base station provides coverage over a cell of the network. Adjacent base stations are grouped into paging groups. Data packets flow from the network to a base station through a series of routers (RTR), which are controlled by a network component called the base station controller (BSC). The base station controller handles the session of a subscriber according to subscriber context information which is maintained in a database (CTXT). The communication between the network and the mobile subscriber is secured by an authentication protocol, controlled by an authentication server (AUTH). The base station controller monitors network incoming data for a mobile subscriber through a proxy router (PROXY).

This component provides a number of key services: *Handover* allows a subscriber to move from one cell to another. *Standby Mode* saves battery and network bandwidth by not keeping track of a subscriber that is not actively communicating. *Paging* allows the base station controller to locate a subscriber that is inactive to deliver incoming packets.

The behavior of the base station controller can be decomposed into the following sub-behaviors. This decomposition is based on the data structures and resources of the system such as communication ports: Session Control (SC), Context Management (CX), Authentication Keys (AK), Standby Mode (SM), Handover (HO), Paging Control (PC), Proxy Monitoring (PY), Router Control (RR). These features are not further described.

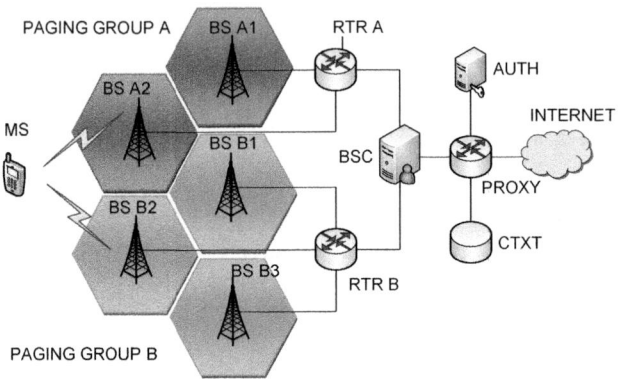

Fig. 1. Cellular Network

The following metrics are used to compare different implementations of the BSC network component.

4.1 Size Metrics

We use size metrics to assess the relative importance and complexity of different entities of the models and to compare the complexity of the different implementation. The metrics used include:

- Lines of code (LOC) of an entity or a feature of the system. When counting the number of lines of code for a transition, we count all the code that is specific to the transition, including the size of operations that are specific to the transition.
- Number of transitions (NT) and number of states (NS) of a region or a state machine. The number of transitions and states reflect the amount of structure of the system.

4.2 Modularity Metrics

We use coupling and concern diffusion metrics to assess the modularity of the system. These metrics are adapted from the work of Garcia et al. [6] [7] to be applicable to state machines.

- Coupling between transitions (CT) indicates the amount of sharing between two transitions. We count one coupling dependency between two transitions when one shared variable or resource such as a timer is accessed by both transitions.
- Coupling distribution (CD) of a transition indicates the number of transitions that it interacts with through shared variables or resources. As the different versions of the system have different number of transitions, we use a normalized version of the CD by dividing the number of transitions by the total number of transitions. A value of 25% indicates that the transition interacts with 25% of the transitions of the system.

- Concern diffusion over transitions (DT) indicates how many transitions implement part of the functionality of a given concern. We use a normalized version of the DT.

5   Case Study Results

We compare two implementations of the network component using size, coupling and separation of concerns metrics. The first version of the system is a monolithic implementation, which is structured according to interface protocols of the system. The second version uses orthogonal regions to encapsulate the features of the system and transactional regions to completely isolate the regions from each other.

5.1   Monolithic Implementation

The monolithic implementation was performed by a third party using a commercial UML tool. The main state machine defining the system behavior is composed of only 3 states: Init, Standby, and Active, which correspond to the standby mode feature. The engineers structured the model according to the interface specifications of the system by grouping the transitions of the system according to the interface protocols described in the requirements. The features described in Section 4.2 are not modularized. The reason for this decomposition is that the requirement documents for the system include detailed descriptions of the action to be performed in response to the different input signals of the system, whereas the features and sub-behaviors of the component are described in more abstract terms in the system-wide system architecture document.

5.2   Transactional Implementation

The transactional implementation was obtained through successive refactoring of the third party model. The design was guided by the features of the system rather than the interface specifications. First, the variables and data structures that contribute to common features were grouped together and encapsulated into regions. Second, the guards and internal signals exchanged between the regions were extracted and expressed as synchs and guards. Third, the global variables that were still shared between regions where eliminated. The environment signals where translated into internal signals using synchs and broadcast to the different regions to propagate the signal parameters and update the data handled by each region. Finally, all the synchs and guards where replaced by transactions, eliminating all dependencies between the regions.

5.3   Metrics Comparison

5.3.1   Size
Figure 2 compares the size of the monolithic implementation to the size of the transactional implementation using lines of code. For the monolithic implementation, the graph displays the sum of the size of the transitions associated with each interface protocol. For the transactional implementation, the graph sums up the size of the

transitions for the transactions (IF) and for the regions. The graph shows that the transactional implementation has about the same size as the monolithic implementation in terms of lines of code.

Figure 3 shows the size of the system obtained by counting the number of transitions of the monolithic implementation and the number of states and transitions for the transactional implementation. As the monolithic implementation only contains a single region, its states are shared by all the transitions of the system. The monolithic implementation counts 3 states for 30 transitions, whereas the transactional implementation has 20 states for 84 transitions. The transactional implementation has almost 3 times more transitions than the monolithic implementation.

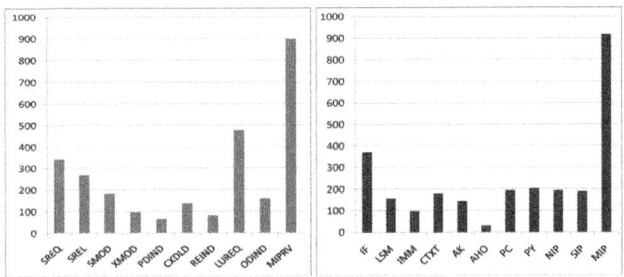

Fig. 2. LOC (a) Monolithic (b) Transactions

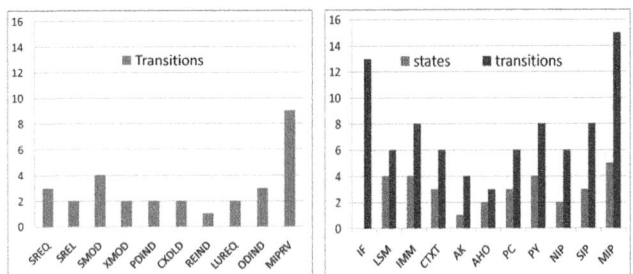

Fig. 3. States / Transitions (a) Monolithic (b) Transactions

5.3.2 Modularity

Figure 4 depicts the amount of coupling between the transitions of the monolithic implementations. The two horizontal axes correspond to transitions. The transitions are grouped according to the interface they implement, indicated by white boxes along the diagonal. The vertical scale corresponds to the amount of coupling between the intersecting transitions. This graph can be interpreted as a Design Structure Matrix [9], where dependencies are weighted based on the amount of coupling. For simplicity, we do not characterize the direction of the dependencies. Hence, all dependencies appear above the diagonal.

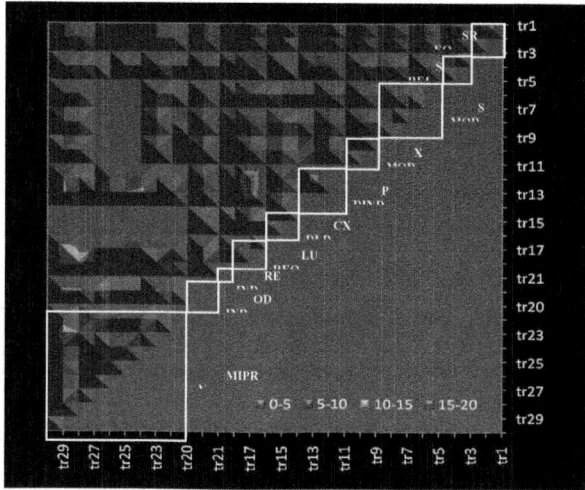

Fig. 4. Coupling between transitions (monolithic)

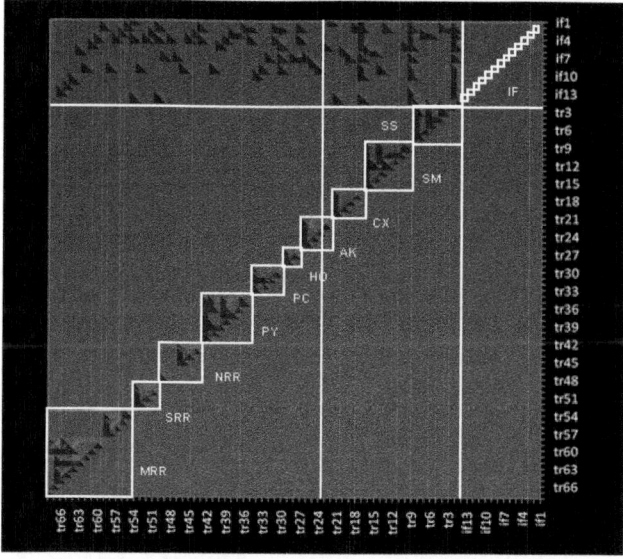

Fig. 5. Coupling between transitions (transactional)

The monolithic implementation contains transitions that interact through up to 20 shared variables or resources. In the graph, we can identify transitions that have a high level of coupling with other transitions. In particular, there is a large amount of coupling between the session request, power down indication, and location update protocols and all the other protocols. On the other hand, the context download and reentry complete protocols appear fairly independent from the other protocols.

Figure 5 shows the amount of coupling between the transitions of the transactional implementation. The transitions are grouped according to the region or the transaction they belong to, again using white boxes along the diagonal to indicate these. The figure shows that each region is completely independent from the other regions of the system. The regions depend on the transactions they are part of. All interactions between transitions are concentrated in the transactions, as seen on the top of the chart. Figure 6 presents a three-dimensional view of Figure 4 and 5, providing a better comparison of the amount of interactions between the transitions of both implementations.

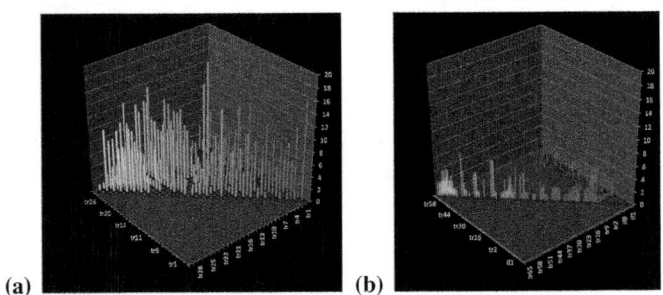

Fig. 6. Coupling between transitions (a) Monolithic (b) Transactional

Figure 7 shows how the coupling between transitions spreads over the system. The transitions of the monolithic implementation interact with a very high percentage of transitions in the system. In particular, the transition that handles location updates interacts with 95% of the transitions in the system. On the other hand, the transitions of the regions in the transactional implementation only interact with the transitions of the same region. Furthermore, the transactions themselves only interact with a small amount of transitions in the system. These interactions consist of guards and internal signals between the transactions and the regions.

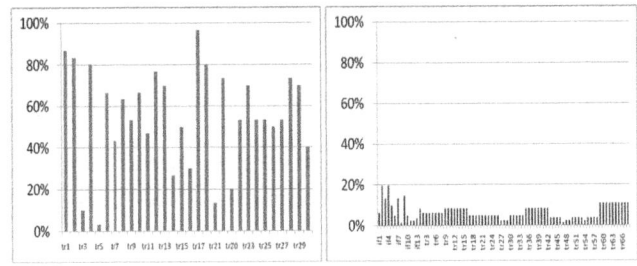

Fig. 7. Coupling between transitions (a) Monolithic (b) Transactional

Figure 8 presents the diffusion of the features that are modularized in one implementation over the transitions of the other implementation. For the monolithic implementation, many features spread over a large percentage of the transitions. In the case of the transactional implementation, the behavior associated with specific protocols spreads over a relatively smaller number of transitions.

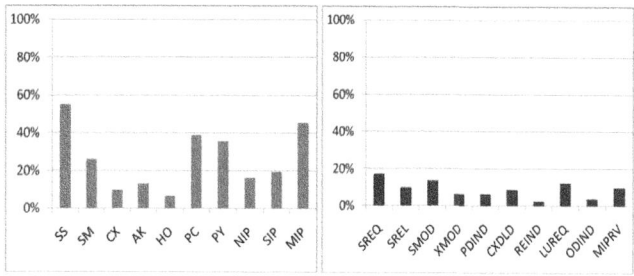

Fig. 8. (a) Diffusion of the features - monolithic (b) Diffusion of the protocols - transactional

5.4 Discussion

The results presented in the previous section can be summarized as follows:

1. **Size:** Both models are about the same size. The impact of the elimination of crosscutting in terms of lines of code is partially compensated by an increased in size due to the additional structure of the model. This impact on the size of the model is moderate because the behavior that is replicated across different transitions is already encapsulated using functional decomposition.

2. **Structure:** The transactional implementation has more structure than the monolithic implementation. The transactional implementation contains two important structuring mechanisms: the states of the regions, which indicate the phase of computation the region is ready to perform and the transaction definitions, which indicates how the regions collaborate to implement a protocol.

3. **Modularity:** The transitions of the monolithic implementation are tightly coupled with each other. In the transactional implementation, there are no dependencies between the different regions. The transactional region composition achieves complete separation of concerns between the regions. The transactions are completely independent from each other as well. The only remaining dependencies are between the regions and the transactions they participate in.

4. **Diffusion:** The shift from a decomposition based on the interfaces of the system towards decomposition based on the features of the system causes diffusion of the interface protocols over the regions. In the monolithic implementation each signal is handled by a specific transition which completes all the tasks required to handle the input. Using the region-based decomposition, the behavior associated with an input is distributed over the different regions. Yet, the diffusion of the protocols over the regions is less important than the diffusion of the features over the transitions of the protocols. The transaction structure controls the diffusion by providing a high level view of all the behaviors associated with the input, as well as the different possible completions (using the transactional exception types).

5. **Flexibility:** The modularization of the different types of routing protocols between the NRR, SRR and MRR regions allows subscriber sessions to load only the routing region that corresponds to its type of subscriber. In the monolithic implementation, these behaviors are entangled and cannot be loaded separately. As the system needs to support many sessions concurrently, the impact of this

modularization on memory consumption is significant. For a typical distribution of subscriber sessions, we measured that the memory used by the transactional implementation is 15% less than for the monolithic implementation.

5.5 Summary

The transactional implementation achieves complete separation of concerns between the behaviors implemented by the regions. Each region depends on the transaction specifications it participates in but is completely independent from the implementation of the other regions. They use the states of the different regions to express pre and post-conditions for the transaction. Hence, the states and triggers of the regions need to be visible to the transaction specifications. Complete separation of concerns between the regions means that they can be refined and tested independently, as long as the states and triggers exposed to the transaction specifications do not change.

6 Related Work

Statecharts [1][2][3] introduce two concepts: hierarchical state diagrams and orthogonal regions. This paper focused on orthogonal regions but did not extend on the concept of hierearchical state diagrams. Transactional composition of region can be seen as a way to impose hierachy on top of a set of completely independent regions. Yet, transactions provide a more flexible hierarchical structuring mechanism than hiearchical state diagrams. Hierarchical state diagrams impose a strict tree-like structure over the regions of the system. Each sub-region is part of a state of an upper-region. Hence, all the states and transitions of the same regions are clustered into the same super-state. On the other hand, transactional composition allows a set of transitions from different regions to be clustered together into a single step of execution, as long as the transactions themselves follow a strict tree structure.

Transactional region composition can be seen as a form of symmetric AOP [8]. Each region provides a stateful view of the behavior of the system, seen from the perspective of the feature modularized by the region. Symmetric AOP approaches such as Hyper/J focus on the symmetric merging of structural features such as inheritance hierarchies. When it comes to the merging of behavior, these approaches come short because of the lack of structure of behavior specifications and resort to join point based merging of behavior using asymmetric expressions. The use of state machines enables our approach to use the additional structure provided by states and transition to merge behaviors without having to resort to pointcut expressions over statements and expressions within the transitions.

Transaction specifications can be seen as design rules [9] or crosscutting interfaces [10][11]. A transaction defines an interface consisting of pre-conditions, triggers and post conditions for transitions of the participating regions. It defines an interface that cuts across the decomposition into features, and enables the system to support a decomposition into features and a decomposition into interface protocols simultaneously.

The work presented in this paper builds on a large body of research in the area of Aspect-Oriented Modeling [12]. Aldawud identifies the similarities between aspect-oriented compositions and the composition of regions in statecharts, and proposes to model aspect-oriented composition using internal signals between orthogonal regions [13]. In [14], Mahoney builds on top of Aldawud's work and proposes a notation to decouple regions by extracting internal signals from statecharts using an aspect-oriented notation which corresponds to the synch concept presented in the paper. Zhang [15] proposes an aspect-oriented notation to modularize crosscutting concerns across different regions of UML state machines. In particular, Zhang proposes a notation to capture synchronization constraints between regions which is similar to the concept of guards presented in this paper. Protocol modeling [16] propose a semantic for the orthogonal composition of behaviors using a state machine-based notation based on CSP. The protocol modeling approach can be mapped to the composition of orthogonal regions, and is similar to the approach advocated by Aldawud.

Neither of these approaches achieves complete independence between the regions. The AOM approaches use small examples to illustrate the proposed syntax and therefore do not address the issue of scalability and maintenance of large systems. Neither of the proposed approach was applied to the development of a real system and the presented results are not evaluated quantitatively.

The transaction semantics used in this paper are inspired from work on exception handling in concurrent asynchronous systems such as atomic actions [17]. Atomic actions define recovery blocks that span over multiple processes and define a semantic for exception handling within these blocks. An exception raised within an atomic action causes all the participating processes to execute their corresponding exception handler. In this paper, the semantics of atomic actions were adapted to simplify the composition of independent modules, rather than to handle failures in concurrent systems.

7 Conclusions

We introduced transactional composition of orthogonal regions. Transactional composition specifications serve three purposes. First, they capture all the dependencies between regions into a separate module using an aspect-oriented semantic, making the regions completely independent from each other. This specification is more concise than descriptions that enumerate the dependencies between regions explicitly, which makes the approach practical for systems that consist of a large number of regions. Second, they expose elements of the regions such as source states, triggers and target states that need to be maintained during the development to ensure the correct composition of the system. Hence, transactional composition specifications define an interface that cuts across the different regions. Each region can be refined and tested independently as long as the entities exposed in the interface are maintained. Finally, transactional composition specifications provide a view of the system from the perspective of the external interface of the system, which is complementary to the decomposition into regions.

We evaluate the approach by comparing a monolithic implementation of a real-world telecom system to a transactional implementation using size, coupling and separation of concern metrics. Our results show that the transactional implementation is more structured and much more modular than the monolithic implementation.

Further research is required to determine how to apply the approach in a systematic way. In particular, we need to determine the criteria to be used to group features and sub-behaviors into separate regions. We also need a method to apply the decomposition recursively, by successively decomposing behaviors into smaller parts. This approach also has repercussions on how the requirement documents should be structured. In the telecom domain, precise requirement documents are structured according to interface specifications rather than features. It is yet to be determined how these requirements can be defined in a way that supports both decompositions simultaneously.

References

1. Harel, D.: Statecharts: A visual formalism for complex systems. Science of Computer Programming 8(3), 231–274 (1987)
2. Harel, D., Naamad, A.: The STATEMATE Semantics of Statecharts. ACM Transactions on Software Engineering and Methodology (TOSEM) 5(4), 293–333 (1996)
3. Harel, D., Kugler, H.: The RHAPSODY semantics of statecharts (or, on the executable core of the UML). In: Ehrig, H., Damm, W., Desel, J., Große-Rhode, M., Reif, W., Schnieder, E., Westkämper, E. (eds.) INT 2004. LNCS, vol. 3147, pp. 325–354. Springer, Heidelberg (2004)
4. Cottenier, T., van den Berg, A., Elrad, T.: The Motorola WEAVR: Model Weaving in a Large Industrial Context. In: AOSD 2007, Industry Track, Vancouver, Canada (2007)
5. Cottenier, T., van den Berg, A., Elrad, T.: Joinpoint Inference from Behavioral Specification to Implementation. In: Bateni, M. (ed.) ECOOP 2007. LNCS, vol. 4609, pp. 476–500. Springer, Heidelberg (2007)
6. Sant'Anna, C., et al.: On the Reuse and Maintenance of Aspect-Oriented Software: An Assessment Framework. In: Proceedings of the Brazilian Symposium on Software Engineering, Manaus, Brazil, pp. 19–34 (2003)
7. Garcia, A., et al.: Modularizing design patterns with aspects: a quantitative study. In: Proceedings of the 4th International Conference on Aspect-oriented Software Development, Chicago, USA, pp. 3–14 (2005)
8. Tarr, P., Ossher, H., Harrison, W., Sutton, S.: N Degrees of Separation: Multi-Dimensional Separation of Concerns. In: Proceedings of the 21st International Conference on Software Engineering, Los Angeles, USA, pp. 107–119 (1999)
9. Baldwin, C., Clark, K.: Design Rules. The Power of Modularity, vol. I. MIT Press, Cambridge (2000)
10. Kiczales, G., Mezini, M.: Aspect-oriented programming and modular reasoning. In: Proceedings of the 27th International Conference on Software Engineering, St Louis, USA, pp. 49–58 (2005)
11. Grisswold, W., et al.: Modular Software Design with Crosscutting Interfaces. IEEE Software 23(1), 51–60 (2006)
12. Kienzle, J., Gray, J., Stein, D., Cottenier, T., Cazzola, W., Aldawud, O.: Report of the 14th International Workshop on Aspect-Oriented Modeling. In: Ghosh, S. (ed.) MODELS 2009. LNCS, vol. 6002, pp. 98–103. Springer, Heidelberg (2010)

13. Elrad, T., Aldawud, O., Bader, A.: Aspect-Oriented Modeling: Bridging the Gap between Implementation and Design. In: Batory, D., Blum, A., Taha, W. (eds.) GPCE 2002. LNCS, vol. 2487, pp. 189–201. Springer, Heidelberg (2002)
14. Mahoney, M., Bader, A., Aldawud, O., Elrad, T.: Using Aspects to Abstract and Modularize Statecharts. In: The 5th Aspect-Oriented Modeling Workshop in Conjunction with the UML 2004 Conference, Lisbon, Portugal (2004)
15. Zhang, G., Hölzl, M., Knapp, A.: Enhancing UML State Machines with Aspects. In: Engels, G., Opdyke, B., Schmidt, D.C., Weil, F. (eds.) MODELS 2007. LNCS, vol. 4735, pp. 529–543. Springer, Heidelberg (2007)
16. McNeile, A., Roubtsova, E.: Aspect-Oriented Development Using Protocol Modeling. To appear in A Common Case Study for Aspect-Oriented Modeling Approaches, Transactions on Aspect Oriented Software Development. LNCS, vol. 7 (2010)
17. Campbell, R., Randell, B.: Error Recovery in Asynchronous Systems. IEEE Transactions on Software Engineering SE-12(8), 811–826 (1986)

Real-Time Signaling in SDL*

Marc Krämer, Tobias Braun, Dennis Christmann, and Reinhard Gotzhein

Networked Systems Group,
University of Kaiserslautern, Germany
{kraemer,tbraun,christma,gotzhein}@cs.uni-kl.de

Abstract. SDL is a formal specification language for distributed systems, which provides significant, yet limited real-time expressiveness by its notion of time (now) and its timer mechanism. In our current work, we are investigating various ways to augment this expressiveness, by proposing language extensions and exploiting degrees of freedom offered by SDL's formal semantics. This paper presents some recent results of our work: a mechanism for real-time signaling, which can be roughly characterized as a generalization of SDL timers. More specifically, we propose to add the possibility of specifying a time interval for the reception of ordinary SDL signals, by stating their time of arrival and expiry. This extension can be used, for instance, to specify time-triggered scheduling, which is required in many real-time systems. In the paper, we present the concept of real-time signaling, propose a syntactical extension of SDL, define its formal semantics, outline our implementation, show excerpts of a control application, and report on measurement results.

1   Introduction

A real-time system is a reactive system in which the correctness of the system behavior depends not only on the correct ordering of events, but also on their occurrence in time (cf. [1]). Execution of a real-time system is usually decomposed into tasks (e.g., local computation units, message transfers), which are initiated when a significant change of state occurs (*event-triggered*), or at determined points in time (*time-triggered*), and which are to be completed before their deadlines.

SDL [2] is a formal description technique for distributed systems and communication systems, and has been promoted for real-time systems, too. By its notion of time (now) and its timer mechanism, SDL provides significant, yet limited real-time expressiveness. In SDL, a task can, for instance, be specified by a single transition (*simple task*) or by a sequence of related transitions (*complex task*).

In our current work, we are looking into various ways to augment SDL's real-time capabilities, by defining language extensions as well as by exploiting

---

* This work is supported by the Carl Zeiss Foundation and the German Research Foundation (DFG) within the priority program SPP 1305 "Control Theory of Digitally Networked Dynamical Systems" under grants GO 503/8-1 and LI 724/15-1.

degrees of semantic freedom (see, e.g. [3]). In this paper, we address the problem of specifying and executing *time-triggered task schedules* in distributed real-time systems, introducing and applying a mechanism called *real-time signaling*, with SDL as design language. In particular, we propose a syntactical extension of SDL, define its formal semantics, outline our implementation, and demonstrate *real-time signaling* in use.

Following this introduction are six sections. In Sect. 2, we present our concept of specifying and executing time-triggered schedules in SDL, and examine possible solutions. Based on our findings, we propose a syntactical extension of SDL for *real-time signaling* and present its formal semantics in Sect. 3. Section 4 gives an overview of the implementation of *real-time signaling*, including signaling to the SDL environment. In Sect. 5, we present excerpts of a networked control system and measurements that provide evidence for the effectiveness of our solution. Section 6 reports on related work. Section 7 contains conclusions and an outlook.

2   Conceptual Considerations

A time-triggered schedule is a list of tasks and their initiation points in time. To keep the list manageable, it can be restricted to tasks that are scheduled strictly periodically. In this case, it is sufficient to have one entry per task, defining period and time of first execution. For timely behavior, decomposition into tasks and their initiation points in time have to be carefully planned to ensure that required resources (e.g., CPU, shared medium) are available, and that tasks are finished before their deadline. In this paper, we assume that proper time-triggered schedules are available (see, e.g. [1]).

Given a time-triggered schedule, a design decision whether individual schedule entries are associated directly with corresponding tasks or whether they are collected in *schedulers* – dedicated components that manage a number of schedule entries and trigger tasks accordingly – is to be made. In the former case, scheduling information would be scattered over the entire system and thus be difficult to maintain. Therefore, we favor a more centralized solution with one or a few schedulers.

2.1   Realization of Time-Triggered Schedulers in SDL

In SDL, schedulers could be realized as components of the SDL Virtual Machine (SVM), which controls, inter alia, selection and firing of transitions. Here, the SVM would have to be configured with a time-triggered schedule before executing a given SDL system. Yet, it is not obvious how tasks consisting of one or more transitions could be identified and triggered by the SVM at runtime in an SDL semantics compliant way. Therefore, we favor another design choice, where schedulers are explicitly specified as regular SDL processes that are executed under the control of the SVM.

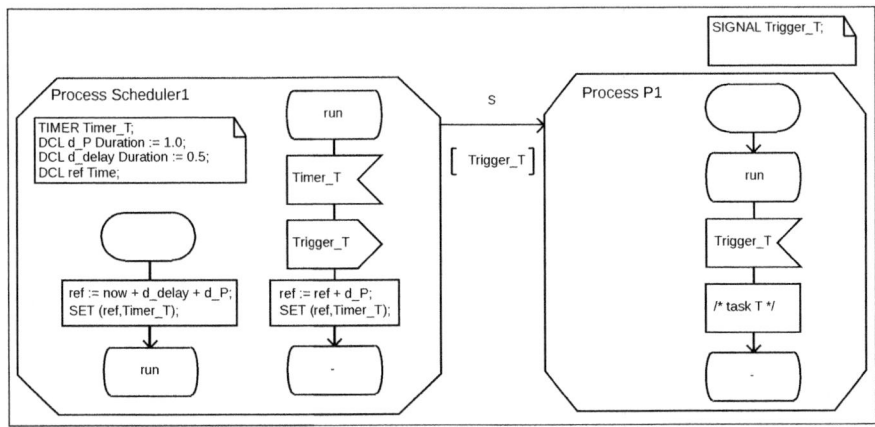

Fig. 1. Timer_T in scheduler triggers execution of task T

There are several ways of specifying schedulers in SDL. To keep examples short, we show two solutions for a single task T only, which is periodically triggered at times 1.5, 2.5, 3.5, ... One solution is to declare, for each task T, an SDL timer Timer_T in the scheduler, which is always set to the next initiation time of T (see Fig. 1)[1]. When Timer_T expires, a specific SDL signal Trigger_T identifying task T is sent by the scheduler to the SDL process P1 hosting the task, and Timer_T is set again. On reception of Trigger_T, task T is eventually executed. While appearing to be straightforward, this solution creates substantial overhead, as a timer is required for each task. Also, there are several sources of delay[2], in particular, delays to create, forward, queue, and consume the signals Timer_T and Trigger_T, preventing T to be executed as scheduled.

The solution shown in Fig. 2 is an attempt to reduce delays. Here, we use one SDL timer Timer_S in the scheduler, which activates the scheduler periodically[3]. When activated, the scheduler triggers all tasks to be executed before its next activation. This is done by sending signals Trigger_T identifying task T to the SDL process P2 hosting the task. However, since the trigger signals are now sent well before the actual initiation time, P2 has to delay execution of task T. For this purpose, the signal Trigger_T carries a parameter of type Time with the task's next execution point in time t. When receiving Trigger_T, P2 sets Timer_T to t, and executes T when Timer_T expires. We note that this solution eliminates several sources of delay, as the trigger signal is exchanged well ahead of the scheduled execution time of T. However, it produces roughly the same overhead in terms of SDL timers and signals.

---

[1] d_delay is the offset of the first executed timer.

[2] When referring to sources of delay, we assume that the SDL system is executed on a real hardware platform.

[3] The period of the scheduler and task T is set to same value d_S. d_off determines the relative starting time of the task relative to the execution time of the scheduler.

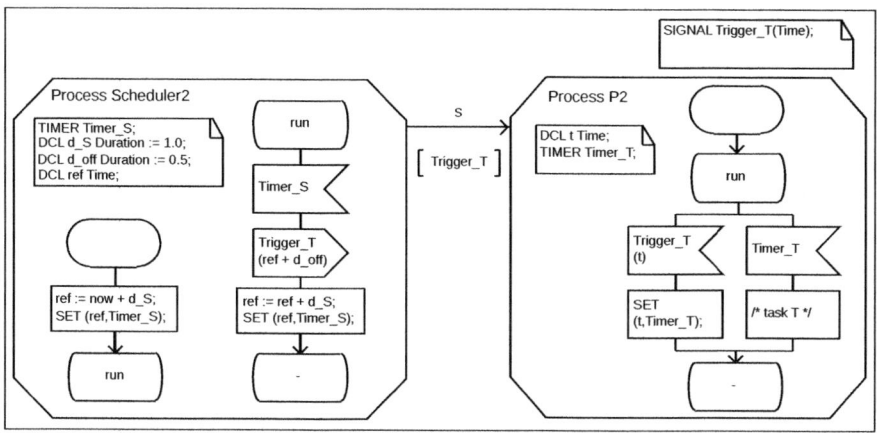

Fig. 2. External trigger and local task-activating timer

2.2   Drawbacks of SDL Solutions

As seen in Fig. 2, a normal *output* statement is used, sending a signal with the scheduled task execution time as parameter. The receiving process sets a local timer and executes the task on timer expiry.

This way of modeling time-triggered executions has several conceptual and execution time related drawbacks. Using an external signal to control a local SDL timer has impacts on the signal parameters and the design of the receiving process. Instead of just reacting and executing the task on signal reception, the process has to adopt the given pattern to be compliant with the scheduler. Thus, knowledge that should be encapsulated in the scheduler is scattered over all processes that host tasks. It follows that the reuse of these processes is limited and only possible in systems using the same type of schedulers. For instance, the use of the same task in a system with event-triggered scheduling requires an adaptation of the process specification because an immediate execution of the task is required.

Besides conceptual shortcomings, the standard SDL approach has also drawbacks concerning resources required at runtime. The process hosting the task has to be executed on reception of the trigger signal from the scheduler to set the local timer, and again when this timer expires to execute the task itself. In case of a temporary higher system load, the delivery of the trigger signal can be delayed. To cope with higher load, the process can be adapted to discard the received trigger signal and defer execution of the task to the next time a trigger signal is received (see Sect. 3.2). In SDL, this can be done by including an additional check before the task is executed. This results in higher overall system load, which is critical in the context of limited resources (e.g., embedded platforms) and has negative impacts on the timeliness of scheduled tasks.

3 Real-Time Signaling in SDL: Concept, Syntax, and Semantics

In this section, we propose the concept of *real-time signaling*, present a syntactical extension of SDL, and define its formal semantics. In particular, we add the possibility to specify the arrival time of signals (Sect. 3.1) and their expiry time (Sect. 3.2), and introduce timestamping of signals (Sect. 3.3) by adding new keywords (**at**, **expiry**, **sendtime**) to SDL. The required syntactic and semantic modifications of Z.100 [2] and Z.100 Annex F3 [4] are summarized in List. 1.1 and List. 1.2, and will be explained in the following subsections. With these preparations, we revisit the example of Sect. 2 and provide an improved solution in Sect. 3.4. In Sect. 2.2, we discuss and compare both solutions.

<output statement> ::= **output** <output body> <end>
<output body> ::= <signal identifier> [<actual parameters>] ...
                   <communication constraints>
<communication constraints> ::=
                   {**to** <destination> | **timer** <timer identifier> | <via path>
                   | **at** <time expression> | **expiry** <time expression>}*
<imperative expression> ::= <sendtime expression> | ...
<sendtime expression> ::= **sendtime**

Listing 1.1. Changes of the SDL syntax

```
1  shared atArg: PLAINSIGNALINST → TIME
2  shared expiryArg: PLAINSIGNALINST → TIME
3  shared sendTime: PLAINSIGNALINST → TIME
4  controlled sendTime: SDLAGENT → TIME
5
6  maxTime(a:TIME,b:TIME):TIME =def
7    if (b = undefined) ∨ (a ≥ b) then a else b endif
8
9  OUTPUT=def SIGNAL× VALUELABEL*× VALUELABEL× VIAARG ×TIME ×TIME
          × CONTINUELABEL
10
11 EVALOUTPUT(a:OUTPUT) ≡
12   SIGNALOUTPUT(a.s-SIGNAL, values(a.s-VALUELABEL-seq, Self), value(a.s-
          VALUELABEL, Self), a.s-VIAARG, a.s-TIME, a.s2-TIME)
13   Self.currentLabel := a.s-CONTINUELABEL
14
15 SIGNALOUTPUT(s:SIGNAL, vSeq:VALUE*, toArg:TOARG, viaArg:VIAARG, atArg:
          TIME, expiryArg:TIME) ≡
16   ...
17     choose g: g ∈ Self.outgates ∧ Applicable(s, toArg, viaArg, g, undefined)
18       extend PLAINSIGNALINST with si
19         si.plainSignalType:= s
20         si.plainSignalValues :=vSeq
21         si.toArg :=toArg
```

```
22        si . viaArg :=viaArg
23        si . atArg :=atArg
24        si . expiryArg :=expiryArg
25        if  atArg = undefined then si.sendTime :=now
26        else  si . sendTime :=atArg endif
27        si . plainSignalSender :=Self. self
28        INSERT(si, now, g)
29      endextend
30      endchoose
31    endif
32
33  DELIVERSIGNALS ≡
34    choose g: g ∈ Self. ingates  ∧  g. queue ≠ empty
35      let  si = g.queue.head in
36        DELETE(si,g)
37        si . arrival :=maxTime(si.arrival, si.atArg)
38        . . .
39      endlet
40    endchoose
41
42  SETTIMER(tm:TIMER, vSeq :VALUE*, t:TIME) ≡
43    . . .
44    endif
45    si . sendTime :=si.arrival
46  endlet
47
48  SELECTTRANSITIONSTARTPHASE ≡
49      . . .
50      else
51          Self. inport . schedule :=cleanSchedule(Self. inport. schedule)
52          Self. inputPortChecked :=Self.inport. queue
53          . . .
54      endif
55
56  cleanSchedule(siSeq:SIGNALINST*):SIGNALINST* =def
57    if siSeq = empty then empty
58    elseif siSeq.head.expiryArg = undefined ∨ siSeq.head.expiryArg ≥ now then
59      < siSeq.head >⌢ cleanSchedule(siSeq. tail)
60    else cleanSchedule(siSeq. tail)
61    endif
```

Listing 1.2. Changes of the SDL semantics

3.1 Specified Signal Arrival Time

To execute time-triggered schedules located in one or more dedicated schedulers, we propose the concept of *real-time signaling* in SDL. A *real-time signal* is an SDL signal for which an arrival time is specified when the signal is sent, with the effect that reception is postponed until this point in time. This is similar to setting a local SDL timer, which generates a timer signal on expiry. The main difference here is that real-time signals can be sent by other SDL processes. Another difference is that there is no reset operation, i.e. once a real-time signal is sent, it can not be deleted by the sender, preserving the signal character. Both normal signals and time-triggered signals are inserted in the same ordered signal queue. The ordering is based on the actual arrival times of normal signals and the specified arrival times of time-triggered signals.

To specify arrival times of signals, we add the communication constraint at <time expression> to the output action (see List. 1.1). In the formal SDL semantics (see List. 1.2), the specified signal arrival time is added to the subdomains of OUTPUT (TIME, line 9), and to the parameter list of the ASM macro SIGNALOUTPUT ($atArg$, line 15). When a signal is created (line 18), the specified signal arrival time is associated with the signal instance (line 23) using the shared function $atArg$ (line 1). When the signal is eventually delivered to the receiving agent, as defined in the ASM macro DELIVERSIGNALS (line 33), the actual signal arrival time is the maximum of specified arrival time ($si.atArg$) and actual arrival time ($si.arrival$) as defined by the shared function $arrival$, which takes the effects of delaying channels into account (line 37). Thereby, signals are never enqueued in the past.

3.2   Signal Expiry Time

With *real-time signaling*, it can be expressed that signal delivery does not occur before the specified signal arrival time. However, there may still be an arbitrary delay until the signal is actually consumed, thereby triggering the scheduled task. On real hardware, this delay will increase during periods of high system load.

To control system load to some degree, we propose the concept of signal expiry in SDL. When a signal is sent, an expiry time can be specified, with the effect that the signal is discarded if it has not been consumed before this point in time. This is particularly useful in situations where a periodic value is delivered, where only the latest value is of interest. When used together with *real-time signaling*, a time interval where signal consumption is valid can be specified.

To specify signal expiry times, we add the communication constraint expiry <time expression> to the output action (see List. 1.1). In the formal SDL semantics (see List. 1.2), the specified signal expiry time is added to the subdomains of OUTPUT (TIME, line 9), and to the parameter list of the ASM macro SIGNALOUTPUT ($expiryArg$, line 15). When a signal is created (line 18), the specified signal expiry time is associated with the signal instance (line 24) using the shared function $expiryArg$ (line 2). Signal expiry time is evaluated at the beginning of the transition selection phase, which is defined by the ASM macro SELECTTRANSITIONSTARTPHASE (line 48). Before the input port is frozen for transition selection (line 52), expired signal instances are removed (line 51). Removal of expired signals is formally defined by the new function *cleanSchedule* (line 56). Systems using expiry time must consider the fact of signal removal as further design aspect, since the removal of expired signals can lead to deadlocks.

3.3   Timestamping of Signals

In real-time systems, *timestamping* is used to refer to the time at which an event has been detected. If the event is reported by a signal, the timestamp can be associated with that signal. In [3], we have considered early timestamping for higher precision, adding the timestamp as signal parameter that was set when the signal was created.

Alvarez et. al. [5] proposed to associate, with each signal, timestamps recording sending and reception times, and to access them using predefined functions `time_sent` and `time_received`, respectively. We follow up on this idea and associate a timestamp with every SDL signal, denoting the time when the signal was sent. To access the timestamp, we introduce the anonymous variable `sendtime` (see List. 1.1), which yields the sending time of the last consumed input signal. In the formal SDL semantics (see List. 1.2), the sending time is defined to be the creation time of the signal (line 25), or, in case of SDL timers, the timer's specified time value (line 45), which is equal to their arrival time[4]. As stated in Sect. 3.1, *real-time signals* are considered as remote timers, hence the sending time is set to their specified arrival time (*si.atArg*, line 26).

When an ordinary SDL signal is processed in a transition, the expression `now - sendtime` can be used to determine the duration of the signal transfer and the waiting time in the signal queue. For real-time signals and local timers, it denotes the waiting time in queue only and can be evaluated at runtime.

3.4   Example of Real-Time Signaling

We now revisit the example of Sect. 2, and use the SDL extensions above. Figure 3 shows a solution that is derived from Fig. 2, where we have used only one SDL timer `Timer_S` for periodic scheduler activation. When activated, the scheduler triggers all tasks to be initiated before its next activation, by sending signals `Trigger_T` identifying task T to the SDL process hosting the task. Different from the solution in Fig. 2, `Trigger_T` now is a real-time signal, for which the time of arrival and expiry are specified using the communication constraints `at` and `expiry`, respectively. Compared to Fig. 2, the specification of process P3 hosting task T is significantly shorter, as the timer `Timer_T` becomes obsolete – process P3 is in fact the same as process P1 in Fig. 1. In this solution, the SDL process hosting the task needs no adaptation.

Another improvement has been achieved by using the anonymous function `sendtime` to express a reference point in time to define arrival and expiry times (`OUTPUT Trigger_T`), and to set timers (see Fig. 3). This makes the use of time variables (variable `ref` in Fig. 2) to store reference points in time obsolete, thereby simplifying the specification of the scheduler further.

---

[4] Compared to the SDL standard, on timer expiry, a new signal with the same name is created and put in the input port of the agent.

We note that the solution in Fig. 3 indeed reduces the number of SDL timers, and thus runtime overhead. Compared to the previous solutions, almost all sources of delay have been eliminated; what remains is the delay of the consumption of the the real-time signal `Trigger_T`.

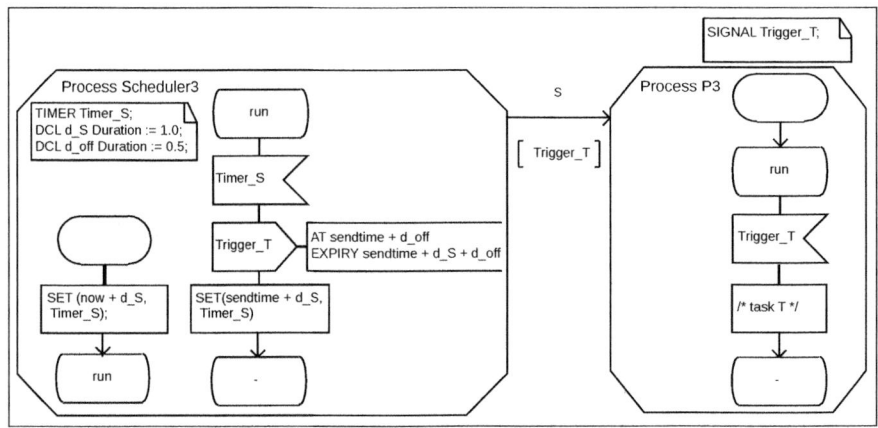

Fig. 3. Real-time signaling

4   SDL Environment Framework (SEnF)

Particularly on embedded platforms, the SDL system under execution needs to interact with the peripherals of the platform, for instance, to communicate with other nodes or to take measurements using integrated or connected sensors. With our tool chain and model-driven development approach SDL-MDD [6], we are able to automatically transform an SDL specification into runtime-independent C++-code using our code generator ConTraST [7]. Next, a platform-dependent compiler is used to obtain executable machine code for the target platform. The generated code is executed under the control of the SDL Runtime Environment (SdlRE), our implementation of the SDL Virtual Maschine (SVM) as defined in Z.100 Annex F3. Currently, SdlRE supports the PC platform[5] and the ARM-based wireless sensor node Imote2 [8] by Memsic.

To interact with peripherals, SDL processes exchange SDL signals with the environment. These SDL signals are processed by hardware-specific drivers, which are provided by our SDL Environment Framework (SEnF) [9]. The usage of signals to the environment to interface with hardware drivers avoids manual coding entirely and enables an holistic model-driven development approach for embedded platforms with SDL.

SdlRE treats the environment SEnF like any other SDL agent: SDL signals to the environment are delivered to its SDL agent and stored in its signal queue. On execution of the environment agent, all pending signals are delivered to the

---

[5] The PC platform uses Linux as operating system.

responsible hardware drivers by calling their input procedure. After processing a delivered SDL signal, execution control is returned to the environment agent. When all signals are processed, execution control is passed back to SdlRE. Regarding embedded platforms, most hardware drivers are based on interrupts. This means that the integrated or connected hardware components generate an interrupt, which is handled by the driver in the responsive interrupt service routine (ISR). Thereby, interrupts allow almost an immediate reaction of the driver to time-critical hardware requests, e.g., to read buffers of a transceiver early enough to prevent overflows.

To implement *real-time signaling* with SEnF accurately, we added a centralized *real-time* queue for all hardware drivers, which contains the SDL signals transmitted to the environment using *output at*. This queue is isolated from the regular signal queue, storing all SDL signals sent to the environment using standard SDL mechanisms. The *real-time* queue is sorted by the specified *real-time signaling* timestamps. A hardware timer is set to the timestamp of the earliest signal in the queue, generating an interrupt on expiration. In the ISR the signal is then removed from the queue and delivered to the responsible hardware driver by calling its input procedure. Thus the input procedure runs in the context of the ISR and therefore yields very high precision. Finally, the hardware timer is updated to the timestamp of the next signal in the *real-time* queue.

On insertions of new signals in the *real-time* queue, the configuration of the hardware timer is checked, and updated if the new signal is earlier than the current timer setting. Before a new signal is enqueued, an optional hardware driver specific callback handler is called, which can adjust the *real-time signaling* timestamp of the signal. Hence, driver-specific delays can be considered, e.g. if the driver needs additional time to communicate with a sensor and to start a measurement, the *real-time signaling* timestamp of the signal is decreased by this constant delay. Accurate *real-time* queues are currently supported on the Imote2 platform, which provides the required hardware timers and gives full control over all system resources. In our implementatin, the SdlRE acts as operating system of the platform.

The centralized *real-time* queue was chosen to achieve high precision of the *real-time signaling* mechanism for all hardware drivers. Furthermore, this yields an encapsulation and clear separation between SDL on the one hand, and driver- and hardware-related timing aspects on the other hand.

5   Evaluation

We illustrate the application of *real-time signaling* by our inverted pendulum system, a wireless networked control system (WNCS), where controllers, sensors, and actuators exchange information over a wireless digital communication network. The main challenge of a WNCS is to achieve predictable performance and stability in all possible dynamic situations. The WNCS Communication

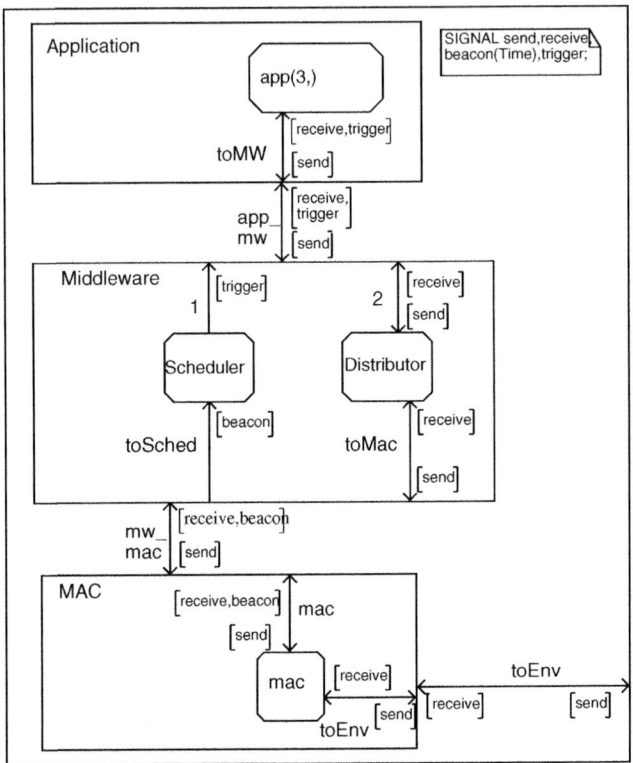

Fig. 4. Excerpt of the WNCS_CoM

Middleware (WNCS_CoM), which is part of the inverted pendulum system, follows a service-oriented approach. Sensor and actuator nodes announce their services and the minimum service time interval. Controllers subscribe to announced services, specifying a periodic update interval, so the service provider is responsible to send the data. In Fig. 4, we show an excerpt of our SDL model, consisting of MAC, Middleware, and Application layer.

The MAC layer provides medium-wide tick synchronization and TDMA-based medium access. Reference ticks are used for medium arbitration and time adjustment of the distributed scheduler in Middleware. The scheduler is responsible for the activation of tasks, based on current service subscriptions and the constant delay of the control application to provide measurement data or to apply actuator values.

In this inverted pendulum system, there are several places where *real-time signaling* is applied. First, there is the MAC layer, which is responsible for periodic tick synchronization and medium slotting (see Fig. 5). For resynchronization, a master node transmits a tick frame every d_{resync}, which is repeated by further network nodes. Synchronization accuracy and therefore guard times within each

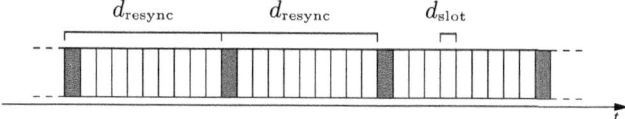

Fig. 5. MAC with TDMA

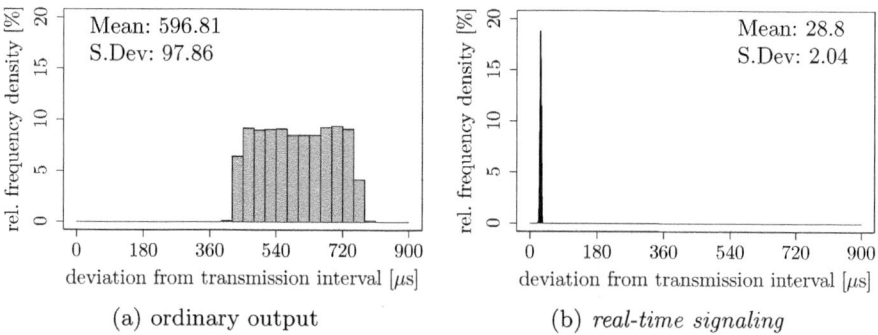

(a) ordinary output   (b) *real-time signaling*

Fig. 6. Tick synchronisation using regular output and output **at** via SEnF

time slot of duration d_{slot} depend on the precise timing of tick frames. Therefore, we use real-time signals to schedule tick frame transmissions, and measure the deviation of actual transmissions from the specified transmission interval. For comparison, we repeat these measurements, using regular SDL timers and signals. The results are summarized in Fig. 6.

All measurements are performed on an Imote2 sensor node [8], using Con-TraST [7]. Each experiment consists of 6000 measured values, where d_{resync} is set to 100 ms. In Fig. 6(a), the difference between the planned transmission time (the time when the SDL timer expires) and the actual transmission time is shown. We measure delays from $\sim 400\,\mu s$ up to $\sim 800\,\mu s$. In comparison, we show the measurements of the same experiment, now using *real-time signaling* (cf. Fig. 6(b)). Since the signal is transferred early to the destination process (environment), the signal is already in the input queue when it has to be processed. Therefore, it can be processed almost instantly at the specified arrival time (see Sect. 4), which yields a significantly smaller average value of only $29\,\mu s$. The measured maximum delay is only slightly higher at about $35\,\mu s$, due the use of a hardware interrupt routine and other non-interruptible routines. Compared to the use of regular SDL signals, there is an improvement by a factor of 22.

Another place to apply *real-time signaling* in the inverted pendulum system is the scheduling of the control application `Application`. For a given schedule (cf. Fig. 7), the scheduler can send the activation signal to the application in advance, which reduces the delay upon task execution. As before, we perform measurements to compare the processing delays of regular SDL signals to real-time signals. We define a schedule for 3 applications (as shown in Fig. 7) on the same node, with an expiry time of 100 ms. The upper schedule was specified

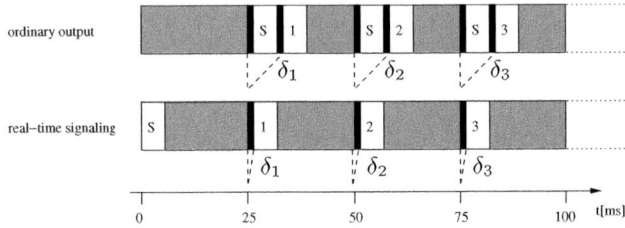

Fig. 7. Control application schedules

using regular SDL signals as shown in Fig. 1. Here, the Scheduler (S) has to be activated just before the task Application (1,2,3) to be scheduled. In case of *real-time signaling* (below), the scheduler is only activated once per period as shown in Fig. 3. For each application i, the difference δ_i between the planned and actual execution time is measured.

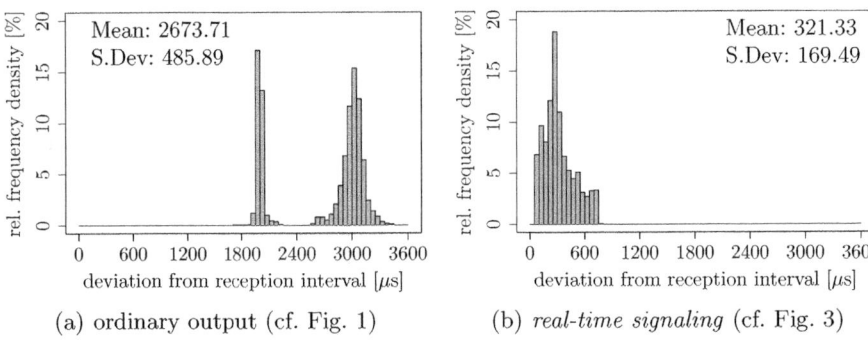

(a) ordinary output (cf. Fig. 1)   (b) *real-time signaling* (cf. Fig. 3)

Fig. 8. Scheduler using output and output **at**

In Fig. 8(a), we show the deviation of the applications between the planned and the actual execution time. The deviation for regular SDL signals ranges from $1600\,\mu s$ to $3600\,\mu s$. In comparison, *real-time signaling* shown in Fig. 8(b) has only a deviation between $0\,\mu s$ and $800\,\mu s$ – this is only $\frac{1}{4}$th of the time of the ordinary mechanism.

6   Related Work

SDL's limited real-time expressiveness and its high degree of implementational freedom have been addressed by quite a number of authors over the past two decades. Although common objectives of all proposals are the improvement of predictability and the handling of overload situations, various approaches can be found, reaching from extensions to SDL on design level (like [5,10,11,12]) to implementation-specific realizations of the SDL semantics (like [13,14,15]). However, to our knowledge, there is no approach based on time-triggered execution of SDL systems. In the following, we restrict the survey on approaches extending the notion of SDL timers and signals, and proposals covering the scheduling of agents.

In [10], the authors introduce extensions to SDL's notion of time progress on specification level. The presented approach targets at simulations and is motivated by timed automata with urgencies. In particular, it is suggested to classify transitions as eager (time must not progress), lazy (time may progress with indefinite amount), and delayable (time may progress within given bounds). Although delayable timers seem to be similar to our approach of signal arrival and expiry, the implication is completely different, since our objective is not the control of simulation time, but the control of system load on real hardware. In [11], the authors extend their approach by introducing cyclic and interruptive timers, and present further annotations such as periodicity of timers or execution delay of tasks, also for simulative purpose only.

In [12], Gotzhein et al. present the concept of input port bounds, an extension to SDL to avoid queue overflows that can cause illegal behavior on concrete limited hardware platforms. Similar to the signal expiry, their approach makes SDL systems more robust against system overload at the cost of less reliable signal transfer within SDL systems. In contrast to the approach in this paper, the number of signals (not an expiry time) is the criterion for removal of signal instances. In addition, they distinguish between three perceivable solutions of treating incoming signals in case of input port overflows (discard, replace, delete/append).

Besides many topics regarding the efficient implementation of SDL, Mitschele-Thiel discusses the handling of limited input queues on implementation side in [13]. He presents four alternatives to handle input queue overflows: Prevention (with hard assumptions on the system's environment), removal of signals (similar to [12]), blocking of the signal's sender (with the risk of deadlocks), and dynamic control (detecting overload situations and throttling the load). With dynamic control, Mitschele-Thiel introduces also a design-based solution to handle overload situations, but in contrast to expiry times of signals, his solution generates additional system load in situations in which high load already exists.

Similar to the predefined variable `sendtime` (see Sect. 3.3), Álvarez et al. [5] introduce a function called *time_ sent*, holding the point in time when an SDL signal has been created. In addition, they propose a function *time_ received*, recording the time when the signal is consumed in a transition. Since our SVM provides non-preemptive scheduling, we have no need for such a function. Álvarez et al. also discuss the problem of timely transition activations. However, their approach is based on local SDL timers and transition priorities, and not compliant to the SDL semantics regarding to the order of signal receptions.

The idea of a centralized scheduler in SDL was realized in [16] in terms of a CPU scheduler simulator for educational purposes. The presented scheduler supports a plenty of scheduling strategies (such as FCFS, SJF, and EDF); however, it simulates operating system processes only and is not intended for the scheduling of SDL systems.

To test schedulability of SDL systems, several approaches with off-line analysis have been proposed. Many of those approaches apply a transformation of the SDL specification to a different formal representation (such as analyzable task networks [17], methods from queueing theory [18], and timed automata [19]). Since the mentioned proposals perform analyses without enforcing an appropriate scheduling of agents, we will not go into further detail.

7   Conclusions and Future Work

In this paper, we have introduced *real-time signaling* in SDL, by extending SDL to specify time intervals for the reception and expiry of ordinary signals, and by associating send times with signals. This extension can be used, for instance, to specify timer-triggered scheduling, which is required in many real-time systems. Our contribution covers syntactical extensions of SDL, their formal semantics, their implementation in the SDL Runtime Environment (SdlRE) and the SDL Environment Framework (SEnF), and their application in case studies. Finally, we have reported on measurement results which have revealed improvements by a factor of up to 22. We have successfully applied the introduced concepts to a realtime communication system for an inverted pendulum [20].

In future work, we will investigate various ways to further improve the real-time expressiveness of SDL. In particular, we will exploit the degrees of freedom offered by the SDL Virtual Machine (SVM) as part of the formal SDL semantics. For instance, to achieve predictability, we need more control of the timing behaviour including the load situation. This requires a priori knowledge on worst-case execution times, and the possibility to suspend non-real-time processes from execution.

References

1. Kopetz, H.: Real-Time Systems – Design Principles for Distributed Embedded Applications. Kluwer Academic Publishers, Dordrecht (1997)
2. International Telecommunication Union (ITU): ITU-T Recommendation Z.100 (11/2007): Specification and Description Language (SDL) (2007), http://www.itu.int/rec/T-REC-Z.100-200711-I
3. Becker, P., Christmann, D., Gotzhein, R.: Model-Driven Development of Time-Critical Protocols with SDL-MDD. In: Reed, R., Bilgic, A., Gotzhein, R. (eds.) SDL 2009. LNCS, vol. 5719, pp. 34–52. Springer, Heidelberg (2009)
4. International Telecommunication Union (ITU): ITU-T Recommendation Z.100 Annex F: Formal Semantics Definition (2000)
5. Álvarez, J.M., Díaz, M., Llopis, L., Pimentel, E., Troya, J.M.: Integrating Schedulability Analysis and Design Techniques in SDL. Real-Time Systems 24(3), 267–302 (2003)
6. Gotzhein, R.: Model-driven with SDL – Improving the Quality of Networked Systems Development. In: Proceedings of the 7th International Conference on New Technologies of Distributed Systems (NOTERE 2007), Marrakesh, Morocco, pp. 31–46 (2007) (invited paper)

7. Fliege, I., Grammes, R., Weber, C.: ConTraST – A Configurable SDL Transpiler and Runtime Environment. In: Gotzhein, R., Reed, R. (eds.) SAM 2006. LNCS, vol. 4320, pp. 216–228. Springer, Heidelberg (2006)
8. Memsic: Imote 2 datasheet,
   http://www.memsic.com/support/documentation/wireless-sensor-networks/category/7-datasheets.html?download=134
9. Fliege, I., Geraldy, A., Jung, S., Kuhn, T., Webel, C., Weber, C.: Konzept und Struktur des SDL Environment Framework (SEnF). Technical Report 341/05, TU Kaiserslautern (2005)
10. Bozga, M., Graf, S., Kerbrat, A., Mounier, L., Ober, I., Vincent, D.: SDL for Real-Time: What is Missing? In: Sherratt, E. (ed.) SAM, VERIMAG, IRISA, SDL Forum, pp. 108–121 (2000)
11. Bozga, M., Graf, S., Mounier, L., Ober, I., Roux, J.-L., Vincent, D.: Timed Extensions for SDL. In: Reed, R., Reed, J. (eds.) SDL 2001. LNCS, vol. 2078, pp. 223–240. Springer, Heidelberg (2001)
12. Gotzhein, R., Grammes, R., Kuhn, T.: Specifying Input Port Bounds in SDL. In: Gaudin, E., Najm, E., Reed, R. (eds.) SDL 2007. LNCS, vol. 4745, pp. 101–116. Springer, Heidelberg (2007)
13. Mitschele-Thiel, A.: Engineering with SDL – Developing Performance-Critical Communication Systems. John Wiley & Sons, Chichester (2000)
14. Bræk, R., Haugen, Ø.: Engineering Real Time Systems. Prentice Hall, Englewood Cliffs (1993)
15. Sanders, R.: Implementing from SDL. In: Telektronikk 4.2000, Languages for Telecommunication Applications. Telenor (2000)
16. Rodríguez-Cayetano, M.: Design and Development of a CPU Scheduler Simulator for Educational Purpose Using SDL. In: Kraemer, F.A., Herrmann, P. (eds.) SAM 2010. LNCS, vol. 6598, pp. 72–90. Springer, Heidelberg (2011)
17. Kolloch, T., Färber, G.: Mapping an Embedded Hard Real-Time Systems SDL Specification to an Analyzable Task Network - A Case Study. In: Müller, F., Bestavros, A. (eds.) LCTES 1998. LNCS, vol. 1474, pp. 156–165. Springer, Heidelberg (1998)
18. Diefenbruch, M., Hintelmann, J., Müller-Clostermann, B.: QUEST Performance Evalution of SDL System. In: Irmscher, K., Mittasch, C., Richter, K. (eds.) MMB (Kurzbeiträge), TU Bergakademie Freiberg, pp. 126–132 (1997)
19. Ober, I., Kerbrat, A.: Verification of Quantitative Temporal Properties of SDL Specifications. In: Reed, R., Reed, J. (eds.) SDL 2001. LNCS, vol. 2078, pp. 182–202. Springer, Heidelberg (2001)
20. Chamaken, A., Litz, L., Krämer, M., Gotzhein, R.: Cross-layer design of wireless networked control systems with energy limitations. In: European Control Conference 2009, ECC 2009 (2009)

Priority Scheduling in SDL[*]

Dennis Christmann, Philipp Becker, and Reinhard Gotzhein

Networked Systems Group,
University of Kaiserslautern, Germany
{christma,pbecker,gotzhein}@cs.uni-kl.de

Abstract. In real-time systems, the capability to achieve short or even predictable reaction times is essential. In this paper, we take a pragmatic approach by proposing priority-based scheduling in SDL combined with a mechanism to suspend and resume SDL agents. More specifically, we define adequate syntactical extensions of SDL and show that they are compliant with the formal SDL semantics. We have implemented all proposed extensions in our SDL tool chain, consisting of SDL compiler, SDL runtime environment, and environment interfacing routines, thereby being compatible with model-driven development processes with SDL. In a series of runtime experiments on sensor nodes, we show that compared to customary SDL scheduling policies, priority scheduling with suspension of SDL agents indeed achieves significantly shortened reaction times.

1   Introduction

In *real-time systems*, correctness does not only depend on functional correctness, but also on the points in time at which results are produced (see [1]). Timeliness is also crucial in *communication networks* applying TDMA for medium access, where nodes transmit frames in their assigned time slots, thereby avoiding frame collisions, or for efficient duty cycling. To support timeliness, the capability to achieve short or even predictable reaction times is essential.

SDL [2] is a formal description technique for distributed systems that is also being advocated for the design of real-time systems. To specify real-time aspects, SDL offers the notion of global system time, referred to by the function now, and the concept of SDL timers. However, timer expiry does not yield an instantly-processed interrupt; instead, a timer signal is produced and appended to the input queue of the local agent. In real implementations of SDL models, this timer semantics may cause substantial delays, thereby inhibiting the timely reaction of the SDL agent to this event. In particular, delays are caused by three sources: First, the SDL runtime environment implementing the SDL Virtual Machine (SVM) has to detect timer expiry, and to place a signal into the corresponding input queue. Secondly, the receiving agent has to be scheduled and dispatched. Especially in high load situations with many agents in the SDL system, the agent's scheduling delay may be high. Reasons for this potentially high delay are

---

[*] This work is supported by the Carl Zeiss Foundation.

I. Ober and I. Ober (Eds.): SDL 2011, LNCS 7083, pp. 202–217, 2011.
© Springer-Verlag Berlin Heidelberg 2011

that neither does the SDL semantics stipulate a particular scheduling strategy nor does SDL provide any means to specify preference rules for agents. Thirdly, there may be further signals in the input queue to be consumed before the timer signal, which implies that the receiving agent may have to be scheduled more than once. Similar concerns apply to scenarios where no SDL timers but regular SDL signals are sent to trigger other SDL agents in a timely fashion.

In this paper, we take a pragmatic approach to improve the real-time capabilities of SDL. More specifically, we propose SDL extensions that can be used by the system designer to influence the agents' execution order. The first extension adds the possibility to assign static priorities to SDL agents, thereby giving privilege to time-critical tasks and shortening their reaction times even in situations with potentially high system load. The second extension is a mechanism to suspend and resume SDL agents, thereby reducing system load and thus reaction times in critical time intervals. This way, the problem that a transition of a low priority agent may be running when a transition of a high priority agent becomes fireable can be solved.

The work reported in this paper makes the following contributions. First, we propose SDL extensions to select among several scheduling strategies and to assign static priorities to SDL agents combined with a mechanism to suspend and resume agents. For compatibility with existing SDL tools, these extensions are defined by annotations (see Sect. 3). Also, we address their compliance with the formal SDL semantics. Secondly, we have implemented all proposed extensions in our SDL tool chain, consisting of the SDL compiler ConTraST [3], the SDL Runtime Environment (SdlRE), and the SDL Environment Framework (SEnF) to interface SDL systems with hardware platforms. Section 4 addresses several implementation aspects. Thirdly, we have performed runtime experiments in order to compare the performance of ordinary SDL scheduling policies to priority scheduling with and without the suspension of low priority agents (Sect. 5). The experiments provide sufficient evidence that the proposed SDL extensions are necessary and effective. The paper is completed by a survey of related work (Sect. 2), and conclusions with an outline of future work (Sect. 6).

2   Related Work

In this section, we survey related work. First, we look at approaches exploiting implementation choices to improve runtime efficiency of SDL. Then, we outline design and analysis techniques to increase predictability of SDL systems.

The improvement of runtime efficiency of SDL implementations is extensively treated in two standard works. In [4], Bræk and Haugen compare the conceptual SDL world to real hardware systems and discuss fundamental differences, e.g., limited hardware resources and processing delays. They introduce step-by-step guidelines to distribute SDL systems to several physical entities, and to dimension hardware resources. They also discuss the software design of SDL, i.e., alternatives how to implement SDL constructs, e.g., regarding communication, concurrency, data types, and the sequential behavior of SDL processes.

The second standard work by Mitschele-Thiel [5] focusses on performance engineering. His comprehensive treatment covers differences between SDL and real-world implementations, too, and introduces alternatives in the integration of SDL systems with an operating system (*tight, light, bare*). He also discusses a variety of implementation alternatives that influence runtime efficiency.

In addition to these standard works, the efficient implementation of SDL is addressed, e.g., in [6] and [7]. Topics in [6] are the realization of SDL signals by method calls and the mapping of SDL entities to physical objects. Since physical distribution cannot be specified in SDL, supporting tools have been developed, e.g., IBM's deployment editor [8], which is based on UML component diagrams.

To improve predictability of SDL systems, adaptations of the SDL runtime model and pure analytical approaches that are based on assumptions on runtime environment and hardware platform have been proposed. In [9], Álvarez et al. present a more predictable but non-standard-compliant execution model for SDL to reduce non-determinism of the formal SDL model. Their solution involves the preemptive and priority-based scheduling of SDL agents. The priority of an agent is calculated dynamically and depends on signals in its queue and transitions in the agent's current state. In order to perform schedulability analysis, transitions are additionally labeled by their *worst case execution time* (WCET).

The assignment of process and signal priorities is also suggested in [4]. Some tools already support priorities, e.g., Cmicro in the IBM Rational SDL Suite [8]. Even though their approach provides an easy way to privilege agents and even transitions, it is not fully compliant to the SDL semantics. In addition, Cmicro suffers from several language restrictions.

There are also tools supporting tight integrations of an SDL system into an underlying real-time operating system (RTOS) (cf. Cadvanced integration strategies [8] or Pragmadev's Real Time Developer Studio [10]). Since such approaches introduce additional overhead compared to bare integrations, require an additional implementation step, and create a strong bonding between SDL system and RTOS, we do not go into further detail.

Bozga et al. propose a set of annotations, grouped into *assumptions* and *assertions* [11]. These annotations include a priori knowledge about the system's environment, such as execution delays and periodicity of external inputs. Additionally, they introduce cyclic and interruptive SDL timers as well as operators to access timer values. They also combine the concept of transition urgencies with SDL to influence the progress of time in simulations. In particular, they suggest to label transitions as *eager*, *lazy*, or *delayable*. Although this approach increases the expressiveness of SDL, it is more on the theoretical side, since progress of time is not controllable in real executions.

In addition, further analytical techniques have been proposed. One example is QSDL that is based on the foundations of *queuing theory* [12]. Further approaches include *timed automata* [13] and *tasked networks* [14]. Thereby, well-known analytical methods, e.g., known from model checking, are brought into the context of SDL. However, most analytical methods consider execution delays

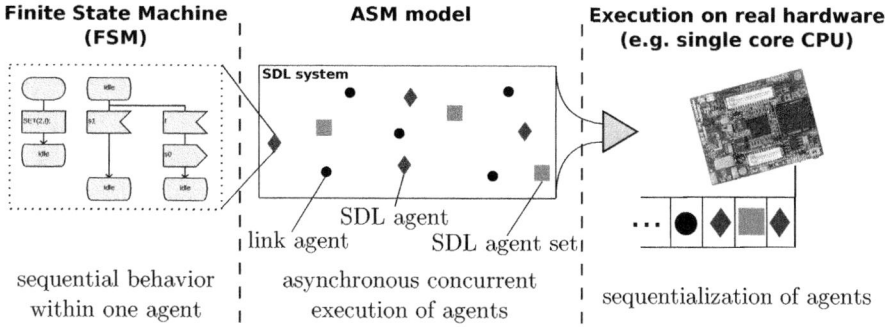

Fig. 1. Gap between SDL's formal semantics and the behavior on real hardware

within single transitions only and ignore overhead of the runtime system (e.g., the selection of fireable transitions).

To our knowledge, our approach is the first to provide priority scheduling combined with temporary suspension of low-priority agents. Different from the analytical approaches, it covers the explicit configuration of SDL runtime models and is fully implemented in an operational SDL tool chain. Unlike existing implementations and the standard works on implementing SDL, our focus is not on more efficient implementations of SDL, but on customized, transparent scheduling of SDL agents compliant with the SDL standard [2]. Moreover, our realization with low-power sensor nodes does not rely on an underlying (real-time) operating system, but states a bare integration on hardware, thereby being more efficient and controllable.

3   Scheduling Strategies in SDL

This section introduces annotation-based extensions to SDL to increase the language's expressiveness [15]. They are part of an ongoing research process with the objective to bring SDL further towards real-time systems. The presented annotations enrich system specifications with information configuring the system's scheduling strategy. By introducing priority scheduling, we establish a basis to privilege time-critical tasks. With the suspension of low priority agents, we provide additional measures to shorten reaction times further.

3.1   Problem Statement

The scheduling of SDL agents is a crucial step when implementing the concurrent runtime model of SDL, since it is critical with respect to reaction times and compliance with deadlines. Fig. 1 illustrates the gap between SDL's concurrent runtime model and its sequentialized execution on real hardware. The figure is subdivided into three parts: The left part shows the specification of a finite state machine (FSM), e.g., in the context of an SDL process. Transitions within one FSM are executed sequentially and must not be interrupted by another transition of the same FSM (*run-to-completion*). The middle part of Fig. 1 shows the runtime model of SDL that is specified by Abstract State Machines (ASMs) in the dynamic semantics [2]. The formal semantics defines three types of ASM agents (SDL AgentSets, SDL Agents, and Links) that are executed concurrently and autonomously by the SDL Virtual Machine (SVM). Nevertheless, the concurrency has to be eliminated by a certain scheduling strategy when the SDL system is executed on real hardware, e.g., on a single-core platform (cf. right part in Fig. 1), which is common in many application areas such as wireless sensor networks. In general, asynchronous concurrency and the vague notion of execution time allow arbitrary scheduling strategies – preemptive as well as non-preemptive – for the sequentialization of SDL agents. However, SDL itself provides no means to specify a particular scheduling strategy.

In our approach, we introduce extensions to SDL, enabling the selection and configuration of the scheduling strategy that is suitable for the concrete scenario. Thereby, scheduling of agents is not only more transparent, but also manipulable by the system developer. In addition, the approach provides the option to privilege certain agents and to temporarily suspend low priority agents in order to speed up time-critical reactions. Further objectives are compatibility with existing tools and the exploit of SDL's semantical freedom. Particularly, we leave the behavior of input ports, which is often manipulated when introducing priorities in SDL (e.g., in [9]), unchanged.

3.2   Supported Scheduling Strategies

When implementing SDL, there is in general no restriction on the scheduling strategy to be used. However, if the whole language is to be supported, off-line time-triggered scheduling strategies are to be rejected and event-triggered strategies are the only remaining alternative to deal with SDL's actor model.

We have devised a scheduling framework within the *SDL Runtime Environment* (SdlRE), our implementation of the SVM, which currently supports three dynamic, non-idling, and non-preemptive scheduling strategies [16]. This means that scheduling decisions are made at runtime, that no idling periods are allowed if there are agents with pending tasks, and that an executed agent must return control to the runtime environment, since there is no enforced interruption of an agent's execution (*cooperative scheduling*). Although non-preemptive strategies can handle less scheduling problems, we do not support preemptive algorithms, since they require more overhead at runtime (coordination, restrictive synchronization of shared variables, ...), and are harder to implement and analyze than non-preemptive ones [17].

Non-preemptive Round Robin (NP-RR). With the *non-preemptive round robin* scheduling strategy (NP-RR), all agents of the system, i.e. SDL Agents, SDL AgentSets, and Links, are executed in a cyclic manner [18]. The order within the cycle is given by the agents' initialization order, which depends on the SDL tool chain and therefore cannot be prescribed during system design. NP-RR

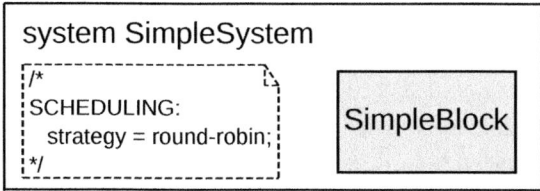

Fig. 2. Global scheduling policy in head symbol of the SDL system

reflects the SDL runtime model one-to-one, in the sense that every agent decides by itself if there is something to do, e.g., if there are SDL signals to process. Note that this is no necessary condition for compliance with SDL's semantics, since an agent without a fireable transition does not show any reaction from an outer point of view. Because many agents are executed without any pending signal, NP-RR usually suffers from low efficiency.

To select NP-RR as scheduling strategy in an SDL system, we specify a scheduling policy in the system's head symbol (see Fig. 2). The policy is specified as annotation, i.e., as formal SDL comment, thereby being compatible with existing SDL tools. Inside the annotation, the keyword `SCHEDULING` marks the beginning of a scheduling policy and is used in our tool chain as indicator to evaluate the annotation (see Sect. 4). Subsequent to this keyword, a set of parameters to choose and configure a desired scheduling strategy follows. In Fig. 2, there is only one parameter assigned, setting the scheduling strategy to NP-RR (`strategy = round-robin`).

Agent-based First Come First Served (FCFS). Compliance of the SVM's implementation with SDL's semantics does not require the one-to-one mapping of all types of ASM agents. Particularly, it is usual to omit the scheduling and dispatching of SDL `AgentSets` and `Links` and to flatten the system's hierarchy, i.e., to transport signals directly between SDL `Agents` holding the actual FSM that is specified by the developer. In these realizations, the functionality provided by SDL `AgentSets` and `Links` is moved into service primitives of the SDL runtime system. Regarding efficiency, it is even recommended to implement a more demand-driven scheduling strategy, i.e., to execute SDL `Agents` only when they hold fireable transitions.

The agent-based *first come first served* (FCFS) strategy realizes such a demand-driven scheduling in SdlRE [18]. It maintains a queue containing all agents with pending signals.[1] In steady state, there are only SDL `Agents` in the queue. SDL `AgentSets` and `Links` are only executed explicitly if new system structures are created (e.g., during system startup or dynamic process instantiation). If an SDL signal is put into the input port of an agent and the agent is not yet in the

---

[1] SdlRE also supports other types of transition triggers like `continuous signals`. However, it is often not easy to decide whether (and when) corresponding conditions yield true (e.g., if the condition contains `now`). Thus, such language features can hardly be treated in a pure demand-driven way.

queue, it is inserted at the end of the queue. On the other hand, if the agent is already enqueued, the signal is inserted in the input port of the agent without changing the agent's position in the queue. Thereby, the resulting execution order is fair on agent level. Compared to NP-RR, execution order of agents with FCFS is significantly more transparent. However, if two agents become fireable simultaneously, e.g., if two timers expire at the same point in time, the behavior of the SDL model also depends on the SDL tool chain. In particular, the system designer can not enforce a desired order in this case. Similar to NP-RR scheduling, FCFS is selected in the system's head symbol (`strategy = fcfs`). This is also the default scheduling strategy in our SVM implementation.

Priority Scheduling. In many systems, privilege of critical tasks has to be provided instead of fairness. Particularly, in event-triggered real-time systems, priority-based scheduling is an indispensable precondition for the timely execution of critical tasks and the shortening of their reaction times.

With *priority scheduling*, SdlRE provides a scheduling strategy with fixed priorities that are assigned on agent level. In particular, only SDL `Agents` can be configured with explicit priorities. SDL `AgentSets` and `Links` always run with system-wide highest priority, since they are executed only when then system structure changes (cf. FCFS strategy). For the same reason, the initiation of SDL `Agents` is privileged with highest priority as well. Thus, the final priority of an SDL `Agent` is assigned after the execution of its start transition.

Even with priorities, there are still situations in which system behavior is nondeterministic. In particular, FCFS is used within each priority class, i.e. if two timers in two agents of same priority expire simultaneously, the execution order is not prescribed by the specification. However, such situations can be resolved by the designer by assigning different priorities.

In contrast to signal priorities in Cmicro [8], priority scheduling leaves the consumption order of signals in an input port unchanged. Particularly, the semantics of `priority inputs` is untouched [2]. Thereby, SDL's implementation freedom is exploited while remaining compliant to its formal semantics.[2]

Similar to NP-RR and FCFS, the system developer selects priority scheduling by setting `strategy = static-priorities` in the SDL system's head symbol (see Fig. 3). In addition, priority scheduling provides parameters that the developer has to configure during system design, namely the number of priority levels (`levels = 5`) and the default priority of SDL `Agents` (`priority = 1`). By setting `levels` to a concrete natural number, the range of valid priorities is determined, which is from 0 (highest priority) to `levels-1` (lowest priority). Default priorities are used for SDL `Agents` without explicit priority assignment.

The assignment of priorities to SDL `Agents` is also defined by the developer in terms of annotations. For this purpose, several possibilities exist on various levels of the system hierarchy to allow priority assignments in a flexible way. In general, a priority is assigned in an SDL comment symbol that is connected

---

[2] We assume that the system is not overloaded permanently. Otherwise, there is no guarantee that a low-priority agent is eventually executed.

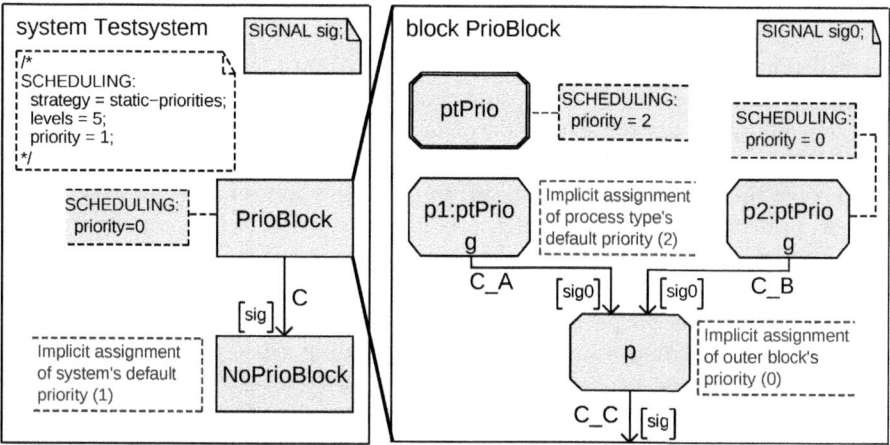

Fig. 3. Priority scheduling: Strategy is selected and configured in the head symbol of the SDL system. Priorities are directly assigned to SDL components.

to a corresponding SDL component (see Fig. 3). Again, annotations within the comment symbol start with the keyword SCHEDULING, followed by priority = <priority> (e.g., PrioBlock in Fig. 3). They can be associated with services,[3] processes, and blocks, in each case with instantiations as well as type definitions. If a priority is assigned to both type definition and instantiation, the instantiation's priority overrides the type definition's priority, resulting in an unambiguous priority assignment (cf. ptPrio and p2:ptPrio in Fig. 3). Otherwise, the instantiation gets the priority of the type definition (cf. p1:ptPrio in Fig. 3).

Although priorities are assigned at design time, the priorities of the resulting SDL Agents must be determined at runtime, since they are in general optional and depend on the agents' positions in the system hierarchy. In particular, the priority of an SDL Agent is determined according to the following constraints of the SDL specification, where the evaluation is applied in descending order:

1. If a priority is assigned to the SDL process or it contains services with assigned priorities, then the resulting SDL Agent gets the highest priority of all these assigned priorities.
2. If a process inherits from another process with assigned priority, the resulting SDL Agent gets the priority of the supertype. If the inheritance affects multiple levels, the priority is evaluated from bottom to top.
3. If a priority is assigned to the block specification containing the process, the resulting SDL Agent gets the block's priority (cf. process p in Fig. 3). If there is a hierarchical nesting of blocks, the process priority is evaluated from bottom to top.
4. If there is no priority assigned at all, the default priority is used as defined in the system's head symbol.

---

[3] Since SDL 2000, services are replaced by state aggregations [2]. Due to missing tool support, we still refer to services.

3.3   Suspension of Agents

All scheduling strategies supported by SdlRE are non-preemptive, leading to an efficient implementation with less runtime overhead. However, the non-preemptive scheduling delays the execution of high-priority agents until the currently running transition is finished.

To solve this problem and to speed up reaction times of high-priority agents further, priority scheduling in SdlRE provides the option to temporarily suspend agents according to their priority level. By this approach, system load can be reduced prior to an expected time-critical task, e.g., before time resynchronization starts. For this purpose, two SDL procedures, Suspend and Resume, have been specified, building a wrapper to corresponding scheduler functions in the SdlRE. The Suspend procedure provides a priority level as parameter, which states the borderline between agents that are dispatched further and agents that are (temporarily) prevented from execution. By calling the Resume procedure, all suspended agents are released.

In general, the decision to suspend particular agents from execution should be taken from some central components with scenario-specific knowledge. By enabling the suspension of agents by means of SDL procedures, components taking this decision can be specified in SDL during system design, e.g., in a centralized SDL process. Thereby, application knowledge and the system's current state can be taken into account to decide which agents are to be suspended.

3.4   Dealing with the SDL Environment

According to SDL's semantics, it is assumed that the SDL environment has one or more agent instances [2]. In our implementation of the environment, the *SDL Environment Framework* (SEnF), there is exactly one agent. Different from ordinary agents within the SDL system, the environment agent requires a special treatment, since it can be triggered by external events, e.g., a hardware interrupt. Therefore, when searching for an appropriate scheduling strategy for SDL systems, the question arises how to schedule the environment.

A naive solution might be the execution of the environment agent in *idle* times of the system, i.e., when no other agent is executable. This solution corresponds to a priority-based solution, at which the environment agent has lowest priority. However, in cases of temporary intra-system load, system input/output would be delayed significantly, which is not acceptable for many scenarios. Another solution would be the immediate execution of the environment agent each time a signal is pending to/from the environment, which corresponds to the assignment of the highest priority in a priority-based solution. But this solution may cause problems in case of polling hardware drivers and can also lead to overload within the system, since adding additional load from the environment to the system would be privileged. In sum, there is no generic solution to handle the environment, since the best strategy depends on the specific scenario as well as the used hardware platform. We propose again an annotation-based solution to let the system developer decide how to deal with the environment during load situations. In particular, we extend the presented scheduling annotations with three optional parameters that are specified in the system's head symbol:

- `env-signal_in-threshold`: Number of signals in the environment's input port that enforces the execution of the environment agent.
- `env-signal_out-threshold`: Threshold on the number of signals generated by the environment that are to be sent to the SDL system. Exceeding this value enforces the execution of the environment agent.
- `env-agent-threshold`: Number of non-environment agent executions that enforces the execution of the environment agent. This parameter defines a maximal interval (in terms of number of agent executions) between subsequent executions of the environment agent.

In general, smaller numbers lead to faster reactions. However, too small numbers may increase system load in situations in which load is already high. Therefore, adequate planning and load estimations are required to determine a suitable configuration. Compared to a scheduling of the SDL environment with one static priority, the solution based on thresholds is stronger and more flexible.

4   Implementation Aspects

In this section, we outline the implementation of the proposed extensions of SDL. Components and dependencies of our tool chain are illustrated in Fig. 4. The figure shows an excerpt of SDL-MDD (SDL-Model Driven Development), a holistic and domain-specific development process with SDL [19]. The excerpt starts with the *Platform-Independent Model (PIM)*, a functionally complete SDL specification. Next, the PIM is transformed to the *Platform-Specific Model (PSM)*, by adding hardware-specific aspects, e.g., to interface with specific communication technologies, and by adding scheduling aspects as introduced in Sect. 3. This transformation is partially guided by a set of heuristics, and supported by reuse approaches, e.g., SDL design patterns and SDL micro protocols. To generate code, the PSM is first transformed to SDL-PR format, using the IBM Rational SDL Suite, which accepts and preserves the annotations specifying scheduling aspects as (formal) comments. With the code transpiler ConTraST [3], the SDL-PR format is then automatically transformed to *Runtime-Independent Code (RIC)*, the C++ representation of the SDL system.

To incorporate the proposed SDL annotations into the generated code, we have modified and extended ConTraST. Before generating the C++ representation, ConTraST checks the correctness of the annotations' syntax and applies additional semantic checks, e.g., if an assigned priority is in the range of allowed priority levels. Afterwards, annotations regarding scheduling are grouped into runtime-independent and runtime-dependent annotations. Runtime-independent annotations describe static configuration parameters (e.g., the selected scheduling strategy) and are transformed into C macros. Thereby, they are already considered at compile time, decreasing the overhead at runtime. Runtime-dependent annotations are more dynamic in the sense that the corresponding configuration

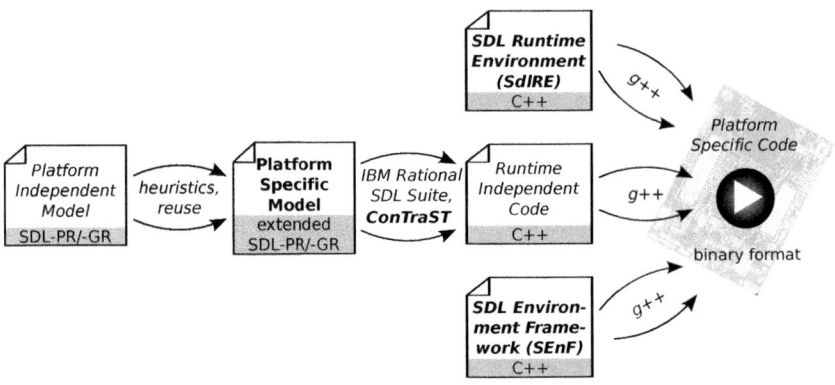

Fig. 4. Model-driven development with SDL and its annotation-based extensions

parameter must be determined at runtime. An example of a runtime-dependent annotation is the priority of an agent.

The RIC is complemented by the SDL Runtime Environment (SdlRE) and the SDL Environment Framework (SEnF). SdlRE, our implementation of the SVM, coordinates the execution of agents and the delivery of SDL signals. SEnF provides environment interfacing routines specific to the selected hardware platform, for instance for communication devices. To realize the scheduling annotations, we have modified and extended SdlRE and SEnF. In particular, an extensible scheduling framework with a well-defined interface was incorporated into SdlRE, in which, up to now, three scheduling strategies have been integrated (see Sect. 3).

To obtain *Platform-Specific Code (PSC)*, SdlRE, SEnF, and the RIC are compiled by a platform-specific compiler, and linked. The generated file is then deployed on the hardware platform, and executed.

5   Experimental Evaluation

In this section, we present quantitative evaluations of priority scheduling with and without suspension of agents, and demonstrate the benefits regarding response times and predictability of critical tasks in comparison to NP-RR and FCFS. In a first series of experiments, we measure the accuracy of SDL timers, i.e., the amount of time the consumption of SDL timer signals is delayed. In a second series of experiments, we investigate the precedence of signal chains. In both cases, we use SDL benchmark specifications for better comparison, and run the experiments on sensor nodes that are fully controlled by SEnF and SdlRE. The results show that our implementation is fully operational, and that the proposed extensions are necessary and effective.

All evaluations are done by benchmark experiments on a customary Imote2 sensor node [20] (on the right-hand side of Fig. 1). The Imote2 is equipped with 32 kB SRAM, 32 MB flash memory, additional 32 MB SDRAM, and a single-core

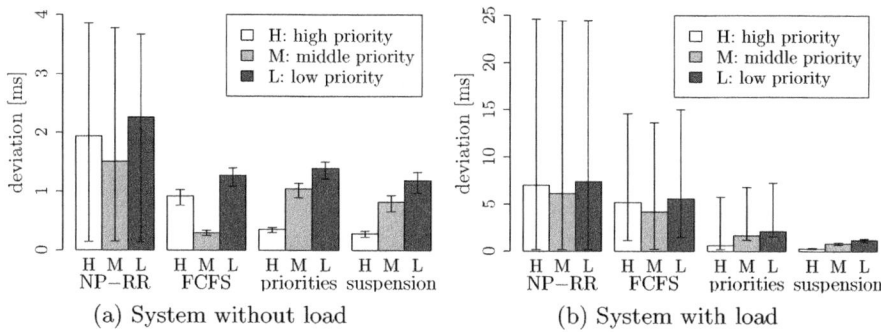

Fig. 5. Deviations of timer signals' actual consumption times from nominal values. Notice that (a) and (b) use different time scales.

XScale CPU, providing clock rates up to 416 MHz. The measured data values are sent to a PC via serial interface. To obtain reproducible results, further external interfaces are disabled. The evaluated SDL systems are deployed on the sensor node without further underlying operating system (bare integration). Thereby, all influences on the measured values, like interrupt handling and execution order of agents, are fully controlled by SEnF and SdlRE.

5.1   Accuracy of SDL Timers

This benchmark examines the deviation of SDL timers from their nominal values. The evaluated SDL system includes three SDL process instances of the same type, each instance setting a periodical timer to absolute and identical points in time. To each process instance, a different priority is assigned, defining an order of precedence between the agents at runtime. In addition, further processes with lower priority are added to the system to quantify the impact of load.

The results of this scenario are shown in Fig. 5 for all supported scheduling strategies. For priority scheduling, the plots distinguish between scheduling without suspension (named `priorities`) and with suspension (named `suspension`). In Fig. 5a, timer deviations from their nominal values are shown without further system load, where in Fig. 5b, random load was added to the system. In case of priority scheduling with suspension, load-generating agents are suspended from execution. Both plots illustrate, for every SDL timer, the average, minimum, and maximum deviation of timer signal consumption times from their nominal values. Each bar is based on 6000 measured samples.

In both plots, deviations are always greater than $0\,ms$ due to the overhead of selecting agent and transition. Both plots also show that average deviations and jitter are significantly higher when NP-RR is used. This is due to the scheduling of all agents with NP-RR, independent of signals in their input queue.

In case of no load (Fig. 5a), deviations with FCFS are in general comparable to deviations with priority scheduling. With FCFS, the precedence order between agents does not fit to the developer's requirements, since priorities can not be considered. However, there is also a clearly visible order when using FCFS (H – middle deviations, M – smallest deviations, L – largest deviations). This can be traced back to the process specification order in the SDL-PR file, a tool-specific property that is hardly ascertainable and influenceable during the creation of the SDL system. Since the system is free of background load, there is no necessity to suspend low-priority agents, thus, the results of priority scheduling without and with suspension are similar.

When load is added to the system (Fig. 5b), priority scheduling shows its full potential. Different from NP-RR and FCFS, average deviations and jitter increase significantly slower, since load-generating agents have lower priority, resulting in less influence in the consumption time of the considered agents' timer signals. In particular, average deviations increase by a factor of about 0.7 with priority scheduling (without suspension), where deviations with NP-RR and FCFS increase by factors of 3 up to 13. Comparing the average deviations with priority scheduling without suspension against FCFS, the high priority agent is executed 4.6 ms earlier (0.6 ms vs. 5.2 ms). This impressive number illustrates the need for priority-based scheduling in SDL. Although the degradation of timer accuracy is significantly smaller when using priority scheduling without suspension, the jitter is higher in comparison to the experiments without load, since load-generating transitions cannot be interrupted. This problem is solved by priority scheduling with suspension of low-priority agents. In particular, scheduling with suspension does not show any difference when load is added to the system, resulting in substantially more accurate and load-independent consumption times of timer signals, and thus in more predictable system behavior.

5.2   Prioritized Signal Exchange

In this scenario, the main focus is on the functional evaluation of NP-RR, FCFS, and priority scheduling by evaluating timing behavior of signal exchange within the SDL system. Therefore, we introduce the term *signal chain* to be a sequence $C = \langle s_1, s_2, \ldots, s_n \rangle$ of signals, started by signal s_1, such that consumption of signal s_i triggers the output of s_{i+1}, for $1 \leq i \leq n - 1$. The evaluated SDL system processes three identical signal chains $C_j = \langle s_{j,1}, \ldots, s_{j,n} \rangle$, $1 \leq j \leq 3$, where $s_{1,i}$, $s_{2,i}$, and $s_{3,i}$ (with $1 \leq i \leq n$) are processed by identical components (SDL processes and services) with different assigned priorities. Each signal chain triggers a total of 14 transitions, allocated into 5 SDL services and 9 SDL processes. By using inheritance and priority annotations on several hierarchy levels (blocks ↔ processes ↔ services), the correct implementation of priority scheduling as described in Sect. 3.2 is validated.

Figure 6 shows completion times of the three signal chains for FCFS, NP-RR, and priority scheduling without suspension. For each scheduling strategy, every signal chain is completed 4000 times. Because no random load was added to the system, completion times only have a small jitter. As expected, completion times with NP-RR are in general significantly higher due to the (non-required) execution of idling agents. In case of NP-RR and FCFS scheduling, there are only marginal differences in completion times of the three chains, where the

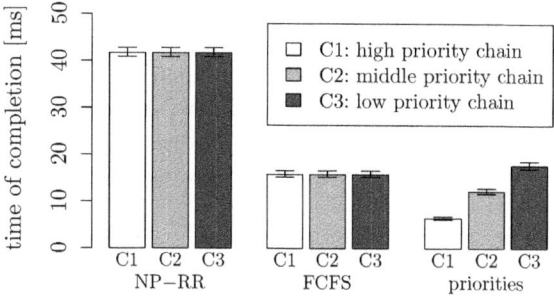

Fig. 6. Time of completion (avg/min/max) of all signal chains

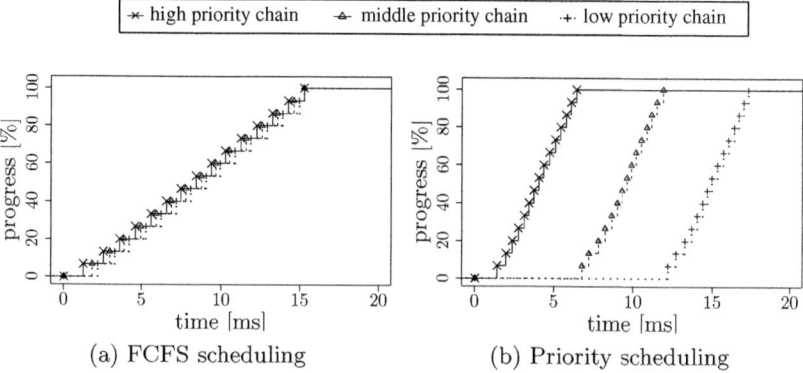

Fig. 7. Comparison of example signal chain progresses

precedence order between tasks is clearly observable in case of priority scheduling. Particularly, the completion time of the high-priority chain is 6.4 times (2.5 times) shorter than the completion time with NP-RR (FCFS) scheduling. Thus, reaction times on critical events are significantly shorter.

To demonstrate the differences in scheduling with FCFS and priority-based scheduling, Fig. 7 depicts showcase signal progresses per signal chain. With FCFS, signal progress is nearly in lockstep, since the scheduling of agents follows their activation order. In contrast, priority scheduling executes agents with fireable transitions according to their priority. Thereby, the high priority chain is finished even before signal forwarding of other chains starts.

6   Conclusions

When executing the concurrent runtime model of SDL on a concrete hardware platform, scheduling of the system's agents becomes necessary. Often, this step is applied in an unpredictable and tool-specific way. In this paper, we have introduced annotation-based extensions to SDL, which enable the developer to better control the execution order of agents by choosing and configuring appropriate scheduling strategies. In particular, we have introduced priority-based scheduling of SDL agents combined with a mechanism for their temporary suspension. The presented approach exploits the implementation freedom of SDL while still being compliant with its semantics. Furthermore, the approach is compatible with existing tools and incorporated into SDL-MDD, our model-driven development approach with SDL [19].

By the realization of a priority-based scheduling strategy, measures were introduced to privilege time-critical tasks and to suspend low-priority agents. Thereby, average as well as worst case reaction times of critical tasks can be reduced enormously, bringing SDL an important step closer to real-time system development. In experimental evaluations on customary sensor nodes, the benefits of priority scheduling with and without suspension were demonstrated. For instance, on a system with random load, consumption delays of expired critical SDL timers were more than 10 times smaller than consumption delays with FCFS scheduling.

During our experiments, it turned out that the priority of the SDL environment agent has a large impact on the predictability of reaction times. Here, pure priority scheduling with a single, static priority of the environment agent is not sufficient. With environment signal thresholds, we have presented an approach that distinguishes between input and output signals to and from the environment. This approach can be seen as a generalization of static priority scheduling: usually, the environment agent has the lowest priority, but obtains the highest priority if the threshold is exceeded - a step towards dynamic priority scheduling.

The SDL extensions proposed in this paper are an important, but not yet sufficient step towards hard real-time system development with SDL. First, tasks often consist of several related transitions, which may be associated with different SDL agents. If these SDL agents have different priorities, task execution can not be performed in a timely manner. Secondly, to design hard real-time systems, Worst-Case Execution Times (WCETs) must be known. While it is already difficult to determine WCETs for single transition bodies, it is even more difficult if the assumption that agent scheduling takes no time is dropped. Thirdly, agent priorities have to be assigned dynamically, if they are time-dependent, or if they depend on the current system state. For instance, an SDL process performing network synchronization should be privileged during resynchronization phases only. In summary, these points call for dynamic priorities, a notion of task in SDL, and WCETs of tasks. We will address these topics in our future work.

References

1. Kopetz, H.: Real-Time Systems – Design Principles for Distributed Embedded Applications. Kluwer Academic Publishers, Dordrecht (1997)
2. International Telecommunication Union (ITU): ITU-T Recommendation Z.100 (11/2007): Specification and Description Language (SDL) (2007)
3. Fliege, I., Grammes, R., Weber, C.: ConTraST - A Configurable SDL Transpiler and Runtime Environment. In: Gotzhein, R., Reed, R. (eds.) SAM 2006. LNCS, vol. 4320, pp. 216–228. Springer, Heidelberg (2006)

4. Bræk, R., Haugen, Ø.: Engineering Real Time Systems. Prentice Hall, Englewood Cliffs (1993)
5. Mitschele-Thiel, A.: Engineering with SDL – Developing Performance-Critical Communication Systems. John Wiley & Sons, Chichester (2000)
6. Sanders, R.: Implementing from SDL. In: Telektronikk 4.2000, Languages for Telecommunication Applications, Telenor (2000)
7. Leblanc, P., Ek, A., Hjelm, T.: Telelogic SDL and MSC tool families. In: Telektronikk 4.2000, Languages for Telecommunication Applications, Telenor (2000)
8. IBM: Rational SDL Suite (2011),
   http://www-01.ibm.com/software/awdtools/sdlsuite/
9. Álvarez, J.M., Díaz, M., Llopis, L., Pimentel, E., Troya, J.M.: Integrating Schedulability Analysis and Design Techniques in SDL. Real-Time Systems 24(3), 267–302 (2003)
10. Pragmadev: Real time developer studio (2011), http://www.pragmadev.com/
11. Bozga, M., Graf, S., Mounier, L., Ober, I., Roux, J.-L., Vincent, D.: Timed Extensions for SDL. In: Reed, R., Reed, J. (eds.) SDL 2001. LNCS, vol. 2078, pp. 223–240. Springer, Heidelberg (2001)
12. Diefenbruch, M., Hintelmann, J., Müller-Clostermann, B.: QUEST Performance Evalution of SDL System. In: Irmscher, K., Mittasch, C., Richter, K. (eds.) MMB (Kurzbeiträge), TU Bergakademie Freiberg, pp. 126–132 (1997)
13. Ober, I., Kerbrat, A.: Verification of Quantitative Temporal Properties of SDL Specifications. In: Reed, R., Reed, J. (eds.) SDL 2001. LNCS, vol. 2078, pp. 182–202. Springer, Heidelberg (2001)
14. Kolloch, T., Färber, G.: Mapping an Embedded Hard Real-Time Systems SDL Specification to an Analyzable Task Network - A Case Study. In: Müller, F., Bestavros, A. (eds.) LCTES 1998. LNCS, vol. 1474, pp. 156–165. Springer, Heidelberg (1998)
15. Christmann, D.: Spezifikation und automatisierte Implementierung zeitkritischer Systeme mit TC-SDL. Master's thesis, TU Kaiserslautern (2010)
16. Stankovic, J.A., Ramamritham, K.: Hard Real-Time Systems, Tutorial. IEEE Computer Society Press, Los Alamitos (1988)
17. Jeffay, K., Stanat, D.F., Martel, C.U.: On Non-Preemptive Scheduling of Periodic and Sporadic Tasks. In: IEEE Real-Time Systems Symposium, pp. 129–139 (1991)
18. Fliege, I.: Component-based Development of Communication Systems. PhD thesis, University of Kaiserslautern (2009)
19. Gotzhein, R.: Model-driven with SDL – Improving the Quality of Networked Systems Development. In: Proc. of the 7th Int. Conf. on New Technologies of Distributed Systems (NOTERE 2007), Marrakesh, Morocco, pp. 31–46 (2007)
20. Memsic: Imote 2 datasheet (2011),
   http://www.memsic.com/support/documentation/wireless-sensor-networks/
   category/7-datasheets.html?download=134

A Model-Based Formalization of the Textual Notation for SDL-UML

Alexander Kraas

Poppenreuther Str. 45, D-90419 Nürnberg, Germany
alexander.kraas@gmx.de

Abstract. The Specification and Description Language (SDL) is a domain specific language that is well-established in the telecommunication sector since many years, but only a small set of SDL tools is available. In contrast, for the Unified Modeling Language (UML) a wide range of different kinds of tools can be used for various purposes, such as model transformation. In order to makes it possible to specify SDL compliant models with UML, a profile for the combined use of SDL and UML was standardized. This profile also embraces a textual notation for the action language of SDL-UML, which is a subset of the concrete syntax of SDL. Unfortunately, a formal specification of that textual notation is not specified. In order to remedy this gap, in this paper, a model-based approach for the formalization of the textual notation for SDL-UML is presented.

Keywords: SDL-UML, Profile, Textual Notation, Formalization.

1 Introduction

Since many years, the Specification and Description Language (SDL) [1] is well-established in the telecommunication sector. In general, SDL can be used to specify telecommunication protocols and the behavior of distributed systems, but its applicability is not only restricted to these domains. In addition to SDL specific tools, SDL compliant models can also be specified with the Unified Modeling Language (UML), which requires that the SDL-UML profile [2] is applied to a UML model. This profile does not only include stereotypes for the specification of structural aspects, but also a set of stereotypes for the behavior specification. This also embraces a particular action language that can be used in terms of graphical SDL-UML elements or with the corresponding textual notation.

Unfortunately, the mapping of the textual notation to the corresponding SDL-UML elements is not formally defined, because associated transformation steps are only specified in terms of textual rules. Furthermore, the transformation of shorthand notations in the textual notation is not defined, too. In contrast, the static semantics of the concrete and abstract syntax of SDL are well-defined in Annex F2 [3] of the Z.100 rec. by using a first order predicate logic.

In the present paper, it is analyzed if the Query / View / Transformation (QVT) [6] technology and the Object Constraint Language (OCL) [4] can be applied in order to specify constraints and transformation rules for the textual

I. Ober and I. Ober (Eds.): SDL 2011, LNCS 7083, pp. 218–232, 2011.

notation of SDL-UML. Furthermore, the specification of a metamodel for the textual notation is discussed, because without such a model neither OCL nor QVT are applicable. However, the mapping of the textual notation to corresponding SDL-UML elements is not addressed in this paper. Instead, the QVT-based transformation of shorthand notations into equivalent code fragments of the textual notation is discussed. That is because this kind of transformations is more complex than the other one. Nevertheless, on the foundation stone of the presented approach, a mapping of the textual notation to SDL-UML elements should also be possible.

Apart from a model-based formalization, an appropriate framework for parsing and processing the textual notation of SDL-UML is discussed in the second part of this paper. This framework rests on the Eclipse Modeling Framework (EMF) [12] and the Scanner-less Generalized Left-Right (SGLR) parser that is a part of the Stratego/XT Project [14].

The rest of this paper is structured as follows. In section 2, related approaches and metamodels are discussed. A brief overview of the textual notation for the SDL-UML profile is given in section 3. A metamodel for the textual notation, associated constraints and transformation rules are discussed in section 4. The framework for parsing and processing the textual notation is presented in section 5. Finally, in the last section a conclusion and an outlook on the future work is given.

2   Related Work

Apart from the SDL-UML profile, in [8] a UML profile for Communicating Systems (UML-CS) is discussed, but this does not embrace a textual notation. Both profiles specify SDL-specific action semantics, but SDL expressions are represented in a different manner. In SDL-UML, expressions are represented in terms of UML expressions, whereas in UML-CS the semantics of expressions is not specified. The advantage of representing SDL expressions in terms of dedicated UML elements is that parse trees for the textual notation of SDL-UML can be stored in the model repository of a UML tool. Hence, the mapping of SDL-UML models to the abstract grammar of SDL should be straightforward. However, before the textual notation can be mapped to corresponding SDL-UML elements, the static semantics have to be analyzed and shorthand notations have to be expanded. But this aspect is not treated in the Z.109.

Another approach for the formalization of a UML profile for SDL is discussed in [10]. On the foundation of a case study, the mapping of stereotyped elements to the abstract grammar of SDL is discussed. In general, the proposed methodology is similar to that used for the formalization of the static semantics of SDL [3]. As in the above-mentioned case, the static semantics of the textual notation is not treated.

A metamodel-based approach for SDL is discussed in [9]. In particular, two metamodels for different purposes are proposed. One metamodel address the abstract grammar of SDL-2000, while the other one is introduced for specifying the manner in which features should be presented to a user. Even if the textual representation is treated in a small example, a few important issues are still open. In particular, these are the mapping to the abstract grammar and the transformations of shorthand notations.

In contrast to the approaches discussed above, the challenges and problems concerning the implementation of a parser for the concrete syntax of SDL-2000 are discussed in [9]. But also in this case, the check of the static semantics and the transformation of shorthand notations are not treated.

All works mentioned above, address issues concerning the formalization and the mapping to the abstract grammar of SDL, but the semantics or the transformation of a textual notation is not treated. In order to fill this gap, the present paper addresses the issue of transforming shorthand notations on concrete syntax level by using the operational language of QVT. In addition, the specification of a metamodel for the textual notation is analyzed.

3   The Textual Notation of the SDL-UML Profile

The SDL-UML profile as specified in the most recent version of the Z.109 Rec. [2] defines a set of stereotypes that can be used for the structural and behavioral specification of a SDL system in terms of UML. The stereotypes that define the action language of SDL-UML extend only a small set of metaclasses related to UML Actions. In addition to the graphical format of UML actions, also a textual notation is defined that is a subset of the concrete grammar of SDL. In general, it is possible to use the graphical and textual format of SDL-UML actions in combination.

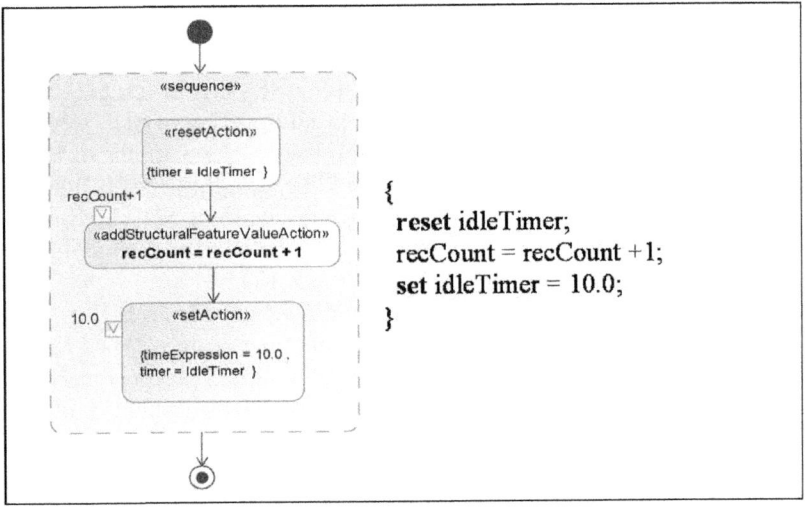

Fig. 1. Compound Statement for Transition T2

The example given in Fig. 1 specifies the behavior of a transition in a «StateMachine». The first statement is a «ResetAction» which resets the `Idle-Time`. In the textual notation, this statement is represented as a `<reset>` symbol. The «AddStructuralFeatureValueAction», which corresponds to an `<assignment>` symbol, is used to increase the `recCount` variable. Finally, the «SetAction» restarts the `IdleTimer` with an initial value of `10` seconds. The corresponding symbol of the textual notation is the `<set>` symbol.

4 A Model-Based Formalization of the Textual Notation

The model-based formalization of the textual notation for SDL-UML is discussed in this chapter. For the considered approach, a metamodel for the textual notation is introduced. On the foundation of this metamodel, the applicability of the Object Constraint Language (OCL) and the Query/View/Transformation (QVT) technology are discussed.

4.1 General Approach

The approach discussed in this chapter is aligned to the static semantics of SDL, which is specified in Annex F2 [3] of Z.100. This document embraces the static semantics for the concrete and abstract syntax of SDL. For the purpose of formalization, various constraints, transformations and mapping rules are defined. However, for the presented approach, only constraints and transformations on concrete syntax level are of interest. The constraints define a set of rules that ensure the well-formedness of the concrete syntax. The purpose of the transformation rules is to specify in which manner shorthand notations have to be expanded on concrete syntax level.

In the presented approach, the Object Constraint Language (OCL) is utilized in order to specify constraints for the textual notation of SDL-UML. This is feasible, because the formalisms of SDL as well as OCL are both first order predicate logics. Furthermore, for the transformation of shorthand notations in the textual notation of SDL-UML, the operational language of the Query/View/Transformation (QVT) specification [6] is used. In contrast to the relational language of QVT, with the operational language mapping rules with a higher degree of complexity can be defined. That is because relational mappings only express the relationship of elements.

Since QVT mapping rules are specified on metamodel level, a source and a target metamodel are required. However, with QVT also in-place transformations can be defined. In this particular case, as source and target of a transformation, the same metamodel can be used. Hence, only one metamodel is required for the transformation of shorthand notations in the textual notation of SDL-UML. That is because shorthand notations are expanded to corresponding statements on the same syntax level.

4.2   A Metamodel for the Textual Notation of SDL-UML

In the most recent version of Z.109 [2], the syntax of the textual notation is specified in terms of Backus-Naur Form (BNF) production rules. Hence, before model-based techniques can be applied to the textual notation, a meta-model has to be derived from the BNF specification. The realization is discussed on the example of the assignment statement and the operation application expression. Later on, the resulting metamodel fragments are used for a detailed discussion of the transformation of shorthand notations in terms of QVT mappings.

The following production rules specify the concrete syntax of a value assignment to a variable. A distinction has to be made between the assignment of a value to a simple variable, a field of a variable for a structured type (field variable) or an element in a variable that represents a multi-valued type (indexed type). As a matter of principle, it is possible to construct a nested structure of field and indexed variables of arbitrary depth. That is because the left parts of indexed variable> and <field variable> consist of a <variable> non-terminal symbol.

```
<assignment>
    ::= <variable> <is assigned sign> <expression>

<variable> ::=
    <variable identifier> <extended variable>

<extended variable>
    <indexed variable> <field variable>

<indexed variable> ::=
    <variable> { ( <actual parameter list> ) }
  | <variable> <left square bracket> <actual parameter list>
      <right square bracket>

<field variable> ::=
    <variable> <exclamation mark> <field name> <variable>
  | <full stop> <field name>

<field name> ::=
    <name>
```

The metamodel fragment that represents the concrete syntax of an assignment statement is shown in Fig. 2. In comparison to the corresponding BNF production rules, this metamodel fragment does not contain any lexical symbols, such as parenthesis (e.g. <indexed variable>) or keywords. That is because elements of the metamodel for the textual notation of SDL-UML shall be instantiated based on an Abstract Syntax Tree (AST) that usually does not contain such syntactical sugar.

As a matter of principle, a metamodel for a textual notation could be generated automatically by applying the algorithm proposed in [15]. However, this kind of metamodel also contains not required syntactical sugar and keywords. Hence, the discussed metamodel for the textual notation of SDL-UML is derived manually.

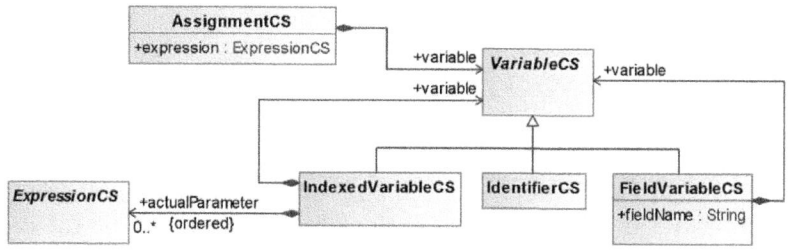

Fig. 2. Metamodel of the Assignment

In general, each production rule is represented as a particular metaclass and attributes represent the terminal and non-terminal symbols of a production. Furthermore, most of the attributes of metaclasses are defined in terms of composite aggregations, rather than associations, because instances of the attributes shall be stored in the scope of its metaclass. A ordered list of symbols, such as <actual parameter list>, is represented as an ordered set of attributes with an (possible) infinite upper bound (see IndexedVariableCS in Fig. 2). A metaclass that is the counterpart for a production rule which only consists of non-terminal alternatives, e.g. <variable>, is defined as abstract. The reason for this is that such kind of symbols and metaclasses shall not be instantiated.

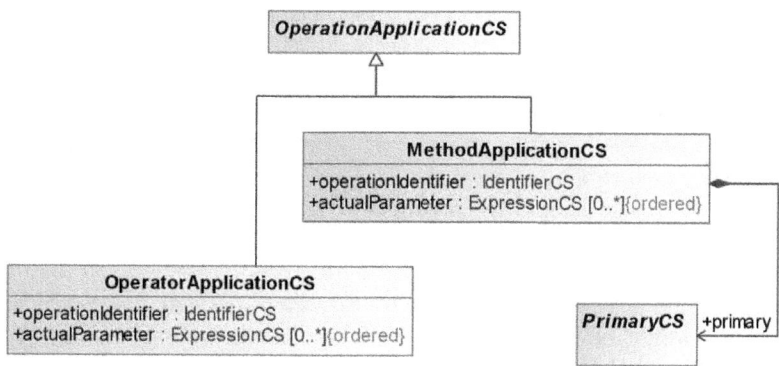

Fig. 3. Metamodel of the Operation Application

The fragment of the metamodel that represents the operation application of the textual notation of SDL-UML is shown in Fig. 3. In contrast to the fragment considered before, attributes are not defined in terms of explicit composite aggregations. Instead, they are specified as owned attributes of metaclasses. In this case, the aggregation kind of an attribute has to be defined as composite, which is the pendant for a composite aggregation.

4.3   OCL Constraints on the Textual Notation

As mentioned in section 4.1, the formalisms of SDL [3] embrace a set of constraints that ensure the well-formedness of the concrete syntax. In general, a subset of these constraints should also apply for the textual notation of SDL-UML. In order to evaluate the applicability of OCL constraints for the metamodel presented in the section before, the following constraint on the concrete syntax of SDL is taken as example:

$$\forall methodApp \in \text{<method application>}:$$
$$getEntityDefinition_0(methodApp.s\text{-<identifier>}, \textbf{method}) \neq undefined$$

Fig. 4. Constraint on a method application of the concrete syntax of SDL

The above shown constraint ensures that the operation identifier in a method application can only refer to an operation which is of kind 'method'. In order to ensure the same conditions for the textual notation of SDL-UML, the following OCL invariant constraint can be defined in the context of the MethodApplicationCS metaclass.

```
context MethodApplicationCS
   inv: not self.getEntityDefinition
        (self.operationIdentifier,'method').oclIsUndefined()
```

First of all, the constraint invokes the `getEntityDefinition()` operation, which determines if an operation of kind method exists for the given identifier. In addition, the leading not operator and the predefined `oclIsUndefined()` operation are used to determine if the first operation returns a result or not.

In general, it also should be possible to translate other constraints of the formalisms of SDL in the same manner, but for this purpose also helper operations, such as `getEntityDefinition()`, has to be taken into account. That is because some of these operations require access to elements of a SDL-UML model that cannot be specified in terms of the textual notation, e.g. instances of «ActiveClass». Hence, an appropriate OCL environment has to provide an implementation for such kind of operations.

4.4   Transformation of Shorthand Notations

In this section, the model-based transformation of shorthand notations in the textual notation of SDL-UML is discussed in detail. As already mentioned, the presented approach rests on the operational transformation language of QVT. The application of this language is considered on the example of the transformation of a field variable occurring in an assignment. The required metaclasses for this transformation are defined in section 4.2.

Transformations on the Concrete Syntax Level of SDL. The formal transformation rule for a field variable of a SDL assignment is shown in Fig. 5. This rule specifies that each `<field variable>` in an assignment has to be transformed to a corresponding `<method application>` that is the new right hand expression (value to be assigned) in the transformed assignment. The name of the method application is derived from the `<field name>` concatenated with the word 'Modify'. Furthermore, the right hand expression of the original assignment is taken as the argument of the created method application. The `<variable>` of the original field variable is used as the new variable in the transformed assignment. In addition, this variable also has to be used as the `<primary>` of the created method application.

```
<assignment>(<field variable>(var, fieldname), expr)
   =8=>
       <assignment>(var, <method application>(var, modifyExtractName(fieldname, "Modify"), expr))
```

Fig. 5. Rule for the transformation of a field variable shorthand notation

For instance, consider an assignment, containing two field variables, which has a shorthand notation as follows: `myVar.fieldA.fieldB = value`. After applying the before mentioned transformation rule two times, an assignment that contains two nested method applications is created.

```
myVar = myVar.fieldAModify(myVar.fieldA.fieldBModify(value))
```

QVT-based Transformations of a Field Variable. In this section, the QVT-based transformation of short hand notations is discussed on the example of the transformation rule explained in the section before. As in the case of OCL queries and constraints, usually, QVT mapping rules are defined in the 'context' of a particular metaclass. When a mapping rule is invoked, the current context instance is passed as context parameter and can be accessed by the predefined 'self' variable. In addition, QVT also introduces the predefined variable 'result' that can be used in order to access the result of a mapping rule. In the presented approach, each mapping rule is defined in the context of an appropriate metaclass so that the 'self' variable refers to the source instance for a transformation.

The QVT implemented transformation of a field variable consists of a set of different mapping rules, because for this purpose several transformation steps are required. The starting point for the transformation is the `fieldVariableTo-Variable()` mapping operation, which is specified in the context of the AssignmentCS metaclass. First of all, it has to be ensured that only instances of an assignment for a field variable are mapped. This can be realized with the optional 'when' clause of a mapping operation that has to contain a Boolean guard condition.

In the body of the mapping rule, the `fieldVar` refers to the field variable and `fVarClone` contains a copy of the same value. That is because in QVT the value of a variable can be mapped only once, but the present mapping operation maps a field variable to a new variable and a primary expression in the result of the mapping. In addition, further mappings are implemented by the `toMethodApplication()` operation.

```
mapping AssignmentCS  ::fieldVariableToVariable():AssignmentCS
  when { self.variable.oclIsTypeOf(FieldVariableCS)}
  {
    var fieldVar:FieldVariableCS
          := self.variable.oclAsType(FieldVariableCS),
        fVarClone:FieldVariableCS
          := fieldVar.deepclone().oclAsType(FieldVariableCS);
    expression
          := fVarClone.map toMethodApplication(self.expression);
    variable := fieldVar.variable;
  }
```

The result of the `toMethodApplication()` mapping operation is a new instance of the MethodApplicationCS metaclass, which has to be used as the value to be assigned in the transformed assignment. Hence, within this mapping operation, the `actualParameter` and the `operatioIdentifier` of the method application are constructed, but the mapping of the primary part is realized by another mapping operation.

```
mapping FieldVariableCS::toMethodApplication
  (param:ExpressionCS):MethodApplicationCS
  {
    primary := self.variable.map toPrimary();
    operationIdentifier := objectIdentifierCS
        { name := self.fieldName+"Modify"};
    actualParameter := param;
  }
```

For the mapping of a variable to the primary part of a method application, the `toPrimary()` operation has to be invoked. In contrast to the mapping operations discussed before, this operation makes use of the 'disjunction' functionality of QVT. Instead of an operation body, a list of mapping operations is specified.

The applicability of each of these operations is evaluated in the order of their occurrence, as long as the type and the 'when' clause of one of these operations matches.

The mapping to a primary is realized in the mentioned way, because the VariableCS metaclass is denoted as abstract and has three specializing non-abstract sub-classes (see Fig. 2). Instead of determining the required mapping operation depending on the concrete type of a VariableCS instance with an if-then-else construct, the handy way of a disjunction is used for this purpose.

```
mapping VariableCS::toPrimary():PrimaryCS
  disjuncts
    VariableCS::toVariableAccessPrimary,
    VariableCS::toFieldPrimary,
    VariableCS::toIndexedPrimary { }
```

Since a variable can consist of a list of field and indexed variables with an arbitrary length, each of them has to be mapped in a separate step. Hence, the mapping operations toIndexedPrimary() and toFieldPrimary() are recursive mappings. In contrast, the toVariableAccessPrimary() mapping operation has not to be recursive, because a variable identifier is always the left most part in a nested assignment.

```
mapping VariableCS::toVariableAccessPrimary():VariableAccessCS
  when { self.oclIsTypeOf(IdentifierCS) }
  {
    identifier := self.oclAsType(IdentifierCS);
    isThis := false;
  }

mapping VariableCS::toFieldPrimary():FieldPrimaryCS
  when { self.oclIsTypeOf(FieldVariableCS) }
  {
    var fieldVar:FieldVariableCS
          := self.oclAsType(FieldVariableCS);
        fieldName := fieldVar.fieldName;
    primary := fieldVar.variable.map toPrimary();
  }

mapping VariableCS::toIndexedPrimary():IndexedPrimaryCS
  when { self.oclIsTypeOf(IndexedVariableCS) }
  {
    var iVar:IndexedVariableCS
          := self.oclAsType(IndexedVariableCS);
    actualParameter := iVar.actualParameter;
    primary := iVar.variable.map toPrimary();
  }
```

Transformation Results. For the proof of concept, the transformation source and its transformed counterpart are shown in Fig. 6. On the left side of this figure, the source AssignmentCS instance is shown, which is the equivalent for the following textual specified assignment: `myVar.fieldA.fieldB = value`.

The AssignmentCS instance shown on the right side of the figure is the transformation result of the `fieldVariableToVariable()` mapping operation. The mapping has to be performed twice, because the source instance contains two nested field variables. In consequence, the transformation result contains two nested method applications and only one variable identifier that refers to `myVar`.

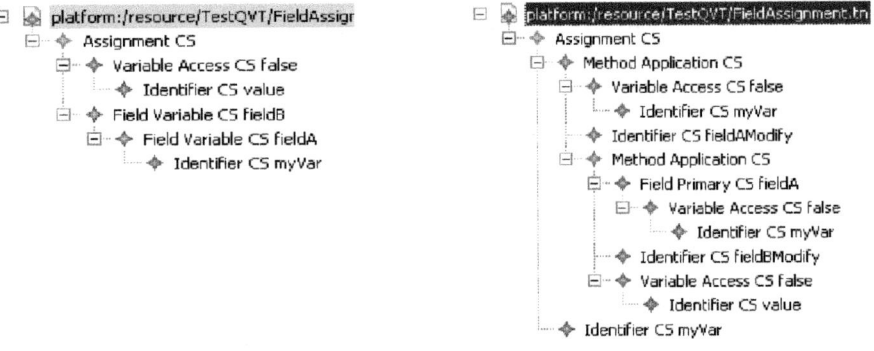

Fig. 6. Source and transformed field variable assignment

5   Framework for Processing the Textual Notation

A framework for parsing and processing the textual notation of SDL-UML is presented in this section. The most important parts of this framework are a parser for the notation, a component that validates OCL constraints and another component for processing QVT transformations.

5.1   Components of the Framework

In general, the prototypical framework for parsing and processing the textual notation of SDL-UML consists of the Scanner-less Generalized Left-Right (SGLR) parser [14] and components of the Eclipse Modeling Projects [13]. In general, Eclipse also provides different Text-to-Model transformation solutions, but they had been assessed as not appropriate for parsing the textual notation. This fact is discussed in more detail in sections 5.2 and 5.3.

The following parts of Eclipse are used for the parsing and processing framework of the textual notation:

- *Eclipse Modeling Framework (EMF)*
  The metamodel of the textual notation is specified in terms of an EMF model. All other components of the framework access instances of this metamodel. In addition, a tree-based model editor for the metamodel is generated.
- *QVT Operation (QVTO)*
  This component of Eclipse implements the operational language of QVT. This component is required for processing the mapping operations discussed in section 4.4.
- *OCL Parser*
  The OCL parser of eclipse is used to evaluate constraints on instances of the metamodel for the textual notation. Before QVT mapping operations are processed, the defined constraints are evaluated in order to ensure the well-formedness of the parsed input.

5.2   Requirements for the Parser

In this section, the most important requirements for a parser, which is able to process the textual notation of SDL-UML, are discussed. The requirements to be fulfilled are as follows:

1. *Ability to parse atomic expressions and statements*
   A parser for the textual notation should have the ability to parse atomic expressions and statements. That is because in SDL-UML it is possible to specify atomic actions in terms of its textual representation.
2. *Ability to automatically construct a parse tree*
   An appropriate parser should support the automatic creation of a parse tree, which makes further processing steps (e.g. model transformations) possible. In addition, a parse tree should be accessible in terms of an Application Programming Interface (API).
3. *Support of user-defined annotations*
   The notation of the grammar definition should support the ability to specify user-defined annotations for production rules so that additional information can be injected into generated code.
4. *Handling of syntactical ambiguities*
   As stated in [11], the concrete syntax of SDL has some ambiguities, which are also inherited by the textual notation of SDL-UML. A disambiguation is only possible with context-sensitive information, but in the case of SDL-UML, the required information can only be determined from elements in a SDL-UML model. Hence, a parser for the textual notation should be able parse non-ambiguous grammars.

5.3   The SGLR Parser

As mentioned in section 5.1, the SGLR parser is chosen for the prototypical framework, because its distinguished features fulfill most of the identified requirements.

The SGLR parser can process atomic expressions and statements (*requirement 1*), because a set of different start symbols can be defined. Furthermore, the SGLR parser can be used in combination with multiple target languages, because it supports different textual as well as binary formats in order to represent parse trees (*requirement 2*). Nevertheless, an appropriate access to parse trees is only possible with a wrapper API. Since such a component is not a part of the SGLR parser, it has to be implemented or generated.

For the specification of production rules, the Syntax Definition Format (SDF) of the SGLR parser has to be used. A notable feature of SDF is the support of user-defined annotations (*requirement 3*), which can be specified in terms of labels and attributes. In SDF, labels can be specified for any kind of terminal and non-terminal symbol of a SDF production rule. The second possibility to specify user-defined annotations is to use optional attributes for SDF production rules. Due to the fact that the SGLR parser produces a parse forest instead of only one parse tree, ambiguities can be represented very efficiently (*requirement 4*). If an ambiguity exists in a parse tree of the textual notation of SDL-UML, this is resolved after the instantiation of corresponding metamodel elements.

As discussed before, the SGLR parser does not provide an API for accessing parse trees. Hence, a generator that creates a wrapper API was implemented. For this purpose, the generator extracts user-defined information from the SDF specification, which contains the syntax definitions of the textual notation for SDL-UML. Based on this information, various Java classes are generated which makes the instantiation of the metamodel for the textual notation possible.

5.4 The Syntax Definition Formalism and Its Relation to Metaclasses

In general, each SDF production consists of at least one symbol followed by an arrow sign -> and the name of the sort, which is introduced by a production. The sort name can be followed by a comma-separated list of optional production attributes. The list has to be written within curly brackets {...}. For instance, information required for constructing an AST have to be specified in terms of particular constructor attributes (cons). In addition, labeled symbols can be used in order to define user-defined annotations. This kind of symbols is prefixed with a name that represents the label, e.g. `"variable":Variable`.

As mentioned in the section before, user-defined annotations are required to generate the wrapper API for the textual notation of SDL-UML. In addition to labeled symbols, the API generator processes constructor attributes, too. The relations of annotations in a SDF specification to corresponding metaclasses are discussed on the following example. In this example, the information that is required by the API generaotr is underlined.

In general, the metaclass to which a SDF production belongs is referred by the constructor attribute. For instance, the Assignment production is associated with the AssignmentCS metaclass. Furthermore, labeled symbols refer to attributes of the corresponding metaclass. When a production is specified only with a non-terminal symbol, e.g. the Variable production, no annotations have to be defined. That is because the counterpart of this kind of productions is an abstract metaclass. For instance, the counterpart of the Variable production is the VariableCS metaclass.

```
variable:Variable "=" expression:Expression
    -> Assignment { cons("AssignmentCS") }

VariableID      -> Variable
IndexedVariable -> Variable
FieldVariable   -> Variable

variable:Variable "[" actualParameter:ActualParameterList "]"
    -> IndexedVariable { cons("IndexedVariableCS") }

variable:Variable "." fieldName:Name
    -> FieldVariable { cons("FieldVariableCS") }

OperatorApplication -> OperationApplication
MethodApplication   -> OperationApplication

operationIdentifier:OperationID
    -> OperatorApplication {cons("OperatorApplicationCS")}
operationIdentifier:OperationID
        "(" actualParameter:ActualParameterList ")"
    -> OperatorApplication {cons("OperatorApplicationCS")}

primary:Primary "."operationIdentifier:OperationID
    -> MethodApplication {cons("MethodApplicationCS")}

primary:Primary "."operationIdentifier:OperationID
        "(" actualParameter:ActualParameterList ")"
    -> MethodApplication {cons("MethodApplicationCS")}
```

6 Conclusion and Future Work

In the recent years, many research activities have considered the model-based formalization of the abstract syntax of SDL. In addition, the mapping from UML profiles to the abstract syntax of SDL has been treated. However, that research work has not covered the formalization of a textual notation. In order to close this gap, a model-based approach for transforming shorthand notations in the textual notation of SDL-UML was discussed.

In a first step, the derivation of a metamodel for the textual notation of SDL-UML was analyzed on the example of a small part of the syntax definition. On this foundation, the successful application of the operational language of QVT could be proofed. Furthermore, also the OCL-based specification of constraints on the textual notation was considered. In summary, it can be concluded that the model-based formalization of the textual notation for SDL-UML could be possible.

For the future. it is planned to complete the presented metamodel. Afterwards, the model-based mapping of textual notation to corresponding stereotypes will be considered.

References

1. International Telecommunication Union: Recommendation Z.100 (11/07), Specification and Description Language (SDL),
   http://www.itu.int/rec/T-REC-Z.100/en
2. International Telecommunication Union: Recommendation Z.109 (06/07), SDL-2000 combined with UML, http://www.itu.int/rec/T-REC-Z.109-200706-I/en
3. International Telecommunication Union: Recommendation Z.100 Annex F2 (11/00), SDL Formal Definition, Static Semantics,
   http://www.itu.int/rec/T-REC-Z.100-200011-IAnnF2/en
4. Object Management Group: Object Constraint Language, OMG Available Specification, Version 2.2 (February 2010), http://www.omg.org/spec/OCL/2.2/PDF
5. Object Management Group: Unified Modeling Language (UML), Superstructure, V2.3 (May 2010), http://www.omg.org/spec/UML/2.3/Superstructure/PDF
6. Object Management Group: Meta Object Facility (MOF) 2.0 Query/View/Transformation Specification, Version 1.0 (April 2008),
   http://www.omg.org/spec/QVT/1.0/PDF
7. Kraas, A., Rehm, P.: Results in using the new version of the SDL-UML profile. In: Joint ITU-T and SDL Forum Society Workshop on ITU System Design Languages, Geneva, Switzerland, September 15-16 (2008)
8. Kraatz, S., Hogrefe, D., Werner, C.: A UML Profile for Communicating Systems. In: Gotzhein, R., Reed, R. (eds.) SAM 2006. LNCS, vol. 4320, pp. 1–18. Springer, Heidelberg (2006)
9. Prinz, A., Scheidgen, M., Tveit, M.: A Model-Based Standard for SDL. In: Gaudin, E., Najm, E., Reed, R. (eds.) SDL 2007. LNCS, vol. 4745, pp. 1–18. Springer, Heidelberg (2007)
10. Grammes, R.: Formalisation of the UML Profile for SDL - A Case Study. Technical Report 352/06, Department of Computer Science, University of Kaiserslautern (2006)
11. Schmitt, M.: The Development of a Parser for SDL-2000. In: Proceedings of the Tenth GI/ITG Technical Meeting on Formal Description Techniques for Distributed Systems, pp. 131–142. Shaker Verlag, Ithaca (2009)
12. The Eclipse Foundation, Eclipse 3.3.2, Open source software,
    http://www.eclipse.org/platform
13. Homepage of the Eclipse Modeling Project, http://www.eclipse.org/modeling/
14. The Stratego/XT Project, http://www.strategoxt.org/
15. Alanen, M., Porres, I.: A Relation Between Context-Free Grammars and Meta Object Facility Metamodels. Technical Report 606, TUCS (March 2004)

Standardizing Variability – Challenges and Solutions

Franck Fleurey[1], Øystein Haugen[1], Birger Møller-Pedersen[2],
Andreas Svendsen[1,2], and Xiaorui Zhang[1,2]

[1] SINTEF, Pb. 124 Blindern, 0314 Oslo, Norway
[2] Department of Informatics, University of Oslo,
Pb. 1080 Blindern, 0316 Oslo, Norway
{franck.fleurey,oystein.haugen,andreas.svendsen}@sintef.no,
birger@ifi.uio.no, xiaorui.zhang@sintef.no

Abstract. Any modeling language can be said to model variability, but our concern is how variability can be expressed generically and thus be standardized on its own and not as an add-on or profile to other languages. In product line engineering feature modeling has been applied to express variants of product models. This paper shows how the Common Variability Language can be designed to enhance feature modeling and automate the production of product models from a product line model.

Keywords: Product line engineering, variability modeling, feature modeling, OMG, standards.

1 Introduction

Modeling languages do express variability. Templates, generics and similar language constructs enable one model to be the source of many similar models coming about by instantiation templates and by providing actual type parameters to generic model elements. Classes, subclasses and interfaces play roles here, as they may be used to express constraints on variability.

This kind of variability modeling is standardized as part of the standardization of each of the modeling languages. SDL and UML are examples of modeling languages that have these kinds of constructs. Some may be more formally defined than others, but in general one may assume that the variability expressed in modeling languages will imply semantically sound specific models (where variability has been resolved), i.e. the specific models adhere to the semantics of the language, and the semantics of the variability constructs are also defined as part of the semantics of the language.

Feature modeling is another kind of variability modeling. There is a de facto standard for how feature models are depicted, however, not what the semantics is, and especially not what a resolution of the variability of a feature model will imply for a model in some modeling language. Feature models are usually defined separately and not tied to any (design or implementation) model that would have (or implement) the resolved features.

Standardizing the variability mechanisms as part of modeling languages would be in contradiction to the 'art of language design', and - if carried out – imply the design and implementation of the same set of constructs for a large number of languages. Standardizing a pure feature modeling language will only give semantics to the variability, not to its effect on models.

I. Ober and I. Ober (Eds.): SDL 2011, LNCS 7083, pp. 233–246, 2011.

The answer is to define and standardize *one* language for specifying variability, and then let variability models in this language apply to models in some base modeling language. Resolving the variability of a variability model will result in a product design/implementation model that has the selected features. This specific product model is created from the product line model by means of transformations that are specified as part of the variability model.

This answer also addresses how variability should be handled in Domain Specific Languages (DSLs). DSLs are often small, focusing on specific domains and their concepts. However, DSLs are many, so having a separate variability language that applies to all of these will pay well off.

OMG has therefore issued an RFP that asks for proposals for a language for modeling variability. The background for this is partly due to the MoSiS CVL [1], a Common Variability Language that has been designed and implemented as part of the ITEA MoSiS project [ITEA 2 - ip06035], and partly due to the fact that both users and tool vendors see the need for standardization. The MoSiS CVL has demonstrated that this is approach is feasible. Users and tool vendors includes users and tool vendors of both general-purpose languages like UML, of DSLs, and of feature modeling languages.

The paper describes the challenges (Section 2) in making a general, separate language for modeling variability that applies to models in any modeling language, the solution (Section 3) by the MoSiS CVL, and its relation to other similar approaches (Section 4).

2 Challenges

2.1 Achieving Generality

We have identified two different approaches to the combination of a DSL (or any language) and a variability language.

- Amalgamated language
- Separate languages

The *amalgamated* language is formed by the DSL and variability language concepts being combined into one language, e.g. by combining the metamodel of the DSL with the metamodel defining language concepts for variability modeling. The combined language either has a new, combined syntax, or a syntax based on the DSL extended by the syntax of the variability concepts (e.g. like profiling UML).

In practice the situation is typically that the creators of the DSL realize that even though the DSL is expressive enough to describe the whole domain, the language is not quite expressive enough to achieve effective reuse and simple model maintenance. Often the DSL designers will look for general language constructs to achieve this.

With the amalgamated approach, the DSL is no longer fully domain specific as there are several concepts that are more general than domain specific. Another challenge for the language designer is how to handle that the metamodel appears cluttered over time and the dedicated domain specific concepts are obscured.

It is hard to make the amalgamated approach general. The combination of metamodels is not something that can be done once and for all. In fact it is necessary to apply a lot of language design competence to associate the general metaclasses with the domain-specific metaclasses.

The *separate languages* approach means modeling the product line in both a Common Variability Language (CVL) and a domain specific DSL and keep the respective models separate. CVL model elements will relate to DSL model elements by simple object references. Even though the variability model and the base model are kept separate, the concrete syntax may choose to combine the representations into a common concrete syntax. We will cover this in more detail in Section 3.4.

Even though variability language concepts like templates, generics and class/subclass are general concepts and as such should be possible to add to any language, the required relation to the type of the language prevents this. Constraints on template and type parameters will typically be described in terms of the type system of the language.

Variability mechanisms that should be able to apply to any language will therefore have to consider variability on model elements independently of their semantics and purely based upon the structure of the model in terms of related model elements. Given a resolution of variability, the resulting (product) model still has to be a valid model (according to the static semantics of the base language).

2.2 Automated Generation

A standard language for modeling variability should support as much automation as possible. In particular this means that when the resolution of the variability is known it should be possible to produce the models of the individual products automatically. Experience has shown that this requirement is not as obvious as it seems, especially when the automation shall work for variability on any model in any DSL.

2.3 Powerful Abstraction Mechanisms While Still Simple

We argued in Section 2.1 that in the normal evolution of a language abstraction mechanisms are introduced. The abstraction concepts are the means to make the language express more than what directly meets the eye.

MAGIC is an acronym for a categorization of mechanisms for abstraction. We shall present these categories in the opposite order of the letters. "C" is the category of "concepts" and conceptualization is often achieved through concepts of type or method/procedure/function. Concepts are defined, identified by a signature and applied several times in the description. "I" is the category of "identity". Mechanisms in this category are identity modifiers such as inheritance, overloading and overriding. Even parameters may be considered identity modifiers. "G" is the category of "generation" which comprises mechanisms of dynamics, generation of objects with or without their own behavior. "A" is the category of "aggregation" and this includes mechanisms for grouping and containment. Finally, the category "M" includes mechanisms to express meta-relations. Executing a meta-construct will modify the description of another process or model or program.

We argued that it is not trivial to add such abstraction mechanisms to a base domain-specific language. This does require general language competence. We may, however, investigate how we could introduce general abstraction mechanisms into the CVL which we want to standardize. This would be a one time job, but the challenge is to perform the abstraction in a way that maintains the perceived simplicity.

2.4 Concrete Syntax

Any language needs to make its concepts visible to its users. With our CVL we face a number of interesting challenges regarding the representation of the variability concepts.

One challenge is related to what already exists. Standardization is often about mediating between existing solutions and representations. In the variability domain there are traditions in representing variability with "feature diagrams" and with tags or stereotypes.

A second challenge is how to make the combined set of models – a base model in any given DSL and the associated CVL model – be perceived as one seamless model?

The third challenge is to distinguish between the concrete syntax and representation of the language on one side, and the appearances of the supporting tools on the other side. Is there a difference between what the tools represent and the concrete syntax of the languages? What defines that difference?

2.5 Generic Tooling

We seek to implement a generic language for variability – CVL. Our final challenge is to support the process of designing and managing variability models in the most effective way. We would like to define and implement a generic reference tool for CVL that can be applied to define CVL models in conjunction with any other modeling language.

3 Solutions

We give our solutions to the challenges and illustrate them with a running example. The running example will apply the Train Control Language (TCL) [2] which is a DSL for modeling train stations to automate the production of code for train station signaling systems.

3.1 Achieving Generality: The Fragment

We want CVL to describe variability in general regardless of how the products themselves are described. We believe that a separate approach is the better and decide that a product line definition will consist of a base model and a CVL model.

Our variability language can be viewed to consist of two layers: a feature specification layer and a product realization layer. Since we can use much of the already existing feature models for the variability specification, in this paper we concentrate on the product realization layer where the concrete connections to the base model are handled.

The core concepts of CVL are substitutions. Models are assumed to consist of model elements in terms of object that are related by means of references. The CVL model points out model elements of the base product line model and defines how these model elements shall be manipulated to yield a new product model. There are three kinds of substitutions: *value substitution, reference substitution* and *fragment substitution*. The most elaborate kind of substitution is that of the fragment substitution. A fragment substitution replaces base model elements defined as a *placement* by base model elements defined as a *replacement* as illustrated in Figure 1. The product model on the right side is produced from the base model to the left by means of a fragment substitution. The fragment is defined in CVL by a set of boundary elements (circles named x^p and x^r) recording the references in and out of the fragment. In Figure 1 the boundary elements and the corresponding placement and replacement are superimposed onto a base model. In the models pointers from the CVL elements to base model elements realize this. A fragment substitution will define a Placement Fragment (solid-drawn circle around 2 and 3) and one or more corresponding Replacement Fragment (dashed line around 5, 6, and 7). The idea is that substitutions define a transformation from a product line model to a product model. Provided the resolution model, the execution of the CVL transformation will bind the boundary elements of the placement to the boundary elements of the replacement e.g. binding a^p to a^r and b^p to p^r. The transformation is generic and relies on reflection; therefore it can be applied to any language defined by a metamodel.

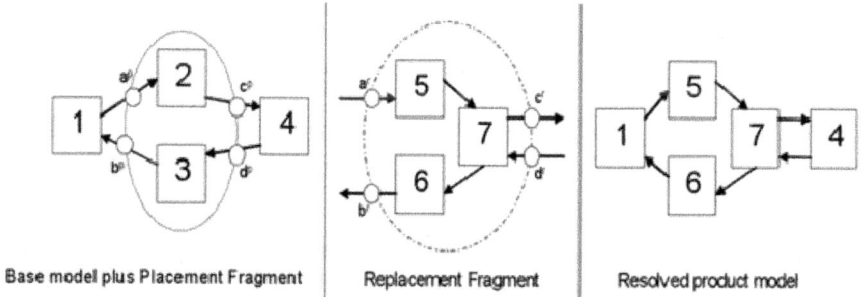

| Base model plus Placement Fragment | Replacement Fragment | Resolved product model |

Fig. 1. A simple fragment substitution

3.2 Automating Generation: Semantics by Transformation

Our CVL semantics is defined by a MOFscript [3] program that transforms the base description into a product description in the base language.

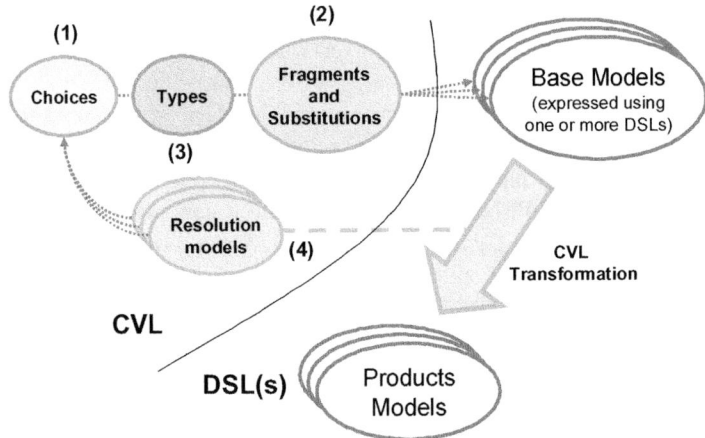

Fig. 2. Producing product models from base models and CVL description

In Figure 2 we indicate the CVL transformation process. The resolution models (4) serve as actual choices and values arguments to the variability descriptions (numbers 1,2,3), which again serve as the input to the transformations of the base model constructs into the final product models.

The CVL execution starts by copying the whole designated base model and this copy will be used for further manipulations. Every involved value substitution will change the referred value by the value given in the corresponding resolution. Every involved fragment substitution will substitute the placement by a copy of the associated replacement fragment. In the end the final product has been produced in the base language.

The CVL operational execution is defined in MOFScript generically meaning that the CVL execution is oblivious of the base language. The CVL execution merely knows that the referred base model is defined through a MOF metamodel. For our concrete implementation we require that it is provided as an EMF Ecore model.

3.3   Abstraction Mechanisms: The MAGIC of CVL

MoSiS CVL is a domain specific modeling language for describing variability. The primitive substitutions will suffice to be able to define all changes from a given base model to a desired product defined in the base language. We want our CVL to be expressive, yet simple, and we shall see how our CVL satisfies the MAGIC concepts that we presented in Section 2.3.

The concepts – C in MAGIC – of CVL are defined through variability elements that appear as nodes in the feature diagrams which are integral parts of our CVL representing the choices that the users can make. In early dialects of feature diagrams the feature models were directed graphs such that a given (feature) node may be referred by several other nodes. The intuition of this is that the multiply referred feature is a subfeature to several higher level features. In CVL we found that this kind of reuse of a feature submodel mixed the concepts of the feature *instance* and the feature *type* definition. Thus we defined a concept of a *type* and a concept of a type *invocation* referring the feature type. This also opens up for a future packaging concept where such feature types can be defined and distributed with the corresponding base model and reused in other contexts.

We also introduce the concept of an *Iterator* to abstract the choosing options of what is commonly known as feature models. Combined with the CVL grouping concept CompositeVariability all common choice options can be defined as explained in the table in Figure 3.

Semantics	Symbol	CVL Element	Comment
Mandatory		:CompVar	*CompositeVariability* makes the resolution of a node mandatory for any instantiation
Optional		:Iterator Lower =0 Upper = 1	The multiplicity [0..1] reflect the fact that the sub-node can be chosen or not.
AND		:CompVar	CompositeVariability makes the resolution of all sub-nodes mandatory for any instantiation
OR		:Iterator Lower =1 Upper = -1 IsUnique = true	The multiplicity [0..*] means that any number of sub-nodes can be chosen. *IsUnique* specifies that each sub-node can only be chosen once (which corresponds to the usual OR semantics)
XOR		:Iterator Lower =1 Upper = 1	The multiplicity [1..1] means that one and only one of the sub-nodes can be chosen (which corresponds to a classic XOR semantics).
Multiplicity	[x..y]	:Iterator Lower = x Upper = y IsUnique = true	The multiplicities associated to a choice are mapped to an Iterator containing the same multiplicities

Fig. 3. Correspondence between common choice options of feature models and CVL iterators

The Iterator has the following definition. An Iterator is a CompositeVariability and a CompositeVariability defines a group of variability elements. For every resolution element that refers to the iterator one of its variability elements will be chosen. The number of resolution elements referring to a given instantiation of an iterator must be between its lower and upper boundary numbers. Furthermore, the Boolean indicator *isUnique* will tell whether the corresponding resolution elements must point out different members or can duplicate members for the given iterator.

The identity modifier of CVL – I in MAGIC – is our special kind of parameterization. Given that we have a type concept it would be possible to introduce a traditional parameter and argument concept, but we decided that CVL may become too much of a traditional programming language. Instead we devised a way to make the fragments and their associated substitutions more powerful. Any given placement can only be used in one execution of a fragment substitution. This is obvious, since when a placement has been involved in a substitution it has been replaced and cannot be recognized again. However, by allowing the replacement fragments to contain placements we achieve added flexibility. In subsequent or nested substitutions the placements inside the used replacements can be changed again modifying the model in new ways that are still well defined.

The generation concepts of CVL – G in MAGIC – are associated with the fact that replacement fragments are always copied when substitutions are executed. Furthermore, when a type is invoked, the invocation defines a returned replacement fragment from the execution of the type definition. In order to be able to modify elements that have been created during the current execution we have fragment references. In this way our CVL can express additive variability where the final product is built from smaller reused building blocks which are conceptually very different from the subtractive variability where the base model defines the union of all products and features are just removed from that oversized product.

Aggregation – A in MAGIC – has already been mentioned since CVL has mechanisms for grouping, the CompoundVariability.

Finally, metaconcepts – M in MAGIC – refer to mechanisms that manipulate the description of other processes. One may say that CVL itself is on meta-level since executing CVL changes the base model into a product model. The essential mechanism that makes CVL execution possible is the fact that every model can be seen as a MOF model. We also apply the MOF reflection mechanisms to assure that the fragment placement and replacement are type consistent regarding their base language types. This means that the references before and after a substitution will refer to objects of the same base type.

3.4   Concrete Syntax: Different Solutions to Different Problems

In Section 2.4 we identified three kinds of challenges: to represent existing notations, to define a seamless yet generic syntax of CVL and any base language, and the relationship to tool behavior.

Representing Existing Notations. Standardization is about compromising what is already existing and what needs to be made. In the realm of variability modeling the feature diagrams have been around since the FODA method [4], but several dialects have emerged to enhance the notation and improve its expressiveness. It was quite obvious that CVL needed to define its version of the feature diagrams.

In Figure 4 we notice some deviations from the traditional feature diagrams. First we notice the explicit invocations shown in small blue rounded rectangles. Secondly we have defined the special iterators as different triangular symbols and not just as

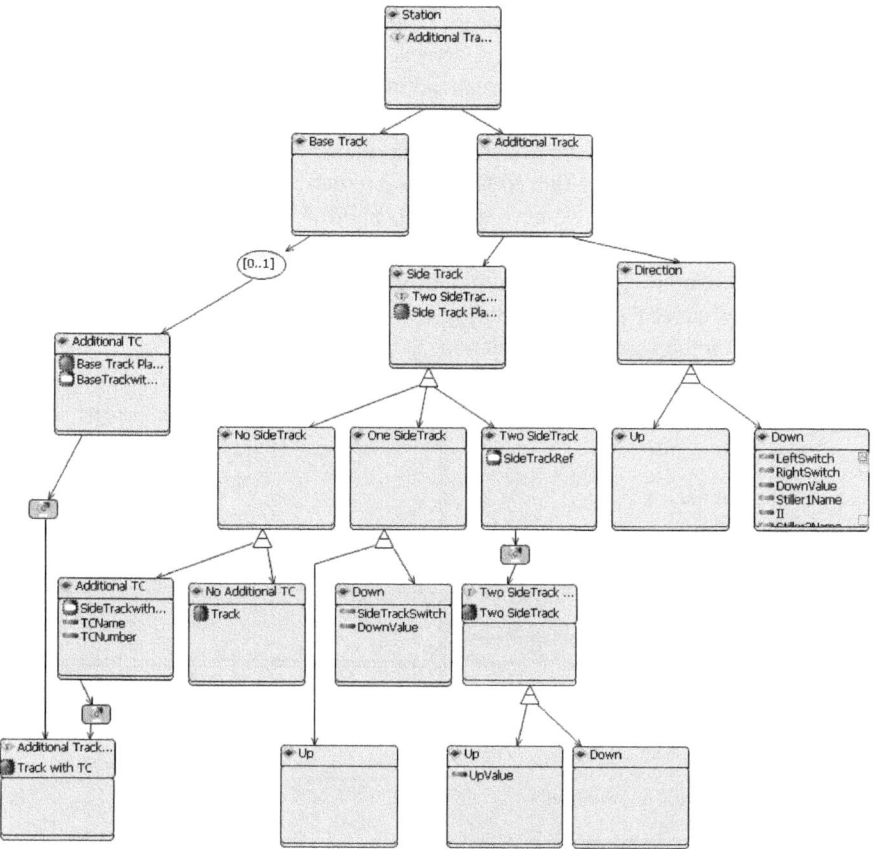

Fig. 4. The CVL Feature diagram of a train station product line

arcs, and third we have the explicit symbol for the general multiplicity iterator notation as a yellow ellipsis. The advantage of our notation is that it can be more easily manipulated by editors created by the Eclipse technology GMF [5]. Still we have chosen to make special symbols for what was considered different concepts in the traditional feature diagrams for user choices even though our CVL language has generalized these concepts into one Iterator concept. This is a concession to the past and recognition of the need to compromise.

How to be Generic and Particular at the Same Time? Our second challenge is about CVL being a standardized language, which should go well with any base language. There is no doubt that a user would like the CVL notation to match that of the base language such that the tools could form a seamless environment for development. This is difficult since base languages come in different shapes, some are graphical, some are textual, some are tabular. Some base languages use proprietary symbols while others apply simple geometric shapes like rectangles and circles. How can CVL syntactically match all these different base language shapes?

Our solution was to define a set of tool interface operations. This corresponds to a configurable syntax. The challenging area is where CVL meets the base language. This is what we call the variability realization layer comprising the actual references from CVL to the base model. The interface operations are about being able to create a set of such references and subsequently make them visible. The fragments are what we need the base language editor to handle and to deliver the information about to the CVL Tool. The other way we have a need to highlight what is defined in CVL as a fragment, in the base language editor. This is configurable in the tools by realizing four interface operations for selection and highlighting of base model elements. We have normally chosen to apply coloring to achieve what can be characterized as a CVL overlay on the base model depictions.

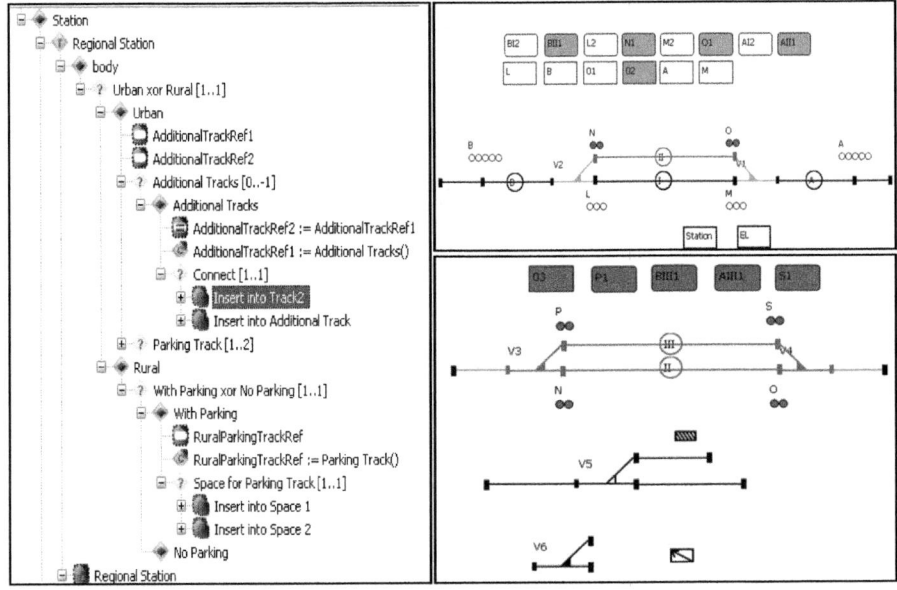

Fig. 5. Example of highlighting as a CVL overlay

In Figure 5 we see how a substitution is depicted as coloring (or shading) of elements in a DSL editor. The upper right pane shows the designated base model copy of a train station with a placement and its immediate surroundings colored in different colors red and orange. The lower right pane shows the replacement in blue and green colors. The left pane shows a browser where the substitution of the given placement with the given replacement is selected.

Another approach to representing the variability realization layer is that of annotating the appropriate base elements by either symbols or text. Typically stereotypes (a la UML) are used for this purpose. Why we do not favor this approach is that it clutters effectively the base model since all these annotation are usually present all the time. As one can easily imagine the same base element may be taking part in many fragments of which only some will eventually be selected for execution and it is tricky to get a proper overview. Therefore, when such permanent annotations are applicable is usually when a rather simple variability model is to be built and typically when the base model represents a full union of all products.

The Relationship between Language Syntax and the Tool. We have already touched upon this last challenge. What distinguishes the concrete syntax of a language from the appearance within a tool? Are we going to standardize the tool appearance? These are difficult questions of which we have no final answer, but our experiences with using the CVL language and tools are that the relationship is far tighter than one might want to think. Modern models are normally so big and complex that printing all of them out is not something anybody would do anymore. Therefore it is no longer fruitful to equate concrete syntax with the representation on paper. Furthermore, while we want competition among tools supporting the same standard (e.g. CVL) language, we need to give them freedom of choosing different solutions. Still we want to be able to migrate between tools and to recognize a CVL description when we see it (or manipulate it).

3.5   Generic Tooling: The CVL Tool

We have already argued in Section 3.4 that the distinction between concrete syntax definition and tool definition is a matter of taste. Our CVL Tool provides an editor for the variability specification layer in the form of a dialect of feature diagrams. This editor can define the CVL elements all the way down to the substitutions and their placements and replacements, but the editor can also hide the bottom layer elements from the view.

The variability realization layer is manipulated through the four interface operations that need to be realized by the base model editor. With the proper competence it has been experienced that implementing the interface is a matter of a few hours. We have normally used coloring or other visual effects such as blinking to represent the highlighting of base elements in question.

We have not yet landed on any specific representation for the resolution model, but our tool accommodates for two different ways to define and view the resolutions. Within the MoSiS project we have integrated with the PLUM[1] tool from Tecnalia in Bilbao and the PLUM tool can be seen as a resolution model editor.

In situations where the PLUM tool is not available, we have implemented our own editor that applies highlighting on the feature diagrams as shown in Figure 6.

---

[1] http://www.esi.es/plum/

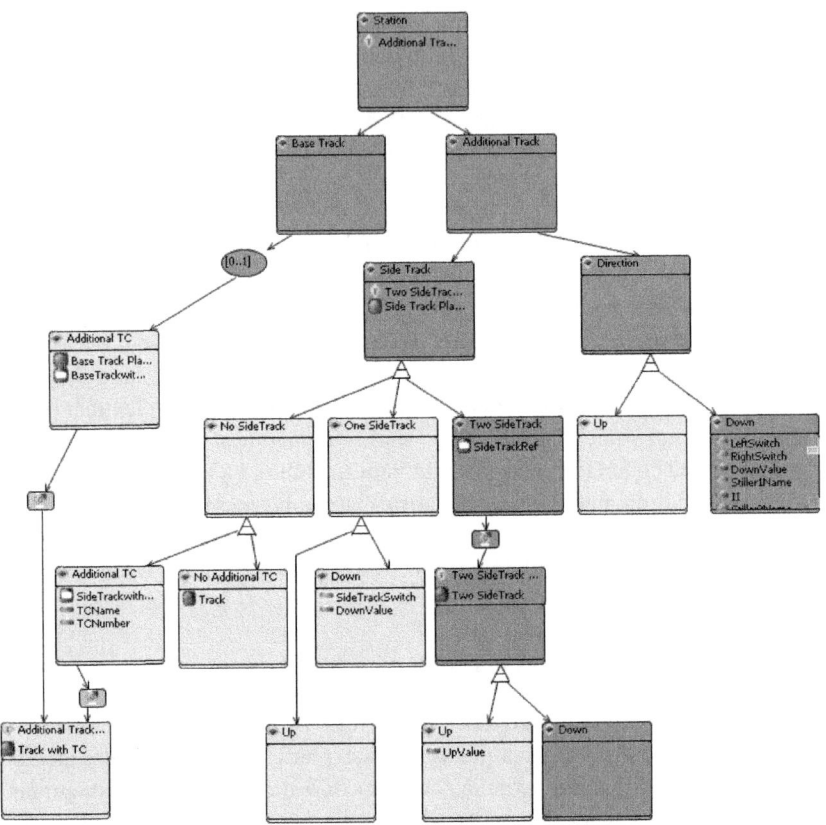

Fig. 6. Resolution shown as highlighted features

4 Related Work

The main idea behind CVL as a language for specifying variability models has been related to other approaches in the SPLC'2008 paper on CVL, [1]. It is not a new idea to make variability models orthogonal to the product line models see e.g. [6] and [7] where the main reason for making a separate variability model is for tracing variabilities across different artifacts, but the new thing with our approach is that elements of the variability models have unidirectional links to the elements of the base product line model that are subject to variation. Other approaches have the links the other way, see e.g. [8] and [9], combined with annotations of the product line model elements, while the CVL approach does not require any annotation of the base product line model. Other approaches to variability just make variability annotations of UML models, e.g. by means of profiles with stereotypes (e.g. [10], [11] and [12]), and thus have no explicit, separate variation models.

Feature diagrams as such have been surveyed in a number of papers. Feature diagrams are not the main subject of this paper, but rather the use of them for generating specific product models. The use of feature diagrams falls in two main categories: as stand-alone specifications of features as part of requirements specification, and as specifications that are linked to base product line models and are executable in the sense that selecting a configuration of features may produce a specific model.

The most primitive way of making feature diagrams executable is by translating them to models/programs in either some general purpose model transformation language or just to a general purpose programming language. Formalizing feature diagrams (as e.g. [13]) helps in this respect, but may also just have the purpose of making stand-alone feature diagrams more precise.

The FeatureMapper [14] approach is similar to the CVL approach in that the tool maps features to elements of the models. It also applies to arbitrary languages defined by metamodels, it has support for recording of modeling steps associated with a feature, but it lacks the support for model fragments with boundary elements as supported by CVL.

A more specific approach is the template-based approach in [9]. This approach has many similarities with our CVL approach, in that feature diagrams are separate from the base product line model, and in that the approach applies to any model in any language defined by a metamodel in MOF. However, it links from the base product line model to the feature diagrams, and it still annotates the base product line model.

The reason that the template approach has annotations of the base model is that often more than one model element has to be removed or exchanged by a given configuration, and the feature diagram modeler has to specify this by means of annotating all the affected model elements. In the CVL approach, selecting a model fragment as subject for variation (consisting of several base model elements), the tool will find the boundary elements to the rest of the base model.

The type concept of CVL may be compared with the notion of feature diagram references [8]. While the semantics of a feature diagram references amounts to a macro-like expansion of the referenced diagram in the place of the reference, CVL supports instantiations of types.

Another main difference from other approaches is that CVL may in fact express the construction of models based upon base model fragments, while other approaches rely on the base model being a model that has the union of all features. Feature models thereby simply specify possible configurations of features, and the transformations are simply removing model elements and possible setting values of model element properties.

5   Summary and Future Work

We have presented our language for variability modeling originating from the MoSiS project, called CVL. We have argued that it can be standardized and that it is possible to make adequate tools that are generic and can work seamlessly with support tools for the base languages defining the products of the product lines. We have seen that there are challenges to concrete syntax and to tooling, but we have pointed out solutions as well.

We have already made a serious effort to standardize CVL. In December 2009 we edited a Request For Proposal for the OMG and it was issued. In December 2010 there were two independent submission teams presenting their initial submissions and in September 2011 there will appear a joint revised submission.

Many of the original ideas presented in this paper will find their way into the revised submission, but not all. Standardization is like politics – it is the art of the possible and there are strong opinions and competences from others that cannot be ignored.

Acknowledgements. The work presented here has been developed within the MoSiS project ITEA 2 – ip06035 part of the Eureka framework and the CESAR project funded by ARTEMIS Joint Undertaking grant agreement No 100016.

References

1. Haugen, O., et al.: Adding Standardized Variability to Domain Specific Languages. In: SPLC 2008. IEEE Computer Society, Limerick (2008)
2. Svendsen, A., Olsen, G.K., Endresen, J., Moen, T., Carlson, E.J., Alme, K.-J., Haugen, Ø.: The Future of Train Signaling. In: Busch, C., Ober, I., Bruel, J.-M., Uhl, A., Völter, M. (eds.) MODELS 2008. LNCS, vol. 5301, pp. 128–142. Springer, Heidelberg (2008)
3. Oldevik, J.: MOFScript Eclipse Plug-In: Metamodel-Based Code Generation. In: Eclipse Technology Exchange Workshop, eTX (2006)
4. Kang, K., et al.: Feature-Oriented Domain Analysis (FODA) Feasibility Study. Software Engineering Institute, Carnegie Mellon University, Pittsburgh, PA (1990)
5. GMF, Eclipse Graphical Modeling Framework (GMF), http://www.eclipse.org/modeling/gmf/
6. Pohl, K., Bökle, G., Linden, F.v.d.: Software Product Line Engineering—Foundations, Principles and Techniques. Springer, Heidelberg (2005)
7. Berg, K., Bishop, J., Muthig, D.: Tracing Software Product Line Variability – From Problem to Solution Space. In: SAICSIT 2005 (2005)
8. Czarnecki, K., Helsen, S., Eisenecker, U.: Staged Configuration Using Feature Models. Software Process Improvement and Practice 10(2), 143–169 (2005) (Special issue on Software Variability: Process and Management)
9. Busch, C., Antkiewicz, M.: Mapping Features to Models: A Template Approach Based on Superimposed Variants. In: Glück, R., Lowry, M. (eds.) GPCE 2005. LNCS, vol. 3676, pp. 422–437. Springer, Heidelberg (2005)
10. Fontoura, M., Pree, W., Rumpe, B.: The UML Profile for Framework Architectures. Addison-Wesley, Reading (2001)
11. Ziadi, T., Hélouët, L., Jézéquel, J.M.: Towards a UML profile for softeware product lines. In: van der Linden, F.J. (ed.) PFE 2003. LNCS, vol. 3014, pp. 129–139. Springer, Heidelberg (2004)
12. Gomaa, H.: Designing Software Product Lines with UML: From Use Cases to Pattern-Based Software Architectures. In: Booch, G., Jacobson, I., Rumbaugh, J. (eds.) Object Technology Series, vol. 736, Addison-Wesley, Reading (2004)
13. Schobbens, P.-Y., et al.: Generic semantics of feature diagrams. Computer Networks 51(2), 456–479 (2007)
14. Heidenreich, F., Kopcsek, J., Wende, C.: FeatureMapper: Mapping Features to Models. In: ICSE 2008. ACM, Leipzig (2008)

MDE4HPC: An Approach for Using Model-Driven Engineering in High-Performance Computing

Marc Palyart[1,2], David Lugato[1], Ileana Ober[2], and Jean-Michel Bruel[2]

[1] CEA* / CESTA,
33114 Le Barp - France
{marc.palyart,david.lugato}@cea.fr
[2] IRIT – Université de Toulouse,
118, route de Narbonne, 31062 Toulouse - France
{ober,bruel}@irit.fr

Abstract. With the increasing number of programming paradigms and hardware architectures, high performance computing is becoming more and more complex in exploiting efficiently and sustainably supercomputers resources. Our thesis is that Model Driven Engineering (MDE) can help us in dealing with this complexity, by abstracting some platform dependent details. In this paper we present our approach (MDE4HPC) based on Model Driven Engineering which – by describing the scientific knowledge independently of any specific platform – enables efficient code generation for multiple target architectures.

1 Introduction

One of the most visionary predictions in computer science forecasts that computer performance would increase by 40% per year. This prediction made in 1965 by Gordon Moore [1], is still remarkably accurate. While for over 30 years this performance increase preserved the sequential programming model, in more recent years multicore architectures became common among desktop computers, raising the need to rethink software evolution in terms of how to best exploit these new parallel architectures.

In a recent study [2], the author makes a critical analysis and examines how "Moore's dividend" was spent, since obviously software performance is far from observing the same performance gain laws. The analysis reveals that "Moore's dividend" was spent on increasing software size, software functionality, and programming complexity. In fact, a "law" on software performance evolution from Philipp Ross [3] states that "software is slowing faster than hardware is accelerating".

Some applications are by nature better suited for a parallel deployment [4], and high performance-computing (HPC) is undeniably one of the fields where the use of parallel architectures fits well.

---

* Commissariat à l'Énergie Atomique et aux énergies alternatives - French Atomic and Alternative Energy Commission.

I. Ober and I. Ober (Eds.): SDL 2011, LNCS 7083, pp. 247–261, 2011.
© Springer-Verlag Berlin Heidelberg 2011

James Larus in [2] highlights the fact that according to the HPC community "each decimal order of magnitude increase in available processors required a major redesign and rewriting of parallel applications". Therefore, in order to ensure that the performance of HPC applications is increasing in step with the computer performance increase, major redesign and rewriting are needed.

In current practice, parallel programming models and in particular those addressing HPC are low level, machine specific and therefore complicate application porting. We believe this could change, and one way to do it is by applying Model Driven Engineering [5] specific techniques.

According to the MDE philosophy, system development should be built upon an abstract platform independent model. We are convinced that applying similar principles to HPC would be highly beneficial, although some effort is needed in order to set up the proper development environment. Our approach follows this direction, by proposing (1) a methodology based on successive model transformations that enrich progressively the model with platform information and (2) Archi-MDE an integrated development environment that supports the use of MDE for the development of HPC applications by implementing the proposed approach.

The rest of this paper is organised as follows: in Section 2 we present typical problems encountered when trying to program efficiently on forthcoming hybrid hardware architecture. In Section 3 we overview the state of the art of HPC development and we give the basic principles of MDE. In Section 4, we introduce MDE4HPC - our approach for applying MDE techniques in the development of HPC applications. In Section 5, we present Archi-MDE - an implementation of our approach that we use to asses the validity of MDE techniques in connection with HPC. Finally, in Section 6 we detail expected contributions of our research, that give directions for future work.

2   Problem Statement

In high performance computing, the development of efficient code for numerical simulations requires knowledge of a highly heterogeneous nature. Besides the fact that the modeling of a physical phenomenon is remarkably complex, developers are compelled to bear in mind the prerequisites for performance (tasks distribution, memory management, calculation precision). Moreover, the current trend is to depend on hardware specific library and instructions (NVIDIA Cuda [6], ATI Stream [7], IBM Cell [8]), hence code is strongly dependent on the hardware platform and often highly target dependent. Even though, as experience shows, good performances can be achieved, this approach has drawbacks: architecture dependency, mix-up of concerns and programming complexity. We discuss below these disadvantages in more detail.

Applications vs. supercomputers lifetime cycle. As shown in Figure 1 the life cycle of supercomputers is five to seven times shorter than scientific applications life cycle in our case. CEA experience shows that the simulation models

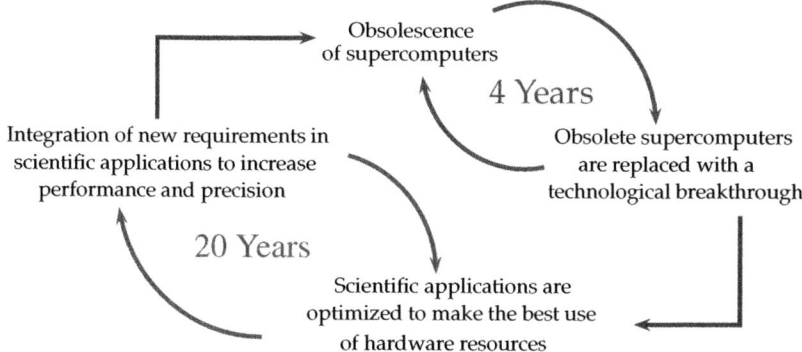

Fig. 1. CEA scientific applications life cycle versus supercomputers lifecycle

and numerical analysis methods associated with our professional problems have a lifetime in the order of 20 to 30 years and must therefore be maintained over that period, with all the additional problems that come with software maintenance over such a period of time (e.g. team turnover).

In parallel, through its TERA program [9], the CEA has decided that every four years its main supercomputer has to be replaced in order to increase its computation power by a factor superior to ten (Tera-1: 2002, Tera-10: 2006, Tera-100: 2010). With a pace faster than Moore´s law [1] hardware technological breakthroughs inevitably appear and software migration problems become an important issue.

Lack of separation of concerns. The problem to solve - the scientific knowledge of the physics - is entirely mixed with target dependent information, added to manage the parallelism. Once a complex system (multi-scale, multi-physics) has been built, it is hard to retrieve afterwards the physical models. As a result, maintenance and evolution become even more complicated.

Inaccessibility to domain experts. Programming complexity reduces the use of these workstations and supercomputers to a few scientists who are willing to spend a significant amount of time learning the specificities of a particular set of machines.

Furthermore, with the new generation of supercomputers made of hybrid machines (multicore CPUs mixed up with GPUs[1] or CELL processor) we will come close to the human limit to manage such systems at a low level. A classical study in human psychology [10], identified some limits on our capacity for processing information, especially in case it has "multidimensional" nature. These theoretical limits are seriously challenged by architectures with numerous processing elements, out of which some are built for very specific tasks.

This new generation of architecture would decrease even more the possibility of separation of concerns by adding more and more information to manage the

---

[1] Central Processing Unit / Graphics Processing Unit.

parallelism within the code. It is easily conceivable that a source code with MPI calls, OpenMP pragmas and CUDA code is not the best starting point to understand or retrieve the physics hidden inside the code. This is why we will look for an alternative solution.

The current tendency of replacing real-life experiments with numerical simulations in industrial systems conception in order to guarantee the reliability and safety of these systems is accelerating. As an example the CEA Simulation Program [11] has been built around three components: *physical modeling, numerical computation* and *experimental validation*. Thus, the use of computation results in order to guarantee the performance of a system is a replacement solution that allows to make up for the lack of directly exploitable experimental data. The credibility of such an approach is assessed through the restitution of past experiences and by domain expert certification. These additional constraints (domain validity assertion, uncertainty of forecasting computation, restitution of unexplored physics) due to the CEA's *Simulation Program* raise the need for a more abstract and formal approach. The progressive use of formal methods must be taken into account by the whole development process and associated supporting tools.

2.1   Current Development Process

The typical development process used is illustrated in Figure 2, using the SPEM [12] notation. Although the *design* phase is represented by only one activity in the diagram, three steps can be observed in reality but their precise limits are not formalized and may vary depending on the project. These three phases are presented below:

- *Physical model conception* – aims at describing the observable reality by finding which parts of the physics are required to solve the problem, and which are the best suited equations.
- *Numerical model conception* – aims at selecting a mathematical model to solve the physics equations selected in the previous phase.
- *Software conception* – aims at designing the software implementing the numerical model.

The design of these three models and of their relationships is critical. Thanks to MDE we believe that we can offer a more formalized way to define these models and the transformations which bind them together. As a collateral effect, we hope to enhance the validation phases.

3   State of the Art

In this section we review the state of the art with respect to the two main technologies we use in this paper: High Performance Computing and Model Driven Engineering. We start with an overview of technologies and research in High Performance Computing which are related to the problems exposed in the previous section. Then we present the Model Driven Engineering principles as well as its potential benefits for HPC.

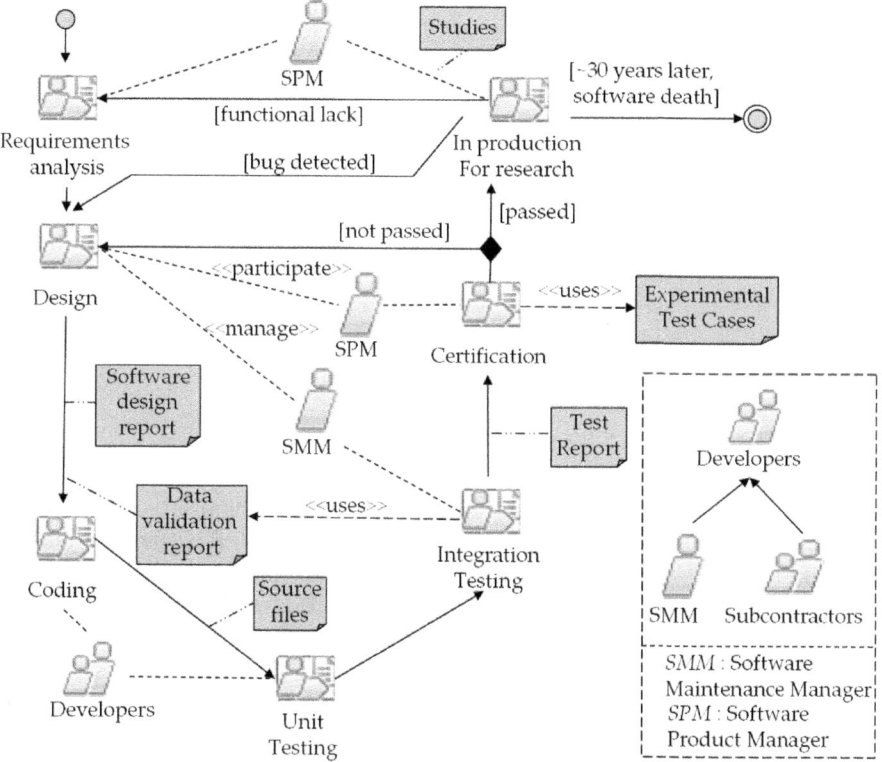

Fig. 2. Actual process development

3.1 The HPC World

Several solutions for the development of HPC applications are currently available. Most of them follow the tendency highlighted in Figure 3 [13]: the more abstract they are, the more specific to a science domain they tend to be.

For instance, two of the most used solutions on supercomputers are MPI (Message Passing Interface) [14] and Open MP (Open Multi Processing) [15]. MPI is a specification of routines which provides a low-level programming model which supports message passing programming. Thus it is suitable for distributed memory systems. OpenMP is an Application Program Interface which targets shared memory systems. It consists of a set of compiler directives (pragma), library routines, and environment variables which influence run-time behaviour. Both of these solutions can be used for nearly any scientific problem, but excluding the fact that they are suited for only a specific type of memory system they have a major problem: the abstraction level offered to the software developer is low. As expressed before, the consequences are multiple: low productivity of the developer, error prone, high complexity.

On the other side, several efforts of abstraction have been successfully attempted such as PETSc (Portable, Extensible Toolkit for Scientific Computation) [16] and

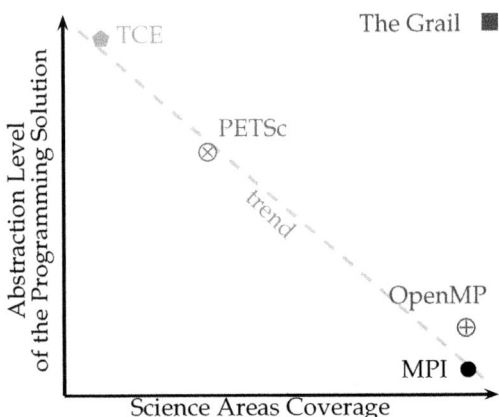

Fig. 3. Overall trend within HPC solutions

TCE (Tensor Contraction Engine) [17]. PETSc is a library built above MPI aimed at facilitating the solving of scientific applications modelled by partial differential equations and TCE is a compiler for a domain-specific language that enables chemists to develop their applications with only high-level descriptions. Unfortunately, these solutions tend to be to some extent specific to a particular scientific domain.

In the meantime, considerable research to tackle problems raised by the use of heterogeneous machines has been performed. Amongst the most noteworthy we can mention StarPU [18] and HMPP (Hybrid Multi-core Parallel Programming environment) [19]. StarPU is a unified runtime system that offers support for heterogeneous multicore architectures (CPU, GPGPUs, IBM Cell). The performances of such a system look promising but although part of the complexity is managed by the runtime, the creation of applications remains tedious for the developer. On the other hand, HMPP adopts an approach similar to OpenMP but is designed to handle HWAs(HardWare Accelerators) such as GPU. Thus it offers a respectable approach for improving legacy code. However, as its use is based on compiler directives which limit the separation of concerns, this solution can appear as less attractive for new developments.

3.2 Model Driven Engineering

In this section we try to review the basic principles of Model Driven Engineering and to analyse the benefits it can bring to the development of HPC applications.

MDE aims at raising the level of abstraction in software development, by using models that make it possible to abstract away from the technological and implementation dependent details. The models are organized in a way that encourages the separation of concerns: business and application logic is disconnected from the underlying platform technology. The goal of this abstraction is to enable domain experts, who can be inexperienced in computer science, to concentrate on the problem to solve and on their expertise.

In MDE, the models are more or less abstract, depending on how much implementation dependent details they contain. High level models are refined by transformations into lower level models, the aim is to finally obtain a model that can be executed employing either code generation or direct model interpretation. The aim is also to generate a wide set of artefacts such as documentation or tests.

Models are commonly used in other engineering and science fields. MDE development led to their widespread use in software development, not only as passive entities or as "contemplative models" [20], but also as productive entities, intensively used in symbolic execution, model checking, model based testing, code generation, etc. Furthermore, MDE enables an increase of the automation of repetitive tasks through the use of models transformations.

Concerning the potential benefits a model based approach, the use of MDE philosophy and model based approaches in general have led to real success in industrial domains other than high performance computing. For instance, real-time and critical systems benefit from the UML (Unified Modeling Language) profiles UML-RT [21] (UML profile for Real Time) and MARTE [22] (Modeling and Analysis of Real-time and Embedded Systems). In fact, models enable the telecommunication [23], aeronautics and automotive industries to reduce cost and time in the development process [24,25]. Closer to our field, ongoing research based on MDE is being pursued on shared memory systems: standard multi-core computing systems [26] and multiprocessor System On Chip [27].

4   Overview of the Proposed Approach MDE4HPC

In this section we introduce the main concepts and technologies of our approach called MDE4HPC. First, we present the key ideas which define the core of our approach and finally we set out the additional services which aggregate around this core.

4.1   General MDA Principles Applied

The core of our methodology follows MDE principles and relies mainly on models and transformations. Figure 4 summarizes the key concepts of our approach.

In our approach, according to the MDE principles, the application developers (conjointly with scientists if they are not the same) start the development process by defining *Platform Independent Models* (PIMs) which are, by definition, independent from any specific hardware, library or even architecture. These models capture the solution to the problem that needs to be solved independently of any technological constraints. In consequence these models are sustainable, if the specifications do not change. Consequently, they are defined once, irrespective of the platform we aim to target.

A typical PIM contains a *data model* and a *tasks model*. The data model represents the data organization (for example the mesh structure) of the simulation

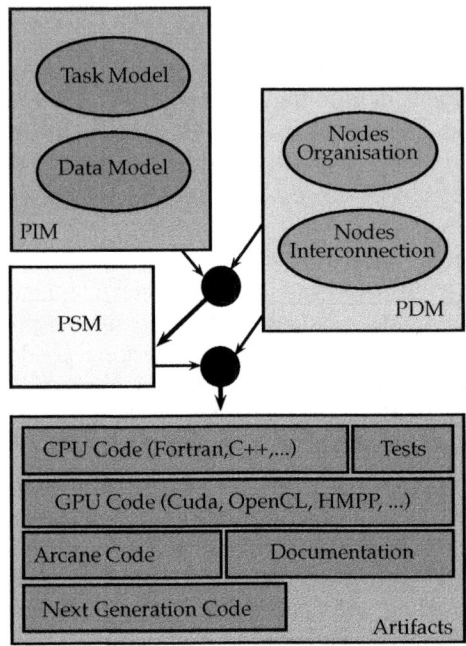

Fig. 4. Simplified description of the sequence of model transformations (represented as black circle) during the development process

and the task model is composed of elementary computational tasks that work on the data model, for example the mesh structure.

On the other side, the development makes use of a target platform model, under MDE vocabulary it is called *a Platform Description Model (PDM)*. In the case of our applications, the PDM covers:

- *Computational nodes organisation*: processing units (CPU, GPU, ...) architectures, memory description (size, type, bandwidth).
- *Computational nodes interconnection*: data link features (bandwidth).
- *File storage system* organisation and capacity.

The task of modelling the platform, that leads to the the PDM, can only be achieved by hardware architecture experts who fully understand the specificities of a particular computer (architecture). The same expert would also work on modelling transformations related to including platform aspects in the PIM.

As recommended by the MDA guidelines, the platform dependent model is combined with the PIM to form a *Platform Specific Model* (PSM). This process is often, a several step process, meaning that the transformation to a PSM is actually done in several stages, each integrating one or several aspects of the PSM. The principles of this multi-step transformation, are illustrated by Figure 5. Ideally, these transformations end up in a code generating transformation.

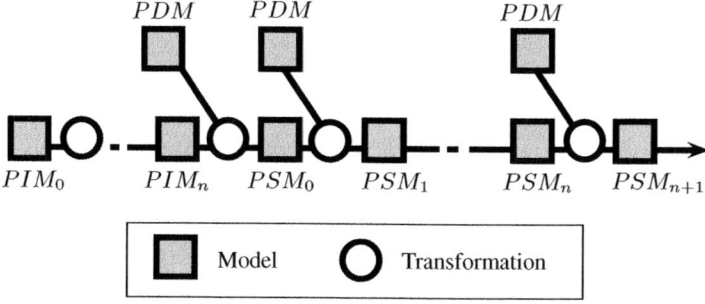

Fig. 5. Succession of transformations during the development process

The combination of different models helps us in dealing with the separation of concern as each model and each transformation are defined by a specialist of the domain modelled (physics, mathematics, software, hardware). However *the order* or *the combination* all of these transformations is not trivial because not all the transformation are commutative, associative or compatibles between them. For example, in the hypothesis of dealing with low level models a few steps before code generation, attempting to apply a set of optimizations, two optimizations such as loop unfolding and inlining could clash with each other if they were applied in the wrong order. As a result, the actual order in which the transformations should be applied is defined by domain experts, for instance by the optimisation expert who can decide the order of the unfolding and the inlining. Note that this problem is not new, the choice of the order of applying optimisations is always meaningful. What is new is the fact that this choice is more explicit.

Our approach does not target the automatic parallelization such as discussed in [28]. Instead, we introduce an approach where experts can focus on their domain of expertise.

The definition of our approach benefits from the exchanges between various domain experts. To achieve this, we have organised mixed team of physicists and numerical computer scientists to define the PIM. The computer system engineers were then in charge with the definition of the PDM. Finally, the transformations from PIM to PSM and from PSM to code were achieved conjointly by software engineers and computer system engineers, with the aid of model transformation tools.

In sum, none of these tasks were done completely automatically, still some of them were performed with automated assistance. The most important aspect here is that each of these tasks focuses on a particular expertise domain, thus was performed by a domain expert, that was able to focus on its own expertiese domain.

The models corresponding to the PIM, PSM and PDM, are described according to a Domain Specific Modeling Language (DSML) called *HPCML (High Performance Modeling Language)*. This DSML stands at level M_2 in the four-level architecture hierarchy [5] and it aims at formalize the description of models. The abstract syntax of a DSML is defined through a metamodel. The choice of a DSML over a UML Profile stems from our previous work [29]. They are both situated at the M_2 level, UML profiles can be seen as an extension of the UML metamodel and DSML are defined with a new metamodel dedicated to the domain. If necessary, and as they both comply with the MOF (level M_3), transformations could be written to transform models compliant with our DSML HPCML into models compliant with its potential UML profile equivalent.

HPCML covers concepts related to task modeling (such as component, service) and data modeling (such as type, mesh). HPCML it is designed to suit constraints imposed by parallelism, and it is actually an evolution after feedbacks from a first version that was deployed and tested on mid-size projects in the context of the IDE Archi-MDE.

4.2   Openings Offered by the Models Use

The use of models in the way described in the previous section, opens the way to a collection of additional services that allow to increase developer productivity, improve code performance and quality. In the context of our approach, some of these services are already included in the Archi-MDE development environment, that will be presented in Section 5.

Model validation is one of the classical gains of using models in the development process, as it allows for early correctness checking and thus it makes it possible to improve quality by verifying the correctness of each component, before arriving to the actual code. The literature abundantly treats this topic and many techniques are available allowing for model based validations, the use of most of them would be beneficial in our approach.

In the context of our concrete setting, our goal, for the moment, is to put up a rapidly functional framework allowing to effectively use modelling in the context of HPC. Therefore, we do not intend, at least not for the moment, to develop specific validation techniques. Instead we will use already existing technologies that can be easily integrated into our setting. As Archi-MDE is developed with the Eclipse framework, for the moment we will use an existing Eclipse based OCL (Object Constraint Language) verification engine capable of inconsistency detection mechanism.

Symbolic execution and automatic test generation are also classical benefits of using modelling and the automatic test generation based on symbolic execution such as the approach presented on [30] can be a factor of both productivity and quality improvement. Although for the moment our approach does not cover this, we find it may bring substantial benefits in our context and we intend to enrich Archi-MDE with such capabilities, by adapting an already existing automatic execution and test generation engine.

Optimization. In the majority of cases, a model contains more and higher level information than the code resulting from it. The use of low level models, as introduced in the previous section, opens the way to start introducing optimizations in the context of these models [31].

In the context of Archi-MDE (that we will detail in Section 5) we generated sequential Fortran code to assess the interest of optimizations injected during model transformations. These optimisations concerned loop unrolling and inlining on Intel Xeon. We analysed the speed-up under the following two settings:

- the version optimized only by the compiler (in our case the Intel compiler);
- the version where the optimisation started at (low level) model stage, in the context of Archi-MDE and was then continued by the compiler.

Benchmarks comparing these optimisations gave us encouraging results, as we obtain a better speed-up when the optimizations started in Archi-MDE.

Software metrics proved their interest in the context of HPC applications [32]. The use of model metrics [33] should allow to perform live analysis of the models in order to determine ratings of the quality of the code produced and thus provide a useful feedback to the developer.

Performance forecasting is currently used in order to make system design decisions based on quantifiable demands of their key applications rather than using manual analysis which can be error prone and impractical for large systems [34]. These approaches could benefit from the existence of models that provide meaningful abstractions of the systems, in order to evaluate which parts of the application are compute-intensive and thus guide the developer as to where he needs to focus his attention to enhance performance.

Anti-patterns [35] provide an interesting mechanism of identifying possible errors before they actually manifest. The use of anti-patterns is more interesting in the context of models than of code. Therefore, our approach that consists in raising the place of models in the development cycle, opens the way to the definition and identification of anti-patterns for HPC models.

We overview here a list of functionalities that are enabled by a model based development of high-performance computing applications. This list is naturally not exhaustive, and was dressed up using feed-backs from HPC specialists on what would be useful and what would be feasible in this context.

The following section overviews Archi-MDE, the development framework that we have built for supporting the model based development of HPC applications. some of the functionalities we overview above are already part of this framework, such as the optimization, some other, such as the OCL consistency verification, can be re-used from a OCL based model analysis tool, while some other are for the moment on our future work list.

5 Archi-MDE

Archi-MDE is a user-supportive integrated development environment which aims to support the methodology associated with our approach.

There are marvellous IDEs and frameworks available. We chose to rely on the Eclipse platform and especially the open source Eclipse Modeling Project

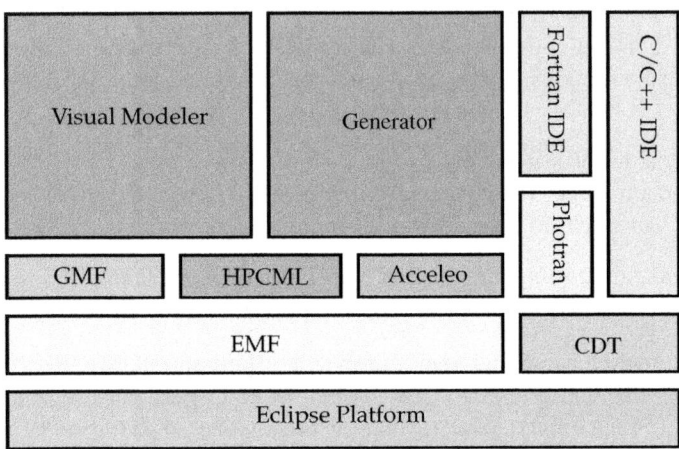

Fig. 6. Archi-MDE Architecture

[36] which focuses on the evolution and promotion of model-based development technologies. The principal reasons for this choice were the integration of code compilation/edition tools, the modularity, the wide and dynamic community behind the project, a robust infrastructure based on a system of plugins with extension points and a vast collection of existing plugins that can be reused. The open source aspect of the tool was also an important advantage.

Figure 6 gives an overview of the Archi-MDE tool architecture. The Eclipse Modeling Project provides a set of tooling, standards implementations and modeling frameworks such as EMF (Eclipse Modeling Framework) [37] and GMF (Graphical Modeling Framework) that we are using. The domain specific modeling language *HPCML*, introduced in in Section 4, is implemented based on EMF, while its graphical view is based on GMF.

Archi-MDE integrates two existing plugins that are used to edit, compile and debug the generated source files:

- **CDT**: Eclipse C/C++ Development Tooling [38] provides a fully functional C and C++ Integrated Development Environment (IDE)
- **Photran**: Photran [39] is an IDE and refactoring tool for Fortran based on top of the CDT plugiun.

The information on the target platform is injected during the model to text transformation, corresponding to the code generation that is performed using the Xpand engine [40]. Archi-MDE uses aspect-oriented programming techniques present in the Xpand templates. The ATL project [41] for M2M transformations seem to be well suited to our needs for the moment.

As the final goal of this process is code generation, Archi-MDE produces code for Arcane [42]. Arcane is a software development framework for 2D and 3D numerical simulation codes used by the CEA and the IFP (French Institute of Petroleum). It already offers a fair abstraction level of the underlying hardware which is close to our task and data models (see PIM definition from Section 4) and provides utility services that we had no interest in developing again for the sake of the demonstration.

6   Conclusion and Future Work

Hardware architectures are evolving fast. Unfortunately present applications do not possess the required qualities to easily adapt to these frequent evolutions while maintaining optimal performances. However, there is an increasing demand advocating the need to add abstraction [43] in dealing with parallel architectures or to perform a more radical paradigm shift [44] in developing HPC software.

The main contribution of this paper is to propose a new way to deal with these problems by using MDE techniques for the development of HPC applications. We present the potential benefits of such approach, that include the more flexibility for maintenance and code porting towards new hardware architectures.

MDE4HPC, the methodology presented in this paper, is ready to offer better separation of concerns and knowledge capitalization. These points are a pillar of our approach by allowing people to focus and contribute fully on their area of specialization. We also presented Archi-MDE a user-supportive integrated development environment to sustain the methodology.

Our experiments on applications with few thousand lines of code are very encouraging and made us confident in the feasibility of this approach and in the added value for CEA simulation code development. Based on these positive feedbacks from the first version of Archi-MDE, we intend to deploy and assess our approach on bigger size projects within the CEA. Moreover, we are about to improve the additional services of Archi-MDE to draw maximum advantage from the use of models. Model verifications, symbolic execution and reverse engineering of legacy code are the next steps to complete the assessment of our approach.

Obviously, a lots of things have still to be done, such as applying MDE4HPC on real-size projects, identifying relevant benchmarks that would allow to quantify the gains of applying this technique, and identifying and implementing more functionalities so that Archi-MDE can exploit the use of models. The preliminary results make us very confident both in the fact that MDA can be applied for the development of HPC applications, and that it can bring serious benefits to it.

References

1. Moore, G.E.: Cramming more components onto integrated circuits. Electronics 38(8), 114–117 (1965)
2. Larus, J.R.: Spending moore's dividend. Commun. ACM 52(5), 62–69 (2009)
3. Ross, P.E.: Engineering: 5 commandments. IEEE Spectrum 40(12), 30–35 (2003)
4. Asanovic, K., Bodík, R., Demmel, J., Keaveny, T., Keutzer, K., Kubiatowicz, J., Morgan, N., Patterson, D.A., Sen, K., Wawrzynek, J., Wessel, D., Yelick, K.A.: A view of the parallel computing landscape. Communications of ACM 52(10), 56–67 (2009)

5. Miller, J., Mukerji, J.: Mda guide version 1.0.1. omg/2003-06-01. Technical report, OMG (2003)
6. Kirk, D.: Nvidia cuda software and gpu parallel computing architecture. In: ISMM, pp. 103–104 (2007)
7. Bayoumi, A.M., Chu, M., Hanafy, Y.Y., Harrell, P., Refai-Ahmed, G.: Scientific and engineering computing using ati stream technology. Computing in Science and Engineering 11(6), 92–97 (2009)
8. Johns, C.R., Brokenshire, D.A.: Introduction to the cell broadband engine architecture. IBM Journal of Research and Development 51(5), 503–520 (2007)
9. Gonnord, J., Leca, P., Robin, F.: Au delà de 50 mille milliards d´opérations par seconde? La Recherche (393) (January 2006)
10. Miller, G.A.: The Magical Number Seven, Plus or Minus Two: Some Limits on Our Capacity for Processing Information. The Psychological Review 63, 81–97 (1956)
11. Cea - The Simulation Program,
    http://www.cea.fr/english_portal/defense/
    the_simulation_program_lmj_tera_airix
12. Software Process Engineering Meta-Model, version 2.0. Technical report, Object Management Group (2008)
13. Bernholdt, D.E.: Raising the level of programming abstraction in scalable programming models. In: IEEE International Conference on High Performance Computer Architecture (HPCA), Workshop on Productivity and Performance in High-End Computing (P-PHEC), pp. 76–84. IEEE Computer Society, Los Alamitos (2004)
14. Snir, M., Otto, S.W., Huss-Lederman, S., Walker, D.W., Dongarra, J.: MPI: The complete reference. MIT Press, Cambridge (1996)
15. Dagum, L., Menon, R.: Openmp: An industry-standard api for shared-memory programming. Computing in Science and Engineering 5, 46–55 (1998)
16. Balay, S., Buschelman, K., Eijkhout, V., Gropp, W.D., Kaushik, D., Knepley, M.G., McInnes, L.C., Smith, B.F., Zhang, H.: PETSc users manual. Technical Report ANL-95/11 - Revision 2.1.5, Argonne National Laboratory (2004)
17. Baumgartner, G., Bernholdt, D.E., Cociorva, D., Harrison, R., Hirata, S., Lam, C.-C., Nooijen, M., Pitzer, R., Ramanujam, J., Sadayappan, P.: A high-level approach to synthesis of high-performance codes for quantum chemistry. In: Supercomputing 2002: Proceedings of the 2002 ACM/IEEE conference on Supercomputing, pp. 1–10. IEEE Computer Society Press, Los Alamitos (2002)
18. Augonnet, C., Thibault, S., Namyst, R., Wacrenier, P.-A.: StarPU: A Unified Platform for Task Scheduling on Heterogeneous Multicore Architectures. In: Sips, H., Epema, D., Lin, H.-X. (eds.) Euro-Par 2009. LNCS, vol. 5704, pp. 863–874. Springer, Heidelberg (2009)
19. Bodin, F.: Keynote: Compilers in the manycore era. In: Seznec, A., Emer, J., O'Boyle, M., Martonosi, M., Ungerer, T. (eds.) HiPEAC 2009. LNCS, vol. 5409, pp. 2–3. Springer, Heidelberg (2009)
20. Bézivin, J., Gerbé, O.: Towards a precise definition of the OMG/MDA framework. In: ASE, pp. 273–280. IEEE Computer Press, Los Alamitos (2001)
21. Douglass, B.P.: Real Time UML: Advances in the UML for Real-Time Systems, 3rd edn. Addison Wesley Longman Publishing Co., Inc., Redwood City (2004)
22. Thomas, F., Gérard, S., Delatour, J., Terrier, F.: Software real-time resource modeling. In: FDL, pp. 231–236. ECSI (2007)
23. Reed, R.: Itu-t system design languages (sdl). Computer Networks 42(3), 283–284 (2003)
24. Lockheed Martin (MDA success story),
    http://www.omg.org/mda/mda_files/lockheedmartin.pdf

25. Objectsecurity: Helping to secure the friendly skies,
    http://www.omg.org/mda/mda_files/objectsecurity_final.pdf
26. Pllana, S., Benkner, S., Mehofer, E., Natvig, L., Xhafa, F.: Towards an intelligent environment for programming multi-core computing systems, pp. 141–151 (2009)
27. Taillard, J., Guyomarc'h, F., Dekeyser, J.-L.: A graphical framework for high performance computing using an mde approach. In: Euromicro Conference on Parallel, Distributed, and Network-Based Processing, pp. 165–173 (2008)
28. Banerjee, U., Eigenmann, R., Nicolau, A., Padua, D.A.: Automatic program parallelization. Proceedings of the IEEE 81(2), 211–243 (1993)
29. Lugato, D.: Model-driven engineering for high-performance computing applications. In: The 19th IASTED International Conference on Modelling and Simulation, Quebec City, Quebec, Canada (May 2008)
30. Lugato, D., Bigot, C., Valot, Y., Gallois, J.-P., Gérard, S., Terrier, F.: Validation and automatic test generation on UML models: the AGATHA approach. International Journal on Software Tools for Technology Transfer (STTT) 5(2), 124–139 (2004)
31. Metcalf, M.: FORTRAN Optimization. Academic Press, Inc., Orlando (1985)
32. Panas, T., Quinlan, D., Vuduc, R.: Tool support for inspecting the code quality of hpc applications. In: Proceedings of the 3rd International Workshop on Software Engineering for High Performance Computing Applications, SE-HPC 2007, p. 2. IEEE Computer Society, Washington, DC (2007)
33. Mohagheghi, P., Dehlen, V.: Existing model metrics and relations to model quality. In: ICSE Workshop on Software Quality, WOSQ 2009, pp. 39–45 (May 2009)
34. Grobelny, E., Bueno, D., Troxel, I., George, Vetter, J.S.: FASE: A Framework for Scalable Performance Prediction of HPC Systems and Applications. Simulation 83(10), 721–745 (2007)
35. Brown, W.J., Malveau, R.C., Mowbray, T.J.: AntiPatterns: Refactoring Software, Architectures, and Projects in Crisis. Wiley, Chichester (1998)
36. Gronback, R.: Eclipse Modeling Project: A Domain-Specific Language (DSL) Toolkit. Addison-Wesley Professional, Reading (2009)
37. Steinberg, D., Budinsky, F., Paternostro, M., Merks, E.: EMF: Eclipse Modeling Framework 2.0. Addison-Wesley Professional, Reading (2009)
38. Eclipse C/C++ Development Tooling - CDT, http://www.eclipse.org/cdt/
39. Photran - an integrated development environment and refactoring tool for Fortran, http://www.eclipse.org/photran/
40. Xpand, http://wiki.eclipse.org/xpand
41. ATL : ATL Transformation Language, http://www.eclipse.org/atl/
42. Grospellier, G., Lelandais, B.: The arcane development framework. In: POOSC 2009: Proceedings of the 8th Workshop on Parallel/High-Performance Object-Oriented Scientific Computing, pp. 1–11. ACM, New York (2009)
43. Kulkarni, M., Pingali, K., Walter, B., Ramanarayanan, G., Bala, K., Chew, L.P.: Optimistic parallelism requires abstractions. Communications of ACM 52(9), 89–97 (2009)
44. Harrison, R.J.: The myriad costs of complexity will force a paradigm shift. In: Community Input on the Future of High-Performance Computing Workshop (December 2009),
    http://www.nics.tennessee.edu/sites/www.nics.tennessee.edu/files/NSF-HPC-Whitepaper-12-09.pdf

AUTOSAR vs. MARTE for Enabling Timing Analysis of Automotive Applications

Saoussen Anssi[1], Sébastien Gérard[2], Stefan Kuntz[1], and François Terrier[2]

[1] Continental Automotive France SAS, PowerTrain E IPP,
1 Avenue Paul Ourliac - BP 83649, 31036 France
{saoussen.ansi,stefan.kuntz}@continental-corporation.com
[2] CEA LIST, Laboratory of model driven engineering for embedded systems,
Point Courrier 94, Gif-sur-Yvette, F-91191 France
{sebastien.gerard,francois.terrier}@cea.fr

Abstract. Automotive software systems are characterized by increasing complexity and tight requirements on safety and timing. Recent industrial experience has indicated that model-based and component-based approaches can help improve the overall system quality, foster reuse and evolution, and increase the potential for automatic validation and verification. In this paper, we discuss some crucial specification capabilities that need to be satisfied by modeling languages to enable scheduling analysis aware modeling for automotive applications. We evaluate the extent to which two major industry-based languages, MARTE and AUTOSAR, satisfy those needs.

Keywords: modeling languages, scheduling analysis, automotive applications.

1 Introduction

The capability to develop highly dependable software solutions in a way that facilitates rapid response to market needs has become one of the decisive competitive factors in the automotive industry. Automotive embedded systems often exhibit hard real-time constraints that need reliable guarantees for full system correctness [1]. For instance, power train and chassis applications include complex (multivariable) control laws, with different sampling periods, conveying real-time information to distributed devices. Thus, a hard real-time constraint which has to be controlled in power train applications is the ignition timing according to the position of the engine, which is defined by a sporadic event characterizing the zero-position of the flywheel. End-to-end response delays must also be bounded. An excessive end-to-end response delay of a control loop may induce not only performance degradation but also cause vehicle instability. For example, an ESP (Electronic Stability Program) corrects the trajectory of the vehicle by controlling the braking system according to 25-second samples from several sensors distributed in the vehicle. These constraints have to be assured whatever the situation. Hence, the "worst case" scenario must be taken into consideration, because of the safety critical nature of automotive applications.

One approach to predict timing properties is scheduling analysis. This technique can be used at different development stages. Early analysis of a design model aids

I. Ober and I. Ober (Eds.): SDL 2011, LNCS 7083, pp. 262–275, 2011.
© Springer-Verlag Berlin Heidelberg 2011

developers to detect potentially inadequate real-time architectures and prevent costly design mistakes. A later analysis of an implemented system allows designers to discover timing faults, or to evaluate the impact of possible platform migrations or modifications of scheduling parameters.

In order to master the system complexity and assess system-level trade-offs, seeking higher quality and dependability, model-based engineering (MBE) is gaining momentum in the automotive domain. One of the advantages expected from this approach is the ability to exploit correct-by-construction, incremental design processes, which rely extensively on automated transformations and synthesis, and formalized computer-based correctness analysis.

A challenging problem in MBE is to integrate architecture models with the information that is relevant for performing different kinds of mathematical analyses. These analyses (e.g., timing and safety analyses) help to validate the system against several quality criteria and to predict the system correctness under various conditions. In order to perform these analyses, the system architecture representation must be first transformed into some form that enables mathematical evaluation. This form is denoted here as "analysis model". Analysis tools accept as input these analysis models and evaluate them mathematically to produce results used for successive refinement of architecture models. An important goal in MBE is to ensure that the analysis model may be derived directly from a suitably annotated architecture model using automated or semi-automated support [2].

The design of modeling languages is at the core of the MBE topics. While growing in number, they vary widely in terms of the abstractions they support and analysis capabilities they provide. In this paper, we particularly focus on two industry-based modeling languages that cover constructs and parameters required for scheduling analysis. First, AUTOSAR (Automotive Open System Architecture) [3] is dedicated to the automotive domain and aims at defining an open standardized architecture in order to face the future challenges in automotive development. Second, we consider OMG's MARTE (Modeling and Analysis of Real-Time and Embedded systems) [4] which deals with time-related aspects and includes a detailed set of non-functional attributes to enable state-of-the-art scheduling analysis.

This paper characterizes the required modeling features in terms of (a) system-oriented aspects, i.e., information completeness and, (b) design-oriented aspects, i.e., features for improving the designer's decision-making capability. Next, we highlight the capabilities and limitations of the two modeling languages with respect to those requirements. The question is how well do these languages meet the current challenges in automotive timing analysis. One main goal is to allow people involved in the design of these languages to identify concepts useful for scheduling analysis that have been either overlooked or are inadequately supported.

2   Modeling Needs for Automotive Applications to Enable Scheduling Analysis

In this section, we catalog some essential modeling features to support state-of-the-art scheduling analysis in automotive architectures. These features suffice for the purpose of the paper, which is to provide an informal, comparative review of the expressive power provided by the two modeling languages relative to this specific aspect. A more comprehensive study of other aspects such as analysis frameworks or design-analysis model transformations is beyond the scope of this paper. We organize the features considered into system-oriented and design-oriented modeling features. System-oriented features are features that reflect the capability of the language to model all the characteristics of the targeted system needed to perform scheduling analysis. These characteristics may involve e.g., the kinds of timing constraints that should be verified during scheduling analysis. Design-oriented features reflect the capability of the language to give constructs and means to make efficient scheduling analysis-aware modeling. For example, these features can reflect the extent to which the language allows separating application parts from resource platform parts when developing analysis models. They can reflect also the capability of the language to enable efficient architecture refinement based on analysis results of previous design phases.

2.1 System-Oriented Features

These modeling features represent the ability to specify the necessary characteristics of a system with accuracy and precision (i.e., information completeness).

Timing constraints. Basic timing constraints include deadlines and maximum jitters. Both can be specified by relative/absolute durations (maximum time intervals) or instants (occurrence of a timeout event). These constraints can apply to the completion of control/data flows in functional chains or to arbitrary events within computation and communication chains. In particular, the time elapsed since a data was read by a sensor and an output processed with this data is passed to an actuator (known as "data age") is of interest for the stability of control models.

Most of the scheduling analyses existing today use the notion of physical time as measured by a unique time base. However, distributed applications often experience problems for agreement on consistent time reading due to clock synchronization. This means that scheduling them depends on different time bases, and therefore constraints must refer to specific clocks. Another kind of timing constraint, as mentioned in Section 1, is related to timing assertions measured according to other variables such as for example the motor cycles. This leads to timing constraints measured in different physical units or via conditional assertions. Modeling languages should account for this diversity to enable useful timing analysis.

End-to-end flows. Scheduling analysis methods are typically scenario-based. This leads to a behavior model supported by the notion of end-to-end flow. An end-to-end flow refers to a unique causal set of execution/communication functions triggered by an activation event (or logical combination of events). All possible end-to-end flows in a given system can be generated by starting from the activation events, and then forming event sequences by recursively considering the output event set for the functions producing the events.

The granularity of the functions involved in an end-to-end flow is often related to the choice of black or gray-box component modeling. For the first case, port to port delays should be considered, while for the second scenario, component internal behavior is modeled by describing end-to-end flow that involve the elementary execution entities that compose it. Whatever the choice, the ordering of functions follows a predecessor-successor pattern, with the possibility of multiple concurrent successors and predecessors, stemming from concurrent functions joins and forks respectively.

Activation events. Both event-triggered and time-triggered paradigms are often encountered in automotive applications. Event-triggered means that tasks are executed or messages are transmitted by the occurrence of events (e.g., a door has been opened). Time-triggered consists of tasks executed or messages transmitted at predetermined points in time (they communicate by means of asynchronous buffers).

The event-triggered paradigm provides a more efficient use of resources but for analysis purposes it needs a richer set of activation models. This may imply activation events modeled by known patterns and their parameters (e.g., periodic, sporadic, burst activations), activation tables, or by workload generator models (e.g., StateFlow models).

SW and HW resources. What is needed for scheduling analysis is to take into account the impact of the Operating System (OS) and hardware resources on applications (e.g., overheads due to the OS and the stack of communication layers, throughputs, and bandwidths). Among these aspects, protocols for access to mutual exclusive resources are of paramount importance in scheduling analysis of modern multiprocessor architectures [5].

2.2 Design-Oriented Features

These features are related to the modeling constructs and facilities used to organize models and, more generally, to support the designer's decision-making capability.

Application vs. platform. In a typical automotive development flow, application and platform evolve separately. Application artifacts center on functionality and control logic, while platform artifacts focus on ECU/bus selection, middleware layers, and OS services. When creating a modeling approach for specifying this kind of systems, the well-known Y-Chart scheme [6] provides a strong foundation. This approach specifies how the different models of the application and the HW/SW resource platform are put together to build the global system model. This scheme can be regarded as an abstraction of a layering architectural pattern, which may include distributed applications, middleware layers, OS services, and hardware.

Allocation. In order to integrate global models, e.g., for performing system-level analysis, we must recombine application and platform models. This can be achieved by means of a third model, often called the allocation model. This model allows exploring different architecture options with respect to a set of functionalities and thereby reusing an architecture platform with different functions. This model also may include the associated timing attributes resulting from the allocation. For example, when allocating a runnable to a given OS task and ECU, one needs to specify its execution time (after e.g., calculation or measurement).

Semantics preservation. Automotive applications as described by component-based approaches do not match the models used in typical scheduling analyses. Beyond structural mismatches (which can be solved by model transformation techniques), semantics shall be preserved for full consistency of analysis results with other development activities such as code generation or simulation. In particular, the semantics of port communication and internal behavior of software components needs to be aligned with the causal model supported by scheduling analysis techniques. For instance, a common pattern in end-to-end flows that is particularly important in control systems is over/under sampling. Automotive applications often consist of periodic tasks possibly dependent through data interchange via ports. In order to perform reliable timing analysis, the semantics of different synchronization patterns must be specified and aligned to predictions obtained by analysis (e.g., data age).

Composition. Integration of IP components from different suppliers is frequent in automotive industry. Therefore, there is a need for specification means and composition rules, to which suppliers should comply, that enable deduction of global timing properties from component properties in order to allow plug-and-play of subsystems in a correct-by-construction manner. To this end, component suppliers would need to provide only a set of parameter values that characterize the time behavior of their components without revealing internal designs.

Analysis scope. Due to the specific tools targeted by scheduling analysis, it is important to bound system model elements to a particular analysis or evaluation scope. An analysis scope may e.g., represent different application-platform allocation scenarios, abstraction levels, operational modes, or different quantitative values of non-functional parameters.

Tool support. To enable accurate scheduling analysis for automotive systems, tools dedicated for both the modeling and timing analysis are of paramount importance. These tools should allow modeling all scheduling analysis related features based on the concepts provided by modeling languages. In addition, tools supporting automatic transformation from modeling tools to scheduling analysis tools are very interesting since they can accelerate the design-analysis phase and save time during the development process. For an efficient tool support in the industrial context, the tool maturity, robustness and the user friendliness should be considered when developing such tools (for modeling, analysis and transformation). Concerning scheduling analysis tools, these tools should satisfy scheduling analysis needs for automotive applications. For example, they should implement scheduling analysis algorithms that satisfy automotive constraints (e.g., the tool should allow using FIFO (First In First Out) as second algorithm for tasks having the same priority). In [18], the authors present a detailed summary of the requirements that should be met by scheduling analysis tools to enable analysis for automotive systems.

3   Modeling Languages Capabilities

We consider two modeling languages with strong support for timing analysis: AUTOSAR and MARTE. In this paper, we do not provide details on these languages. Further information on publications, tutorials, tools, and links can be found via their respective websites: [3], [4]. The study presented here is based on the version 4.0 for AUTOSAR and 1.0 for MARTE.

Table 1 contains a summary of the extent to which the two modeling languages cover the features considered. Full explanations are given below.

Timing constraints. Modeling of time and timing constraints differ significantly in these two languages. AUTOSAR allows expressing timing constraints such as maximum delays, repetitions rates, synchronizations, and data ages, by adding timing information to events and event chains. To set these bounds, the parent concept is timing constraint. A timing constraint can specify an upper bound, a lower bound, a nominal value, and a jitter. These parameters are measured in time units and other physical units used in automotive systems such as for example angular degrees and cylinder segments.

MARTE extends the basic time model of UML with synchronous/asynchronous, physical/logical time models as well as provisions on relativistic effects that can occur in distributed systems. We can distinguish at least three layers of time constructs:

- In the first layer, time is presented as a set of fundamental notions such as time instant, duration, time bases, or clocks.
- In the second layer, MARTE provides mechanisms to annotate timing requirements and constraints in models. One key modeling feature is the concept of observation. Observations provide marking points in models to specify assertions. Some typical assertions have been pre-packaged in ready-to-use patterns, such as jitters or conditional time expressions.
- In the third layer, time concepts are defined as part of the behavior, not as mere annotations. This set of constructs cover both physical and logical time.

Hence, both AUTOSAR and MARTE give good coverage for timing constraints modeling for automotive systems. In fact both of them allow modeling the different timing constraints involved in automotive domain (deadline, maximum jitter, synchronization constraints, etc). In addition, both of them allow describing timing constraints related to different time bases. However, the AUTOSAR timing model, as based only on the notion of timing constraint that can be attached to events and event chains seems to be more simple and easy to understand. Nevertheless the MARTE model seems to be richer. But, this makes it difficult to decide which concepts to use when developing a timing model using MARTE.

End-to-end flows. This aspect is supported by the two languages with more or less formality.

AUTOSAR calls this concept event chain (or time chain). An event chain relates a set of stimuli to a set of response events. Time chains can be composed of non-concurrent time chain segments. Figure 1 shows an example of an AUTOSAR event chain with join and fork precedence relations. In this chain, end-to-end constraints such as reaction constraints and data age constraints can be applied. The semantics of these constraints are discussed later in this section.

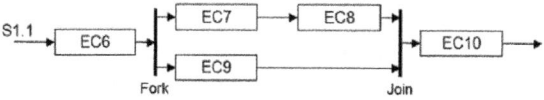

Fig. 1. Example of an AUTOSAR event chain

In MARTE, the term used is actually end-to-end flow. MARTE end-to-end flows describe logical units (steps) of processing work in the system, which contend for the use of processing resources (processors, buses, etc.) and activated by triggering events called workload event. Figure 2 shows an example of MARTE end-to-end flow. In this language, data and control can be part of the processing. Like AUTOSAR, different kinds of timing constraints can be attached to end-to-end flows (deadlines, output jitters, etc.). One important feature in MARTE is that end-end-flows can be represented in behavioral views complementing component models. This approach allows modelers to specify multiple end-to-end flow configurations that could be likely related to (a) specific operational modes, (b) alternative execution chains, or (c) different quantitative scenarios of activation parameters or other non-functional annotations. Thus, unlike AUTOSAR, one behavior model that has been extended in MARTE with data communications is the sequence diagram. Sequence diagrams capture structural entities (including ports) in the vertical axis, and interchanging of control and data messages in the horizontal axis. MARTE end-to-end flows can also be modeled using UML activity diagrams.

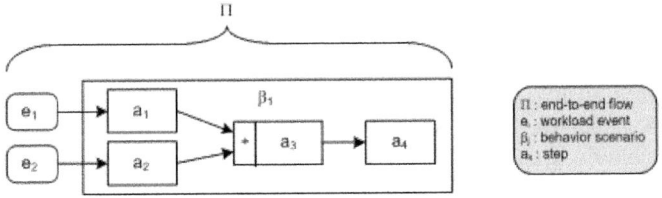

Fig. 2. Example of MARTE end-to-end Flow

Activation events. Specification of activation events differ in the two modeling languages.

The activation events are modeled via events with repetition rate constraints in AUTOSAR. In AUTOSAR, a repetitive event describes whether the stimulus is periodic, sporadic, burst, concrete or arbitrary [4].

In MARTE, activation events are modeled by means of workload events. From a specification viewpoint, MARTE is richer than AUTOSAR as workload events can be modeled by known patterns (e.g., periodic, aperiodic, sporadic, burst) but also by irregular time intervals, by trace files, or by workload generator models (e.g., state machine models). The workload event element contains additional parameters for periodic and aperiodic patterns such as jitters, burst parameters, and distribution probabilities.

SW and HW resources. The taxonomy of platform resources diverges from one to the other language.

AUTOSAR allows specifying the system hardware resources when describing the system topology at the system level. The AUTOSAR ECU instance concept allows defining the ECUs used in the topology. Communication networks can be specified through the concept Communication Cluster that represents the main element to describe the topological connection of communicating ECUs. For each communication cluster, one or more Physical Channels can be defined. It describes the transmission medium that is used to send and receive information between two communicating ECUs as well as the protocol used for the communication.

AUTOSAR allows describing the software resources involved in the system when defining the OS configuration (which is part of the ECU configuration step). Tasks are specified through the concept Os Task that represents an OSEK task (OSEK, Open Systems and the Corresponding Interfaces for Automotive Electronics, is an industry-standard operating system used for automotive applications).

The MARTE analysis model distinguishes two kinds of processing resources: execution hosts, which include for example processors and coprocessors, and communication hosts, which include networks and buses. Processing resources can be characterized by throughput properties as for example processing rate, efficiency properties such as utilization, and overhead properties such as blocking times and clock overheads.

Unlike AUTOSAR, which includes all the required parameters for FlexRay or CAN (Controller Area Network) bus configuration, MARTE does not provide sufficient details to describe all the analyzable aspects in these specialized buses. There are, however, some approximation approaches that allow modeling time-triggered communication by means of static schedules (time tables), but they have not been fully formalized with concrete parameters in this language.

Application vs. platform. The two considered modeling languages support separation of application from platform models. They differ in the way these models are created.

For example, MARTE supports this separation of views at different abstraction levels. In particular, at scheduling analysis abstraction level the modeling concepts are organized into a "workload behavior" model dealing with application-specific annotations, and a "resources platform" model dealing with computing and communication annotations. Figure 3 shows an overview of the organization of a MARTE scheduling analysis model into workload behavior and resource platform models. The two models constitute together a root model called analysis context model.

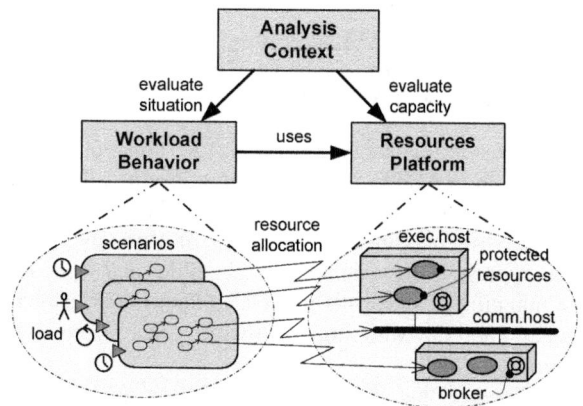

Fig. 3. Workload behavior and resource platform models in MARTE

In AUTOSAR, this is rather done through considering different views when designing the system. At the Virtual Functional Bus (VFB) view, only application software components are considered without platform-related details. At ECU (Electronic Control Unit) view, the software platform is described as part of the ECU configuration process. At system view, details about the topology and the hardware platform (computation & communication) are introduced. In addition, AUTOSAR provides a layered software architecture that allows separation between the hardware independent application software and the hardware dependant basic software. Figure 4 shows an example of the architecture of an AUTOSAR ECU, which basically identifies an application layer and the AUTOSAR basic software layer. These parts are linked via the AUTOSAR Runtime Environment (RTE) (the RTE is the runtime implementation of the VFB on a specific ECU).

The RTE realizes, hence, an intermediate layer between the hardware independent application software and the hardware dependant basic software components.

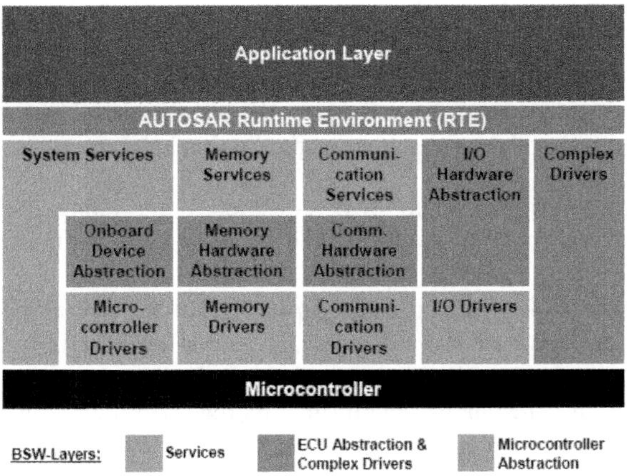

Fig. 4. The AUTOSAR ECU layered architecture

Compared to AUTOSAR, MARTE allows only modeling the application elements separately from resource platform elements. But, it does not give any concepts equivalent to the RTE concept of AUTOSAR.

Allocation. The two modeling languages define the concept of allocation but with different terminology. In MARTE, the allocation concepts allows for different kinds of spatial and temporal binding. In AUTOSAR, this is called mapping, AUTOSAR deals with three kinds of mapping: the mapping of Runnable Entities to OS tasks (runnable entities represent the smallest executable and schedulable entities in AUTOSAR), the mapping of OS tasks to ECUs (This is performed during the ECU configuration process) and the Mapping of Software components to ECUs (during the system configuration process).

An important difference that matters for scheduling analysis is the capability to represent allocation-specific information. MARTE allows for specifying arbitrary non-functional properties attached to allocations such as the execution times of the steps that compose the end-to-end flows involved in the system. This feature is supported differently by AUTOSAR. In fact, through the notion of software component implementation, the language allows specifying the resource consumption (execution time, memory consumption) needed for each runnable entity.

Another timing analysis modeling capability is related to the abstraction of OS layers by means of allocation relationships. For instance, automotive applications are typically centered on functional design during early development phases. Functional models commonly do not account for scheduling parameters (priorities, scheduling policies, etc.), required for timing analysis. In order to perform scheduling analysis in early phases, it is necessary to make assumptions about the mapping of functional entities (e.g., runnables) into OS tasks, and allowing for annotating estimated values directly into such entities. Figure 5 illustrates these two allocation options, which can be used at different abstraction levels of the same architecture. In the more abstract level, alternative (b) assumes that Runnable1 and Runnable2 will be allocated to one OS task each, and subsumes scheduling-specific parameters. Unlike AUTOSAR, this mechanism is available in MARTE.

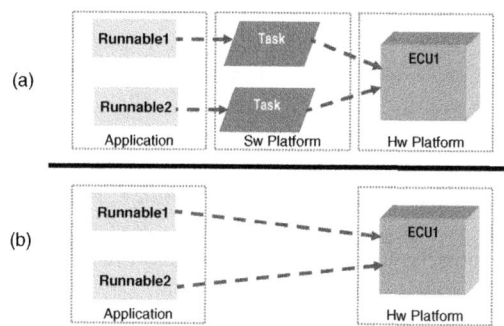

Fig. 5. Allocation at different abstraction levels (a) and (b)

Semantics preservation. Due to its importance in automotive system design, the calculation of end-to-end delays, jitters and data age in the presence of multi-rate data communication has been recently considered in literature.

In [8] the authors distinguish four different semantics of end-to-end data communication, which are included in the timing extensions of AUTOSAR. Among these, the "last-to-last" (maximum data age) semantics is needed for delay calculation in control engineering, while the "first-to-first" (first reaction) semantics is also of interest e.g., for body electronics where "button-to-action" latency is critical.

In another work, André et al. [9] extend some calculations for arbitrary schedules by using MARTE. This work separates the logical semantics that determines the relative order of dispatched events and data (modeled as a sequence of execution steps), from the chronometric semantics that determines a total order (modeled as steps deployed in multi-rate tasks and, the latter in hardware resources).

Composition. Unlike AUTOSAR, MARTE does not formally account for the issue of composition of end-to-end flows for scheduling analysis. In MARTE, however, assumed/guaranteed non-functional properties can be annotated in component interfaces by using specialized constraint annotations. This is particularly useful to specify contract-based component applications. On the other hand, Composition is the core concept in AUTOSAR. Application design is based on the description of different software components that may be part of an application composition. Therefore, AUTOSAR proposes calculating end-to-end delays for black-box compositionality, a feature that is not supported by MARTE. AUTOSAR vertical compositionality makes the approach applicable to different schedulers (Time Division Multiple Access, Round Robin, and Earliest Deadline First) and for realistic task models, e.g., periodic tasks with jitter or burst, as long as a response-time analysis is available [8]. Its horizontal compositionality makes it applicable to distributed systems with several ECUs and buses, be it synchronous (e.g., with FlexRay) or asynchronous (e.g., with CAN). As among the most important goals of AUTOSAR is to deal with this composition issues, this language seems to have more capabilities than MARTE concerning this aspect.

Analysis scope. MARTE introduces the notion of analysis context. An analysis context is the root concept used to collect relevant quantitative information for performing a specific analysis scenario. Starting with the analysis context and its parameters, a tool can follow the links of the model to extract the information that it needs to perform scheduling analysis. Analysis results can also be inserted back in MARTE models to take them into account during architecture refinement.

Analysis contexts, together with SysML parametrics [10], can be also used to formalize the design space for architecture exploration. In [11], MARTE and SysML are used in system evaluation and optimization scenarios, by explicitly defining objective functions, costs, and the search space (multiple candidate architectures and design constraints).

Unlike MARTE, AUTOSAR itself does not give any mean to bound modeling elements and properties participating in analysis scenario.

Tool support. To develop MARTE models, it is possible to use some tools such as the open source tool Papyrus [12] and the commercial tool ARTISAN Studio [13]. Both of these tools support the MARTE profile and hence, allow annotation of UML diagrams using MARTE concepts. Moreover, in [14], the authors present a tool chain called Optimum that allows transforming MARTE models developed in Papyrus to an input model understandable by the open source scheduling analysis tool MAST [15].

To develop AUTOSAR models, a tool called CESSAR-CT based on the ARTOP framework [16] has been developed by Continental engineering services. This tool allows modeling a self contained AUTOSAR architecture (application software components, timing, software/hardware resources, allocation, etc). However, users have noted that[1], for an efficient use for large systems, the user-friendliness of this tool should be improved. From a timing analysis perspective, a transformation between AUTOSAR models to the commercial scheduling analysis tool SymTA/S [17] is being developed by the SymTA/S provider, Symtavision. From a scheduling

---

[1] This statement is based on discussions with the users of the tool.

analysis point of view, SymTA/S, the scheduling analysis tool for AUTOSAR systems is more mature than MAST as it meets all the requirements presented in [18] to enable scheduling analysis for automotive systems. For efficient use for industrial development the tool support for both AUTOSAR and MARTE still need to be improved further.

Table 1. Modeling Support for Scheduling Analysis

Features - Languages		AUTOSAR	MARTE
System-oriented features	Timing constraints	Timing Constraint (Input/output synchronization, repetition rate, reaction, data age). Timing measurement units including time units, angular position, and other engine variables.	Physical and logical time constraints. Clock constraints. Time expressions for conditional assertions, indexed timed events, jitters, etc. based on time observations.
	End-to-end flows	Event chains. Event chains related to architecture events. Joins and forks precedence relations	End-to-end flows with join, forks, and conditional precedence relations. Modeled as separated behavior models (e.g., sequence diagram, activity diagrams) complementing component models.
	Activation events	Repetition rated events (periodic, sporadic, burst, concrete, arbitrary)	Patterns (e.g., periodic, aperiodic, sporadic, burst), irregular time intervals, by trace files, or by workload generator models.
	SW and HW resources	Hardware resources: ECU instance, communication cluster, physical channel. Concepts for CAN and Flexray buses modelling Software resources: described through OS configuration mechanisms, OS tasks, OS task priorities, OS resources.	Execution and communication resources characterized by throughputs, utilization, overheads, scheduling parameters. OS (tasks, semaphores, etc.) and hardware
Design oriented features	Application vs. platform	Separation of modelling views: VFB view (modelling of application components), ECU view (modelling of software platform), System view (modelling of hardware platform and topology)	No predefined layers. Modelling support for different application and platform views
	Allocation	Description of the mapping of runnable entities and basic software entities to OS tasks, mapping of OS tasks to ECUs, mapping scenarios of software components to ECUs.	Allocations with non-functional properties. Refinement of non-functional properties though VSL variables and expressions.
	Semantics preservation	In AUTOSAR timing extensions, four semantics for synchronization in end-to-end flows: first-to-first (first reaction), first-to-last, last-to-first, last-to-last (data age).	Logical relationships between read/write events
	Composition	Black-box composition rules for event chains	Required/offered/contract non-functional annotations in component interfaces
	Analysis scope	None	Analysis context, variables/parameters, analysis results
	Tool support	CESSAR-CT for modeling. Transformation from AUTOSAR models to SymTA/S tool	Papyrus, ARTISAN Studio for modeling. Optimum for transforming MARTE models to MAST tool

4 Conclusions

In this paper, we discussed some crucial specification capabilities that need to be satisfied by modeling languages to enable timing analysis in automotive applications. We evaluated the extent to which two major industry-based modeling languages, MARTE, and AUTOSAR, satisfy those needs.

The purpose of this paper is to raise questions and encourage discussion, rather than to argue that a particular modeling language is the answer. We think that a good modeling language should be general enough to capture appropriate constructs to perform useful system analysis at different abstraction levels. As can be expected, different architectural styles, fidelity levels, and language formalities in the two surveyed languages lead to diverging capabilities. On the other hand, these constructs must not be too disconnected from the system execution semantics so that analysis results can be reliable. This wide-open area needs more research in the two modeling languages discussed.

Finally, although both languages seem to be expressive enough to enable scheduling analysis, care must be taken. The design of modeling languages should typically involve a trade-off between expressive power and analyzability. The more a language can express, the harder it becomes to understand what instances of the formalism to use. Thus, more expressive languages commonly require additional effort to define methodological frameworks and tools well suited, in this case, to the automotive domain.

References

1. Navet, N., Simonot-Lion, F. (eds.): The Automotive Embedded Systems Handbook. Industrial Information Technology. CRC Press / Taylor and Francis (December 2008) ISBN 978-0849380266
2. Espinoza, H.: An Integrated Model-Driven Framework for Specifying and Analyzing Non-Functional Properties of Real-Time Systems. PhD Thesis (English), University of Evry, FRANCE (September 2007)
3. AUTOSAR Partnership, http://www.autosar.org
4. MARTE website, http://www.omgmarte.org
5. Schliecker, S., Rox, J., Negrean, M., Richter, K., Jersak, M., Ernst, R.: System Level Performance Analysis for Real-Time Automotive Multi-Core and Network Architectures. IEEE Transactions on Computer Aided Design (2009)
6. Chen, R., Sgroi, M., Martin, G., Lavagno, L., Sangiovanni-Vincentelli, A.L., Rabaey, J.: UML for Real. In: Design of Embedded Real-Time Systems, pp. 189–270. Kluwer Academic Publishers, Dordrecht (2003)
7. André, C., Mallet, F., Peraldi, M.-A.: A multiform time approach to real-time system modeling: Application to an automotive system. In: IEEE Int. Symp. on Industrial Embedded Systems (SIES 2007), Portugal, pp. 234–241 (July 2007)
8. Feiertag, N., Richter, K., Nordlander, J., Jonsson, J.: A Compositional Framework for End-to-End Path Delay Calculation of Automotive Systems under Different Path Semantics. In: 1st Workshop on Compositional Theory and Technology for Real-Time Embedded Systems CRTS 2008 (2008)

 9. André, C., Mallet, F., de Simone, R.: Modeling of Immediate vs. Delayed Data Communications: from AADL to UML MARTE. In: ECSI Forum (FDL), Spain (September 2007)
10. SysML website, http://www.omgsysml.org
11. Espinoza, H., Servat, D., Gérard, S.: Leveraging Analysis-Aided Design Decision Knowledge in UML-Based Development of Embedded Systems. In: SHARK-ICSE 2008, Leipzig, Germany (May 2008)
12. Papyrus website, http://www.papyrusuml.org
13. ARTISAN Studio website, http://www.atego.com
14. Mraidha, C., Tucci-Piergiovanni, S., Gérard, S.: Optimum: A MARTE-based Methodology for Schedulability Analysis at Early Design Stages. In: Third IEEE International Workshop UML and Formal Methods, Shangai, China (November 2010)
15. MAST website, http://mast.unican.es
16. ARTOP User Group website, http://www.artop.org
17. SymTA/S website, http://www.symtavision.com/symtas.html
18. Anssi, S., Gérard, S., Albinet, A., Terrier, F.: Requirements and Solutions for Timing Analysis of Automotive Systems. In: Kraemer, F.A., Herrmann, P. (eds.) SAM 2010. LNCS, vol. 6598. Springer, Heidelberg (to appear, 2011)

Author Index

GPSR Compliance

The European Union's (EU) General Product Safety Regulation (GPSR)
is a set of rules that requires consumer products to be safe and our
obligations to ensure this.

If you have any concerns about our products, you can contact us on
ProductSafety@springernature.com

In case Publisher is established outside the EU, the EU authorized
representative is:

Springer Nature Customer Service Center GmbH
Europaplatz 3
69115 Heidelberg, Germany

Batch number: 09490872

Printed by Printforce, the Netherlands